IMPORTANT:

HERE IS YOUR REGISTRATION CODE TO ACCESS
YOUR PREMIUM McGRAW-HILL ONLINE RESOURCES.

For key premium online resources you need THIS CODE to gain access. Once the code is entered, you will be able to use the Web resources for the length of your course.

If your course is using **WebCT** or **Blackboard**, you'll be able to use this code to access the McGraw-Hill content within your instructor's online course.

Access is provided if you have purchased a new book. If the registration code is missing from this book, the registration screen on our Website, and within your WebCT or Blackboard course, will tell you how to obtain your new code.

Registering for McGraw-Hill Online Resources

TO gain access to your MCGraw-Hill web resources simply follow the steps below:

1. USE YOUR WEB BROWSER TO GO TO: **http://www.mhhe.com/burrows9**

2. CLICK ON **FIRST TIME USER**.

3. ENTER THE REGISTRATION CODE* PRINTED ON THE TEAR-OFF BOOKMARK ON THE RIGHT.

4. AFTER YOU HAVE ENTERED YOUR REGISTRATION CODE, CLICK **REGISTER**.

5. FOLLOW THE INSTRUCTIONS TO SET-UP YOUR PERSONAL UserID AND PASSWORD.

6. WRITE YOUR UserID AND PASSWORD DOWN FOR FUTURE REFERENCE. KEEP IT IN A SAFE PLACE.

TO GAIN ACCESS to the McGraw-Hill content in your instructor's **WebCT** or **Blackboard** course simply log in to the course with the UserID and Password provided by your instructor. Enter the registration code exactly as it appears in the box to the right when prompted by the system. You will only need to use the code the first time you click on McGraw-Hill content.

Thank you, and welcome to your MCGraw-Hill online Resources!

Higher Education

REGISTRATION CODE

0MAZ-NPEN-T6X5-TT85-IRLV

*YOUR REGISTRATION CODE CAN BE USED ONLY ONCE TO ESTABLISH ACCESS. IT IS NOT TRANSFERABLE.

0-07-301684-5 T/A GROSS: DISCIPLINES AND TECHNIQUES, 9E

Video Production

Ninth Edition

Video Production

DISCIPLINES AND TECHNIQUES

Lynne S. Gross
California State University, Fullerton

James C. Foust
Bowling Green State University

Thomas D. Burrows
Professor Emeritus
California State University, Northridge

Boston   Burr Ridge, IL   Dubuque, IA   Madison, WI   New York   San Francisco   St. Louis
Bangkok   Bogotá   Caracas   Kuala Lumpur   Lisbon   London   Madrid   Mexico City
Milan   Montreal   New Delhi   Santiago   Seoul   Singapore   Sydney   Taipei   Toronto

Higher Education

VIDEO PRODUCTION: DISCIPLINES AND TECHNIQUES

Published by McGraw-Hill, a business unit of The McGraw-Hill Companies, Inc., 1221 Avenue of the Americas, New York, NY 10020.

Some ancillaries, including electronic and print components, may not be available to customers outside the United States.

This book is printed on acid-free paper.

1 2 3 4 5 6 7 8 9 0 DOW/DOW 0 9 8 7 6 5 4

ISBN 0 07 293548 0

Publisher: *Phillip A. Butcher*
Sponsoring editor: *Phillip A. Butcher*
Developmental editor: *Laura Lynch*
Editorial coordinator: *Marcella Tullio*
Senior marketing manager: *Leslie Oberhuber*
Lead media producer: *Erin Marean*
Senior project manager: *Christina Thornton-Villagomez*
Production supervisor: *Janean A. Utley*
Designer: *George J. Kokkonas*
Lead supplement producer: *Marc Mattson*
Associate photo research coordinator: *Natalia C. Peschiera*
Cover and interior design: *Maureen McCutcheon*
Typeface: *10/14 Palatino*
Compositor: *The GTS Companies, Inc.*
Printer: *R.R. Donnelley and Sons Inc.*

Library of Congress Cataloging-in-Publication Data

Gross, Lynne S.
    Video production : disciplines and techniques / Lynne S. Gross, James C. Foust, Thomas
D. Burrows.—9th ed.
      p. cm.
    Rev. ed.: Video production. c2001.
    ISBN 0-07-293548-0 (softcover : alk. paper)
    1. Television—Production and direction. I. Foust, James C. II. Burrows, Thomas D. III.
Title
PN1992.75.B8 2005   2004040184

Dedication

To our many students who have helped make teaching the most rewarding of all professions.

About the Authors

Lynne Schafer Gross

She has taught television production full-time at a number of U.S. colleges, including California State University–Fullerton, Pepperdine University, UCLA, Loyola Marymount University, and Long Beach City College. She has also taught production internationally in Estonia, Australia, Guyana, Swaziland, and Malaysia. Her professional experience includes serving as director of programming for Valley Cable TV and producing series for commercial, public, and cable television. She is past president of the Broadcast Education Association and has served as governor for the Academy of Television Arts and Sciences. Her honors include receiving the BEA's Distinguished Education Service Award and the IRTS Frank Stanton Fellow Award. She has published 10 other books and numerous journal articles. Her doctorate is from UCLA.

James C. Foust

He is an associate professor and head of the Broadcast Journalism sequence in the Department of Journalism at Bowling Green State University. He has worked in commercial video production and as a television news videographer and editor. He currently works on freelance video and interactive media production and has published several journal articles and book chapters. He also has written a book, *Big Voices of the Air: The Battle Over Clear Channel Radio,* and he is working on an online journalism textbook. He holds a Ph.D. and M.S. degree from Ohio University.

Thomas D. Burrows

He now holds the title of Professor Emeritus in the Radio, TV, and Film Department at California State University–Northridge. Retirement from full-time teaching has provided him the opportunity to pursue a number of activities relating both to his academic background and to his work as a professional broadcaster. He continues to work with the Radio, Television, and Film Department at California State University–Northridge and with several community broadcasting projects. During his earlier career as a producer and director in commercial and public broadcasting, he received the Christopher, Emmy, and Peabody awards. He holds an M.A. degree from the School of Journalism at the University of Southern California.

Brief Contents

Contents

7   Audio   153

8   Graphics and Sets   183

9   Video Switchers   205

13 Video on the Internet and Optical Discs 301

Preface

This edition of the text has been greatly revised and reorganized to take into account the many changes that have occurred in video production. Updating is nothing new for this text because it covers a very dynamic field. When the first edition was published in 1978, television was dominated by three TV networks and some local stations. As the years have passed, TV has added cable TV, corporate video, direct broadcast satellite, CD-ROMs, DVDs, the Internet, and various other distribution technologies. Equipment, too, has changed from analog based to digital based while all the time getting smaller, cheaper, and more user-friendly.

Underlying Disciplines

Although the techniques and equipment of television may be changing, the disciplines that serve as the underlying strength of any operation remain much the same. The basic concepts of *advance preparation*, the constant *checking of detail*, and the *necessity for teamwork* assume a position of even more importance as technology progresses. Disciplines involve a number of attitudes and behaviors such as responsibility, self-control, initiative, and respect for the work of others. These disciplines are, in many ways, the most important part of any university-level production course. We firmly believe that these disciplines can be learned only within the structure of production exercises that involve full class participation and the rotation of students within the various crew positions.

Chapter Organization

The text is organized into 13 chapters, the same number as the last edition, but the chapter order has been changed so that producing and directing are closer to the front of the book. In addition, the chapter on interactive media that appeared in the last edition has been recast and renamed, "Video on the Internet and Optical Discs."

Chapter 1 has been largely rewritten to bring up-to-date all the changes that have occurred in the video production field. It also emphasizes the role convergence plays in production and delineates the differences among studio, field, and remote truck production.

Chapter 2 gives an overview of the duties and responsibilities of cast and crew and should be useful as students begin production exercises.

Chapters 3 and 4 have been moved forward at the suggestion of the book's reviewers. These chapters enable students to understand the crucial producing and directing functions early in the course. The producing chapter includes new material on legal considerations and record keeping.

The specific equipment chapters begin with Chapter 5 and cover cameras, lighting, audio, graphics and sets, the switcher, recording equipment, and editing equipment. Much of the camera chapter has been rewritten to discuss new digital and HDTV technologies. The audio chapter has received major rewriting to reorganize and update it. More space is devoted to how graphics are constructed because graphics have become a major element on the modern TV screen. The material on sets has been restructured to take into account that this function is now often outsourced. The recording chapter has received updates on new types of tapeless recorders. The editing chapter includes a stronger emphasis on nonlinear editing and has many rewritten parts to highlight new features.

Chapter 12 on field production contains a new section on remote truck production. The final chapter on the Internet and optical discs covers how to put a completed video project on the Internet and how to save it on a DVD. Both these distribution means are becoming more common for all video production products.

The book ends with a glossary and an index. The glossary can be particularly helpful as it contains definitions for all the words that are boldfaced within the text.

State-of-the-Art and Real-World Equipment

As in previous editions, we have presented equipment that in our view serves as an example of the technologies that students work with in their institutions or will work with as they first enter the job market. Some equipment used for illustration will be close to state of the art, but in other cases, we have deliberately shown some older, proven units because they are typical of the technology in general use.

Web Material

The book has extensive interactive web materials that can be accessed over the Internet. Anyone who purchases this book can access this material at http://www.mhhe.com/grossvideo9.

For students, web material includes:

- Audio, video, and teamwork exercises
- An illustrated glossary
- Self-tests
- Links to useful sites

For instructors, web material includes:

- Summaries of the scope and purpose of each chapter
- Training exercises

Test Questions

A set of multiple choice and true/false questions are also available for instructors. Please contact your McGraw-Hill sales representative or call the Customer Service number at 1-800-338-3987.

Authors

Some changes have taken place in the authorship of this textbook. Tom Burrows, who was responsible for the original creation of the text, is now in retirement and did not actually participate in this revision, although many of his original words and ideas, such as disciplines and techniques, are still the underpinning for the text. Don Wood, now in retirement, is no longer actively involved with the book, but we thank him for his many years of dedicated service and his contributions to the structure and content of the book.

Acknowledgments

We have had the advice and assistance of many colleagues and students in putting this text together. Although we cannot single out everybody, we would specifically like to thank the following video professionals who shared their expertise with us and arranged for us to visit TV facilities and view production processes:

Victor M. Webb, *Director/Associate Director (DGA), KCBS 2/KCAL 9 News*

Barry Zegel, *Vice President, West Coast Technical and Production Operations and Engineering, CBS Broadcasting Inc.*

Steve Schifrin, *Vice President, Program Production Services, CBS Broadcasting Inc.*

Tim Saunders, *President, Broadcast Design International*

Jerry Butler, *Senior Director, DTV Strategic Services Group, Public Broadcasting Service*

Paul Lopez, *Production Manager, WBGU-TV*

Tom Zapiecki, *Producer/Director, WBGU-TV*

Jose Cardenas, *Field Production Coordinator, WBGU-TV*

We also wish to thank those who reviewed the book for us. They are:

Juliet Dee, *University of Delaware*

Eric Freedman, Ph.D., *Florida Atlantic University*

John Hoerner, *University of Montevallo*

Gary Larson, *University of Nevada–Las Vegas*

Patricia Sanders, *University of Northern Alabama*

Again, we wish to provide a text that serves as an efficient teaching and learning vehicle for introductory and secondary courses in television production. As always, we welcome suggestions and corrections from our colleagues.

Video Production

Introduction to Video Production

Video production is an exciting field. Whether you are putting together a video of your college graduation ceremony or directing a hit show for network TV, you will find that the art of combining elements into a meaningful whole is a creative process that is both stimulating and rewarding. To undertake production, you must interact with both people and equipment. This book gives you the skills to do both. That is why the book is subtitled "Disciplines and Techniques." Disciplines will make you a valued member of a crew, and techniques will enable you to do your job, especially as it relates to equipment operation.

The first chapter of this book is devoted to an overview of the production process and some of the factors that account for the current state of video production. The chapter starts with a definition of the *disciplines* and *techniques* that underlie a successful career in video production. It then goes on to discuss the following:

- What is meant by a professional attitude (1.1)

- How attitude and self-image can affect your work (1.1)

- The differences and similarities related to studio, field, and remote productions (1.2)

- The physical characteristics and equipment found in studios and control rooms (1.2)

- Some of the real-world considerations of field production (1.2)

- How trucks and cameras operate in remote productions (1.2)

- The basic control functions of transducing, channeling, selecting/altering, monitoring, and recording/playback (1.3)
- Differences between analog and digital (1.4)
- How digital technologies have contributed to HDTV and convergence (1.4)
- A brief historical background of video production (1.5)
- Aspects of employment in the video industry (1.6)

1.1 Personal Disciplines in Support of Technique

In the study of media production, it is important for you to develop an early understanding of two differing but related aspects of the creative process. First, definite operational *techniques* are put into practice during such diverse activities as equipment operation, scriptwriting, and team organization. Some of these are precise physical actions; others are a matter of often-repeated mental patterns. Second, there are some equally important individual *disciplines* that relate more to personal attitudes in such matters as an acceptance of responsibility and a careful manner of performance that the person can bring to these techniques.

To define these terms further, take the example of one camera operator who uses off-air time to double-check all aspects of focus for upcoming shots, allowing for possible unexpected variables in camera-to-subject distance. Another operator does only a cursory check and makes last-second adjustments if changes occur. Both individuals may know the specific techniques needed to operate their cameras equally well, but only the first one will be prepared for the surprises that often occur. To go a step further, consider that, with prior permission from the director, the camera operator has the discipline to look for special but unplanned shots during a rock concert. One shot he or she gets uses the camera lens and a light source to create a flare effect around a performer. Here we have an example of creativity relating to both discipline and technique.

This text takes a number of opportunities to extend the idea of self-discipline into the related concept of *teamwork*. Producing a television program is a team effort. You cannot produce a program (especially a studio-based production) all by yourself. There is no way to be on camera at the same time you are focusing the camera, adjusting the sound, and operating the recorder. Any productions you are in charge of will need the cooperation and skill of your classmates. Conversely, your fellow students will depend on your techniques and discipline. The positive side of this is the personal bonding that occurs during a production class and often lasts a lifetime. The downside is that the productions are only as good as the weakest link. In a team effort, everyone must help everyone else. There is no room for cliques or biting comments.

When you are the director, you will be the leader of the production team. Most other times you will be a follower, but one who contributes ideas and is in charge of specific chores. You must learn to handle both roles equally well. As a leader you should listen to ideas of others (see Chapter 4), and as a crew member you should learn how to make suggestions to the director in a constructive and amiable manner.

If you intend to make a career of video production, you, as a student, have entered into a process of *development* that must continue throughout your career. You must be concerned with techniques and also develop your own sense of production discipline so that others can depend on you with confidence. One of the most revealing tests of your production capabilities will be to answer this simple question: Do other people really want you on their production team? Attitudinal qualities have much to do with how this question is answered.

Development of a Professional Attitude

When you and others work together, ongoing success is very much a matter of what other people think of you (especially those in charge of getting things done). In these circumstances, you are judged by a set of values that are usually summed up under the term *professional attitude*. How do others view your manner of approaching tasks that fall within your area of responsibility?

Dependability is probably the most basic virtue in a time-oriented industry like telecommunications. Do you make a conscious effort to be on time and to be in the physical and mental condition that enables you to give your best effort? Do you handle equipment with proper care to avoid costly maintenance work? Do you meet deadlines? Do you make an attempt to communicate your suggestions as well as your uncertainties to those in charge? Do you show respect for the work of others and for their operational needs during the production sequence? Finally, and of great importance, have you learned to discipline yourself to remain calm and focused on your tasks, especially when difficulties occur? The answers to these and similar questions determine how you rank with your peers.

For many students, their most important career contacts will go back to the people with whom they worked closely in their production courses. In terms of future employment, it is not so much *who you know* as it is the status of the people *who think well of you*. It therefore behooves any student, beginning on the first day of class, to quietly but confidently start doing those things that create the impression of being one who is articulate, reliable, and skilled. Yes, big talkers for a while can make an impression without much to back it up, but eventually the realities of production are their undoing.

Attitudes and Self-Image

In building interpersonal relationships, it is important to keep in mind that others' opinions about you relate in many ways to what you think of yourself. Much has been written about how people need *self-esteem*. A reality, too often ignored, is that people do not simply *get* self-esteem . . . they must *earn* it. On a production crew, you earn the good opinion of others by consistently doing the sort of job that brings approval and, along with it, self-satisfaction. Good work does not just happen. It comes from thinking through the things you must be prepared for in order to function in any given position. Do you really understand the signal flow through the audio board, or are you planning on figuring it out during the setup period? Where are the tight places in the script when a lot happens at once? A few minutes spent in preparation can save hours of wasted time during final production.

An interesting process of interaction becomes evident as groups of four and five people begin to work together on a project without a specific leader. Such teams quickly find that it is difficult to function properly when everyone tries to have an equal say on all matters. One designated person must be responsible for final decisions. Those decisions are best made after the leader makes sure there has been an open exchange of ideas and opinions on every aspect of the production. The successful leader maintains the position not only by consistently presenting a good plan of action but also by acknowledging and adopting other team members' ideas when they are appropriate. Teams usually function best when everyone has a chance to exhibit creative thinking as well as production-related skills. The ability to balance both the competitive and cooperative aspects of human nature successfully within a group is one of the surest tests of good leadership.

Another balancing process can be observed as each new semester begins. A course starts out with a new mix of students. Some are old friends, while others are going through the process of proving themselves. Some who have done well in earlier classes tend to take their status for granted. During the normal competitive process of crew performance in production exercises, new people begin to emerge both as leaders and/or as persons with other production-related talents. It is then that the student who is simply coasting either works extra hard to catch up or loses status. The ability to respond positively in these situations says a lot about a person. In the long run, the individual with a firm *ego energy drive*, balanced with an ability for honest *self-evaluation*, will be sought after not only for school projects but also throughout a professional career.

1.2 Types of Productions

A great deal of television production occurs within the controlled environment of a television **studio** and **control room**—news, game shows, talk shows, morning information programs, situation comedies, soap operas. Many of these programs also contain material shot through **field production**—interviews with witnesses of a robbery for inclusion in a newscast, the scene at an airport incorporated within a soap opera, footage of vegetables being grown on a farm that is part of a cooking show. Sometimes out-of-studio production is used for an entire program—a documentary about fly fishing, a movie that takes place in a jungle. Another form of production, called **remote production,** is a combination of studio and field production. A truck serves as the control room and the "studio" is in the "field"; it might be a football stadium, a parade route, or a classroom.

Studio Production

Studio production is the main focus of this book, but many of the principles related to the studio apply equally well to field and remote production. The main difference is that field and remote production must take into account the technical problems created by the "real world," such as rain, traffic noise, and annoying shadows. The studio is a controlled environment specially made for television.

The Studio

A television studio is usually a large room at least 20 feet by 30 feet without any posts obstructing its space. (See Figure 1.1.) Usually a set occupies one end of the studio and the cameras move around in the other part; if a studio is large enough, however, there may be several sets and the cameras move back and forth among them. The floor is level, usually made of concrete covered with linoleum so that the camera movement can be smooth. The ceiling is 12 feet to 14 feet high to accommodate a pipe **grid** from which lights are hung.

Figure 1.1

A TV studio. Note the open space and high ceiling.   *Photo courtesy of KABC-TV.*

A studio is best located on the ground floor with large doors that open to the outside so that set pieces and other objects can be brought in easily. Walls and ceilings should be soundproofed, and the studio should be reliably air-conditioned for the comfort of both people and the equipment. The air conditioning needs to be quiet so that the microphones do not pick up the sound. Although lights and other equipment do not need as much power as in earlier times, studios should be built so that they can use greater amounts of electricity than ordinary rooms. Wall outlets are needed not only for power but also for use in connecting cameras, microphones, and other equipment to the control room.

Not all studios are built this way, however. For example, some news studios are right in the middle of the newsroom. These are usually rather small spaces where the anchors sit to deliver the news while the other people who are gathering and editing news continue their work in adjacent spaces. You will probably find that your university studio does not meet all the specifications mentioned in the previous paragraph; for example, it may only have a 10-foot ceiling, or it may not have large access doors. Not having a "perfect" studio can make production a little more difficult, but certainly not impossible.

It is within the television studio that talent performs. Three, four, or more cameras pick up the image of the performers, and microphones pick up the sound. Lights are necessary so that the camera electronics can "see" what is happening. Each camera's shot is slightly different so that the director has a choice as to which shot to use.

A studio often has TV sets, called **monitors,** that crew members, and sometimes talent, can look at to see what is being recorded. The people operating the cameras wear **headsets** that are part of an **intercom** system through which they can communicate with other crew members, especially the director. There usually is also a **studio address** system that the director can use from the control room to talk to everyone in the studio, both talent and crew. This, of course, cannot be used during production because the microphones would pick up the sound as part of the program audio. That is why there is an intercom, so that the director can communicate with the studio crew while a program is being recorded or aired.

The Control Room

Near the studio is a control room, which is the operation center for the director and many other crew members. (See Figure 1.2.) It usually has a raised floor so that all the cables from the studio equipment can be brought into the control room and connected to the appropriate pieces of equipment. Often there is a window between the studio and control room so that those working in the control room can see what is happening in the studio. This window consists of two panes of glass, each of which is at a slightly sloped angle so that sounds do not reflect directly off the glass and create a sound that contains echo. The window should also be well sealed so that sounds from the control room do not leak into the studio. Some control rooms, especially those used in teaching situations, have an area where people can sit to observe what is happening.

The control room contains a great deal of equipment, which will be discussed in detail in the following chapters. But basically, the images from the cameras go to a **switcher** that is used to select the pictures that can be sent to the recording equipment, which is also usually located in the control room. The sound coming from the microphones goes to an **audio console** where its volume can be adjusted and sounds can be mixed together so that they, too, go to the recording equipment (or are aired live). A **graphics generator** is used to prepare titles and other material that needs letters, numbers, and figures. These, too, go through the switcher where they can be combined with images from the cameras. Other inputs that might go to the switcher and audio board include a satellite feed and previously taped material that is rolled into a show from a videocassette recorder.

There are many monitors in the control room, generally one for each input to the switcher and several to show what has been selected to go to the recorder or out over the air. By the same token, there are speakers for audio and there are headsets so that the equipment operators can be on the intercom. In addition, numerous timing devices are needed to ensure that the programs will be the right length. The **dimmer board** that controls the studio lights may be in the control room or may be in the studio. The same is true for the controls for the **prompter,** the device that places the script in front of the camera lens so that talent can read from it.

There may also be equipment in the control room that adjusts features on the studio cameras, such as the amount of light coming into the lens.

Other Studio-Related Spaces

Studios attached to TV stations or other entities that send a signal into the airwaves or to some other outside destination have an area called **master control.** The end product from the control room goes to master control where it is processed in various ways to be sent on its journey. Sometimes programs and commercials are stored on large computers called **servers** and are sent out from master control in an automated fashion that involves computer software. Master control is also where satellite feeds or feeds from remote locations are received.

Most studio complexes have editing suites where material shot in either the studio or the field can be edited. There also is an area for storing portable and infrequently used equipment. Buildings often have an area where sets and props can be built and stored. Because constructing sets is usually noisy, that area should be at some distance from the studio, but storage should be as close as possible.

A **green room** is an area where people about to go on a program, such as a talk show or game show, can wait. It is called a green room because the walls are often painted green in line with the theory that green is a soothing color that will relax potential performers. The makeup room should be close to the studio and, of course, there should be toilet facilities in the vicinity. The engineer and others who are in the studio area frequently should have their offices nearby.

As a student, you probably can't change how your school's studio facility is designed, but you can decide what features you like best and remember them in case you have a chance during your career to give input regarding the building or remodeling of a facility. (See Figure 1.3.)

Field Production

Field production usually involves shooting and recording with a single **camcorder.** (See Figure 1.4.) The image that comes through the lens goes directly to the recorder without going through a switcher. Sound is recorded with a microphone but it, too, usually goes directly to the recorder.[1] At a later time the desired images and sounds are edited together in the proper order.

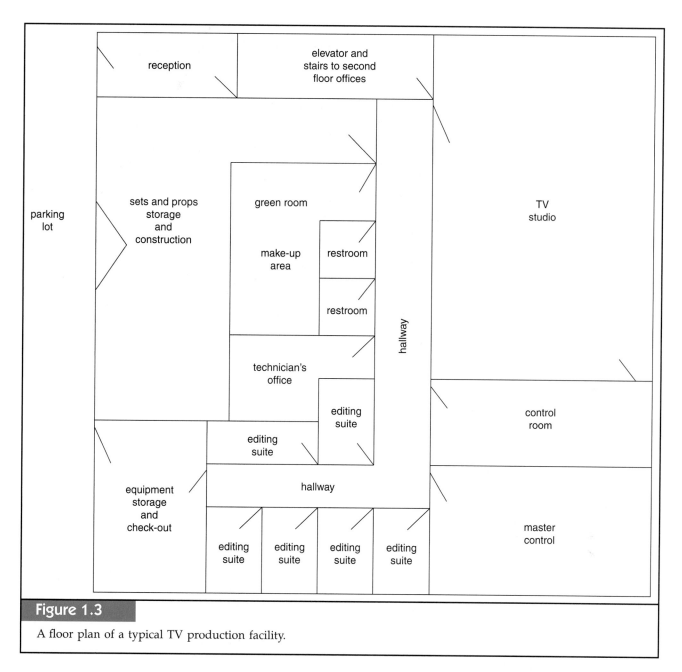

Figure 1.3

A floor plan of a typical TV production facility.

Because the "real world" is both the studio and the control room, there may be no need for a set, and the natural lighting coming from the sun or from lights in a room may suffice. This is usually the case for news and documentaries where what you want to show is the actual situation. But for other programs, especially dramas and comedies, you may find that natural lighting and sets are inadequate and that you need to spend a good deal of time obtaining acceptable picture and sound.

In general, field production uses a smaller crew than studio production because there is not as much equipment involved. Some news crews consist of one person who sets up the camera and attaches the microphone and then goes in front of the camera to report the story. Various types of field production are discussed in more detail in Chapter 12.

Remote Production

Remote productions greatly resemble studio productions in that the outputs of the cameras are fed into a switcher and from there go out live or are recorded. However, remotes, such as the coverage of a football

Figure 1.4

Field production takes place outside the studio and involves much less equipment than a studio shoot.

game, can be more complicated than studio productions and require a larger crew. In fact, coverage of sports productions (or parades or awards ceremonies) usually requires many more camera operators than a studio production because of the size of the venue and all the angles that need to be covered. Similarly, obtaining audio can be difficult because of all the extraneous noises, some of which are unwelcome. Although the sun may provide sufficient illumination, lighting can be a definite challenge if there is not enough light and lights must be brought in to cover a large area.

The truck that constitutes the control room often resembles a studio control room, albeit a little more cramped. (See Figure 1.5.) There may be more recording

Figure 1.5

A remote truck setup used to broadcast a volleyball tournament.

and playback devices because of the need for instant replays and feature inserts. Editing equipment may also be used during production. It might be used, for example, to put together game highlights to be shown during halftime. The van may have an antenna so that what it is shooting can be sent back to master control or to a satellite.

Sometimes studio, field, and remote production are all used during the course of a program. For example, a newscast coming from a studio may include an edited story that was shot in the field earlier in the day as well as a live feed from a remote unit about to start televising a baseball game.

1.3 The Production Path

Another way to look at production is to consider a model that consists of five basic control functions related to audio and video—transducing, channeling, selecting/altering, monitoring, and recording/playback. (See Fig-

ure 1.6.) This isn't the only model that can represent production, but it serves as an appropriate one to understand how the video process operates.

Transducing

Transducing involves converting what we hear or see into electrical energy or vice versa. For example, a microphone transduces spoken sound into electrical **waveforms** that can travel through wires and be recorded. A **diaphragm** within the microphone vibrates in response to the sound waves and creates a current within electronic elements of the mic (see Chapter 7). It vibrates slightly differently depending on whether the sounds are loud or soft, high-pitched or low-pitched. In essence, the microphone arranges electrons in a type of "code" that represents each particular sound. These electrons then travel through equipment as electrical energy until they come to a speaker. The speaker does the opposite of what a microphone does; it transduces the electrical waveforms back into sound waves that are almost the same as

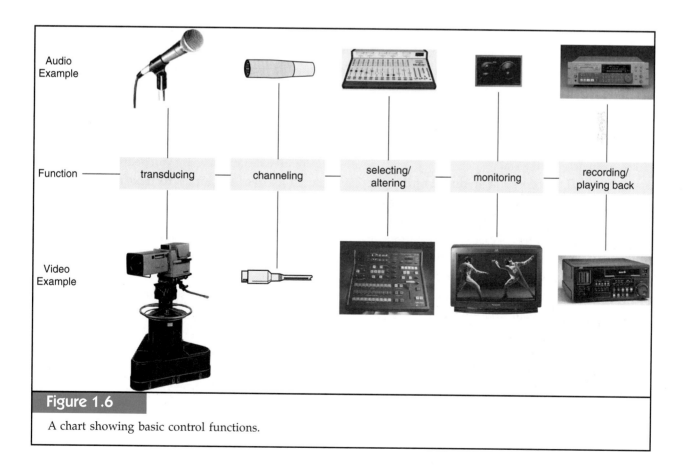

Figure 1.6

A chart showing basic control functions.

those that were originally spoken into the microphone and that can be heard by the ear.

A camera operates in the same way. It transduces light waves into electrical waveforms that can be stored or moved from place to place. When this electrical energy reaches a TV set, it is transduced into a moving picture that the eye can see. Whether the production is studio, field, or remote, microphones and cameras act as transducers.

Channeling

Channeling refers to moving sound from one place to another. In television studios this is usually accomplished over wires, but sometimes **wireless** mics are used. These mics have a small transmitter on them that sends the transduced electrical energy to a small receiver located at the other end of the studio or in the control room. The audio and video signals from a field or remote location are often sent to the master control area through wireless technology.

But usually wires connect equipment. That is why studio walls have equipment outlets—so that the **cables** for the cameras and mics that contain many wires can run through the walls to reach the control room rather than being strewn all over the studio floor. The most common way for the electrical signal to leave or enter a piece of equipment is through a **connector.** Cables have connectors on both ends that can attach to the equipment. For example, one end of a camera cable will plug into a connector on the camera and the other end will plug into a connector in the wall.

Sometimes a signal does not go directly from one piece of equipment to another. Instead it goes through a **patch bay.** This patch bay is out in the open and enables signals to be sent various places. For example, at times you may want the sound from a microphone to go to the audio console, and at other times you want it to go to a cassette recorder. Rather than crawling around on your hands and knees behind the audio console to find the microphone's cable and connector so you can pull it out and move it, you can make a simple change in the patch bay with a wire that has connectors on both ends (see Chapter 7).

The channeling in studios and remote trucks is fairly similar. The walls of the truck and studio will have places to plug in cameras and microphones, and these signals will then be transported through connectors and wires to audio consoles, switchers, recorders, monitors, and other equipment.

Channeling is much simpler in the field. Because the camera and recorder is one piece of equipment, no external wires are needed to carry the picture. A microphone will need channeling to the camcorder, either through a wire and connector or through a wireless signal.

Selecting and Altering

Signals that are transduced by microphones and cameras and channeled with wires and connectors usually go at some point to an audio console or a switcher where they can be **selected.** The switcher has buttons, each of which serves as an inpoint for one of the video signals—camera 1, camera 2, videocassette player 2, graphics generator, satellite feed, and so on. The person operating the switcher pushes the button of the signal that should go on to a video recorder. It is possible, however, to mix signals so that, for example, the title from the graphics generator appears on top of the picture from camera 2 or the picture from the satellite feed gradually fades away while the picture from camera 1 gradually fades in. Most switchers also allow for **altering** pictures to some degree. For example, you can take the picture from camera 1 and squeeze it so it only appears in the upper left-hand corner of the frame. (This will be explained in more detail in Chapter 9.)

Similarly, the audio board can be used to select one sound to go over the air or to mix together several sounds such as music under a spoken announcement. Most audio consoles can also alter sounds, such as making a person's voice sound thin and tinny perhaps to represent a character from another planet.

Once again, these functions are similar for studio and remote production because both trucks and control rooms have switchers and audio consoles. Sounds and pictures produced in the field are also selected and altered, but usually this is done during the editing process after the material has been shot. Most computer editing software can select, mix, and alter so that the end result looks or sounds just like what would come from a switcher or audio console.

Monitoring

Monitoring allows you to hear and see the material you are working with at various stages along the way. Not surprisingly, the pieces of equipment that enable this are often called *monitors*. On the video side, these look like TV sets but generally they do not receive all the channels available on your home set. In addition to one monitor for each signal, there is usually a **preview monitor** that the director and switcher operator use to set up effects before they go out on the air, and there is a **program monitor** to show what you are currently sending out from the switcher.

Audio speakers act as monitors, with some of them being used to hear the current program audio while others are used to hear the sound from a particular piece of equipment. Sometimes the sound is not fed into a speaker but rather into a headset that only the audio operator wears. In that way the sound does not interfere with what crew members are saying to one another.

Picture and sound can also be monitored with specialized electronic equipment. A **VU meter,** for example, shows how loud audio is and a **waveform monitor** shows how bright different parts of a camera image are. These pieces of equipment show things you cannot necessarily see or hear by using TV sets and speakers (see Chapters 5 and 7).

Studios and trucks both have many monitoring devices. Monitoring in field production is often limited to seeing the picture you are taking through the viewfinder of the camera and listening to the audio you are recording through **earphones** plugged into the camera.

Recording and Playing Back

Recording equipment retains sound and picture in a permanent electronic form for later **playback** (see Chapter 10). A wide variety of equipment accomplishes this purpose. Generally it can be characterized as tape-based (a **VCR,** a **DAT,** an audiocassette **recorder**), disc-based (a **CD-R** or **DVD-R**), or computer-based in terms of recording on the **hard drive** of the computer.

Some equipment, such as a **CD player,** does not record but only plays back. Some records both audio and video (e.g., a VCR), and some only records audio (e.g., a DAT). Obviously material can be played back from one piece of equipment and recorded onto another. This is undertaken to make copies of programs and to roll prerecorded material into the program tape that is being produced.

The camcorders used in field production serve as the recording medium but do not lend themselves to roll-ins from other recorders. Both studio and remote production configurations usually have multiple recording devices both for roll-ins and for backup.

Some of the equipment discussed in this section encompasses more than one function. For example, some recording devices allow for several channels of audio and have controls that enable you to *select* which sound you want. Monitors, although they are used for *monitoring*, are also *transducers*. There is no need to specifically categorize each piece of equipment according to its basic control function, but there is a need to acknowledge that both picture and sound go through a process. When you are sending someone's voice into a microphone, you should consider the way that the sound might be channeled, selected, altered, monitored, recorded, and played back so that you record it in a manner that will enable it to make it to the final stage. The same is true for an image created in a camera.

1.4 Convergence and the Digital Age

During anyone's professional career in video production, one thing is certain—there will be change. One of the changes taking place at present is the convergence of media forms made possible, in part, by digital technology.

Differences Between Analog and Digital

Originally video sounds and pictures were **analog,** so named because the electronic waveform that resulted from the transducing process was an analog of the original sound or light wave. (See Figure 1.7.) In other words it contained representations of the same essential

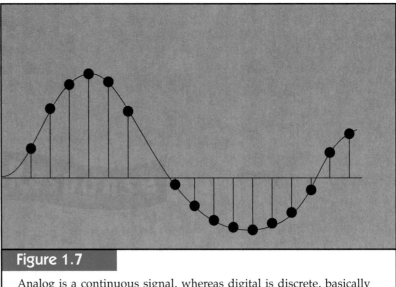

Figure 1.7

Analog is a continuous signal, whereas digital is discrete, basically consisting of many samples of the analog signal. The curved line represents analog, and the dots indicate how the signal would be sampled digitally.

elements—such as loudness, brightness, pitch, and color—that characterized the original sound or light wave. This analog signal then traveled through other equipment such as switchers, audio consoles, and video-cassette recorders to eventually reach a speaker and television screen. In the United States, this analog form was referred to as **NTSC,** which stood for National Television Systems Committee, the government-sanctioned group that devised standards that were adopted for television in the United States. One of these standards dealt with the number of lines of picture information from the top to the bottom of the TV set—it was established at 525, referred to as 525 lines of resolution.

In the 1980s, when people first started to think that the old NTSC standard should be improved, the government formed an Advanced Television Systems Committee (**ATSC**) to look into standards related to digital television. ATSC standards are more complicated than NTSC standards because the committee decided that multiple standards should be allowed. As a result, there are a number of ATSC formats that differ in lines of resolution—some have 480 lines of resolution, some 720, some 1080 (see Chapter 5). To make matters more complicated, some ATSC formats have an **aspect ratio** (the relationship of the height of a TV screen to its width) that is roughly rectangular (like a NTSC TV set), and some have a widescreen aspect ratio more akin in shape to that of widescreen movies. But all ATSC formats are digital rather than analog.

Digital video technology is based on the same on-off (0, 1) arrangement that is used for computers. The electronic waveform is sampled many times and the characteristics, such as brightness and pitch, are coded into off-on pulses called **bits,** which are then formed into groups called **bytes.** These bytes can be sent from one piece of digital equipment to another until they reach the speaker or monitor. Here they must be converted back into analog because the human ear cannot hear and the human eye cannot see digital bytes. Likewise our voices and images are analog, so the beginning of the audio/video process must be analog.

So why go to all the trouble to convert from analog to digital when digital must, in the end, be converted back to analog? One answer lies in the ability to duplicate with a consistent quality. An analog signal, as it moves from one place to another, deteriorates slightly. The waves representing the characteristics waver and slide so that the end product is not exactly like the original wave. If you have seen a VHS tape containing material that has been copied several times, you have seen the result of this deterioration—the colors run together and the picture is washed out. This does not happen with digital technology. The discrete 0-1 pulses representing a byte do not change. They are the same at each stage of the production process. The difference is akin to trying to redraw the waves of an analog signal—you are bound to draw them a little differently when you redo them—as opposed to copying down the numbers 1 and 0 in the correct order. In addition to duplication superiority, digital technologies create sharper images and crisper sound than analog.

High-Definition Television

Digital technology has been instrumental in the development of **high-definition television (HDTV or simply HD).**[2] This is due, in part, to the fact that digital characteristics help enhance the qualities of a higher-resolution picture.[3]

High-definition TV contains about twice as many lines of resolution as the older NTSC analog television, making for a much sharper picture, and it also uses the widescreen aspect ratio. (See Figure 1.8.) As HDTV was being developed, the older NTSC version of television started being referred to as **standard-definition television (SDTV or SD).** But it became more complicated than that. Some of the ATSC formats had about the same number of lines of resolution and same aspect ra-

tio as the NTSC format, but they were, of course, digital rather than analog. They, too became known as SD formats. In other words, NTSC formats are always analog, always have 525 lines of resolution, and always have the roughly rectangular aspect ratio; ATSC formats are always digital, but some ATSC formats are high definition and some are standard definition.

If all of this sounds complicated, it is. The concepts and terminologies are fairly new and change as technology improves. We discuss NTSC-ATSC-HDTV-SDTV-analog-digital more thoroughly in Chapter 5, but, hopefully, the terminology will become less complicated as high-definition television becomes more commonplace. And HDTV *is* becoming more commonplace. People need to buy new TV sets to view it, but more and more HDTV or HDTV-ready sets are being sold. Production of HDTV programming is picking up also, particularly at broadcast and cable networks. Many of the production techniques will remain the same as those for NTSC TV, but some will change. In this book, we discuss production techniques as they relate to HDTV even though most universities have not found the funds to convert their studios to HD. When you begin working in the industry, however, you are quite likely to encounter this new technology.

Convergence

Digital technologies also allow for **convergence** among various media forms. Digital video signals can be placed in a computer allowing them to be edited with computer software and also enabling them to be distributed over the Internet. It is possible to have both television programming and e-mail (or other Internet services) on the same computer screen at the same time, and both these forms of communication can appear on other digital technologies such as cell phones and satellite TV. Movie theaters are slowly converting to digital so that at some point they, too, may be part of the overall digital entertainment distribution scene. (See Figure 1.9.) Procedures for delivering material over these new and varied distribution forms will be discussed in more detail in Chapter 13.

Convergence has a political aspect as well as a technological one. The government has been encouraging companies to enter a variety of communications businesses—telephones, radio, broadcast television,

Figure 1.8

This high-definition TV set has a wider aspect ratio than the standard sets that have been used for many years. *Photo courtesy of Panasonic.*

Figure 1.9

George Lucas's *Star Wars: Episode I—The Phantom Menace* was one of the first movies projected in a few selected theaters by means of a filmless, totally electronic process. *Star Wars: Episode I—The Phantom Menace* ©*Lucas film Ltd. &*[TM]. *All rights reserved. Used under authorization.*

cable television, satellite broadcasting, the Internet. Some have done so. Rupert Murdoch's News Corporation, for example, owns the Fox Broadcasting Network, several cable TV networks including Fox News Channel and Fox Sports Network, DirecTV satellite system, and 20th Century Fox movie studio, among others.[4]

When companies own a variety of distribution means, they try to engage in *synergy* and use the advantages of convergence to help all their operations. For example, a company that owns a book publishing house and a TV network may make movies from the books it publishes hoping to boost the sales related to both. Most TV shows have websites that give additional information and also try to bring in additional revenue. A company that owns several entities that distribute news may use the same reporters to report stories for various outlets—a newspaper, a broadcast channel, a cable network, a website. People need to develop multiple skills for multiple roles. Convergence has a definite impact on employment. Sometimes consolidation of ownership leads to layoffs, but other times it can open new opportunities as companies try to find new ways of enhancing their combined media operations.

1.5 A Short History of Video Production

The challenges being caused by convergence are not new to the history of electronic media. Throughout its short life it has seen technological processes disappear, equipment shrink, and the methods for getting programming to an audience change.

Early Television

Experiments with television date back to the 1880s when a mechanical, rather than an electronic, process dealt with very small still photos. The closest thing to a "program" was an experimental "science fiction thriller" where an aerial photo of New York moved closer and closer and then disappeared to the sound of an explosion.

By the 1930s a primitive form of black-and-white electronic television had been developed that was able to scan an image of Felix the Cat. (See Figure 1.10.) Largely due to the efforts of David Sarnoff, president

Figure 1.10

This is how Felix the Cat appeared on an experimental 60-line black-and-white TV set in the late 1920s. This picture was transmitted all the way from New York City to Kansas. *Photo courtesy of RCA.*

of RCA, TV was displayed at the 1939 New York World's Fair. (See Figure 1.11.) During a brief period in 1941 prior to America's entry into World War II, the Federal Communications Commission (FCC) granted permission for a few television stations to do experimental broadcasting, but this early broadcast period was cut short by the demands of war.[5]

It took awhile for TV to reestablish itself after the war, but by 1948 it was back in business, still in its black-and-white form. Many of the first broadcasts were live remotes. Bulky cameras attached to enormous trucks showed boxing and wrestling matches, baseball games, and dance bands from local ballrooms. TV sets were relatively expensive, so very few people had them in their homes and a lot of the viewing was done in bars. But people loved television, and by 1949 it was well ensconced in living rooms.

Sports remotes continued, but studio production became popular. Milton Berle's *Texaco Star Theater*, a

Figure 1.11

Television being demonstrated at the 1939 New York World's Fair. *Photo courtesy of RCA.*

studio-produced comedy-variety show, became a phenomenal hit and was the reason many people bought their first TV set. Children's programs were also popular during the late 1940s and 1950s, often featuring a clown or some other character who interacted with children in the studio audience and introduced cartoons. Commercials were usually done live from the studio by freelance announcers with a few slides and a hand prop such as a vegetable slicer or a knife set.

Uses of Film and Live Camera

There were no portable video cameras for capturing news, but film cameras were used for this purpose. Because of the expense of film, however, they were used sparingly. Local newscasts would show still photos that came over the syndicated news wires to cover stories that had not been covered on film.

Although some programming was technically and creatively primitive during TV's early years, a number of excellent musical and dramatic programs were produced in New York using a multiple video-camera technique. Done straight through from start to finish with only short breaks for commercials, the actors gave gripping performances with the feel of a stage play. Timing was crucial because there was no way to edit the programs. Sometimes a scene would be written for near the end of a drama where a character had to look for something. If the program was running long, the actor could find the object right away. If not, he or she would hunt for a while.

The only way to record a live program in these early years was through the use of the **kinescope** film process. With few refinements, this was basically a matter of running a film camera in front of a TV set, the result being a noticeable loss of picture and audio quality. (See Figure 1.12.) In the late 1950s, many people in the western states were seeing prime-time network studio productions by means of these filmed recordings because the infrastructure had not been built for transporting signals across the country.

In the early years, film was not used to shoot entire programs because of its cost. Aside from reshowing the program on the West Coast, no one could envision a reason for having a copy of a show. Reruns did not cross people's minds in these early years. But when *I Love Lucy* started in 1951, its creators decided, in what

Figure 1.12

The lack of resolution seen in this kinescope of a late 1950s KABC-TV program resulted in equally weak audio as a result of the recording process.

was then a maverick move, to film the programs. (See Figure 1.13.) Later the filming more than paid for itself because the programs could be sold overseas to a burgeoning international TV market. As filming began to pay off, more programs, especially westerns, were filmed and shown on 1950s TV.

The Impact of Recorded and Edited Video

Video, however, soon developed its own recording medium. Introduced by Ampex in 1956, the **videotape recorder (VTR)** became a standard for studio production during the 1960s. The first VTRs used tape that was two inches wide, and they were as tall as the operator. (See Figure 1.14.)

They changed television production procedures, at first simply because programs could be taped at a different time than they were aired. This was a big help for covering different time zones and for cast and crew members who could work during normal business hours rather than the wee hours of the morning or evening.

Figure 1.13

I Love Lucy was filmed, enabling it to be seen over and over, as it still is today.
Photo courtesy of Viacom, Hlwd.

Soon, however, people developed methods to edit videotape so that different variety acts, for example, could be taped one at a time and later could be strung together. The original editing was done with razor blades and plastic adhesive tape. This process was quickly replaced by electronic **transfer editing** that recorded selected segments from a playback machine to an edited master tape on a second machine.

Figure 1.14

Until the late 1960s many stations were still using large standing models of video recorders for basic playback and recording purposes. This machine was as tall as its operator and about three feet wide.

Color

Another important technological change of the 1960s was the conversion to color TV. A color TV standard was actually approved by the FCC in 1953, but it had had a rancorous history because CBS and RCA-NBC were promoting competing and incompatible color systems. The RCA-NBC system won, but for many years only NBC programmed in color. CBS refused to participate and ABC, strapped for money at the time, broadcast only color shows produced by the movie

studios. But color did eventually take hold and with it a new array of aesthetic production possibilities.[6]

Portable Video Equipment

By the 1970s three-quarter-inch videotape packaged into a cassette was giving rise to small portable video systems. (See Figure 1.15.) At first the portable camera was separate from the portable **videocassette recorder (VCR).** But as time progressed, the recorders became even smaller, using half-inch and narrower tape. This gave rise to the very portable camcorder and changed the way field production was undertaken.

For news production there was no waiting for film to be delivered back to the lab to be developed before editing. TV production, as a whole, became less studio-bound. Even though a large portion of a program might emanate from a studio, sections of it could incorporate the "real world" either through live reports from the field or through something that had been prerecorded in the field and then edited.

Computer-Based Technologies

During the 1980s and 1990s, television production profited greatly from the digital technologies originally developed for computers. One of the first changes was in the area of graphics. Prior to this period, opening and closing credits and any other words, numbers, or charts had to be drawn or printed. Stacks of graphic cards were placed on easels in the studio and as they were needed one of the cameras would focus on them. In the 1980s, **character generators** were developed wherein letters could be typed onto a computer screen and incorporated within a program as needed. The first character generators were primitive, lacking word wrap or centering or font variety, but they eventually evolved into the elaborate graphics generators used today.

The next step was that computers could be used to control videotape equipment used to transfer material from one recorder to another in a **linear editing** fashion. As computer storage increased from megabytes to gigabytes, audio and video could be stored on a hard drive. This, in turn, made possible flexible **nonlinear editing.** The computer controlled instant access to any audio or video point on the hard drive just as a person

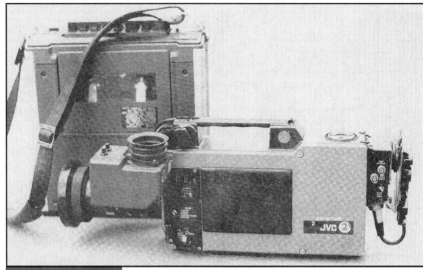

Figure 1.15

A camera attached to a three-quarter-inch U-matic VCR—one of the first portable configurations.

with a personal computer could almost instantly find the beginning of a sentence and then add or subtract any amount of copy on a document. The time previously spent rolling tapes back and forth was eliminated (see Chapter 11).

Computer-based digital technologies also led to digital cameras (see Chapter 5) that were superior in quality to the older analog ones. They also facilitated all of the visual effects now present in movies and television programs. We are now firmly in the digital age, but, as with previous times, change is still the watchword. Those people most likely to succeed in electronic media careers are those who are flexible enough to embrace new techniques while still maintaining the discipline that has always been needed in this field.

1.6 Aspects of Employment in the Video Industry

To the outsider, and probably to some newer entry-level workers, video production might seem to be an endlessly fascinating combination of glamour and excitement. While it is true that status and income levels are often impressive and that the intensity found in many production situations can make the pulse race, other aspects of a video production career also make it very attractive.

Most video professionals feel a definite sense of pride in functioning as a part of a team that creates a product generally valued by our society. Whether you work on a TV news program or on developing a corporate training tape, the process of working together and creating a worthwhile end product provides a strong sense of continuing inner satisfaction as well as a good deal of mutual respect among colleagues.

Work Patterns

Although many prime network and cable shows are produced in large, fully equipped video studios often located on movie lots, many other programs are recorded through smaller **production houses,** with or without union sanction. They employ many recently graduated students working at entry-level wages. The reality is that all too often during the early years of a media career, you must make the decision to trade experience for the kind of salary you would prefer.

But most of those who can survive the difficult early years find themselves in responsible positions with a fairly secure future. You can take heart in the knowledge that those early career problems facing today's students are not very different from those entry-level people faced over the past decades. The oversupply of people wanting to get into TV has always existed.

Another problem is that your work may not be steady. Often people in the video business are employed on a **daily hire** basis. These workers are not on staff, and even though they may work three or four days a week, they are not eligible for health care or other benefits. One result of this **freelance** employment is that many people now make their living working simultaneously in cable, corporate, satellite, Internet, and broadcast production. The production techniques and equipment are very much the same. Crew members are often called upon to perform a wide range of tasks such as audio, lighting, camera, and graphics. Those wishing to direct and produce are usually selected from the crew positions.

Types of Jobs

Many different types of positions are available for people who are trained in video production. Obviously, you are qualified for numerous jobs in entertainment and news over conventional television. But another area for jobs today is *corporate video*. Large and small companies produce a variety of material, such as orientation tapes for new employees, training tapes for new products, and video "newsletters" to keep employees up-to-date. Sometimes these companies have staff people who use company equipment to produce the material in-house; other times they hire freelancers or people who have small production houses. In both cases jobs are created for people with television production skills.

One of the largest employers of media people is the government. Local, state, and federal agencies are involved in a myriad of telecommunications projects. Military applications, including the Armed Forces Radio and Television Services, account for worldwide operations. The medical field, too, needs video production people. Most hospitals use television and related media for patient education, in-service training, and/or public and community relations. (See Figure 1.16.) Another specialized field is *religious production*. The production level seen on many broadcasts of evangelical groups rivals that of many network programs. Many church bodies operate their own networks.

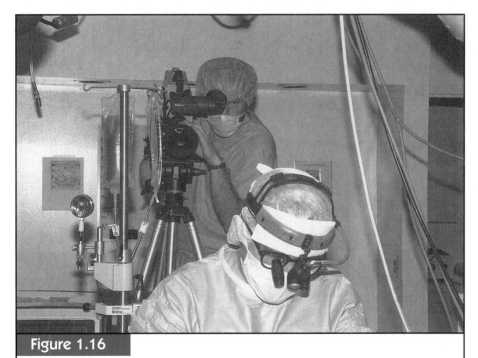

Figure 1.16

The taping of a medical procedure. The use of TV by the medical industry provides jobs for people trained in video production.

Interactive video, made possible by the instant access possibilities of **CD-ROMs, DVDs, video games,** and the **Internet,** is having an important impact on the variety of new jobs that have been established related to designing web pages and developing interactive products for a variety of clients. One of the more intriguing applications of video and computer technologies is **event video,** wherein entrepreneurs produce videotape recordings of weddings, birthdays, school yearbooks, and other significant events.

Employment Preparation

Although a beginning video production course may seem a little early to be thinking about a job résumé, consider that you could be writing a short résumé for an internship or some other production-related position sooner than you think. Many schools offer or require internships, and holding down a part-time job in your area of interest is an excellent way to gain valuable experience.

Also keep in mind that some of your final projects in more-advanced video classes may give you material for the first edition of a *portfolio* that shows what you can do. If you can handle simple school projects well, the people interviewing you for jobs will spot it. Also keep in mind that many of your classmates, especially those with whom you have worked on a team project, are people who may help you get a job or are the ones you may hire someday. It happens.

Discussion Questions

1. Discuss the concept of disciplines and techniques in terms of your own athletic participation, hobbies, schoolwork, and/or employment experiences.

2. In what ways is your school studio complex similar to and different from what is discussed in section 1.2?

3. What do you think video production will be like 10 years from now?

4. In your estimation, what have been the most important technical developments in video production over the years?

Notes

1. As you will learn later, sometimes sound from the microphone goes through a portable mixer where it is combined with other sounds. At other times sound is sent to a separate recorder. The difference here is often referred to as *single-system sound* and *double-system sound.* For single-system sound the audio is recorded along with the video. For double-system sound, the picture is recorded one place and the sound another, such as a DAT. Double-system is used, particularly in movies, so that the sound can be more carefully controlled during recording and more easily manipulated during the editing process.

2. Actually HDTV started out in the 1970s as an analog system developed by the Japanese. But by the time the United States decided to develop a standard for HDTV, it opted for a digital configuration. For more details, see S. Merrill Weiss, "DTV Standard: The Grand Compromise," *TV Technology,* 27 Feb. 1997, 35.

3. Another factor that will be discussed in Chapter 10 is the fact that digital signals can be compressed. See "Digital Compression," *CTI,* Oct. 2000, 46–51.

4. "Rupe Finally Bags His Bird," *Variety,* 10 Apr. 2003, 1; and "Top Media Deals 2001," *Electronic Media,* 31 Dec. 2001, 4.

5. A good source that covers this early material is Erik Barnouw, *The Golden Web: A History of Broadcasting in the United States, 1933–1953* (New York: Oxford University Press, 1968).

6. David E. Garvey, "Introducing Color Television: The Audience and Programming Problems," *Journal of Broadcasting* 24 (Fall 1980): 515–26.

CHAPTER 2

Cast and Crew

When television was first being introduced, radio comedian Fred Allen quipped, "Television is the triumph of equipment over people." There are times (when the camera focus goes out and the computer graphics generator crashes and the audio cable develops a short—all in one day) that cast and crew members may feel that equipment has, indeed, triumphed over them. But as important as equipment is to the production process, it is really the *people* behind and in front of that equipment who are the driving force and the deciding factor regarding the quality of any TV production.

This chapter gives an overview of the duties of the various people involved in production. For the most part, it discusses the positions and tasks required for studio production with the assumption that the program is being sent out live or is being recorded from beginning to end with very few, if any, stops. This type of production requires a large crew because many things must be done all at once.

However, the cast and crew for studio productions vary from place to place and time to time. Facilities that are unionized are likely to have more people than nonunionized shops where people switch jobs and often undertake several functions. Other factors that can affect crew positions are the degree of the production facility's automation and the health of the economy.

The crew positions covered in this chapter are the ones that are at least somewhat standard in the business. Each crew position is discussed in terms of what you would need to do before the actual production process begins, what you do during rehearsal and while the program is being recorded (or aired live), and what you do after production is over. This will give you a general overview of what you should do for your very first production exercise. Because many of these positions are involved with producing or directing or with operating specific pieces of equipment, the chapters that follow will, by nature, give even more detail about the jobs. This chapter should allow you to get started with production, and then you can hone your skills as you learn more details.

You and all the other people involved in a production must undertake certain *techniques* in order to accomplish the given tasks. A technical director must know which buttons and levers to push in order to dissolve from camera 1 to camera 2; the videotape operator must know how to check various meters to make sure picture and sound are actually being recorded; an actor must be able to memorize lines. But you also need the *disciplines* that will ensure a smooth production. Television production can involve a great deal of "hurry up and wait," and cast and crew members need to be at the ready so that they can undertake their duties when the need arises. To delineate the techniques and disciplines involved with production, this chapter covers the following:

- The intensity of the producer's work during preproduction (2.1)
- The "orchestra conductor" role of the director (2.2)
- The timing of a production and the other duties undertaken by the AD (2.3)
- The various ways the stage manager keeps control in the studio (2.4)
- The basic functions of the camera operators (2.5)
- The prompter operator's role in relation to the script and the talent (2.6)
- The preproduction role of the lighting director (2.7)
- The audio operator's duties in terms of both the studio and the control room (2.8)
- The technical and aesthetic duties of the graphics operator (2.9)
- How the technical director assures that the proper picture gets on the air (2.10)
- The videotape operator's responsibilities in terms of recording and playing back (2.11)
- Work that the editor does, especially after the production (2.12)
- Other positions that are often needed for production (2.13)
- The difference between performers and actors (2.14)
- Performing tips for people who are in front of the camera (2.14)
- Clothing, makeup, and hairstyling considerations for those on camera (2.14)

2.1 Producers

Producers are in charge of the *overall organization* of a production, be it a network comedy, a local station newscast, a cable TV sportscast, a syndicated soap opera, an interactive video game, or a corporate training tape. As a producer, you are responsible for seeing that all the elements of a program are in the right place at the right time. (See Figure 2.1.) Have the actors been cast? Has the fog machine been ordered? Where will the cast and crew eat? Producers often initiate a project

Cell phones have become invaluable for producers, such as Wendy Mogol, as they stay in touch with the intricacies of the production process.

and see that it is finished *on time* and *on budget* (see Chapter 3).

Before Production Begins

Your most intensive work as a producer is accomplished during **preproduction.** This is the period when everything must be carefully planned so that **production** (shooting) and **postproduction** (editing) can progress smoothly. You oversee the script and the budget (see Chapter 3), make sure all the necessary people have been hired (often in conjunction with the director), attend to legal matters, and see that all facilities and equipment are available. In general, a producer handles the logistics of a production while a director makes the creative and aesthetic decisions.

During Rehearsal and Recording

For most student productions, a producer is present during rehearsal and recording to give the director moral support and to handle any last-minute details. On the professional level, a producer's role during rehearsal and recording varies according to the nature of the project, the relationship between the producer and director, and how smoothly things are going. If a drama is shot outside the country, the producer may stay home and not witness a single day of shooting; if a talk show is taped in the same building where the producer works, the producer will probably stop in and welcome the guests. Producers are usually in the control room during the entire broadcast of a live news program because so many decisions must be made at the last minute, and producers have the ultimate say regarding what stories appear on the newscast.

When producers and directors work together frequently and harmoniously, the producer comes to trust the director and may never appear on the set. A producer will exert more control if the director's ability is uncertain. A director who is still shooting two days after production was to have finished can most assuredly expect a visit from the producer. So can one who is spending money at a rapid clip.

After the Production

The producer's role if a program needs editing has the same variations as the role during production. A producer stationed at some distance from the editing facility who trusts the director may never appear in the editing room, although the producer almost always looks at a rough cut of an edited program and gives opinions as to what needs to be changed. A student producer will be more involved.

As producer, you should handle the social and legal aftermath of the production. Have the guests been sent thank-you e-mails? Have the music copyright fees actually been paid? The producer also oversees the distribution and promotion of the program and evaluates the program and the process so that things can operate more smoothly (or as smoothly) next time.

2.2 Directors

A **director** has been likened to a symphony conductor. The various crew members are each playing their own "instruments" (camera, audio board, switcher, etc.), and it is the director who coordinates them and sets the overall pace of the program (see Chapter 4). In some situations, the director will have helped to shape the script. In many other situations you, as director, will have the script handed to you and will take the production from there.

Before Production Begins

Your first concern should be to determine the *specific purpose* of the script. Ask yourself several questions: What is the objective of the show? How do you want the audience to react to the program? Then you can begin to think in terms of the overall "feel" and image of the program. What kinds of settings, lighting, and graphics would be most effective?

Next, you should check the script for rough timing. Is the length all right or does the script need to be cut or lengthened? The script should be put in its final television production format and duplicated for all personnel involved. How many copies do you need?

Once you are completely comfortable with the script, you should be able to start specific *facilities planning*. In the case of a remote coverage of some event, you have to scout the location (often in conjunction with other crew members). In other professional situations, you may have to rent studio facilities. Local TV stations own studios that are used for station news and other programs. In most academic situations, the studio will be assigned to you for a definite period of time.

As a student, you may not have to be concerned with securing personnel. The technical crew will be assigned from your class or from some other participating class. There may be some occasions, however, when you will be involved in selecting specific individuals for particular crew assignments.

Casting for actors or other performers may also be done on an informal basis in the academic setting. You may work through the drama department, or you may prevail upon your personal friends or classmates. In securing such volunteer help, make certain that you have a firm commitment; many a student production has been ruined because some friend or casual acquaintance backed out of a production at the last moment. In professional situations, of course, casting is quite an involved process (see Chapter 4).

Next comes the job of pulling the production together. In any kind of major production, the director should plan on holding one or more *production conferences* involving the chief production personnel. (See Figure 2.2.) You must now make sure that all the preproduction elements are properly requested and constructed. The lighting and staging plans are developed at this stage. If any special costumes or props have to be ordered or fabricated, the process is initiated now. Music and other special audio or video material must be chosen and/or produced.

During the entire preproduction process, you have to be working within a very tight interlocking schedule of *checkpoints* and *deadlines*. Many production elements cannot proceed until other items are taken care of first. The costumes must arrive before the exterior video can be shot. The set must be designed before set pieces can be constructed.

Figure 2.2

Prior to production, the director holds a conference with the associate director, stage manager, technical director, and lighting director. *Photo courtesy of Melissa Bossenmeyer.*

In the midst of this activity, you also must be concerned with preparing your script for the day of production. What pacing do you want to achieve? What images and sounds do you want to create to achieve your purpose? You should *mark* your copy of the script indicating which cameras you are going to use for which shots and what instructions you are going to give cast and crew (see Chapter 4).

During Rehearsal and Recording

The director is *the* person in charge during rehearsal and recording. During rehearsals you must make sure that the people both behind and in front of the camera know what they are to do. Never assume that people can read your mind. Some programs, such as dramas, need extensive rehearsals, because everything must take place in a very precise manner. Other programs, such as talk shows, require less rehearsal. In fact, re-

hearsing a talk show too thoroughly can ruin its spontaneity because all the participants will know what everyone else is going to say. For these types of programs, it is often best to discuss only the general topics and the logistical aspects, such as when you will be cutting away for commercials.

After rehearsal, you are ready to start calling shots on your production. If you are a first-time director, you will probably feel some anxiety. However, regardless of what might be churning inside, try *not* to let it show. Force yourself to sit back and take a deep breath. Remember that the composure or anxiety you communicate to the crew will surely be returned to you.

Your actual commands will depend on the type of production, but usually you must do the following: call up the music and graphics needed for the opening credits; make sure the cameras are on shots you are likely to need as the program progresses; call for the proper camera to be on the air at the proper time; bring in prerecorded video or audio material as it is needed; and execute the closing credits.

During the course of your program, always be *looking ahead* two or three minutes. What possible problems lie ahead? Did the mic boom get repositioned all right? Are the closing credits ready to roll? Usually, it is a good idea to delegate many of these "look-ahead" duties to your associate director, but you, as director, have the ultimate responsibility to make sure everything goes as planned.

After the Production

When the program is finished, don't let either talent or crew leave their positions until the videotape operator has played back a bit of the program to make sure it recorded. Then use the **studio address** to thank the crew and talent. Even if you are feeling extremely tense or relieved, keep your composure. Make certain you and your crew clear the studio and control room of all scripts, notes, props, and everything else connected with your production. Don't expect the next group using the studio to clean up your mess.

If there is any postproduction editing to be accomplished, your job is far from done (see Chapter 11). If it is a simple matter of inserting a clean shot to cover the one bad blunder, you may be able to get it done right away. If it is a major editing job of assembling video pieces from several different sources, you will need to schedule editing sessions.

2.3 | Associate Directors

The **associate director** (sometimes referred to as the **assistant director,** or **AD**)[1] helps the director with various tasks. For this reason, some of the duties the AD is assigned differ from program to program, depending on the philosophy and work style of the director. One director may want you to set up all the on-air camera shots so he or she can concentrate on last-minute details, aesthetic decisions, and the actual takes on the air. Other directors want you to sit nearby to remind them of what is coming up next. (See Figure 2.3.) If a show is taped in front of an audience, but the scenes are not taped in order, the director may ask the AD to prepare taped mate-

rial compiled from rehearsals that can be shown to the audience so they understand how the story progresses.

With just about every kind of studio operation, however, one of the AD's primary jobs will be that of timing the production. You will time individual segments during rehearsals, get an overall timing of the program, and then be in charge of the pacing of the program—speeding up or stretching as required—during the actual recording.

Before Production Begins

In any major production undertaking, the AD will work with the director well in advance of the actual production period—attending production conferences, working with talent, and assembling props and other materials. You may be in charge of the rest of the crew—checking to make certain that everyone is present. In nonunion productions, you may be in charge of arranging substitute assignments, thus ensuring that every position is covered.

During Rehearsal and Recording

During the rehearsals, the director will mention various production items that need attention before the actual take. You will jot down the "critique notes," as the director spots problems. Additionally, you should be making notes of similar items that might have escaped the attention of the director. If you notice a major item, such as a missing prop, it should be called to the director's attention before the rehearsal proceeds. Minor items, such as a distracting shadow on the talent's shoulder, are simply written down to be cleaned up later.

You will be especially concerned with noting all the script changes that are made. If any segments are going to be taped out of order, you should note any **continuity** problems that could arise. For example, if a vase of flowers is needed for the first segment and is removed during the second segment but is needed again for the third segment, you should make a special note to double-check that the flowers are returned before the taping of segment three begins.

You may also use the rehearsal period to time as much of the program as possible, including individual segments, tape inserts, and opening and closing elements. All of these will help you with crucial timing that will be needed during the actual production of the program. For

Figure 2.3

The associate director (*front*) sits next to the director (*center*) during taping. *Photo courtesy of Melissa Bossenmeyer.*

example, the final segment of a program might be very crucial to the understanding of the entire program and need to be shown in a specific way. You can time that segment during rehearsal and then **backtime** (count backward from the end of the program). Thus, you will know exactly when the preceding segment must end so that the final segment can be completed properly. Then during production, you can give time signals to the talent regarding when they should wind up the next-to-last segment and begin the final segment.

After the rehearsal and before the actual take, it is your job to make certain that the director *follows through* on all production notes that were jotted down during rehearsal. Often, at this point, the director has a meeting with the entire crew to go over what needs to be changed before the program is actually taped or broadcast. This meeting is based largely on your notes.

Next, you must make sure that everybody involved has all script changes marked down. As surely as one person did not get a crucial script change, that omission will lead to an on-the-air mistake. Additionally, you should remind the director of how much time is remaining before recording is scheduled to start or before the live program goes on the air.

Just prior to production, you will *read down* the clock, letting the director know how many minutes or seconds until air or until recording is to begin. Once on the air, you should follow the script and remain alert to any and all potential problems—ready to call major troubles to the attention of the director.

Your primary job, however, is handling *timing*. The AD must ensure that the entire production is the right length. If the program is to be edited, timing all of the segments to be electronically glued together is an important consideration here. You need some way of keeping track of the various timing notes and reminders. The digital clock readouts available in most control rooms are essential, but many ADs also use stopwatches and timing sheets (see Chapter 4).

As AD, you are also in charge of making sure the talent receives proper time cues. Either directly or through the director, you will tell the stage manager when to give each time signal to the talent. Time signals are given to the talent in terms of *time remaining.* Thus, as you approach the end of a program, you will have the stage manager signal the performer that there are "five minutes remaining," "one minute to go," "30 seconds left," and so forth.

Also during the production, you will be taking notes for postproduction editing—both those items that the director points out (a missed shot, an opportunity to insert a reaction shot) and the items that you notice need to be corrected. Finally, you must be ready to take over at any time. The AD is literally the standby director. Should the director be unable to complete the program, you will assume responsibility for calling shots.

After the Production

Once the production is completed, you still have a few obligations. You should help clean up the control room of extra scripts, notes, and other materials, and debrief the director on any errors that occurred during the program.

A crucial postproduction job of the AD in many situations is the final editing session. You may need to set up a schedule with the director for any planned editing. You may simply continue as the director's right-hand assistant in these assignments or, depending on the nature of the production arrangements, you may be substantially in charge of the postproduction editing session—following the director's instructions, of course.

Some productions, mainly due to budget concerns, do not employ an AD. The director does all the duties usually assigned to the AD. If a production is simple and repetitive, this can work all right, but not having an AD opens the door for errors that would not occur if the director had an assistant taking up some of the workload and double-checking on the program's needs.

2.4 | Stage Managers

The **stage manager** (also called the **floor manager** or the **floor director**)[2] is the director's key assistant in charge of what is happening in the studio. When you assume this role, your main job is to communicate with the talent. The director is in the control room during the actual production and gives you instructions that you relay to the talent mainly through hand signals.

As with the AD position, some studio productions do not employ a stage manager. The performers wear earphones that are part of an **interruptible feedback (IFB)** system and the director gives instructions directly into their ears. Again this increases the difficulty of the director's job and also makes it harder for the talent who must be listening to the director at the same time they are talking. Using an IFB is common for live-from-the-scene news reports where reporters can hear each other as well as the director, but most studio shoots still use a stage manager as a communicator and overseer of the studio.

Before Production Begins

How much you do before production begins depends, to some extent, on how experienced the talent is. Anchors who read the news every day don't need much in the way of basic instruction from the floor manager. But if the talent is new to television, you should attend to their *emotional-physical* needs. Can you offer a glass of water? What production mysteries should be explained to the talent?

This last point is important with inexperienced performers. Because they are not tied into the **intercom,** they are not aware of what is going on most of the time. Explain to the talent why there is a delay (a result of a computer malfunction—not because the talent sat in the wrong chair); explain why the crew is laughing (at the AD's story—not at the talent's clothing).

Prior to production, you should also work out with the talent the *technical-production* requirements. Where is the talent to stand for the demonstration? What kinds of special cues might be needed? All these details should be considered carefully, so that both you and the talent know what to do during the actual taping. In addition, you should demonstrate the various hand signals (stand by to start, begin talking, talk to this camera, cut, etc.) to inexperienced talent and decide exactly what time cues will be given. (See Figure 2.4.)

In addition to handling talent, the other main job of the stage manager is that of handling all production details on the studio floor. This area includes a variety of concerns: broadly supervising staging and lighting setups,[3] directing studio traffic, distributing scripts to everyone who needs them, making sure props are in their right positions. You should exercise authority, because every other floor position is concerned with the production from only one specific viewpoint. For example, the camera operator, the boom operator, and the lighting director all have their particular perspectives to take care of. Perhaps each of these three will have selected the same spot on the floor to position a camera, a mic boom, and a light stand. It is up to you, working from a broader perspective, to coordinate these needs and decide what goes where.

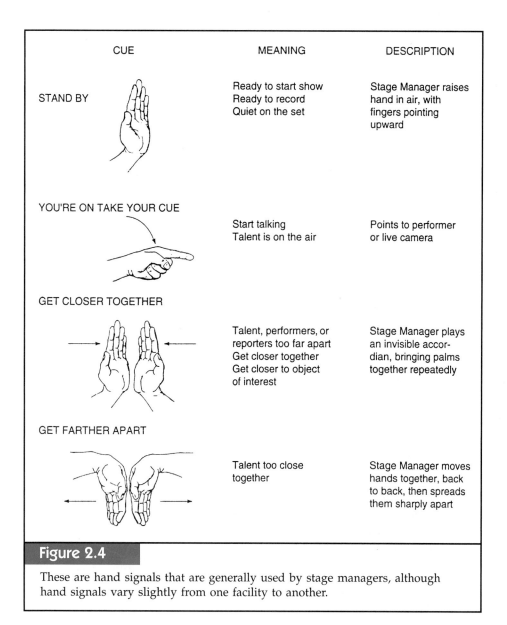

CUE	MEANING	DESCRIPTION
STAND BY	Ready to start show Ready to record Quiet on the set	Stage Manager raises hand in air, with fingers pointing upward
YOU'RE ON TAKE YOUR CUE	Start talking Talent is on the air	Points to performer or live camera
GET CLOSER TOGETHER	Talent, performers, or reporters too far apart Get closer together Get closer to object of interest	Stage Manager plays an invisible accordian, bringing palms together repeatedly
GET FARTHER APART	Talent too close together	Stage Manager moves hands together, back to back, then spreads them sharply apart

Figure 2.4

These are hand signals that are generally used by stage managers, although hand signals vary slightly from one facility to another.

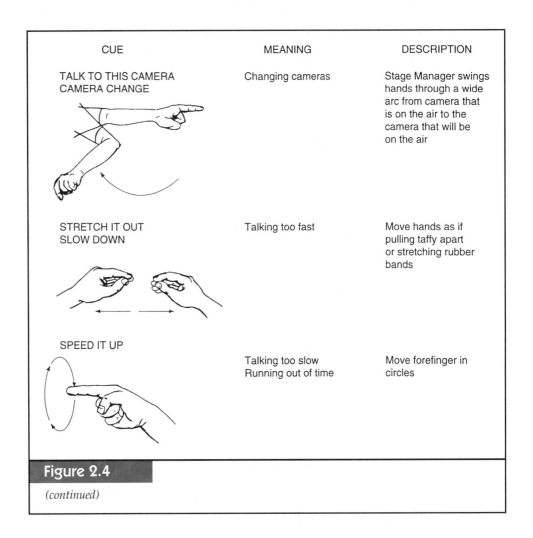

CUE	MEANING	DESCRIPTION
TALK TO THIS CAMERA CAMERA CHANGE	Changing cameras	Stage Manager swings hands through a wide arc from camera that is on the air to the camera that will be on the air
STRETCH IT OUT SLOW DOWN	Talking too fast	Move hands as if pulling taffy apart or stretching rubber bands
SPEED IT UP	Talking too slow Running out of time	Move forefinger in circles

Figure 2.4

(continued)

During Rehearsal and Recording

During rehearsal, the stage manager should give the talent hand cues so they can become familiar with them. In doing this, you should always be in a position to be spotted easily by the talent. The performers should never have to turn their heads or search the studio with their eyes to find you. Often it is good to crouch below the camera that the talent should be addressing. You must, however, make sure that you stay out of the way of the camera lens so that your head or arm does not inadvertently pop up in the shot. During rehearsal, you should also make sure of what your other duties will be. Do you need to move a prop? Do you need to replenish a bowl of fruit?

Once the production begins, the stage manager is the primary contact the talent has. The studio door is shut and the director is in the control room. At this stage, your main job is to give hand cues to the talent and possibly move elements on the set, such as props. You must remain extra alert for any problems and double-check to ensure that all crew and talent are in their places. In general, you must guarantee that everything for the studio that was worked out during the rehearsal period is executed during production.

After the Production

When the taping is over, the stage manager helps collect props and generally polices the studio to see that everything is returned to where it belongs, ready for the next production. After the production, as well as before and during it, you must think of yourself as *the* pivotal individual in charge of the studio—the person who must take the initiative in getting things done.

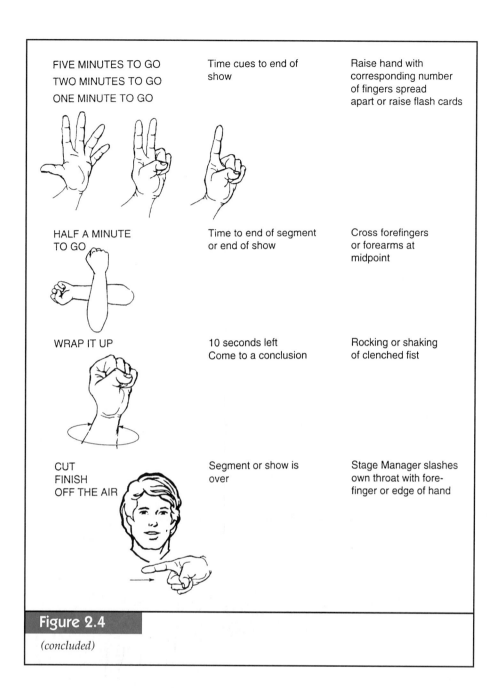

FIVE MINUTES TO GO TWO MINUTES TO GO ONE MINUTE TO GO	Time cues to end of show	Raise hand with corresponding number of fingers spread apart or raise flash cards
HALF A MINUTE TO GO	Time to end of segment or end of show	Cross forefingers or forearms at midpoint
WRAP IT UP	10 seconds left Come to a conclusion	Rocking or shaking of clenched fist
CUT FINISH OFF THE AIR	Segment or show is over	Stage Manager slashes own throat with forefinger or edge of hand

Figure 2.4

(concluded)

2.5 Camera Operators

Camera operators are the people who, based on instructions from the director, frame the shots for the program. To do this job, you must understand the operation of the camera thoroughly (see Chapter 5) so that you can physically move the camera while keeping the image steady and in focus. You must pay particular attention to how the camera interacts with the lighting so that the picture is not overexposed or underexposed. In addition, you must have an aesthetic sense so that the pictures are properly composed. The camera operator frames, from a broad panorama, what the viewer will see.

Most studio productions require at least three camera operators who stand behind their cameras and operate them throughout the taping. If there is no stage manager, one of the camera operators may be asked to signal the talent when to start and stop. Some productions use

robotic cameras; the cameras are located in the studio but have no operators. One person in the control room or the studio operates all the cameras by handling levers that focus and move the camera remotely. (See Color Plate F.)

Before Production Begins

Before the production begins, camera operators ready the cameras for operation. Often this involves wheeling the camera out from beside a wall where it is stored, turning it on, taking a cap off the front of the lens, opening and adjusting a number of levers and knobs that allow the camera to move freely, and generally checking to make sure everything is working properly. (See Figure 2.5.)

Once all the lighting is set, you often need to make some adjustments to the cameras so that their pictures will be optimized for the lights. Sometimes an engineer in the control room, usually referred to as a **video operator** (or **shader**) operates a **camera control unit (CCU)** that handles the more technical adjustments for the cameras. For example, this person operates remote controls on the CCU that govern the relationship of the cameras to the lighting.

During Rehearsal and Recording

Rehearsals are when you find out exactly what will be required and iron out any potential problems. If the program is not rehearsed, you should definitely meet with the director before taping to find out what shots you will be covering. Then during the production, you follow the instructions given by the director over the intercom.

You should always try to think ahead to your next shot. Is the talent going to rise, and, if so, have

Figure 2.5

The camera operators practice their shots during setup time. *Photo courtesy of Melissa Bossenmeyer.*

you unlocked the lever that allows you to tilt the camera up? Are you going to need to get out of the way of another camera operator who has to make a wide move? Are there any cables or other obstructions that will get in the way of your own camera move?

After the Production

After the production is over, you should put the cameras away properly. Usually this involves coiling the cable attached to the camera and moving the camera back to where it is stored. You should cap the lens and lock down all levers and knobs. It is not always necessary to turn the camera off. If it is going to be used again within a short period of time, it should be left on because turning electronics off and on too frequently shortens a camera's life.

2.6 Prompter Operators

Prompters (also called *auto cues* or *TelePrompTers*)[4] are mirror/monitor computerized systems that allow the talent to see words of the script roll up in front of the camera lens. (See Figure 2.6.) Usually all the cameras are equipped with a prompter so that talent can turn from one camera to another and still see the same script. The viewer does not see this script, but the talent can read it while looking directly at the camera lens. Someone has to control the rate that the script

Figure 2.6

A prompter operator types a script before production begins.   *Photo courtesy of Melissa Bossenmeyer.*

crawls up the prompter so that it does not get either ahead of or behind the talent. That someone is the **prompter operator,** although in some situations the talent controls the operation of the prompter.

Before Production Begins

Most prompters are computerized so that whatever script is written for the program can also be fed into the prompter computer without having to be retyped. If the script must be retyped, however, it is your job, as prompter operator, to do that before the production begins. Even if the script does not need retyping, you should check it carefully before taping to make sure it is formatted properly and does not contain anything that will confuse the talent. Are stage directions included in such a way that the on-camera person might accidentally read them? Are any commas missing that could cause the talent to stumble over words?

During Rehearsal and Recording

During rehearsal and production, the prompter operator (who may be physically located in either the control room or the studio) must position the script properly. Many prompters have a variable speed control or a mouse that the operator uses to move the computerized copy. The words that a performer is reading at the moment should be close to the center of the screen with enough of the upcoming script showing so that there is no chance the talent needs to hesitate.

After the Production

After the production is over, you generally delete the script from the computer so that it does not clog up the storage capacity. If production is over for the day, you may want to turn off the computer, although in some facilities the computers are left on most of the time.

2.7 | Lighting Directors

The **lighting director (LD)** is in charge of seeing that the lights are properly set for the telecast and that any lighting effects needed during the telecast are executed (see Chapter 6). Usually this person has a crew that

actually places and adjusts the lights while the LD makes sure the overall effect is accomplished. If the same set is used day after day and there are no major lighting changes, the LD may be on call and not in the studio on a daily basis.

Before Production Begins

Most of the work that you do as LD takes place well before the production begins. For a studio shoot, you and your crew members make sure that the proper amount and type of light reach all the studio locations that need it. For studios that can afford a large number of lighting instruments, this may involve identifying, from the many lights on the **grid** (a series of interconnected pipes that hang just below the ceiling), the lights that are needed and then turning them on. If a studio does not have a large number of lights, then the crew members may have to climb ladders and reposition lights on the grid so that they illuminate the proper areas. (See Figure 2.7.)

Whether the lights are moved or prepositioned, crew members may have to readjust them slightly so that they cast the best possible illumination. Lights are usually plugged into a **dimmer board** so they can be manipulated easily. As LD, you must make sure that the lights give the proper amount of illumination and the proper emotional feeling.

During Rehearsal and Recording

During rehearsals, you and your crew make whatever adjustments you or the director deem necessary. During the production, the LD and crew may have nothing to do. If the same lighting is needed throughout the taping, they may actually leave the studio to work on another show. Often for student productions, these people assume other positions during the production. However, if lights need to be dimmed or changed in some other way during production, then at least the LD will remain to execute these changes.

After the Production

After the production is over, someone must make sure that all the lights are turned off. If studio procedures so require, any lights that were moved should be put back where they were.

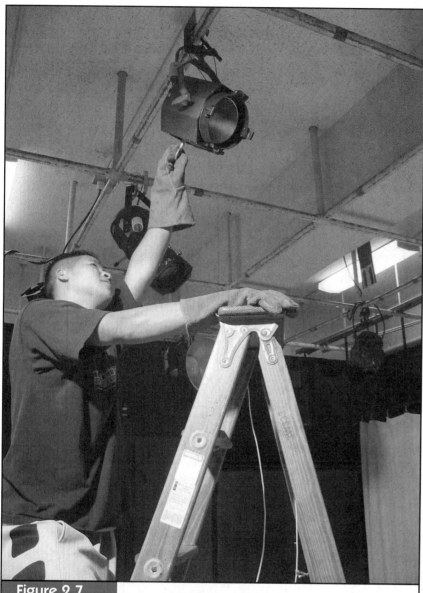

Figure 2.7

This lighting crew member has climbed a ladder to position a light so that it covers a precise area. *Photo courtesy of Donald McLaren.*

2.8 Audio Operators

Some of the work that is done in connection with audio is undertaken in the studio and some is in the control room (see Chapter 7). Audio work can employ one, two, or more people depending on the complexity and budget of the program.

Before Production Begins

Someone must select the appropriate microphones and position them in the studio before the production begins. Do you need to attach a mic to the talent's clothing? Will you be placing any mics on stands, and, if so, do you have the stands? The mics must be connected to receptacles located somewhere in the studio that send the audio signal to the **audio console** in the control room.

Once you have positioned and connected the mics, you must test them to make sure they are working properly. Usually this job involves two **audio operators,** one talking into each mic in the studio and another adjusting it through the audio console in the control room. If only one audio operator is available, the floor manager can talk into the mics. The talent can also talk into the mics (and should in order to set levels), but it is a good idea to make sure the mics are actually working before the talent arrives. You do not want high-priced talent sitting around while you replace a mic battery or trace down a bad cable.

If the program is going to contain music, sound effects, or other audio elements, you should also check these and cue them up before production so that when they are needed during rehearsal or taping, they will come in exactly as the director desires.

It is a good idea to mark on the audio console, with tape that is easily removable, what each of the inputs is handling. For example, for each mic input you can write the name of the talent using the mic. This will help you bring up the right person's sound at the right time. Similarly the inputs from the CD, DAT, and such should be clearly marked.

During Rehearsal and Recording

During rehearsal and/or production, audio operators may be needed in both the studio and control room. If a mic needs to be moved (on a **boom** or other apparatus) during taping, then someone must be in the studio to do this job. If all the mics are attached to talent's clothing, then a studio audio operator really has nothing to do. Two operators may be needed in the control room, however. If a show has complicated audio (and if the control room audio area is large enough), one person can operate the audio console while another starts and stops tape recorders, the CD player, or other equipment. More commonly, however, one audio operator handles all the control-room audio. (See Figure 2.8.)

During rehearsal you should make sure to have all performers speak at the voice level they will be using during performance so that you can set the levels of their mics. All too often beginning audio operators say, "Have him speak louder," or "Have her move closer to the mic." This is the wrong approach. The person (especially one who is seated) who moved into the mic or speaks louder during the test will probably lean to a more natural position and lower his/her volume level during the show. It is the audio operator's responsibility to get consistent quality sound. Can you move the mic closer to the person? Can you increase the volume without creating distortion?

Once the production begins, you should bring in sounds when the director calls for them. Your main job is to make the sound audible and consistent. For example, in most instances you should make sure the music does not drown out what someone is saying, and you should make sure that someone who talks softly can be heard as well as someone with a booming voice.

After the Production

After the production is over, the audio operator(s) should coil the audio cable and put away all the microphones, generally in boxes that are specially made for them. Some microphones have batteries that need to be removed when they are not in use. Any CDs or tapes used during production should be stored away or given to the director or producer.

You should put the board in the generally agreed-upon configuration for the facility. Because audio boards contain a large number of buttons, knobs, and faders, the audio personnel of a facility should agree on commonly used settings for everything and then set the board that way at the end of each production. An enormous amount of time can be wasted if one operator has a need to turn on a little-used knob and then doesn't turn it off again and the next operator can't figure out what is wrong. This is a particularly common problem in colleges where many students who are just learning the board use it during the course of a day. For this reason, college facility engineers often make drawings of how the board should be set or carefully indicate the desired positions of the various controls.

Figure 2.8

Working at the audio board, the audio operator combines sounds and adjusts their volume.
Photo courtesy of Donald McLaren.

2.9 Graphics Operators

The **graphics operator** is in charge of the computer system that is used to create words, drawings, and various visual effects (see Chapter 8). These include such things as opening and closing credits, temperatures used for the weathercasts, short animated sequences used in commercials, statistics for sportscasts, and bar graphs used for corporate productions.

Originally graphics operators were called **character generator (CG) operators,** because the early graphic computer systems were capable of displaying only characters such as letters and numbers. As the sophistication of the equipment has grown, so have the duties of the CG operator, so although that term is still used, *graphics operator* or *graphic artist* is now more commonplace.

Before Production Begins

While the rest of the crew is setting up, you must create the visuals needed for the program. (See Figure 2.9.) If these are extensive, you may have to come in a day or two early to create them and store them in the computer or on an external storage disk. If they consist only of opening and closing credits, the job is fairly simple. You, as a graphic artist, should have a good sense of composition and color, because you usually are creating something that will make an aesthetic statement.

The graphics operator prepares material for broadcast. *Photo courtesy of Donald McLaren.*

During Rehearsal and Recording

During rehearsal and recording you must make sure that the proper graphic is ready when the director wants to display it and that it is displayed in the manner requested. Should it roll or blink? Do credits come on one after another or is there time in between? As with other positions, you should exhibit the *discipline* of thinking ahead so everything you are responsible for comes off smoothly.

After the Production

After the production, you should remove at least most of the graphics from the computer so that they do not take up storage space on the hard drive. Some stations or studios use the same graphics over and over. Those graphics are usually stored permanently on the hard drive. One of the graphics you constructed for a partic-

ular program may be something that another program wishes to use with slight modifications. In that case, you should save the graphic in a predetermined file so it can be found easily.

2.10 | Technical Directors

The **technical director (TD)** operates the **switcher,** the piece of equipment that selects which video signal (camera 1, a videotaped segment, camera 2 with graphics over it, etc.) will go out over the airwaves or be recorded. This piece of equipment can be used simply to **cut** from one picture to another, but most modern switchers are capable of executing a large number of effects—wipes, swirls, squeezes, and so on (see Chapter 9). Like the audio console, the switcher has a large number of buttons, knobs, and levers, and you must become adept at operating them quickly.

The TD is also the head technical person for most studio productions. Although the director actually gives the commands to the various equipment operators, the TD oversees and assists the crew members if they are having trouble executing something the director wants done or if the equipment is malfunctioning.

Before Production Begins

Before the production begins, you as the TD are responsible for ensuring that all the equipment will work throughout the production. If one of the monitors is flickering, should you replace it, try to fix it, or leave it as it is? You also must ensure you know about any particularly difficult picture-switching maneuvers the director might want. Often special effects can be partially set up ahead of time so that they are easy to execute when they are needed.

During Rehearsal and Recording

During the rehearsal and recording, the TD operates the switcher. As with many other crew members, you follow the instructions of the director. Usually you sit right next to the director so you can communicate fairly easily. (See Figure 2.10.) On occasion, the director will also operate the switcher without the aid of a TD, but, as indicated earlier, overloading the director with too many chores is a recipe for disaster.

After the Production

After the production, you set the switcher to its normal configuration in the same manner that the audio operator sets the audio board. Usually resetting the switcher

Figure 2.10

During production the technical director operates the switcher. *Photo courtesy of Melissa Bossenmeyer.*

involves pushing all the buttons that indicate "black" so that no pictures are coming through the switcher. You have the responsibility for the technical **strike** (the turning off and putting away) of the equipment and, as part of this duty, should note any equipment that needs repair or adjustment and inform the studio engineer.

2.11 Videotape Operators

The person who plays back and/or records video signals has historically been referred to as the **videotape operator**. However, devices with no tape, such as **video disk** recorders and computer drives, are now used to record video and audio (see Chapter 10), so the term is somewhat outdated. No new term has become standard, but **video recordist** is sometimes used. We will continue (at least for this edition) to refer to this person, as most production facilities do, as the *videotape operator* or the *VCR operator*—if the person is operating a **videocassette recorder**.

This person is responsible for recording the program being produced. Sometimes even programs that are shown live (such as news or sports) are recorded for archival purposes or so the footage can be used in other programs. In addition to recording, the videotape operator often plays back video material that was previously recorded. For example, the videotape operator may play back a news story that was edited in the early afternoon into a newscast going out live at 6:00 P.M.

Before Production Begins

Before the program begins, you, as the videotape operator, must make sure each playback tape or other recorded material is properly cued up so that when the director calls for it, the right material will play. In line with this, you should also make sure the machine playing back the tape is properly set up so that the signal will go where it is supposed to go. You must also make sure to insert a blank tape or disk in the machine that is to record, and you should check that all the controls are properly set. If the tape has a button or tab that can be set so that the tape is not accidentally erased, you should set that tab or button so the tape will actually record.

During Rehearsal and Recording

During rehearsal, you are likely to play back tapes but not record the rehearsal itself, although sometimes final dress rehearsals are recorded so that material can be used if something goes wrong during production. During production you start the recorder when the director so instructs and monitor all the vital signs to make sure the program is actually recording. Are the audio signals going to the right channels? Is the video meter indicating that the machine is getting a strong enough signal? You also play back prerecorded tapes (**roll-ins**) when they are needed. (See Figure 2.11.)

After the Production

After the production is over, you should carefully label the master on which the program is recorded. Most studios have a standard labeling system that includes the title and length of the program, the date on which it was recorded, and the name of the director. Usually it is a good idea to label both the recording medium and the box it is stored in. You should file the program in the appropriate place or give it to the appropriate person. The same is true for all the material that was rolled into the program.

2.12 Editors

The **editor's** job is to piece together different shots or scenes taped in the studio or the field to create a unified piece of work. Sometimes all the editor's work occurs before a production is taped and sometimes it all occurs afterward. With some of the newer editing systems, editors can even edit while a program is in progress. Of course, some shows, such as a live telecast of a telethon, do not require an editor at all.

Before Production Begins

An editor works before a program is taped to piece together material that will be rolled into a production. For example, you may assemble a background piece about an Olympic athlete to include in a magazine show. You usually work alone in a small room called an editing suite that contains all the equipment needed for editing (see Chapter 11).

This videotape operator readies the recorders so that the program can be recorded and prerecorded tapes can be rolled in to the program.
Photo courtesy of Donald McLaren.

Sometimes the director (or a reporter, in the case of news) is also present for editing. (See Figure 2.12.) Editors who work alone are usually given a script or a list of shots so they have a general idea of what they are to assemble, but they also use their own creativity to present material in an aesthetically pleasing manner.

During Rehearsal and Recording

If editing occurs during production, it is often so that a summary of something that has happened during the course of the telecast can be presented. For example, you might pull together a collage that shows a basketball player sinking six baskets at six different times during the first half. Then the sportscasters could comment on these during halftime.

After the Production

Most editing, however, occurs after the production has been shot when you place shots in juxtaposition with each other. There may be hours of footage that must be

Figure 2.12

The editor, under the guidance of the director, is in the editing suite assembling footage.

cut down to a 30-minute show. You and the director (and/or associate director) must organize the footage, decide what to use, and assemble it.

Sometimes the editing job is broken down, with one or more people editing the picture and several others working on the sound. This is most likely to be the case for dramas and comedies, which often need special audio enhancements such as a laugh track, sound effects, or music. Other editing is much simpler, with both sound and picture being edited by the same person. As an editor, you may need to shorten a game show that ran too long, or piece together parts of a music show taped stop-and-go fashion over the course of an afternoon, or eliminate some dull parts of a talk show.

2.13 Other Positions

A raft of other people are needed for TV production. Sometimes people called **production assistants** undertake all the little jobs that need to be done—distributing scripts to cast and crew, moving flowerpots, getting coffee for everyone. For a large unionized production, specialists undertake specific jobs—a **propmaster**

places and handles all props, **painters** and **carpenters** are available to touch up sets, **makeup artists** apply makeup to talent, **grips** carry cable and other things, a **unit production manager** schedules equipment and facilities. All of these people are usually around before, during, and after production to handle setup, production miscellany, and cleanup on an as-needed basis.

The overall look of a production comes under the province of the **production designer, art director, and/or set designer.**[5] These people work to ensure that all the artistic aspects of a program (set pieces, props, graphics, costumes) work together without clashing or giving different psychological messages. Most of this work takes place before the production is begun, as does the work of **costume designers.**

In the sound area, a music **composer** is often hired to create theme music for a series or to add music to a finished program. Theme music can be composed prior to production, but atmosphere music is almost always composed after the editing is complete. If audio is complicated, a **sound designer** may be hired to handle the overall sound of a production.

People who execute **special effects** and **video effects**[6] have been in great demand in recent years. Even for studio shoots, pyrotechnic effects are used more frequently than in the past, and many shots that used to be shown fairly straight are now enhanced through postproduction digital manipulation. This has led to numerous new positions such as visual effects supervisor, matchmove artist, fleece fabrication assistant, and compositor.[7]

Different types of programs require various specialists. Are you featuring dogs, monkeys, or more exotic animals? If so, you need an **animal handler.** Are real plants and flowers in evidence? A **greensperson** will keep them looking fresh. Do you have children in the class? Then you must hire a teacher. Are there dance numbers? **Choreographers** stage these.

Overall, job classifications are in a state of flux. Technological advances eliminate jobs (e.g., camera operators eliminated by robotic cameras), but just as quickly other technological advances create new jobs (e.g., digital manipulation). The people most likely to succeed in behind-the-scenes employment are those who have a variety of skills and who are willing to learn new tasks and new equipment.

2.14 | Cast

This book, because it is aimed more at the behind-the-scenes aspects of video production, does not dwell on acting techniques, which are covered very well in the many books written on the subject.[8] However, people who are in the television business and members of the general public often have to appear on the screen, and certainly, within the classroom setting, producers and directors often call on their classmates to appear in front of the camera. Therefore, in this chapter, we give some rudimentary tips on what you should do when you are talent for a TV show.

A distinction is often made between two groups of talent: (1) those who serve essentially as communicators, portraying no role except as a host or reporter or themselves; and (2) those in dramatic roles who are portraying some theatrical character. The first category is referred to as **performers,** while the second group is referred to as **actors.** Although the two groups share many characteristics and concerns, it may be helpful to look at them separately in terms of what you need to do when you are in one of these roles.

Television Performers

The category of performer includes announcers, hosts, reporters, people on reality shows, game show contestants, interviewers, panel members, and the like—talent who are portraying themselves and often communicating personally with the audience.

Those who communicate directly with the audience, such as news anchors and program hosts, must realize that even though millions of people may be watching a particular TV program, television is an intimate medium. It is usually received in the privacy of the home, as a rule by an audience of one or a few people. You will be most successful when you conceive of the audience in that manner—one to four people sitting just a few feet away. Other performers, such as interviewees and panel members, communicate with other people on the set but still should keep in mind that their primary responsibility is to the audience.

Voice and Eyes

For this reason, a natural conversational speaking voice is best. The mic is usually clipped on your shirt or blouse so there is no need to speak to some far-off viewer. If you can project the feeling of spontaneity and intimacy in your speaking style, you will be on the way to capturing one of the most sought-after qualities of any television performer—*sincerity.* (As one comedian wisecracked, "If you can fake sincerity, you got it made.") You are probably more likely to talk too quickly than too slowly. Don't rush your words; you may have thought and said them many times, but your audience is hearing them for the first time.

Just as important as vocal directness is the intimacy of specific visual directness. If you are speaking to the audience, you should maintain direct and personal eye contact with the camera lens at all times, looking straight into the heart of it. This direct eye contact is the secret of maintaining the illusion of an exclusive relationship with each individual member of the audience. In maintaining the illusion of direct eye contact, you must become skilled in some of the artifice and techniques of the medium. In many productions, the director will cut from one camera shot of the performer to another. You will have to reestablish eye contact with the new camera immediately. One way to make this transition look as natural as possible is to glance downward—as if glancing at some notes or trying to collect your thoughts—and then immediately establish eye contact with the new camera. The director should inform you if one camera is being used exclusively for close-ups of some object you are demonstrating or discussing. Then you won't need to worry about ever having to look at that camera, even though it is on the air.

If you are speaking to someone else on the set, you should look at that person, even if he or she is off-screen, but you should keep in mind that the camera is most likely on your face, and the audience is very aware of your expressions. Don't grimace inappropriately or let your eyes roam a wide area. Most people are at least subconsciously aware of how to perform on TV because they have watched TV for so many years and been part of family "home movies." This is part of the reason reality shows have been successful. Untrained people can come across well on television if they at least sound and look relaxed.

Mannerisms

Because television is such an intimate, close-up medium, any visually or vocally distracting mannerism you have will certainly be captured with full impact. Some nervous mannerisms, such as a facial twitch or the unconscious habit of licking lips, may be hard to control. On the other hand, some fidgety distractions, such as playing with a pencil or pulling an earlobe, can be corrected if someone calls them to your attention. Ask for such advice; it will help you come across better.

Vocal habits and mannerisms can also be distracting. The use of vocalized pauses (saying "um" or "ah") every time there is a second of dead air is a problem many people share. The ubiquitous "I see" can easily become part of the interviewer's basic vocabulary. Try to avoid these mannerisms.

Handling the Script

Depending on the specific program, you may be working from a full script, speaking extemporaneously, or something in between. Some performers, such as guests on a talk show, may speak spontaneously or *ad-lib* with no preparation at all. Other times performers, such as interviewers, work from notes. These enable the talent to have enough of a solid outline to speak or interview with confidence; yet, by composing the exact words on the spot, they can add vitality and sincerity that is difficult to achieve with a prepared text.

You can handle fully scripted material in one of several ways. *Memorization* is one, but seldom can untrained television performers deliver memorized copy without sounding artificial and stiff. You are better off reading from a physical script in your hands, or, better yet, from a prompting device. Reading directly from a *script* is satisfactory if you are quite familiar with the material and do not have to keep your eyes glued to the script. Some people can handle a script very well, glancing down only occasionally. Others, because of insecurity or nervousness, get completely buried in the script and never establish eye contact. If you do use a script, you should make sure the pages are unstapled so you can slide the pages to the side unobtrusively without creating noise on the microphone. Also, make sure the pages are in the right order before starting the final take.

Occasionally, especially for short reports out in the field, performers read from **cue cards.** These are large pieces of poster board on which the words of the script are written, usually with felt-tipped pens. Someone holds them next to the camera so the talent can read them but still appear to have eye contact. In a studio situation, talent, such as a news anchor, reads from a prompter. (Review Figure 2.6.) This enables you to read the copy while staring directly at the lens. You should try to keep your eyes from going back and forth across the screen so you do not look like you are reading.

Regardless what you are using for a script, it may turn out to be too long or not long enough. It is a good idea to have some material near the end of the program that can be cut and also to have some extra material in mind that can be added, if need be.

Other Performing Tips

To achieve good camera angles, performers have to work close together. Some performers feel uncomfortable with the close physical proximity they must maintain to other talent. As a result, they will start out in a chair close to the other talent but gradually, during the course of rehearsal and taping, move farther and farther away. The result is that a gap develops that looks inappropriate in the TV frame. (See Figure 2.13.) As a performer, try to get used to this "closeness" and check every once in a while to make sure you and the other performers are positioned properly.

Make sure you know where the microphones and lights are, and don't walk out of the light or out of the range of the sound pickup. Don't acknowledge the stage manager's hand signals in any way (such as nodding your head), because this will show on camera. Do, however, respond to the stage manager's cues quickly. For example, when the stage manager cues you, start talking. Otherwise, you will be staring into the camera with "egg on your face." You should be

aware of where the stage manager is, but it is the stage manager's job to stand where you can easily see him or her.

Don't make any big or sweeping gestures, because the chances are that the camera will be on a fairly tight shot. Whenever you can, help the director prepare for important shots by telegraphing them ahead of time. Say, "Now let's look at the first demonstration . . . ," as this will warn the director that you are going to move to the demonstration area. However, don't give direct instructions such as "Now, if I could just get a shot of this wristwatch!"

In a similar vein, if you are going to make a big move, you should lean into it gradually, giving the director, the camera operator, and perhaps the audio boom operator ample warning. In general, you should develop a habit of moving slowly as you go from one area of the set to another. This gives the camera operator

Figure 2.13

Although these two people are sitting at what is normal distance for ordinary conversation, when the television camera frames both of them, there is an undesirable gap between them. They should sit closer together. *Photo courtesy of Melissa Bossenmeyer.*

a good chance of moving along gracefully. (And it looks fast enough to the viewer.)

If you hold up some object in front of the camera for a close-up, hold your arm tightly against your body to steady the hand. Even better, rest the object on a table or stand so there is no possibility of it moving. Don't handle microphones, except hand mics, and avoid playing with the mic cords, because both can ruin audio. When you are asked to give an audio level, speak as you will speak during the program.

Clothing

Usually performers wear their own clothes, not specially designed costumes. If you are going to perform on a program, you should try to find out something about the set so you do not clash with it. If you are going to be sitting in a tan chair, you should not wear a tan shirt or dress because you will disappear. If the set is basically green, don't wear red clothing—unless you want to give the impression of Christmas.

Unless a deliberately colorful, dazzling effect is advised, stick to clothing of a *dull saturation*—muted aqua rather than chartreuse, tan rather than brilliant yellow. Brightness and tonal balance also should be considered in terms of the overall emotional effect that is desired.

Line is also an important design consideration. Vertical lines tend to emphasize tall and slender proportions; horizontal stripes tend to exaggerate weight and mass. Performers who are concerned about appearing too heavy are advised to stick to vertical lines.

With some cameras, dark clothes will make a pale person look even more pale while light-colored clothes next to a tanned complexion will make the skin appear darker. Dark-skinned performers should be careful of light-colored clothing that can tend to heighten the tonal contrast and wash out facial details in the dark areas.

Generally, finely detailed patterns should be avoided. Whereas clothing with a rich thick texture will photograph well on television, clothing with a fine pattern usually will not, because it is too busy and distracting and hard to make out once it has gone through the standard TV process. Thin stripes, herringbones, and small checks can also create the **moiré effect**—a distracting visual vibration caused by the interference of the clothing pattern and the TV scanning lines.

One other clothing consideration involves **chroma key.** This is an effect wherein talent is taped against a colored background, usually blue; then the blue is removed and something else, such as a picture of a building, is inserted in its place (see Chapter 9). The problem is that anything, even a tie, that contains the blue used for the chroma key will disappear and the background picture will show through. Imagine the effect if you have a scene from the fire keyed in behind you—and the audience sees flames coming through your shirt. Ask if chroma key is going to be used, and, if so, avoid wearing chroma key blue.

Makeup

Many productions (such as public-affairs shows) do not require formal makeup. Guests can "come as they are" and look perfectly fine. However, many guests will look better if makeup is used to enhance or correct appearance. Depending on the program, makeup to cover the body as well as the face is sometimes called for.

The object of television makeup for performers is to have them look as natural as possible. A good, basic, unobtrusive makeup job should help enhance normal colors (evening up flesh tones, cutting down on the shine of a bald head), minimize any blemishes or distortions (covering up birthmarks, toning down a beard, eliminating bags under the eyes), and emphasize good points. However, with the close-up lens, any exaggerated makeup certainly would be perceived as unnatural.

If you are performing at a TV facility, a makeup person may be available to apply the makeup, but sometimes, if you want to wear makeup, you will have to apply your own. Such applications are not all that difficult. Before applying any makeup, clean your face with either a moisturizer for dry skin or an astringent (such as alcohol or witch hazel) for oily skin. Try to make sure you are in a room with the same kind of lights that will be used in the studio. Then apply the *base*. This is the initial covering (often *pancake makeup*) that is usually applied to the entire face or exposed area (arms and hands) being treated. This base is to provide the color foundation upon which all the rest of the makeup is built.

Next, apply *powder* to help keep the base from smearing. Usually, powder that is a little lighter than the base color is best. You can use *highlights* and *shadows* to emphasize or minimize facial features. Your forehead, nose, cheekbone, and jaw can all be highlighted with lighter shades or de-emphasized with darker tones. Normally, *rouge* is next applied to the cheeks, nose, forehead, and chin as needed to give you a healthy complexion and to counteract the flatness of the base color.

Finally, you should give special attention to those most expressive features of the face—the eyes and the lips. Use specific drawing tools and accessory items as necessary: *lipstick, eye shadow, eyeliner, eyebrow pencil, mascara,* and possibly *false eyelashes.* The extent of the use of these accent items depends on the need for remodeling and your individual taste.

Hairstyling

Hairstyles with a definite shape or firm silhouette usually compliment the performer more than wispy, fluffy hairdos. You should comb your hair carefully, because backlight will tend to make loose strands stand out. Avoid fancy hair treatments and fresh permanents, because they will make you look unnatural.

Handling all these aspects of performing is part of the overall *discipline* of being in front of the camera.

Television Actors

Many of the observations made regarding television performers apply equally to television actors. Actors, too, must be concerned with their relationship with the audience. Are you talking conversationally as your character would talk? Are you aware of the demands of the mics and lights? Do you understand the stage manager's hand signals?

However, acting involves special considerations. First, actors have to learn to adjust to the concept of a moving audience perspective; there is no firm boundary separating the audience from the actors. The audience perspective is switched every time the camera is changed. The viewer can be transported sideways, in or out, or into the mind of the actor. Actors must, therefore, be aware of how their actions will appear from all angles.

Precision

Actors must move very *precisely*, because they must be within the bounds of what the camera is shooting. If the actor's head is tilted at the wrong angle, the framing for a given shot may be off. If a moving actor does not "hit his mark" at exactly the right spot behind the sofa, he may ruin the impact of an emotional close-up. Sometimes directors have actors "cheat to camera." An actor, in a two-shot for instance, will be directed to turn his or her face slightly toward the camera—rather than looking directly at the other actor straight on. Such *cheating* is not perceived by the viewer, but it does result in more of a head-on shot into the camera.

Television exists generally in a demanding and nonflexible time frame. Most dramatic programs have to be squeezed (or stretched) into given time slots—multiples of a half hour, minus requisite time for commercials. This means that you, as an actor, may need to adjust pacing very precisely, speeding up or slowing down delivery of lines or action. This is especially a concern with soap operas and situation comedies where there can be little flexibility in timing. It is less of a concern for filmed dramas, however, where the exact timing can be worked out in the editing process by cutting or augmenting silent footage, panoramic long shots, and chase sequences.

Quick Study

Compared with the stage and with theatrical motion pictures, television drama is a quick-study medium. Whether working with single-camera or multiple-camera techniques, regular actors in a continuing series must learn up to an hour-long script every week—the equivalent of two feature-length motion pictures every month. For the actor in the hour-long daytime soap opera, the pace and discipline is even more demanding—up to an hour of dialogue every day! Scripts can be placed on prompters for actors, but often they are not looking in the direction of the camera. For this reason they generally prefer cue cards, and, of course, many memorize their lines.

Performers and actors are very important to any video production. They are what the home audience sees. All positions are important, however. A mistake by anyone, cast or crew, affects the overall quality of the production.

Discussion Questions

1. Of all the jobs listed in this chapter, which would you prefer? Why?
2. Discuss what you think would be the main disciplines needed by stage managers, camera operators, audio operators, graphic operators, and videotape operators.
3. If a friend who was going to be on a television talk show for the first time asked you for some helpful hints about what to wear and how to perform, what would you tell him or her?
4. What are some of the major differences between being a TV performer and a TV actor?

Notes

1. Depending on the actual production setup and the traditional organization of the studio/station, the AD may be labeled either "assistant director" or "associate director." The Directors Guild of America officially refers to the position as "associate director" because the "assistant director" title is traditionally used in the film industry.
2. "Stage manager" is a term brought over from the theater. The first TV term used for this person was "floor manager," but because the person is the director's studio representative, some studios/stations use the term "floor director." "Stage manager" is now the most commonly used term.
3. In union situations, the stage manager may be restrained from crossing jurisdictional lines, such as giving orders to the lighting crew.
4. *TelePrompTer*™ is a registered trademark of the Teleprompter Corporation, the first company to manufacture and sell a large number of prompters. Many companies now produce prompting equipment, but the word *teleprompter* has stuck, and sometimes devices manufactured by other companies are generically referred to as teleprompters.
5. A production designer is a person who determines an overall look for a series or movie, especially a highly stylized production that needs a great deal of design coordination. An art director also deals with overall look, usually for a particular show. The set designer just works with the elements of the set, not the overall look.
6. The term "special effects" usually refers to something that is accomplished while the shooting is in progress; it is done on a stage or at a location. The term "visual effects" refers to something undertaken in a computer to enhance or add to what was shot.
7. A visual effects supervisor oversees the people who create computerized effects. Matchmove artists undertake various actions such as walking and sitting down that are transferred into a computer and then used as a basis for the construction of fantasy characters such as animated space people. Fleece fabrication assistants were used in the movie *Babe* and their job was to digitally enhance shots of real animals so they looked more like people. Compositors join together various effects so that they meld in a credible manner.
8. Several books that can be consulted for overall information on acting are as follows: Patrick Tucker, *How to Act for the Camera* (New York: Routledge Press, 1993); Tony Barr, Eric Stephen Kline, and Edward Asner, *Acting for the Camera* (New York: HarperCollins, 1997); and Cathy Haase, *Acting for Film* (New York: Allworth Press, 2003).

CHAPTER 3

Producing

As mentioned in Chapter 2, producing involves bringing everything together for a successful production. The *discipline* of thorough preproduction planning in this process cannot be emphasized strongly enough. The success of every production is determined, to a very great extent, by the way that problems are solved—before they occur. The *techniques* needed for producing involve a great deal of organizational ability and attention to detail. Successful producers develop a feel for the type of material that has the potential for success. They also develop a good instinct for people that allows them to hire the appropriate cast and crew members who will bring the project to fruition.

Producers are involved with a project from the idea stage to execution and beyond. Many of the disciplines and techniques of producing come through experience, but, as a starting point, a producer should have a good grasp of the material covered in this chapter, which includes the following:

- The different types of producers (executive, line, associate) and how their jobs differ (3.1)

- Why producers sometimes opt to be hyphenates and what their duties involve under those circumstances (3.1)

- How to construct and utilize a treatment and/or proposal (3.2)

- The different forms of scripts (film-style, two-column, rundown, outline, storyboard) and how and when to use each (3.2)

- How to build a budget and then adhere to it (3.3)

- The process of casting and selecting a crew (3.4)
- Methods for preparing schedules for different types of shoots (3.5)
- How to deal with legal issues such as copyright (3.6)
- The types of records producers need to keep on computers and as hard copies (3.7)
- The need to promote and evaluate programs (3.8)

3.1 Types of Producers

The nature and scope of a project may determine how many people are involved in producing. A public-access cable talk show may have one "guiding light" who produces, writes, and hosts the show and handles the expenses out of his or her own pocket. A network situation comedy series may have one or more executive producers, one or more producers, a line producer, and a number of assistant and associate producers. Sometimes producer credits are given to people who are not involved in the start-to-finish production process but who render some special service, such as introducing an executive to someone who provides funding for the show. Sometimes writers are given producer credits so that they can earn extra money in the form of **residuals** when the program is rerun.

Executive Producers

Executive producers are generally people who oversee a number of different productions. If an independent production company (such as John Wells Productions) produces a show or series, the owner of the company (John Wells) may take an executive producer credit on all the productions from that company (e.g., *The West Wing, ER*). Each series has a hands-on **producer,** who does the day-to-day work, but the owner of the company, who made the deals with the networks and who is in the process of making other deals, makes decisions regarding the overall scope and direction of the series—hence the term executive producer. In a similar vein, if the network itself produces its own programs, it has employees who serve as executive producers and oversee several projects. Your instructor probably serves as executive producer for your class projects.

Associate Producers

Many productions have **associate** or **assistant producers**—people who help producers who would otherwise have too much to do. For example, a game show may have one assistant producer whose job is to acquire free prizes for contestants, while another assistant producer is in charge of screening potential contestants. Whether someone is an assistant or associate producer is not related as much to what job the person is in charge of as to his or her level of experience and skill; an associate producer is paid more than an assistant producer so people often start out as assistant producers and move up to associate.

Line Producers

Some productions have a **line producer** (also known as a **supervising producer**). This is a person representing the producer who is on the set each day, mainly making sure that all is progressing properly so that the movie will be finished on budget and in time for its scheduled airing.

Line producers sometimes work closely with **unit production managers (UPMs).** UPMs deal primarily with aspects of budgeting and scheduling equipment. Sometimes they are hired by the line producer, other times they are hired by the producer, and often they are employees of a production facility. Occasionally a show will have a UPM but not a line producer.[1]

Hyphenates

Sometimes people are **hyphenates.** They take on multiple roles such as producer-director, producer-writer, or even producer-writer-director. There are advantages and disadvantages to handling a number of different roles. Most people evolve into becoming hyphenates because they want *creative control*. A writer who has been displeased with how a director has interpreted his or her script might decide to become the director for the next script. Directors who feel that cost-conscious producers unnecessarily curtail them may want to make their own decisions about how to prioritize spending. Producers who work hard to develop a project and raise the funding may want to ensure that their vision is carried out during the production phase.

Although being a hyphenate can lead to greater creative control, it is also more work. Given the time pressures of most TV productions, one person can become exhausted trying to polish a script, find Civil War–era guns, and plan camera angles all at one time. Also, few people have all the aptitudes necessary to undertake multiple jobs. Someone who is highly skilled in getting the best performance from actors may not be equally skilled in handling financial statements. Multiple inputs, undertaken *harmoniously,* can also enrich a production. One person, given too much responsibility, can flounder—or become an egomaniac. Often the reasoned judgment that comes from bouncing ideas off others can lead to a richer end product.

Regardless of how the producing chores are divided, however, somewhere along the way they will involve idea generation, budgets, personnel, schedules, legal and production paperwork, promotion, and evaluation.

3.2 Idea Generation

An idea for a TV show can come from anywhere—a story in a newspaper, a dream, a casual conversation, research on the Internet, a brainstorming session with other writers.[2] Getting from the idea to an actual production is a tedious road full of potholes, but in most instances it starts with a written explanation of the idea in the form of a treatment or proposal.

Treatments and Proposals

Most drama and comedy series start with a **treatment.** (See Figure 3.1.) This is several pages, written in regular prose form, that tell the overall premise of the series, describe the main characters, outline the basic

plots for several of the episodes, and highlight the strong points of the idea. In some cases a producer (or executive producer) from an outside production company (with a track record of success) makes an appointment to see the appropriate network executives for a **pitch** meeting. During this session, which lasts about half an hour, the producer tries to convince the network executives that they should buy the series idea. Often they do this by comparing their idea to something that is already popular. (The show will have six *Friends* in a *Dawson Creek* type of setting.) The producer presents the information in the treatment orally and sometimes leaves written material behind for the executives to study.

If the network executives like the idea, they will commission (pay for) one or more complete program scripts. If they like the scripts, they will order a **pilot,** a produced program that is to be one of the series. If they like the pilot and decide to schedule the series on a regular basis, they will give the go-ahead for more scripts and productions. Throughout this whole process, the production company producer negotiates with the network regarding both creative and financial elements.

In other instances, ideas come from people within the network. In these cases a treatment is still needed but the pitch meeting and pilot process are more informal. One-shot dramas, such as made-for-TV movies, often have a treatment as a starting point, but, obviously, it outlines the idea for the single movie, not several episodes.

Many other types of programs that are not fiction oriented also start with an idea that is written on paper. Sometimes these are called treatments, but more often they are referred to as **proposals.** Magazine, talk, documentary, and game shows that are planned for **syndication,** cable TV, or local broadcast often evolve from proposals. So do children's programs and programs intended for educational or corporate outlets. Proposals define the purpose of the project, list the objectives, indicate the **demographics** (statistics of a population such as age and gender) and **psychographics** (lifestyle characteristics of a group such as environmentalists or free spenders) of the audience that will be targeted, give some details as to how the programs will be produced (e.g., animation, field production, studio), outline some of the planned segments, and sometimes

TREATMENT

"THE CAMPUS"

"The Campus" is a high energy series aimed at teens and young adults. It takes place on a college campus and features the adventures, problems, and experiences of four roommates.

Mark, a sophomore, is good looking and athletic. He is on the basketball team and seems destined to become one of its stars. He attracts coeds easily, but deep down he is uneasy with them. He comes from a wealthy family and seems to "have it all." However, he has trouble knuckling down and studying and is constantly on the verge of academic problems that will disqualify him from basketball. He's such a nice guy, however, that his friends try to come to his rescue and figure out ways for him to get through his classes.

Frank, on the other hand, has an easy time in classes, but always seems to have hard luck in social situations. He says the wrong things, wears the wrong clothes, spills his soft drink on a girl he is trying to win over, and generally falls prey to social indiscretions. He and Mark do not get along very well.

Juan tries to smooth the waters between Mark and Frank. He's not as bright as Frank or as athletic as Mark, but he's well rounded and a good mediator. He is on a scholarship and does not have much spending money. Mark sometimes tries to buy his allegiance by giving him material things, but Juan does not respond well to that. He works most evenings so does not have much time for social life.

George is the jokester of the group. In trying to make light of situations, he often utters what turns out to be prophetic philosophy. He likes to play practical jokes on people, especially Mark's girl friends, but he does not mean any harm. He is not particularly good looking, but he is a likable person.

In the first episode of the series, all four arrive back on campus for their sophomore year. Frank, Juan, and George had planned to room with each other and had thought their fourth roommate would be someone they had all befriended in their freshman year. However, that person has dropped out of school and Mark has been assigned to their room. He is unhappy about the situation. He thought he would be in special housing for athletes, but there had not been room for him.

Frank and Mark clash immediately and Frank goes to the housing authority to try to get Mark removed from the room. However, he is unsuccessful. Juan, realizing they will probably all have to live together, talks separately to both Mark and

1

Figure 3.1

An example of how the first page of a treatment might appear.

give information about the proposed budget and potential sponsors. (See Figure 3.2.)

A newscast script proceeds very differently. If a network or station has decided to present the news, no one needs to spell out specific ideas with a treatment or proposal—the ideas come from the news of the day. Parts of the newscast script are written during the course of a day (or several hours) as the producer and news director decide what is the most important news. Reporters and writers put together individual stories and transitions between stories that are eventually read by newscasters. Most newsrooms have a computerized form for individual sections of the newscast that all writers use. It contains such elements as the **slug** (story title), the date, the length, the writer's name, and the newscast producer's name. Usually each element of the newscast is on a separate piece of paper so stories can be juggled easily as news breaks—even during the newscast itself. (See Figure 3.3.)

Varying Script Forms

Because programs and circumstances differ, script forms also differ.[3] The type of script needed for a drama would be overkill for a talk show. A music video that is highly postproduced can use a script with less structure than a news script that must give accurate

Overview: "Tell Me a Story" features a friendly teddy bear who takes children to a library where books come alive and the stories are illustrated in various colorful and exciting ways. It is an excellent program to fulfill the FCC's requirement for educational/instructional programming.

Objectives:

To make listening to stories an enjoyable experience for children.

To interest children in going to the library to check out books.

To show ethnic interaction among children.

Target Audience: Children 2 to 7 who are reading or starting to show an interest in reading.

Series Idea: For each half hour program a large teddy bear takes a group of children of various ethnic backgrounds to the local library where they look through books. As they do so, the pictures in one of the books that one child is looking at will come alive. Sometimes they will come alive in an animated way and sometimes the picture will turn into a group of real people who will act out the story. The children and the teddy bear will intervene in the story from time to time to ask questions or make comments. When one story is finished, another book that a child is looking at will come alive and the same type of interaction will take place. If time permits in the half hour show, a third and maybe a fourth book will come alive.

The Pilot: The show will open with the teddy bear (a man dressed in a teddy bear suit) and three children—one Caucasian girl, one Latino boy, one oriental girl—entering the library. Theme music and opening credits will be over this shot. The bear and the kids will go to the children's section and start looking at the books.

The camera will zoom in on the book the boy is reading called *Hawaiian ABC's*. The Hawaiian boy holding the A will come alive as an animated character and say the lines about "Aloha" meaning "hello." He will jump back in the book and then jump out again with a B and a butterfly fish and read the text about the fish. This will continue for the whole alphabet. Hawaiian music will play throughout. Occasionally the teddy bear or one of the children will ask to interact with something the boy brings out of the book. For example, one of them will ask to blow the conch shell, one will ask to eat a piece of the pineapple and then comment on it, and one will play the ukulele. They will all learn to dance the hula.

When the Hawaiian book is finished, the teddy bear and children will look at other books. This time the camera will zoom in on one of the girls looking at "The Three Bears." The bears and Goldilocks will come alive as real people and act out the story. The teddy bear will tell the children that baby bear is his cousin and on occasion will interact with baby bear in a playful way.

The third story will be "The Crayon Box that Talked." The crayons in the book will come alive as real crayons and the other girl will become the girl in the story who is taking the crayons home with her. At the point in the story where she is coloring, the other children and the teddy bear will help color the picture. At the end of the story, the crayons will all jump back into the page.

The teddy bear will lead the children out of the library as the theme music plays and the closing credits roll.

Figure 3.2

An example of a proposal for a children's program.

---

mistake-proof guidance for a live broadcast. A multimedia game that is interactive needs a different type of script than a TV game show that is not interactive. Although many different script forms have evolved over the years, the main ones that you, as a television student, are likely to encounter are film-style scripts, two-column scripts, rundowns, outlines, and storyboards.

Film-Style Scripts

As might be evident from their name, **film-style scripts** are the type that have been used for years to produce theatrical movies. (See Figure 3.4.) Within the movie business they are referred to as **screenplays,** but the same general form is used for TV programs (especially dramas) and is usually referred to as a script. The main characteristic of this script is that each scene is *separated* from the next so that each can be considered individually. Materials produced from film-style scripts are usually shot in a number of different locations with all the scenes from one location being shot on the same day or succeeding days. A script that highlights times of day, locations, and whether these locations are inside (interior—INT) or outside (exterior—EXT) can help a producer with preproduction planning. The producer uses the descriptive paragraphs to determine what will be needed in the way of props and set pieces.

```
SLUG: DRIVE-BY                        DATE: 5/8
WRITER: THOMPSON                      PRODUCER: JONES
DURATION: :35                         ANCHOR: OSCAR


            VIDEO                              AUDIO


    OSCAR                        ((OSCAR))
                                   RELATIVES OF A TEENAGER
                                 KILLED IN A DRIVE-BY SHOOTING ARE
                                 APPEALING FOR HELP TO FIND THE
                                 PERSON OR PEOPLE WHO SHOT HIM.


    TAKE VO                        18-YEAR OLD PHILIP JOHNSON
    VCR 3: ALLEY WAY             WAS WALKING HOME WITH A FRIEND IN
    CG: DOWNTOWN                 THIS ALLEY DOWNTOWN ABOUT ONE
                                 OH-CLOCK YESTERDAY MORNING.


    OSCAR                          SOMEONE STARTED SHOOTING
                                 AND JOHNSON WAS HIT IN THE HEAD.
                                 RELATIVES SAY HE WAS CHASED
                                 BEFORE BEING SHOT.


    TAKE VO                        HE WAS TAKEN TO SAINT
    VCR 4: HOSPITAL             MARGARET'S HOSPITAL BUT DIED
    CG: ST. MARGARET'S          SHORTLY AFTER ARRIVING.


    OSCAR                          ANYONE WITH INFORMATION ON
                                 THE SHOOTING IS ASKED TO CALL THE
                                 POLICE.
```

Figure 3.3

A sample of a form for writing news stories.

Also, the director shoots each scene a number of times usually using only one camera. For example, the first time the camera might film a two-shot of a man and woman arguing. The second time the scene is shot, the camera would record a close-up of the woman delivering her lines and reacting to the man's lines. The third time through, the close-up would be of the man. Then, during editing, the various shots are cut together. The script form, by showing each distinct scene, helps the director figure out what to shoot. The dialogue is indented, keeping it separate from the writer's descriptive material about the scene. This gives the director room for notes and helps the actors pinpoint their lines.

Film-style scripts are very complete. They include all the words that will be spoken by the actors, describe all the primary action that will take place, and indicate basic moods and emotions. Of course, sometimes the actors or director alter the words, and the interpretation and execution of actions and emotion are the province of the director (hence, the occasional conflict about *creative control*).

Two-Column Scripts

The film-style script is not appropriate for multicamera productions that are shot live or live-on-tape. The descriptions would get in the way, and location does not

```
INT. - ELEGANT RESTAURANT - NIGHT

Joan and Philip, both dressed in stylish clothes, sit at a table.
Philip has leaned forward and is talking softly to Joan.  She is
leaning back and appears to be somewhat distant.

                          PHILIP
              I really want to come back, Joan. I miss the
              children and I'm tired of living out of a suit-
              case.

                          JOAN
                       (sarcastically)
              That's tender.

                          PHILIP
                       (exasperated)
              Now what did I do wrong?

                          JOAN
              You're just acting like your same old selfish
              self.  Everything revolves around you.  No
              consideration for me.  Not even any sign of
              love.

                          PHILIP
              But, of course, I care about you.  I don't need
              to tell you that.

                          JOAN
              That's a matter of opinion.

                          PHILIP
              Now you're being like your old sensitive self.
              I just don't get it.

                          JOAN
              That's right, Philip.  You just don't get it.

Joan gets up from the table angrily and walks away.  She realizes
she has forgotten her purse, returns for it, glares at Philip and
walks toward the door.  Philip looks hurt and confused.

EXT. - CITY STREET - NIGHT

Christopher is seen driving his car, weaving in and out of
traffic.  He pulls over to the curb and blinks his lights off and
on.  A large dark figure carring a briefcase emerges from the
shadows, opens the car door, throws the briefcase in the car, and
receeds back into the shadows.  Christopher drives off.

INT. - PHILIP'S OFFICE - DAY

Philip is going through a stack of papers, but he seems to be
having trouble concentrating.  Mildred comes in the door with a
stack of phone messages.
```

Figure 3.4

An example of a page of a film-style script. Note the separation of the scenes and the indentation of the dialogue.

change. More appropriate is the **two-column script** that pairs the video elements on the left-hand side with audio elements on the right-hand side. (See Figure 3.5.) This layout makes it easy for the producer to find all the materials that will need to be gathered together.

The director, who must act quickly, can easily see what visual images should be on the screen as the talk progresses and can set up cameras for what will be coming next. Usually the left-hand margin of a two-column script is fairly wide so that the director can make notes.

There are many variations on two-column scripts, depending on the type of program for which they are used. Some include every word of dialogue. Editorials and commercials, for example, need to be precise—no ad-libbing allowed. Dramas, such as soap operas, that are shot in-studio with multiple cameras can also use fully scripted, two-column scripts, although they often use scripts that are in more of a film style. Other programs, such as magazine shows and newscasts, include all the words to be spoken by the anchors but include just basic information about edited field reports that are to be rolled in so that the director can bring them in and take them out without any flubs. Still others, such as talk shows and game shows, indicate the

<u>VIDEO</u>	<u>AUDIO</u>
SERVER: OPENING MONTAGE	SOUND FROM SERVER: Runs :30. Ends with cash register sound.
TWO-SHOT - STEVE AND SHARON	STEVE: I'm Steve Anderson. SHARON: And I'm Sharon Hendricks and we're here with some tips that we hope will help you lead a healthier life.
STEVE C.G. Steve Anderson	STEVE: Our topic today is the labels you find on supermarket products. What do all those terms mean and how can they help you decide what foods to buy?
SHARON C. G. Sharon Hendricks	SHARON: We're going to start with a trip I made to the grocery store recently.
VCR 3: GROCERY STORE	SOT. Runs 3:56. Ends with "help you make intelligent decisions."
TWO SHOT	STEVE: Well, it looks like your family is going to be well fed. But what about a family that is on a really tight budget but still wants to cut down on salt?
C. G. Salt chart	SHARON: Low-salt food is not always more expensive. Look at this chart, for example.

Figure 3.5

A sample page from a two-column script. Note how the video and audio items line up with each other. Also note that the news copy in Figure 3.3 is written in a two-column format that varies somewhat from this one. Different production facilities and different types of programs have slightly different ways of preparing two-column scripts, but the video-audio split is a standard element of all two-column scripts.

general topics to be discussed or questions to be asked, because the answers, of course, cannot be scripted ahead of time.

Rundowns

Rather than using a two-column script, some talk and game shows (and other programs for which little can be scripted ahead of time) use **rundowns.** (See Figure 3.6.) These list the various segments that will be included in the program and are most often used for routine programs that are produced on a daily or weekly basis, such as *Today* and *Meet the Press.*

Specific information is given for each segment. This information may vary from one format of program to another, but generally, it includes the source for that segment (videotape roll-in, studio cameras,

```
                    RUNDOWN SHEET

                    "PROFILES" - NO. 37

                                          SEGMENT   TOTAL
SEGMENT    SOURCE          ITEM              TIME    TIME

   1       VCR             Opening Credits.         :25     :25

   2       Cam 2           Host welcomes Jane
           Host mic        Collins from Personnel.  :20     :45

   3       Cam 1,2,3       Host and Jane discuss purpose
           Studio mics     of the department, how it
           Graphics for    interfaces with each employee,
              guest ID     and its organzation.
                           ENDS: We can see this on a
                           chart.                  3:00    3:45

   4       Graphics of     Jane discusses the chart of
              chart        the department's organiza-
           Studio mics     tion.                   1:00    4:45

   5       Cam 1,2,3       Host and Jane discuss com-
           Studio mics     pany benefits.
                           ENDS: Let's look at the tape
                           your department produced
                           about this.             1:30    6:15

   6       VCR             Tape about benefits.
                           ENDS: Music and copyright
                           credit.                 5:35   11:50

   7       Cam 1,2,3       Host and Jane discuss how
           Studio mics     employees get additional
                           information.            2:10   14:00

   8       Cam 2           Host thanks Jane and closes
           Studio mics     program.                 :30   14:30

   9       VCR             Closing credits          :30   15:00
```

Figure 3.6

This is a rundown for one of a series of 15-minute programs that might be produced as a corporate video to highlight the job functions of people within the company. Note that exact wording cues are written in some places so that the director can move smoothly from one element to another.

graphics, remote feed), what the segment contains, and how long the segment should run. If a program has a set length, such as one hour, the total running time may be indicated so that the director can tell if the overall program is running short or long. Cues in and out of segments help the director prepare for transitions.

Producers use the rundowns to make sure all the guests are confirmed and ready to appear in the proper order. Usually these programs are directed by the same person day after day, so the director has a routine and

is mainly concerned with knowing about anything unusual that is incorporated within a particular segment.

News programs usually use both rundowns and two-column scripts. The rundowns indicate the order of the stories, and the scripts have the actual words. The rundown is generally placed on computer screens that are near the anchors and most of the crew members. (See Figure 3.7.) The producer, stationed in the control room, changes the order of program elements as need dictates while the program is on the air, and

Figure 3.7

A rundown for a newscast as it appears on a computer screen. *Photo courtesy of Forrest Carr, Cliff McBride, photographer.*

the computers near everyone else change accordingly. The anchors, director, and others quickly rearrange their two-column scripts to take into account the producer's changes.

Sometimes rundowns include fully scripted material that can be written ahead of time. When they do, they look somewhat akin to a two-column script in that they include a column for video and another for audio. The line can blur between a *detailed rundown* and a *nonspecific two-column list,* but how to categorize the script is not nearly as important as whether or not it is useful for the talent, producer, and director.

Outlines

The line also sometimes blurs between rundowns and outlines. **Outlines** list the various elements of a program but usually in less specific terms than rundowns. They are often used for pieces such as music videos that are shot and then edited. (See Figure 3.8.) Because

of this, they can include some of the type of detail found in film-style scripts. The producer and director both have time to digest the information, and the shooting itself is usually undertaken with one camera from a variety of angles.

Documentaries often lend themselves to outlines. They can indicate general items, issues, or circumstances to be investigated, but the real conclusions and findings cannot be planned until the material has been shot.

Outlines do need to indicate to the producer the props, sets, locations, and other production elements that will be needed to ensure a successful shoot. They must give the director a general idea of what to shoot, but they allow plenty of room for improvisation.

Storyboards

Storyboards show pictures of each visual element and describe the actions and/or indicate the dialogue be-

```
                        MUSIC VIDEO FOR
                    "I LOOK SO GOOD IN YELLOW'
                             BRIAN

The video will consist of four different set-ups:
     1. Brian, dressed in a variety of yellow clothes, lip
syncing in a nightclub setting.
     2. A chorus of children dressed in yellow singing the "Oo la
la la la la la" refrain.
     3. Brian, dressed in a yellow shirt and lip syncing, walking
a dog dressed in a yellow dog jacket.
     4. The three back-up singers in a department store trying on
ugly colored shirts and finally finding yellow ones they like.

We will build two sets in the studio, one for the nightclub scene
and the other for the children's chorus.  The nightclub scene
will have a 1940s look to it and will consist of a sequined
curtain and a floor stand microphone.  The audience will not be
shown.  An intense spotlight will highlight Brian's yellow
clothing.

The children's chorus (about twenty 8 to 10 year olds) will be on
risers against background flats that are painted with geometric
shapes in primary colors.

The dog walking scene will be shot on a street that has many
trees and colorful flowers that will show in the background.

The scene with the back-up singers will be shot in the men's
clothing store late at night when the store is closed.

As the track begins, we see Brian in the nightclub scene dressed
in yellow pants and a black shirt.  As the first verse
progresses, he adds (in jump cut fashion) additional yellow
clothing--a shirt, shoes, a jacket, and finally a large floppy
hat.

At the first "Oo la la" chorus, we cut to a long shot of the
children singing.

Next, Brian is seen walking the dog.  At first the dog is not
seen, but it is obvious from the leash and the way Brian is being
pulled that a dog is present.  When the next "Oo la la" section
comes, the dog and its yellow jacket will be revealed.  Both the
children and Brian will be heard for this "Oo la la," but the
children will not be seen.

The video returns to the nightclub lip syncing until the words "I
hardly know anyone who wears yellow shirts" at which point the
back-up singers are seen rummaging through shirts on a "sale"
counter in the men's clothing store.

                            page 1
```

Figure 3.8

An outline for a music video. Both general and specific ideas are given, and the various set and remote locations are enumerated.

low each picture. (See Figure 3.9.) They are usually used for short productions such as commercials or music videos. A drama could certainly be storyboarded, but it would involve a great deal of tedious artwork and pages and pages of paper. Sometimes directors will storyboard complicated scenes of a drama to better visualize them, but the storyboard, as a script form, is usually associated with short productions.

In general, directors like to work from storyboards because they are so visual.[4] Although a director may superimpose his or her own ideas over the storyboard script, it gives a good starting point. Producers have to examine storyboards very closely to make sure all the props and other elements needed for production will be ready.

The type of script you choose to use—film-style, two-column, rundown, outline, storyboard—will depend on the type of program you are undertaking and the type of material you feel most comfortable with. Scripts are primarily a blueprint for production. People who try to produce without a script are asking for trouble in the same way that builders would be asking for disaster if they tried to construct a house without following a basic blueprint.

Figure 3.9

A storyboard for a commercial. This enables the director to visualize all the action and how it juxtaposes with the words. The accuracy of this visualization is much more important than any artistic considerations. There are computer programs available to help with the construction of a storyboard.

3.3 Budgets

Students often do not give much thought to budgets, because their monetary needs are small. The college provides the equipment; cast and crew members come from the class and do not need to be paid; props can be borrowed from dorm rooms or willing relatives. But in the "real world" of TV production, budgets are *very important*. A producer who goes over budget is not likely to stay employed.

Graduating students who understand the procedures of budgeting are likely to be looked upon as more *valuable* than graduates who have mastered only creative or technical talents. For that reason, it behooves you to practice budgeting by figuring out what it would cost to produce your class projects if you were doing them in the outside world.

Costs of Productions

TV production expenses are usually divided into **above-the-line** and **below-the-line.** The above-the-line costs are creative in nature and include the pay given to talent, producers, directors, and writers. Below-the-line costs are more technical in form and include the salaries of the crew, the cost of the staging area and equipment, and the money needed for supplies such as scenery and makeup.

Costs vary greatly depending on many factors: whether the crew is union or nonunion; the recognition value and reputation of the talent; the length of the production; the number of complicated effects needed; the part of the country or world in which the production is taking place; and whether the equipment and facilities used belong to the production company or are rented from other companies.

Pay Rates

Most major production companies, networks, and some local stations are unionized and agree to pay at least the minimum cast and crew wages stipulated by the various **unions** that represent the technical people—International Brotherhood of Electrical Workers (IBEW), International Alliance of Theatrical Stage Employees and Moving Picture Machine Operators

(IATSE), and others—and the **guilds** that represent the creative people—Screen Actors Guild (SAG), Directors Guild of America (DGA), American Federation of Radio and Television Actors (AFRTA), Writers Guild of America (WGA), and the like. The rates and other factors related to the working environment are renegotiated periodically. Over time, the contracts have become quite complicated, but Figure 3.10 shows some of the major pay provisions for performers, directors, producers, writers, and technical and crafts people that should help students practice budgeting their own productions.[5]

Shoots that are nonunion can pay whatever people are willing to work for, but the unions and guilds fine their own members if they work for anyone for less than union rates. Of course, people who are highly prized can demand much higher pay than that stipulated by the union and guild minimums.

The trend within the television industry is to hire **freelance** cast and crew by the hour, day, or project as indicated in Figure 3.10. However, sometimes people are hired on a more permanent basis, usually referred to as **staff** positions. A local station, for example, would hire a news producer to work with the local news day after day, year after year. That same station might have a staff director who directs a public-service show one day and a sports program the next. Staff people usually receive less per hour than freelancers, but they are assured of steady employment and benefits, while their freelance counterparts must be constantly seeking new jobs.

Facilities and Equipment

Facilities and equipment are also major costs associated with production. If something is produced **in-house**—that is, within a production facility that has its own studio and equipment—the cost could be considered to be next to nothing, because everything that is needed is already in place. However, the facility must be maintained and the equipment must eventually be replaced, so even a local show produced at a local station is usually "billed" (on paper only) for use of the facilities.

When a producer rents an outside facility, costs are real and can be easily budgeted. Most organizations that rent studios and/or equipment have a **rate card** listing

SELECTED TELEVISION INDUSTRY PAY RATES

Directors

If the program length is:	the director is paid a minimum of approximately:
0 to 7 minutes	$ 1,500
8 to 30 minutes	8,000
31 to 60 minutes	$15,000

Producers

Producers are paid about the same as directors.

Writers

If the program length is:	the writer is paid a minimum of approximately:
0 to 15 minutes	$ 5,000
16 to 30 minutes	8,000
31 to 60 minutes	19,000

Performers

These types of performers:	receive approximately this amount of pay:
Principal performers	$680 per day
Singers	560 per day
Bit Performers	520 per day
Extras	110 per day

Technical and Crafts People

Technical Director	$52 per hour
Camera Operator	46 per hour
Video Operator	35 per hour
Prompter Operator	29 per hour
Lighting Director	36 per hour
Lighting Crew	25 per hour
Audio Operator	45 per hour
Boom Operator	35 per hour
Graphics Operator	43 per hour
Videotape Operator	35 per hour
Editor	41 per hour
Associate Director	53 per hour
Stage Manager	38 per hour
Set Designer	35 per hour
Set Decorator	30 per hour
Set Carpenter	29 per hour
Propmaster	32 per hour
Costume Designer	32 per hour
Costumer	25 per hour
Make-up Artist	35 per hour
Hair Stylist	27 per hour
Production Assistant	23 per hour

Figure 3.10

Selected TV industry pay rates. These are approximate rounded-off figures based on guild and union minimums. Note that some of these people are hired by the day, project, or hour. In reality, union provisions are much more complicated, taking into account such factors as how long a person has been in the union, how many hours or days they work total, overtime pay, meal breaks, and working conditions. These figures are intended simply to help students approximate their production costs if they hired union and guild people.

the cost for a fully equipped studio or for the various pieces of equipment that the client might wish to use. The rate card shown in Figure 3.11 lists the costs for a studio with three cameras and other commonly used production equipment as well as the rates for additional equipment. (Rates for portable equipment and editing are given in Chapter 12.) Again, students can use these numbers to practice budget construction, keeping in mind that the numbers can vary greatly depending on the city in which the production is taking place.

Supplies are figured at what they actually cost. If the production calls for a wig, the producer (or assistant producer) must actually locate an appropriate wig (often with the help of the Internet) and find out how

Studio and Control Room Rental . . . . $600 per hour

(Includes a 35′ by 35′ studio with cyc, lighting grid and lights, 3 prosumer digital cameras
with pedestals and prompters, and up to 5 microphones; and a 12′ by 20′ control room
with an 8-in 4-out audio mixer, a CD player, a switcher with 2 effects buses, graphics
generator, and 1 play and 1 record digital VCR.)

Additional Equipment

Extra microphones . . . . $5 each per hour
Extra cameras . . . . 40 each per hour
Extra CD players . . . . 10 each per hour
Digital video effects . . . . 40 per hour
VHS VCR . . . . 15 per hour
DAT . . . . 15 per hour
Nonlinear editing. . . . . 50 per hour

Set Pieces

Podiums . . . . 10 each per hour
Plain flats . . . . 15 each per hour
Chairs. . . . . 5 each per hour
Tables . . . . 5 each per hour
Risers . . . . 10 each per hour
Piano . . . . 20 per hour

Figure 3.11

A facilities and equipment rate card. Studio rental fees and the cost
for renting individual pieces of equipment vary greatly depending on
the size of the studio, the quantity and sophistication of the equipment, and the part of the country where the rental is taking place.
These figures are based on a facility and equipment similar to that
found on many college campuses.

much it costs. One supply that is necessary for all
taped programs is videotape. The actual cost of this depends on which tape format is being used.

Constructing and Adhering to the Budget

Once all the information regarding costs has been
gathered, the producer must actually construct the
budget. It is laid out with the above-the-line costs

separated from the below-the-line costs. After all the
costs have been added, a contingency of 15 to 20 percent is added to take care of the unexpected.

Figure 3.12 shows a worksheet that can be used for
a typical TV production budget. You can use this form to
devise theoretical budgets for your productions or you
can make up your own layout. Many different budget
forms are used in the industry. Some list the associate
director as above-the-line rather than below-the-line.

Budget Worksheet

Production Name:_____

Producer:_____

Director:_____

Date of Production:_____

DESCRIPTION	Number	Cost	Time	Estimate	Actual	Notes
ABOVE-THE-LINE						
Producer	1	8000		8000		
Producer's supplied		50		50		mostly copying
Director	1	8000		8000		
Director's supplies		25		25		mostly copying
Writer	1	5000		5000		
Principal performers	2	680	1 day	1360		
Bit performers	1	520	1 day	520		
Extras	3	110	1 day	330		
SUBTOTAL ABOVE-THE-LINE				23,285		
BELOW-THE-LINE						
CREW						
Associate director	1	53	3 hours	159		
Stage manager	1	38	3 hours	114		
Technical director	1	52	4 hours	208		
Camera operators	3	46	3 hours	414		
Video operator	1	35	3 hours	105		
Prompter operator	1	29	3 hours	87		
Audio operator	1	45	3 hours	135		
Boom operator	1	35	3 hours	105		
Graphics operator	1	43	4 hours	172		
Videotape operator	1	35	3 hours	105		
Production assts.	2	23	4 hours	184		
Propmaster	1	32	4 hours	128		obtain props early
Lighting crew	2	25	1 hour	50		
SUBTOTAL CREW				1966		
FACILITIES						
Studio & control	1	600	4	2400		
DAT	1	15	3	45		
Flats	6	15	4	360		
Chairs	3	5	3	45		
Knick-knacks	3	5	3	45		Get at B&G
Tape	3	5		15		
SUBTOTAL FACILITIES				2910		
SUBTOTAL BELOW-THE-LINE				4876		
SUBTOTAL ABOVE AND BELOW-THE-LINE				28,161		
Contingency at 20%				5632		
TOTAL				33,793		

Figure 3.12

A budget worksheet. This spreadsheet, which assumes a 10-minute production, should be helpful as a guide for preparing budgets. The "Actual" column is filled in after the production is completed and should not be too far away from the estimate. Forms differ from one production to another—sometimes the AD's pay will be considered above-the-line; sometimes contingency (the amount budgeted to take care of the unexpected) will be at 15 percent rather than 20 percent.

Not all of them have one column for "estimate" and another column to list what the production actually costs, but comparing estimates with the actual costs is a good experience for someone just learning to budget. Undoubtedly, you will need things or people for your productions that are not listed on this budget. Doing a little research to find the cost is another good way to learn the intricacies of budgeting.

Computer spreadsheets are particularly helpful for budgeting.[6] Using them, producers can determine what costs would be under various circumstances—with three cameras versus four cameras; hiring two different audio operators versus paying one audio operator overtime; with and without the scene that requires renting a helicopter.

Budget Overruns

If too much money is being spent, the producer is the one who must solve the problem. At times the producer can raise additional money to cover the shortfall; sometimes the producer can convince the director to work faster; other times some element of a program must be cut to save money.

Budgeting is a difficult process. Costs must not be exaggerated or people will not be willing to undertake the production. But sufficient money must be provided so that the program is successful. As money becomes tighter, more care must be given to drawing up and adhering to the budget.

3.4 | Personnel

In addition to seeing that the script and budget are generated, another major duty of the producer is hiring the various people needed for the production. The most important person the producer hires is the director. Sometimes the producer steps out of the hiring process once he or she hires the director; then the director hires the rest of the cast and crew. Of course, if the producer, director, and crew members are all on staff at a production facility, no actual hiring takes place, but the producer may lobby to have the most appropriate (and skilled) of the directors and crew members assigned to the project.

Casting

If the project is a drama or sitcom, **casting** is very crucial and producers often want to be involved. The usual procedure is that the producer and/or director draws up a list of the characters needed, along with their physical and psychological traits. (Often this is taken from the treatment or script.) This list is given to various **agents,** who then select actresses and actors they represent and send them to an audition where they read lines of the script. Then the director, producer, and others who have a vital interest in the production select the cast members. Big-name actors usually do not audition; the producer and director know of their talents and negotiate with the agents to bring them on board. Sometimes specialized **casting agencies** are hired for productions with large casts, such as made-for-TV movies. The director may be involved with hiring the principal actors, but the casting agency alone fills the minor parts.

Although dramas present the greatest challenges for finding talent, other forms of shows also involve hiring or selecting talent. For example, great care goes into selecting contestants for game shows. The number of people wishing to try their luck on these shows far exceeds the number needed, so producers (or associate producers) look for people who are lively or unusual and who have the potential to perform well when the cameras are on. Reality-show producers are interested in the potential dynamics among the people they select. Talk-show producers try to line up people who are well known (or eccentric) and who will interact well with the host or hostess. Public-affairs producers look for people with something to say who can present their points in a dynamic (or at least not boring) manner.

Actors who appear on dramas or sitcoms sign *contracts* that stipulate how much they will be paid and what their general obligations and working conditions are. Nonprofessionals should also be asked to sign **performance releases** so that they cannot come back at a later time and ask for money or other privileges. (See Figure 3.13.) One student producer learned this lesson the hard way. He had a sword swallower appear on his student production and neglected to get the proper release form signed. Later he showed the production on a cable-TV public-access channel, and someone called the sword swallower to say she had seen him. The sword swallower, thinking the student was making huge amounts of money distributing the tape, sued for $100,000 in retroactive pay and residuals. Although the student managed to avoid paying the sword swallower, he had to hire and pay a lawyer to fight the suit.

Crew Selection

The producer for any show will hire the unit production manager and assistant producers, if needed. She or he may also be involved with selecting camera operators, scenic designers, makeup people, and the like. One of the most important considerations is gathering a group of people who work together harmoniously. Frequently, producers and directors have worked with people in the past that they want to work with again

```
                    PERFORMANCE RELEASE

          In consideration of my appearing on the TV program

_____
                          (title)
and for no subsequent remuneration, I do hereby on behalf of
myself, my heirs, executors, and administrators authorize

_____
                        (producer)
to use live or recorded on tape, film, or otherwise my name,
voice, likeness, and performance for television distribution
throughout the world and for audiovisual and general education
purposes in perpetuity.

          I further agree on behalf of myself and others as above
stated that my name, likeness, and biography may be used for
promotion purposes and other uses.  Further, I agree to
indemnify, defend, and hold the producer harmless for any and all
claims, suits, or liabilities arising from my appearance and the
use of any of my materials, name, likeness, or biography.

Conditions:




Signature_____

Printed Name_____

Street Address_____

City and Zip Code_____

Phone Number_____

Date_____
```

Figure 3.13

A sample performance release. All people who appear on a television program who have not signed official contracts should be asked to sign a form such as this.

because they have a common understanding of the TV production process. This makes it hard for new people to break into the business, but it usually ensures a successful production.

If talent or crew must be brought in from a great distance, if the production lasts for many hours, or if any of the shooting is done at a remote location, then the producer must make arrangements for *transportation, lodging,* and *meals.* Creature comforts are definitely the domain of the producer.

3.5 Schedules

Scheduling is another part of the producer's duty. Sometimes this is relatively easy. An ongoing series produced in a studio is likely to tape at the same time each day or each week. The set will be the same each time, and for the most part, the cast and crew will remain unchanged. For such productions, the producer usually posts a **call sheet** on the studio door or

```
┌────────────────────────────────────────────────────────────────┐
│                          CALL SHEET                              │
│  Date_____                                          │
│                                                                  │
│  Program Title_____                   │
│                                                                  │
│  Episode Number_____                                       │
│                                                                  │
│  Producer_____               │
│                                                                  │
│  Director_____               │
│                                                                  │
│  Studio Location_____                                       │
│  ───────────────────────────────────────────────────           │
│                          PERFORMERS                              │
│  NAME                POSITION              REPORT TIME           │
│                                                                  │
│                                                                  │
│                                                                  │
│  ───────────────────────────────────────────────────           │
│                            CREW                                  │
│  NAME                POSITION              REPORT TIME           │
│                                                                  │
│                                                                  │
│                                                                  │
│                                                                  │
└────────────────────────────────────────────────────────────────┘
```

Figure 3.14

An example of a call sheet.

somewhere that is easily accessed by cast and crew. (See Figure 3.14.) This lists the time that everyone is to appear and gives a general idea of what will be shot. The time may generally be the same from week to week, but the call sheet takes into account aberrations. For example, if a complicated makeup job is called for in a particular episode of a series, the person being made up and the makeup person will need to report earlier than usual.

Scheduling is more complicated for a studio show that is produced only once. The producer must find a time or times when all the performers are available, often a difficult task because people appearing on a one-time-only basis are likely to have other obligations. The pro-ducer must also make sure that a studio will be available at a time when all the performers are free. If a producer wants a particular crew member, such as a certain audio operator, that further complicates the scheduling process. Many producers like to work with time lines where they list everything that needs to be done for a production according to when it needs to be completed—a month before production, a week before, a day before, the day of production.

Whether the programming is ongoing or one-shot, someone needs to fill out a **facilities request form** (often abbreviated **FACS**) reserving specific equipment or a specific studio and control room. (See Figure 3.15.) Such a form is needed (even in university settings) so

FACILITIES REQUEST FORM
YOURTOWN UNIVERSITY

Date Facilities Are Needed _____

Time Facilities Are Needed_____
  (Maximum is 4 hours unless special permission has been obtained)

Your Name_____

Address_____

Phone Number(s)_____

E-mail Address _____

FACILITIES REQUESTED
_____ Studio
_____ number of cameras needed (maximum=3)
_____ number mics needed (maximum=5 lav, 3 stand, 1 boom)
_____ Indicate type(s) _____
_____ number of lights being used (maximum=20)
_____ news set
_____ talk show set
_____ other. Specify_____
_____ Control Room
_____ audio board
_____ graphics generator
_____ switcher
_____ prompter
_____ record VCR
_____ roll-in VCR
_____ other. Specify_____
_____ Editing Suite
_____ nonlinear editing system
_____ digital video recorder
_____ microphone
_____ other
_____ Dubbing Bay
_____ video rack
_____ audio rack
_____ other. Specify_____

Figure 3.15

A sample facilities request form that might be used by a university.

that people don't show up and find other people using the equipment they need.

Shoots that cover real events, such as news and sports, have their schedule set for them. The equipment and crews must be available and in place when the event takes place. The scheduling is easiest if the time of the event is known well ahead of time. However, news, by definition, does not occur that way. For this reason, most stations and networks have equipment that is dedicated to the coverage of news events.

Scheduling field production and remotes is quite complicated. Multiple locations are added to the problems associated with having cast and crew available. Also, everyone is usually a long distance from the studio and cannot return for something that was forgotten. For these reasons, producers draw up thorough **breakdown sheets, shooting schedules,** and **stripboards** that list all the elements needed at each location (see Chapter 12). If a studio shoot is particularly complicated, the forms used for field production might be very helpful in the studio setting to ensure that everything goes smoothly.

3.6 | Legal Considerations

It is the producer's responsibility to oversee legal procedures related to a production. If problems occur, a lawyer should be brought in to deal with them. Often producers have law degrees because legal considerations have become a larger and larger part of the producing job.

Copyright Clearance

Copyright is one of the major legal considerations. Nothing that has been copyrighted (e.g., a poem,

photograph, music, film footage) can be used on a show unless the owner has granted permission. Obtaining permission involves sending letters or e-mails to copyright holders and then keeping careful track of what has and has not been cleared. (See Figure 3.16.) Sometimes copyright holders specify particular stipulations, such as a special wording in a credit at the end of the program. Producers must make sure these requirements are executed.

The most commonly used copyrighted material in programs is music. Some TV stations and networks pay **music licensing companies** (ASCAP, BMI, and SESAC), then have the right to use music represented

Date

Name
Licensing Department
Music Publishing Company
Street Address
City, State, and Zip Code

Dear Person's Name:

I am producing a student television production entitled ("Name of Program") for which I would like to use part of your musical composition ("Name of Music"), composed by (Name of Composer.) I would like to acquire a non-exclusive synchronization license for this musical composition.

I would like permission to use this material for broadcast, cablecast, webcast, or other means of exhibition throughout the world as often as deemed appropriate for this student production and for any future revisions of this production. Your permission granting me the right to use this material in no way restricts your use for any other purposes.

For your convenience, a release form is provided below and a copy of this letter is attached for your files. I will appreciate your signing and returning this letter as soon as possible.

Sincerely yours,

Your Name
Your Address
Your Phone Number
Your E-mail Address

I (We) grant permission for the use requested in this letter.

Signature_____

Printed Name_____

Title_____

Phone Number_____

E-mail Address_____

Date_____

Figure 3.16

A sample of a letter you might write to obtain clearance for music.

by those companies, which is most of the popular music. However, most independent productions (including student productions that are going to be shown outside the classroom) must clear copyright or use material that is not copyrighted.

Clearing copyright can be a difficult chore for the producer. Often just finding who owns the copyright can require extensive research, although the search features of the Internet make this much easier than it used to be. With music, the copyright holder could be the composer, the arranger, the publisher of the sheet music, the record company, or some combination of them. Usually when they are found, they want money, so copyright clearance can be *expensive.*

Music that is old enough to be in the **public domain** can be used without copyright clearance. Usually that means the composer has been dead at least 50 years, but sometimes a particular arrangement of a song can be copyrighted, and someone who is still alive can hold the rights to that arrangement.

A way to get around copyright clearance is to have music composed specially for the production. This, too, can be expensive if the composer is to be paid. Student productions have an advantage in this regard, because universities usually have music students eager for the experience of composing in return for a credit. There are also services that provide copyright-cleared music very inexpensively,[7] and computer programs exist that include snippets of copyright-cleared music that you can piece together easily to create your own music.

The producer's problems are similar when it comes to videotape or film footage. If the opening credits require a shot of an airplane taking off, you cannot simply tape a takeoff from some movie you have seen on TV and use it without permission. You could have someone take portable equipment to the nearest airport and shoot the shot, or you could acquire it from a company that supplies **stock footage.** The price is high (a minimum fee of $300 is not uncommon), but these companies have videotape and film to cover a wide variety of situations.

Permission to use written material (poems, stories, charts) can usually be obtained from the publisher of the book in which it appears, while permission to use a painting that is in an art book may require permission of the artist, the photographer who took the picture of the painting, the publisher of the book, the museum where the painting is hanging, or some combination thereof.

Other Legal Issues

Congress, the Federal Communications Commission, and state and local governments pass laws and create regulations that affect TV production. For example, it is legal for someone who feels he or she has been **libeled** by something shown on TV to sue a station or network. News producers must be particularly careful to make sure reporters have checked facts so that someone's character is not falsely defamed. There also are laws related to **invasion of privacy,** most of which state that a person has a right to be left alone. Again, this affects how news is gathered, particularly in relation to hidden cameras and microphones, but it can also come into play in dramatic projects. For example, a person has the right to sue a network planning to make a movie about his or her life if the person does not want the movie made.

The laws governing **indecency** and **obscenity** affect costuming and nuances of the script for drama and comedy programs. During election periods, there are regulations that govern the appearance of political candidates on TV. Producers, with the aid of legal counsel, are the ones who are charged with making sure programs do not run afoul of the law.

3.7 Record Keeping

The producer must keep careful records of legal documents, receipts for purchased supplies, damage done to sets or locations, and other paperwork that is generated during preproduction, production, and postproduction. This paperwork is necessary for a variety of reasons. First, if the producer leaves and a new producer is hired, he or she will have the necessary information to continue production. It also supplies the cast and crew with specifics so that they can do their jobs correctly. Some of the paperwork is used for tax purposes, while some is needed in case of (or, it is hoped, to prevent) lawsuits.

```
            COMMUNICATIONS 350 - STUDIO PRODUCTION
                          GROUP 2
                          PROPS

ITEM                  WHO IS BRINGING IT              NOTES

umbrella              Jorge M.

world globe           Susan T.              will get from library

purse                 Kim S.

waddling duck         Chris B.              bring it a week early
                                            to test it on camera

lamp                  Maria G.              get permission form
                                            signed by dorm coun-
                                            selor
```

Figure 3.17

A list of props as a student producer might prepare it for a class production.

Computers make record keeping relatively easy. To the extent possible, a producer should create a computerized folder and a hard-copy folder for each production. In addition to the items mentioned in the last paragraph, this folder should contain a copy of the treatment or proposal, the budget, the script, the various schedules, contracts and releases, and a list of cast and crew that includes their contact information—e-mail address, cell phone number, fax number, and so on.

Because one of the duties of the producer is to make sure all elements of the program are in the right place at the right time, a producer usually makes and double-checks lists. The type of lists needed vary from production to production. A drama needs lists that detail costumes, sets, props, and who is responsible for each. (See Figure 3.17.) An ongoing talk show needs a list of potential guests and dates when they are to appear. A game show needs a list of prizes that have been or may be acquired for free. A producer, and the people who work for the producer, must be very organized. Production is expensive and forgetting about a simple prop can lead to cast and crew standing around with nothing to do—a very expensive proposition indeed.

3.8 | Promotion and Evaluation

Promotion has become much more important in relation to program production than it used to be. When there were fewer networks, it was easier for people to find shows, so they did not need to be promoted as heavily. Now it is possible for an excellent program to simply get lost in the crowd. Promotion used to be handled primarily by the promotion department of a network or station, but now people involved with a production must do some of their own promotion. Producers usually ensure that there are photographers on the set to take pictures that can be used in advertisements. Sometimes producers write promotional copy or oversee the production of promotional ads that are aired on the network. Often producers oversee the creation of a website that is launched in conjunction with a program. They must integrate the website with the program and make sure that anything mentioned as being on the website is actually there. If audience members are asked to e-mail the program, the producer needs to assign someone to deal with the e-mails.

Once a program is finished, the producer has another function—evaluation. The program should meet its goals. For network TV, the main evaluation process is **ratings.** A series with high ratings stays on the air, and one with low ratings is canceled. But many other forms of programs need much more sophisticated evaluation. The producer of a cooking show designed to show people how to bake a cake should test participants after they have viewed the program to see if people really can bake the cake. Demographic studies should be undertaken to make sure a program designed to appeal to 8- to 11-year-olds is actually watched by that age group. Web-based material, either stand-alone programming or sites that are built in conjunction with TV programming, requires a great deal of evaluation, some of it to make sure the goals are being met and some just to make sure the technical aspects are working. Only by honestly evaluating past productions can producers create even better programming.

Discussion Questions

1. How do the duties of executive producers, line producers, and associate producers differ? Which one do you think you would prefer to be, if any?

2. Come up with an idea for a sitcom series and discuss the major points you would include in a treatment. What type of script do you think you would eventually use?

3. Come up with an idea for a video that highlights some program or event at your university. What points would you include in the proposal? What type of script would you eventually use?

4. What differences would you encounter between budgeting an action-oriented movie-of-the-week for a network and budgeting a company president's "state-of-the-company" talk for an in-house-produced corporate video? What would be some differences in terms of casting and selecting the crew? In terms of coming up with a production schedule?

Notes

1. This job and its title have evolved. It used to be that a unit manager worked for a production facility and a production manager worked for an independent production company. For example, a unit manager might work for a network that produced some of its own shows and rented out its facilities to others (corporations, advertisers, or production companies). The unit manager would be in charge of drawing up and adhering to the rate card and scheduling the facilities for use by both in-house producers and outside clients. Production managers were usually associated with a particular project rather than a particular facility. They determined what costs would be incurred by the project in terms of people, facilities, supplies, and other requirements. But this line is blurring, so, for many projects, the two titles have been combined and the person dealing with schedules and budgets is called the unit production manager.

2. This book does not pretend to be a text in scriptwriting. What is given here is merely an overview of script forms. For more information on scriptwriting, see such books as Syd Field, *Screenplay: The Foundations of Screenwriting* (New York: Dell, 1998); Robert L. Hilliard, *Writing for Television, Radio, and New Media* (Belmont, CA: Wadsworth, 2000); Milan D. Meeske, *Copywriting for the*

Electronic Media (Belmont, CA: Wadsworth, 2003); Claudia H. Johnson, *Crafting Short Screenplays* (Boston: Focal Press, 2000); William Miller, *Screenwriting for Film and Television* (Boston: Allyn and Bacon, 1998); Ray DiZazzo, *Corporate Scriptwriting* (Stoneham, MA: Focal Press, 1992); and Timothy Garrand, *Writing for Multimedia* (Boston: Focal Press, 1997).

3. A large number of computer programs are available to help television writers compose their scripts. Some of the most commonly used are Movie Magic Screenwriter, QNews, Final Draft, and Scriptwriter.

4. Software is available to help with the creation of storyboards. Most of it contains a large number of predrawn people and objects and can be placed in a frame and manipulated—turned, made larger, made smaller, and so on. One popular program is Storyboard Quick from Power Production Software—http://www.powerproduction.com.

5. For more information on wages and salaries, see *Paymaster* (in book or CD-ROM format), a publication put out by Entertainment Partners in Burbank, CA. Phone: 818-955-6000; Web site: www.ep-services.com.

6. Although any spreadsheet can be used to prepare a budget, ones that are specially made for the entertainment industry are helpful because they contain film and television terminology. The program most frequently used is Movie Magic Budgeting, which is tied closely to Movie Magic Screenwriter.

7. Some libraries that supply copyright-cleared music are Blue Ribbon SoundWorks Ltd. (404-377-1514), Canary Productions (800-368-0033), DeWolfe Music Library (800-221-6713), FirstCom Music House (800-858-8880), Killer Tracks (800-877-0078), Metro Music (800-697-7392), and Sound Ideas (800-387-3030). A list of music libraries can be found in "Sound Trackers," *Hollywood Reporter,* 23–29 April 2000, S-16.

CHAPTER 4

Directing

Techniques and disciplines that directors use should fit their own personalities, the capabilities of the on-air talent, and the needs of the particular show they are directing. Some directors are, by nature, more authoritative than others and give concrete direction. Others rely more on psychology and attempt to obtain disciplined performances by letting the talent and technicians feel they are the ones in charge of their own actions. Professional actors, such as those participating in a drama, require different handling than nonprofessionals who might be making a first-time appearance on an interview program. A children's program with many youngsters on it requires a more patient approach than a late-night talk show.

Equipment also affects methods and duties related to directing. If **robotic** cameras (see Chapters 2 and 5) are being used, the director gives commands to one person operating all cameras rather than commands to individual camera operators. If the studio is equipped with **high-definition** TV equipment (see Chapters 1 and 5), the director must consider the frame composition for the wider **aspect ratio** while making sure the composition will work for **standard-definition** TV, the kind most people currently have in their homes. Directors should definitely be familiar with the equipment in the studio. They don't necessarily need to know the intricacies of each piece of equipment, but they should know the underlying principles so that they can communicate effectively with crew members who actually undertake equipment operation.

Also, as mentioned in Chapter 2, what the director does is sometimes affected by what the producer has done. Many series TV programs have been cast by the producer and others before the director sets foot in the studio. For other types of programs, such as a movie of the week, the director might have a large say as to which actors are chosen for the parts. These variations in techniques, discipline, and styles are considered as this chapter discusses the following:

- How the director blocks talent, marks a script, and prepares other paperwork (4.1)
- The nature of prestudio, floor, and control room rehearsals (4.1)
- How the AD uses a timing sheet and handles talent timing cues (4.1)
- The difference between program time and body time (4.1)
- Principles related to calling commands appropriately (4.1)
- The long shot, medium shot, close-up pattern (4.2)
- Placement of cameras (4.2)
- Aesthetic principles related to cutting ratio, shot similarity, position jumps, and the axis of action (4.2)
- The use of transitions such as cuts, dissolves, fades, defocusing, wipes, and digital effects (4.2)
- The proper timing of transitions (4.2)
- How the director interacts with cast and crew (4.3)

4.1 The "Manager" Role

A director is part manager, part artist, and part psychologist. Directors give instructions to cast and crew, make sure the production is aesthetically pleasing, and handle the reasonable (and unreasonable) demands or quirks of those involved with the production.[1]

As the overall "boss," the director must oversee what everyone else involved with the production does. In addition, the director has many specific tasks that are primarily his or her domain and that are part of managing the program. These include blocking the production, marking the script, preparing other paperwork, conducting rehearsals, and actually calling shots. In addition, the associate director, working with the director, must plan the exact timing procedures for the show.

Blocking

Once you, as the director, have determined the purpose of the script and are sure it is the approximate length you want (see Chapter 2), you should start thinking about **blocking**—placing of talent and cameras in particular spots and figuring out how and where they are going to move during the course of the show. This process (also referred to as **staging**) is more complex for dramas and comedies than it is for news and public-affairs programs, but all programs need some form of blocking.

Think through how the actors or performers will best relate to each other. Should the talk-show host sit between two guests or to the right of both of them? Can the weathercaster interact with the anchors while standing on the weather set or will you need to allow time for him or her to walk to the anchor area? Should the husband lean against the back of the wife's chair or sit down in the chair next to her? Don't forget to think about actor comfort. An actress who has to turn her head unnaturally to see the leading man is going to be too uncomfortable to deliver her lines well.

Also think through the relationship of the actors to the cameras. Where should the daughter be positioned so that camera 2 can capture a good close-up of her reaction to her father's chastisement? On which burner of the stove should the chef stir the pudding so that camera 3 can obtain an effective shot?

Directors often draw **blocking diagrams** to help them visualize the shots ahead of time. (See Figure 4.1.) Using these diagrams, they can plan moves and think through how the people and the equipment will inter-

act with each other. One useful blocking technique for directors is to *start blocking in the center of the program.* Pick the most crucial or difficult part of the production and figure out your camera pattern for that segment first. Once you know how that segment has to be blocked, you can figure backward to see how you will want to work your way up to that position.

In planning multicamera blocking, you must keep in mind that the action is continuous, and you will not be able to stop to readjust the prop in someone's hand. You must also keep in mind the position of all the cameras so that they are not visible in any of the shots. And you must consider the position of actors and cameras so that shots can flow appropriately from one camera

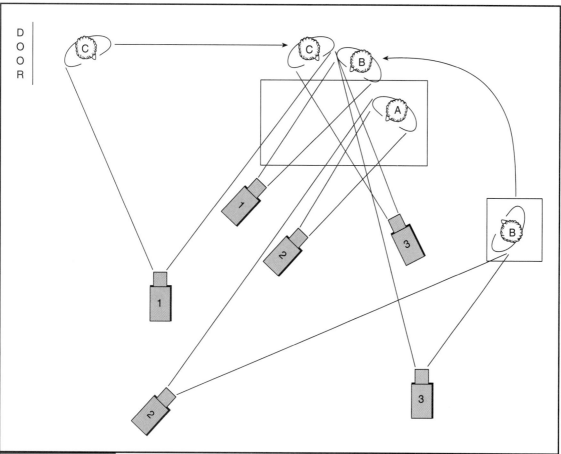

Figure 4.1

A blocking diagram as a director might draw it. In this scene, characters A and B are talking when character C comes in the door angrily and goes behind the sofa. Character B rises from the chair and goes behind the sofa where characters C and B argue. Character A reacts to the argument. Camera 1 pans with C as he moves from the door to behind the sofa and later has a close-up of B. Camera 2 shows A and B talking and then gets a reaction shot of A. Camera 3 follows B from the chair to behind the sofa and later gets a close-up of C.

to another. With single-camera shooting, you can stop, but actors must perform in exactly the same fashion over and over again so that all takes are consistent (see Chapter 12).

Marking the Script

Once you have thought through the blocking, you can *mark* your copy of the script so that you can call commands effectively during the program. Indicate which cameras you are going to use for which shots, what instructions the technical director and camera operators will need, where the audio cues will have to be, what cues the talent will need, and so forth. Most directors develop their own shorthand for marking their scripts, but some commonly used symbols are shown in Figure 4.2.

Depending on the program and the director's experience, scripts are marked in varying degrees. A major studio comedy special might involve hundreds of

abbreviated cues, instructions, and notes. With a fairly routine ongoing program, script preparation may take no more than a few penciled reminders of unusual cues. (See Figure 4.3.)

As a beginning director, you will probably feel more comfortable with a heavily marked script. Just the process of noting all the commands you will need to make will help you when you are in the director's chair. As you gain more experience, you can cut down on the number of markings. For example, you may initially mark a "T" for each **take** (quick cut from one shot to another). As you become more experienced, you can assume that changes from one camera to another will be takes unless they are indicated otherwise and drop the "T" from your markings. Also, once you become more experienced, rather than writing in many markings, you can underline elements that are already in the script to remind you of needed instructions.

Preparing Other Paperwork

The amount of paperwork you prepare depends on your level of experience and the type of program material you are directing. You want to make sure that you do whatever it takes to be well prepared when you enter the studio. For example, you may wish to **storyboard** (see Chapter 3) certain complicated parts of the script so that you can see in your mind's eye exactly how each shot will look.

You may wish to make a **floor plan** of the entire studio setup. (An example of one is shown in Figure 8.20 of the graphics and sets chapter.) This can help you with your blocking and also enable you to keep the overall environment in mind as you think through the show.

Some directors prepare **shot sheets** for their camera operators. (See Figure 4.4.) These are abbreviated descriptions of every shot that each camera has to get. A shot sheet is compact enough to be attached to the rear of the camera, where the operator can quickly refer to it. They are not particularly useful for interview shows, where the director is calling shots on the fly depending on who happens to be talking. But they are very valuable for complex, fully scripted programs, where every shot has been carefully worked out by the director—and where the cameras will have to be moving quite a bit to get various shots as requested.

③	Camera number three
⟨ or F.I.	Fade in
KEY or K	Key
T	Take
⟩⟨ or D	Dissolve
W	Wipe
⟩ or F.O.	Fade out
Q	Cue
⌐⌐⌐⌐⌐⌐⌐⌐⌐	At this point, cut, dissolve, or cue
D.I.	Dolly in
D.B. or D.O.	Dolly back or dolly out
PREP ②	Prepare camera 2
③ TO___	Camera 3, get ready for . . .
2-sh	Shot of two persons
3-sh	Shot of three persons
O/S	Over-the-shoulder shot
CU	Close-up shot
MS	Medium shot
LS	Long shot
ECU or XCU	Extreme close-up
MLS	Medium long shot
MCU	Medium close-up

Figure 4.2

Standard script-marking symbols.

PREP server

< credits

HEALTHY LIVING

VIDEO	AUDIO
SERVER: OPENING MONTAGE	SOUND FROM SERVER: Runs :30. Ends with cash register sound.
PREP W ②	
Open mic	
Q	
W ② 2-sh	
TWO-SHOT - STEVE AND SHARON	STEVE: I'm Steve Anderson.
	SHARON: And I'm Sharon Hendricks and we're here with some tips that we hope will help you lead a healthier life.
PREP graphics	
T ① ms	
STEVE	STEVE: Our topic today is the labels you find on supermarket products. What do all those terms mean and how can they help you decide what foods to buy?
C.G. Steve Anderson	
K graphics Lose graphics	
PREP graphics	
T ③ ms	
SHARON	SHARON: We're going to start with a trip I made to the grocery store recently.
C. G. Sharon Hendricks	
K graphics Lose graphics	
PREP VCR 3	
Roll tape	
VCR 3: GROCERY STORE	SOT. Runs 3:56. Ends with "help you make intelligent decisions."
②	
TWO SHOT	STEVE: Well, it looks like your family is going to be well fed. But what about a family that is on a really tight budget but still wants to cut down on salt?
PREP graphics	
T C. G. Salt chart	SHARON: Low-salt food is not always more expensive. Look at this chart, for example.
① to demo area	

Figure 4.3

This is an example of how a novice director might mark a script.

CAMERA 1	CAMERA 2	CAMERA 3
3. LS Mary in doorway.	1. Wide shot of kitchen, high-angle, boom down.	2. CU coffee cup.
5. LS David in doorway.	4. MS Mary. Follow her.	6. MS Mary. She rises.
7. MS David. He walks into O/S.	12. 2-shot. Pan left as David crosses behind Mary.	8. O/S Mary.
9. O/S David.	15. MS David. Double back as he comes to Mary. Open to 2-shot.	10. CU Mary.
11. CU David.	17. CU Mary.	13. MS David.
14. MS Mary. She sits.	19. 2-shot. Tight.	16. MCU David (bust shot).
20. Loose 2-shot. Mary rises.	21. Crane up. High-angle 2-shot. Dolly in and crane down to single of David.	18. CU David.
22. O/S Mary in doorway. She walks toward David. David turns to camera.	25. Wide shot of David. Dolly out to follow as he walks.	23. 2-shot as Mary turns.
24. CU David.	27. CU Mary's hands.	26. 2-shot. Dolly in to ECU Mary.
28. 2-shot. Mary walks past camera. Hold on David.	31. MS Alice.	29. MS Mary.
30. MS David. Pan to door as Alice enters.	34. MS David. He sits.	32. Loose 2-shot Mary and David.
33. 3-shot favoring Alice.	37. ECU David.	35. Loose CU Mary.
36. CU Alice.	40. Crane down. Loose MS Alice. Follow her to table. Follow action with cup.	38. ECU Mary.
39. CU Alice.		41. ECU Mary.
42. Wide 3-shot. Follow action.		43. CU of flowers.

Figure 4.2

Shot sheets that might be used for a multicamera situation comedy shoot. All the shots have been numbered in the order in which they will occur. The camera operators tape or clip these shot sheets near their viewfinders. Sometimes all the camera operators have all the shot sheets, so they know not only what they will be shooting but also what the other cameras will frame. In other instances, each camera operator would use only his or her own shot sheet.

Conducting Rehearsals

Program types differ greatly in the number and types of rehearsals they have, ranging from essentially none for live news coverage to several days for a sitcom. You want everything to be well enough rehearsed that the program runs smoothly, but at the same time you do not want to overrehearse to the extent that the material becomes stale to both talent and crew. Sometimes outside factors, such as the amount of money budgeted to pay the actors or the amount of time the studio is available, affect your rehearsal schedule. In considering rehearsals, you may wish to think in terms of several different kinds: **prestudio rehearsals, floor rehearsals,** and **control room rehearsals.**

Prestudio Rehearsals

For many extensive productions, especially dramas and comedies, you will want to have some rehearsals prior to coming into the studio. Studio time is too precious to start from scratch with basic blocking. Using a rehearsal hall, an empty studio, or a living room, you can begin working with actors. Specific areas can be measured off and marked with masking tape or furniture to represent major staging areas, and much of your blocking of action can take place—as well as quite a bit of the dramatic interpretation and working on lines.

For nondramatic productions, there are also many good reasons for prestudio rehearsals. Demonstration shows, educational programs, and the like can benefit from having an early **dry-run** session, where the director and talent can work together on the basic staging of the program. For both dramatic and nondramatic shows, it is a good idea to rehearse **business** prior to going into the studio. *Business* involves what people will be doing while they are talking, such as cutting up tomatoes or mopping the floor, and often it is the most complicated part of the show.

Production meetings are also a form of prestudio rehearsal. Whenever possible, the director should gather together all the significant people who will be involved in the studio and go over the entire show with them so that each person knows his or her role in relation to the overall production.

Studio Floor Rehearsals

When the director and the production crew start to work in the studio, the director usually spends some amount of time on the studio floor before assuming the director's chair in the control room. If the talent is particularly insecure or if the technical coordination of a production is really complicated, you might spend quite a bit of your time on the studio floor. On the other hand, if the talent is in control of the situation and the technical elements are no special problem, you probably would benefit from getting into the control room as early as you can.

The main rehearsal you will most likely conduct from the studio floor will be a **walk-through rehearsal.** This might be either a *talent* walk-through if they are not really sure of their positions and movements or a *technical* walk-through (also called a **technical rehearsal**) to explain major camera moves, audio placement, and scene changes. In many instances, the walk-through is a combination, taking both the talent and crew through an abbreviated version of the production. During this time it is beneficial to have a monitor in the studio that can show all the camera outputs at the same time by having each camera output in a different quadrant of the monitor. That way it is easy to explain to the actors and crew how the different shots will interrelate.

Control Room Rehearsals

More complete rehearsals are usually conducted with the director calling shots from the control room. The first rehearsal may be a **start-and-stop rehearsal.** In this approach, you interrupt the rehearsal every time a major problem occurs, correct it, and then continue the rehearsal. It is quite a time-consuming process, although it can be effective if you have the luxury of enough studio time.

Another approach to rehearsing is the **uninterrupted run-through.** In this approach, the director attempts to get through the entire production (or the production segment that is about to be taped) with a minimum of interruptions. Unless problems are major, you keep plowing through the rehearsal regardless of what happens. After the rehearsal is complete, you point out all the mistakes that need to be corrected.

Finally, there is the **dress rehearsal.** Theoretically, this is the final rehearsal—a complete, uninterrupted, full-scale rehearsal after all the problems have been straightened out. In practice, this stage is rarely reached. Realities of the medium are such that there simply is never enough studio time to do as polished a job as you want. In many instances, the director winds up with a combination start-and-stop and dress rehearsal.

When time is short, you must economize and try to make the most efficient use of the time available. Do not stand around waiting for others to finish their jobs before starting your rehearsal; you can rehearse even while the lighting crew is still trimming the lights and while the audio technician is establishing music levels. In an abbreviated rehearsal, at least make certain you get through all the rough spots in the production; *rehearse the open and the close* and *the crucial transitions* that call for coordination of several kinds of movement. Pick your priorities; do not get hung up on small details (such as worrying about the possibility of a boom shadow) when you have only a few minutes to work out major problems (the talent doesn't know where to move next).

Using Communication Devices

When you are in the control room and need to talk to people in the studio, you obviously cannot just holler to be heard. There are several communication devices to facilitate talking with the cast and crew. The main way the director communicates with the crew is through an **intercom** system (sometimes referred to as the **PL** for **private line**). It is, in essence, a closed-circuit audio network that connects all primary production personnel by **headsets** with earpieces and small microphones. Technically, any crew member with a headset can talk to anyone else. In practice, the director is heard most of the time during a production.

When directors (or others) need to talk to talent and/or talent and crew during setup, they often use the **studio address (SA)** system. This is a loudspeaker system that uses a monitor in the studio. A talkback microphone in the control room enables the director or others to activate the studio speaker so they can talk to everyone regardless of whether or not they are wearing headsets. Most studios also have a talkback feature with a mic hanging in the studio so that anyone in the studio can be heard in the control room.

You can also use the studio speaker when talent needs to hear program audio. For example, dancers need to be able to hear the music they dance to. Sound should not be piped into the studio whenever mics are live, however, because the sound feeding back into the equipment through the mics will create the nasty squeal of **feedback.** Most studio monitors automatically cut off microphones when they are activated.

If the director needs to talk to talent during the production, the talent can be wired with an **interruptible feedback (IFB)** system (also referred to as a **telas**). This is a small monitor that fits in the talent's ear. It is often used for news, when the director must tell an anchor about a story change while the anchor is reading another story. Field reporters use them, too, so the director can tell the reporter when to begin a live stand-up.

Sometimes crew or talent needs to hear program audio in addition to commands from the director. For example, boom operators need to hear program audio so they know if they are picking up sound properly, but they also need to be able to hear the director. PL, SA, and IFB systems can all be wired to transmit program audio as well as crew comments.

Timing

As a director, you want to make sure that your **associate director (AD)** is effectively handling timing of the program. One way for the AD to do this is through the use of a **timing sheet.**

Timing Sheets

Timing sheets may take different forms and be used in various ways, but basically they ensure the program is the right length. Computer programs have made it easy to calculate times because they can quickly do the math from any point to figure out how much time a particular segment has taken, how much time remains to the end of the program both with and without commercial breaks, and how much time has lapsed since the beginning of the program. A whole raft of calculations can be displayed continuously while the program is in progress, including how long a segment is taking compared with how long it should be taking.

As a student, you may not have access to computer timing programs, but you can design your own sheets, similar to the one in Figure 4.5. In this example, there are five columns for the AD to use. The first column is for a brief description of each segment in the program. The next four columns are for timing notations of one kind or another. "Unit" means the actual length of the *individual segment.* "Cume" is for the *cumulative time* of the program up to that point.

The "Ideal" column is the estimated time that each segment *should* run and should be figured out prior to setting foot in the studio. The "Rehearsal" column is for jotting down the unit times as various segments are worked through in a start-and-stop rehearsal. It is difficult to get an accurate picture of the actual cumulative times at this point, but the total of the unit times should give the AD a rough picture of how long or how short the program is likely to be. The "Dress" rehearsal column should give the AD a clear picture of how the actual cumulative times compare with the ideal times. The "Air" column is filled in as the program progresses. It lets the AD know how much to tell the talent to *stretch* or, in Figure 4.5, how much to *cut* in order to come out on time. In this program, for example, we can see that several segments ran long, so the interview segment had to be cut short (from an ideal of five and a half minutes to an actual five minutes).

Talent Timing Cues

In many programs, such as the one illustrated in Figure 4.5, the talent would need time-remaining cues in specific segments. Thus, working from the *ideal* times, the host would get, for example, a "30 seconds

SEGMENT (Description)	IDEAL (Unit)	Cume.	REHEARSAL (Unit)	Cume.	DRESS (Unit)	Cume.	AIR (Unit)	Cume.
1. TEASER	(:20)	0:20		:25		:25		:25
2. OPENING TITLES	(:30)	0:50		:40		1:05		1:10
3. INTRO	(1:05)	1:55		1:30		2:15		2:20
4. CHART	(2:00)	3:55		1:50		4:00		4:10
5. DEMO.	(4:00)	7:55		4:45	(4:15)	8:15	(4:20)	8:30
6. INTERVIEW	(5:30)	13:25		6:00		13:45	(5:00)	13:30
7. WRAP-UP	(:30)	13:55		:20		14:05		13:55
8. CLOSE	(:35)	14:30		:45		14:50		14:30
				16:15				
				(+1:45 over)				

Figure 4.5

Sample handwritten timing sheet.

remaining" cue at 3:25 into the program (as a reminder that there are 30 seconds left in the chart talk) and at 7:25 (30 seconds left in the demonstration). The talent might want time cues to get out of the interview segment on time (that is, a 30-second cue at 12:55) or simply time cues to get through with the wrap-up summary on time (that is, a 30-second cue at 13:25).

Care must be taken that the talent clearly understands what these intermediate segment cues are so that they will not be confused with time remaining in the body of the program.

Program Time and Body Time

This brings up one other point of potential confusion. The AD must be concerned both with *getting the talent wrapped up on time* and with *getting the program off the air on time*. In Figure 4.5, the talent needs a 30-second cue at 13:25 because he or she has to be completely wrapped up and finished at 13:55 (leaving the director 35 seconds for the closing credits). Also, the director has to have a 30-second cue at 14:00 in order to get the program off the air and into black at precisely 14:30. Thus, the AD has to work with both **body time**, the actual *length of the program content* including the host's

closing summary but not the show's closing credits, and with **program time,** the *total length of the show* from fade-in to fade-out.

Calling Commands

Once rehearsals are finished and you, the director, and your AD have solved any potential timing problems, you are ready to actually tape the show (or send it out live). You are the one who makes sure all the audio and video material is ready when you need it, and you make the decisions as to what happens when. In actuality, you may delegate some things to your AD, such as making sure the proper camera shots are set up, but you have the overriding authority and responsibility.

Most successful television directors work to develop a calm, articulate manner when giving commands. Whenever possible, they speak in a very casual style and even use a bit of humor. Those not used to being on the intercom should not be misled by this apparent easygoing banter. It is designed to mask the intensity and ongoing pressure under which the director and all key members of the crew are working. Good directors know that to betray anxiety is to risk losing the confidence of the crew. Inexperienced directors who speak in loud and commanding voices are very hard to put up with on a long-term basis. All directorial commands must be delivered in a precise, decisive manner so that crew members know exactly what they are supposed to do. The director must understand the practical consideration of the realities of the production. To request that any crew member do too many things in too short a time is to invite a series of problems. Once an operator falls behind in a sequence, a "domino effect" can occur, which can put a whole series of production elements at risk.

Crew Commands

Each production varies in terms of the exact commands you need to give, but a director might give different crew members the following kinds of commands:

Technical director—Various transitions, such as cuts and dissolves (see Chapter 9 for more about commands to the TD). The TD will also set up special effects, but those are usually planned ahead of time because the director does not have time during production to give elaborate instructions as to what type of effect he or she desires. When the effect is needed the director will call for "effect 1" or "effect 5."

Associate director—Quick comments regarding things such as pickup shots that need editing. Actually, the associate director is more likely to be giving information to the director (such as time remaining in the program) than the other way around.

Audio operator—Fade music or other audio elements in and out; open and close mics.

Graphics operator—Change graphics and bring them in and out (unless they are brought in through the switcher by the TD).

Videotape operator—Start and stop the recorder and any roll-in material.

Lighting director—Bring up or fade out lights if lighting changes are part of the show.

Prompter operator—Usually this person rolls the script without instruction from the director, keeping pace with the talent. Commands would come only if there are problems.

Stage manager—Cues and timing information to relay to the talent.

Camera operators—Shot designations such as close-ups or medium shots and zooms or pans.

Boom operator—This person usually works independently following the talent, but the director might need to instruct the boom operator to raise the boom if it or its shadow looks as though it is going to appear in the picture.

Figure 4.6 gives examples of commands a director might give to get into and out of a talk show. It also indicates the actions these commands should bring. You may want to review this figure after you have read the rest of the book because you will understand the technical terms more thoroughly once you have read the appropriate chapters.

Usually the hardest part of directing is getting the program started because many things need to happen at once. You need to make sure everyone is ready to start the program and then make sure the VCR or other recording device starts recording. Once you have started this procedure you need to place color bars, tone, a slate, and countdown on the recording. **Color bars** are the red, green, blue, cyan, magenta, yellow, white, and black bars that an engineer will use to make sure the color recorded on one machine plays back appropriately on another machine. **Tone** is an audio sound used to calibrate volume; it records along with the color bars. By making sure the sound registers the same place (0 dB) on all meters, technicians can ensure that the volume will be the same on all pieces of equipment. A **slate** gives identifying information such as the name of the program, the date it was recorded, and the name of the director. The **countdown,** which is the numbers 10 to 2 progressing one second apart, is used to cue the tape so it will play back at the appropriate time. The numbers stop at 2 so that there is less chance of the countdown accidentally getting on the air.

Once you (or your AD) are through color bars-tone-slate-countdown, you need to direct the program opening, which is often a complicated arrangement of music, voice, video, and graphics effects. Usually the middle of the program (especially a nonfiction show) is the easiest part because it takes on a regular rhythm. The ending, again, can be complicated by effects and

DIRECTOR'S COMMAND	RESPONSE
(Usually the AD gives all the preshow commands.)	
Ready in studio?	Stage manager says "Yes" or says "No" and tells the director what the problem is
Ready in control room?	Anyone who is not ready says why
Stand by	Stage manager says "Stand by in studio"
	Lighting director makes sure all lights needed are on
	Cameras get on first shots
	Talent gets in place
	Mics are properly positioned
	Prompter operator has first copy up
	Audio board has master fader up but all sound down
	VCR operator gets ready to hit play and record
	Graphics operator gets slate on monitor
	Video operator makes sure levels are correct
	Technical director puts switcher in black
	AD makes sure clock is at 00:00
Roll tape	VCR operator pushes play and record
Take bars and tone	TD pushes button for color bars
	Audio operator pushes tone button and makes sure tone is at 0 dB
	AD starts the clock and makes sure that bars and tone are on for 30 seconds
	VCR operator checks to make sure tone is at 0 dB and there is a video level
Lose tone, take slate	Audio operator pushes tone button off
	TD pushes button for graphics
	AD makes sure slate is on for 20 seconds
Roll countdown, take VCR	VCR operator rolls precued countdown tape
	TD pushes button for VCR and displays countdown tape until number 2 appears
	Graphics operator gets up opening credits
	AD counts with the countdown tape and continues with 2, 1
Take black	TD pushes black button
	VCR operator stops countdown tape VCR

Figure 4.6

Commands that a director might give for a talk show. To simplify this, most of the "ready" commands have not been included. Because the equipment and configuration are different in each studio, this is just a sample of how the program might go. In some circumstances the AD might give fewer commands, the VCR operator might not need to say "speed," the graphics might come on a different way, the bars-tone-slate-countdown may already be on the tape, and so on. However, this is a basic "script" that can be modified to fit particular circumstances.

(Figure 4.6 *Continued*)

(Usually this is where the director takes over from the AD.)

Fade in music	Audio operator fades in music on whatever (CD, cassette, etc.)
	AD starts timing the program
Fade in (whatever—cam 1, 2)	TD fades from black to whatever
Take opening credits	TD puts credits over picture
Lose credits	TD takes off credits but keeps picture under them
Fade out music	Audio operator fades down music
Stand by to cue talent	Stage manager gives talent standby cue
Open mics	Audio operator raises mic faders
Cue talent	Stage manager cues talent and they start talking
Take whatever (Cam 1, 2, 3)	TD takes whatever
Director directs the show	Cameras get whatever shots the director says
	AD keeps track of time and gives time cues
	Stage manager gives talent time cues
	Prompter operator keeps up with talent
	Audio rides levels, adjusts control room monitor volume, and sets up and brings in any needed sounds
	VCR operator checks levels periodically and cues and plays any roll-ins
	Graphics operator cues lower 1/3rds and any other graphics
	Video operator adjusts camera brightness levels, if needed
	TD gets the proper picture on air as the director calls for it
Take (whatever—cam, color)	TD takes whatever
Fade in music, fade out mics	Audio operator brings music up on CD or whatever and lowers faders on mic inputs
	Graphics operator makes sure closing credits are up
Take closing credits	TD brings in closing credits
Lose credits	TD takes credits off
Fade to black	TD fades from picture to black
Fade out music	Audio operator fades out music

(Often the AD once again takes over at this point.)

Stop tape	VCR operator stops recording 10 seconds after end of program
Check tape	VCR operator makes sure audio and video recorded
That's a wrap	All crew members start to clean up their positions

the need to end at a precise time. If you are a novice director, it is often a good idea to practice the beginning and ending of the show by going off to a separate room with a stopwatch and saying the commands you need to give until they feel smooth and natural.

Command Principles

There is really no right or wrong way to give commands, but adhering to certain principles will enable you to give directions as clearly as possible. For example, refer to talent (when talking to the stage manager) by name—"Cue Dr. Morgan," not "Cue him"—to avoid misunderstandings. Refer to camera operators, on the other hand, by numbers; you are less likely to slip up and get confused.

Make sure you use correct and precise *commands of preparation* as well as *commands of execution.* The commands of execution are those cues that directly affect what goes out over the airwaves or is recorded. "Fade in music" or "Take 2" commands call for an immediate action at a precise point in time. For a crew member or performer to respond with this immediate action, however, he or she needs adequate preparation time to be mentally ready and physically prepared. For this reason, commands of execution should be preceded at some point by a related command of preparation. The phrase *"Stand by . . .* music, announcer, graphics" is probably the most functional preparatory command. It alerts the equipment operator—and all other personnel—to listen carefully for the subsequent command of execution. Other terms used for this preparatory purpose are *"ready"* and *"prepare."*

The verb *cue* is quite often used as the first word of a command of execution—"Cue talent." Other commonly used verbs are *fade* (as in "Fade in camera 1" or "Fade out music") and *roll* (as in "Roll VCR" or "Roll credits").

Keeping the lag time of various equipment and personnel in mind, give your cues in a sequence designed to get things happening when you want them to. In opening your program, say "Fade in music" and then "Fade in camera 2." It usually takes a second or so before the music will be heard, but the camera is there with the push of a lever. Similarly, always cue talent before putting his or her camera on the air. "Open-mic-cue-talent-dissolve-to-two" is often given as one command of execution. By the time the stage manager re-acts and throws the cue and the talent takes a breath and starts to talk, the camera will be on the air.

Watch and *listen* to your monitors. Always be aware of exactly what is going on over the air. If a picture is not what you want, then change it. The viewer watching his or her home receiver could care less about your sinus headache or the camera cable with the bad connection; all he or she knows is what comes out over the receiver, and if it is bad, it is bad. Also, always check your camera and preview monitors before calling a shot to be put on the air. Make sure the camera you want to take or the special effects you want next are ready. You cannot afford to get buried in your marked script while ignoring the realities of the picture and sound you are sending out.

4.2 The "Artist" Role

Many things related to managing also affect aesthetics. For example, the director must think of the aesthetics of the picture frame while planning blocking or marking the script. But beyond that, the director must think of artistic principles that will make a program pleasant to watch. Many of these principles involve **continuity**—a broad term that refers to keeping things the same throughout an entire program.

These principles have developed over the years as part of the language of film and television. People viewing a movie or TV program expect certain conventions, and violating them confuses the audience. However, these principles are not laws of the land. In fact, they are made to be violated, because sometimes you want to disorient (or frighten or shock) your audience. Music videos have certainly breached every camera and cutting continuity principle—and have done so effectively.[2] But if a program is straightforward information or entertainment, a director should abide by the conventional language. In addition, understanding a principle better enables you to know how and when to violate it.

We next discuss a number of production conventions that directors should keep in mind. Although the focus of the discussion is on multicamera production, some of these conventions also hold true for single-camera shooting. In addition, some of these principles are important in terms of camera operation and editing and will be discussed in those contexts in Chapters 5 and 11.

Shot Juxtaposition

Early filmmakers[3] quickly came to the conclusion that when one picture is immediately replaced by another, an interaction occurs in the viewer's mind that communicates something more than if each picture were viewed separately. This concept obviously can have direct bearing on the process of shot selection for any television program. Each shot must be thought of as being part of a flow of images, each with a relationship to the one that precedes it and the one that follows it.

LS, MS, CU Pattern

For this reason, the succession of pictures should be motivated by the basic tenet, "Give the viewers what they need to see when they need to see it." To a great extent, this is determined by a juxtaposition of *collective* shots showing the whole picture and intimate *particularized* shots giving the viewers the closer details they want. (See Figure 4.7.)

Figure 4.7

The picture on the top is a long shot that could be considered a collective shot. The picture on the bottom is a close-up, a more particularized shot.

The generalities of a scene or program situation are established by the **long shot (LS)** (also referred to as a **wide shot [WS]** or **establishing shot**). Then the director cuts to a **medium shot (MS)** or a series of medium shots to give the audience particularized details. When something small or intimate needs to be seen, the director uses the **close-up (CU).**

Of course, the terms *long shot, medium shot,* and *close-up* are relative and vary from one type of program to another. The top picture shown in Figure 4.7 is probably a long shot for a discussion program. However, if this were a children's program with toys to be demonstrated flanking the four people, this shot would be considered a medium shot. Likewise, the bottom shot in Figure 4.7 would be considered a close-up for a talk show, but for a drama in which the girl's earring played a major role, this might be the medium shot and the earring would be the close-up.

Nevertheless, the pattern of LS to MS to CU should be observed so that the audience comprehends the total environment and can then relate to particular areas of that environment. Of course, as already mentioned, this "rule" is often violated for perfectly good reasons. Starting with a close-up of a dagger builds suspense and draws the audience into the scene. Where is this dagger and why is it sitting there? Only after the audience's curiosity has been aroused does the director use a wide shot to reveal the location. (See Chapter 5 for more on types of shots that are used in productions.)

HDTV Possibilities

Principles of shot juxtaposition are changing slightly with the introduction of the 16:9 aspect ratio and the greater resolution of high-definition TV. For example, a wide shot of a basketball game can cover the whole court with enough clarity for the audience to discern exactly what is happening. For this reason, there may be less need for medium shots with HDTV than with standard-definition TV, which has a narrower aspect ratio and lower clarity. However, at present, most people are viewing on older sets with a 4:3 aspect ratio, so directing is geared more toward a square screen size.

Camera Selection

Even with the opportunity to plan or block out the camera work in multicamera television programs such as

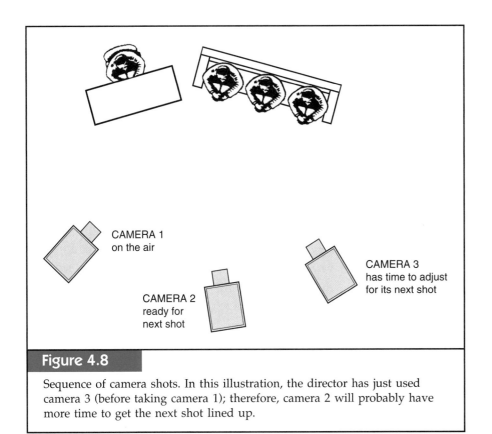

Figure 4.8

Sequence of camera shots. In this illustration, the director has just used camera 3 (before taking camera 1); therefore, camera 2 will probably have more time to get the next shot lined up.

soap operas, the ongoing production technique forces the director to make some rather quick, on-the-air editing decisions, because the exact moment of the take is crucial. Even though these decisions are instantaneous the principles underlying them are similar to the decisions made in postproduction editing discussed in Chapter 11. With talk and game shows there is an ongoing series of changes in camera use every time someone new breaks in to talk. A basic challenge with live programming is to have the proper camera ready for a shot at the exact moment the situation calls for it. On the part of the director, this requires an ability to be able to think *simultaneously* on at least two levels—what is on the air right now and what is going to be on the air next.

Thought Process

With a three-camera structure, the thinking process might work something like this: Camera 1 is on the air. You, as director, have the choice of using camera 2 or 3 for the next shot. Camera 3, however, has just been used on the previous shot. Camera 2, therefore, has

more time to make a framing adjustment or even change position. (See Figure 4.8.)

It is accepted studio procedure in a three-camera setup to place camera 1 on the left, camera 2 in the middle, and camera 3 on the right. This setup allows the director to keep track easily of the relative positions of cameras on the floor and the angle of shots available to them.

Obviously, cameras usually are not employed in a repeated 1-2-3-1-2-3 rotation. To observe the LS, MS, and CU requirements of any program, at least one of the three cameras at any given time will usually be designated as a wide-angle cover-shot camera. This is especially important in shooting unrehearsed programs, such as talk shows, where there are sudden changes of the individuals speaking. The technique on such a program is to cut to a wide shot on the change of voice if a close-up of the new person is not immediately available. The director then has a chance to ascertain who is talking and call for the close-up. The most glaring error on any kind

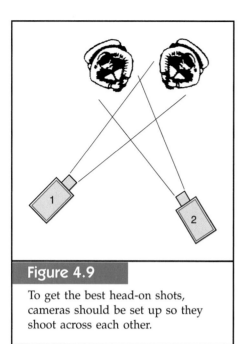

Figure 4.9

To get the best head-on shots, cameras should be set up so they shoot across each other.

of program is for an unprepared director to be caught with a speaker or performer still on camera when that person is no longer speaking or performing. In a rehearsed program, when the camera blocking has been worked out in advance, the director can temporarily commit all cameras to close-up shots, having planned to return to a cover shot at a later specific time.

Crossing Camera Angles

Another principle involving camera selection deals with *crossing camera angles* (see Chapter 11 for the editing corollary to this). In many staging setups, the natural pattern has two people facing each other. To frame the best headshots, cameras should shoot across each other's angles; that is, each camera should be shooting the person or object farthest away from the camera. (See Figure 4.9.) The camera on the right (camera 2) should be getting the shot of the person on the camera left, and vice versa. In this way, each camera gets a view of most of the talent's face. If camera 1 shoots the talent on the left, it will get no more than a profile of the talent. The same holds true for camera 2 if it shoots the person on the right.

Shot Relationships

When changing from one shot to another, the two pictures should relate to each other in both an informa-

tional and aesthetic setting. The subject in two successive shots should maintain continuity in that it should be *readily recognizable.* You would not want to cut to such a different angle that the viewer would not immediately recognize the subject from the previous shot.

Cutting Ratio

One of the most common errors of shot relationship involves long shots and close-ups. If you were to cut from the left-hand shot in Figure 4.7 to a close-up of the girl's earring, most of your viewers would be totally lost, because they would not have noticed the earring in the long shot. One good rule to follow is that you should always keep your camera cuts within a **three-to-one cutting ratio;** that is, do not take to a shot that is *three times larger* or *three times smaller* than the preceding shot.

Shot Similarity

For aesthetic reasons, you should avoid cutting between cameras that have almost exactly the same (matching) shots. The result would be that the scene remains essentially the same, but the picture jumps slightly within the frame. On unrehearsed shows, the camera operators may inadvertently come up with almost identical shots; therefore, it is up to the director to watch carefully for this similarity on the control room monitors.

Position Jumps

Another problem to avoid is the **position jump**—having a primary subject jump from one spot on the screen to another position in the next shot—an apparent loss of continuity. This can occur, for example, if three people are lined up facing two cameras and each camera is getting a two-shot of two adjacent persons. The center person will be on the left of one picture and on the right side of the other camera's picture. (See Figure 4.10.) This position jump can be avoided by having one camera go to a three-shot before cutting or, conversely, by cutting to a close-up single shot.

Axis of Action/Conversation

Another basic principle involves **screen direction.** In successive shots, we want to make certain that all action is flowing in the same direction and that each screen character is facing in one consistent direction. If

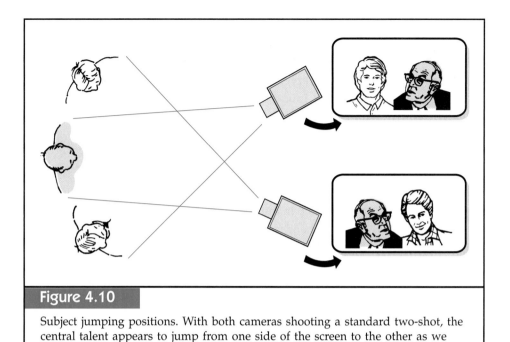

Figure 4.10

Subject jumping positions. With both cameras shooting a standard two-shot, the central talent appears to jump from one side of the screen to the other as we take between shots.

an imaginary line is drawn extending the path in which a character is moving, we can call this the **axis of action.** As long as all cameras are placed on the same side of this axis, the action will continue to flow in the same direction. If cameras are placed on different sides of this axis of action, however, the apparent screen direction will be reversed when cutting between the cameras. (See Figure 4.11.) Directors, therefore, always try to avoid having cameras **crossing the line.**

Closely related to the axis of action is the **axis of conversation.** If the imaginary axis is drawn through two persons facing each other, all cameras should be kept on the same side of this line. Otherwise the screen direction (the direction in which a person is looking) will be reversed when you cut to the other side of the line. This imaginary line—the axis of conversation—will shift, of course, as performers move. Figure 4.12 shows two common errors in crossing the axis of conversation.

Cutting ratio, shot similarity, position jumps, and crossing-the-line problems are all examples of mistakes that are easier to spot in a multicamera production, where the shots can be seen in relation to one another as they are being selected, than they are in the field, where shots cannot be compared. It is much easier for a director to accidentally cross the line when a long shot is recorded in the morning and its accompanying close-up is shot in the afternoon than it is for a studio director who is watching all the monitors.

Transitions

Many of the mechanics of continuity are carried out by the actual **transitions**—the manner in which the director changes from one picture to another. Over the years, these transitions have adopted meaning that audience members readily understand. The director must be aware of the psychological and visually conditioned impact of each. These transitions can be accomplished in postproduction editing (see Chapter 11) as well as with the switcher (see Chapter 9) during a multicamera studio production.

Cuts

The instantaneous **cut** or straight take replaces one picture immediately with another. It implies that there is *no change in time or locale.* It happens right now. The audience is not moved anywhere, except to a different perspective of the same scene. It is the device that the

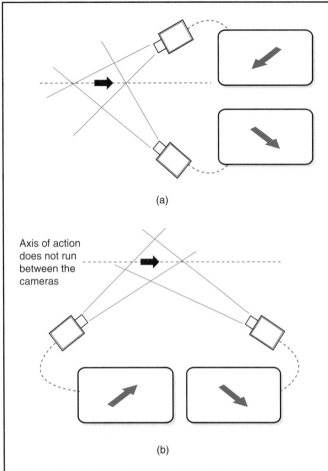

(a)

Axis of action
does not run
between the
cameras

(b)

Figure 4.11

Axis of action. (*a*) *Wrong.* If cameras are placed on both sides of the imaginary axis of action, the screen direction will be reversed when cutting between cameras. (*b*) *Correct.* When both cameras are on the same side of the axis of action, they will both perceive the action moving in the same direction.

audience has accepted since the beginning of the motion-picture film for changing a point of view without making any major dramatic change. In terms of grammar, it is the end of a sentence—a period—and the beginning of a new sentence.

Dissolves

The **dissolve,** simultaneously fading out of one picture and fading into another, creates a temporary overlapping of images. Dramatically, this implies a *change of place* or a *change in time* (usually a lapse of time). It shows a relationship with the previous shot, but there has been a change; the audience has been moved somewhere else or somewhere later in time. Grammatically, the dissolve corresponds to the end of a paragraph or possibly even to the end of a major section of a chapter.

In some programs, particularly music shows, the dissolve is often used purely for aesthetic reasons—a slow dissolve of a singer from a medium to a tight close-up profile, or a close-up of the dancer's feet dissolving to a long shot of the dancer. No change in time or locale is implied in this case—just a pleasant visual effect. In musical productions, the dissolve can be used as an artistic connecting or relating transition, whereas it has the opposite effect in dramas.

Most dissolves are slow and therefore have an effect on the *pace* of a program. For example, an effective series of fast camera cuts can lose its intensity if a dissolve is suddenly used. If a director does not want to lose intensity, the dissolve should not be used. However, dissolves can also be quick, creating an aesthetic that is slightly slower than a cut but faster than a traditional dissolve. If the dissolve stops for a while in the middle, creating a **superimposition,** this serves to intensify whatever is being expressed by the individual images.

Fades

A **fade** from a camera to black or a fade up from black implies a very *strong separation.* It is used in going from one segment of a program to another—from the talk-show interview to the used-car commercial. Dramatically, the fade is the curtain falling—the end of a scene or an act. Grammatically, it would be the visual counterpart of the end of a chapter or story.

Defocus

One specialized transition that can be used with no fancy electronic effects is the **defocus;** the camera on the air defocuses and is dissolved to a similarly defocused shot on another camera, which then comes back into focus. This usually implies either a *deranged state of mind* or a transition *backward in time.* It tends to call attention to itself and must be used very sparingly.

Wipes

The **wipe**—taking one picture off the face of the screen and replacing it with another—also calls attention to itself. Grammatically, its use is most like an exclamation mark. Some wipes, however, have developed

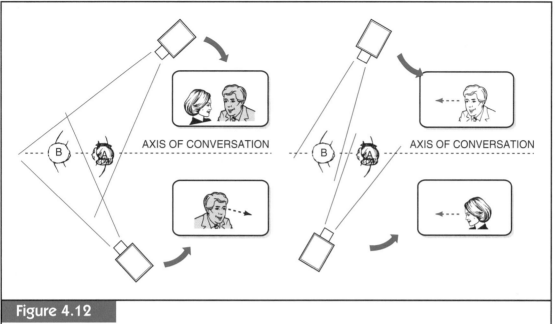

Figure 4.12

Axis of conversation. In the *left* illustration, actor B changes screen direction as we cut from one camera to the other. In the *right* illustration, both actors appear to be looking in the same direction, making it difficult for the viewer to establish the relationship between the two.

more concrete significance. For example, in sports productions, a wipe from the center to the sides indicates an instant replay.

Digital Effects

Digital technology has brought new dimensions to transitions (see Chapter 9). Graphics programs and digital manipulators allow for an array of bursts, flips, tumbles, and spins. These are used mainly as attention getters and are often employed during opening credits to *grab the audience*. Usually, they should be used sparingly during the body of the program because they draw attention to themselves and away from the content of the show.

Timing of the Transition

Understanding the different types of transitions helps to explain the *how* and *why* of changing cameras, but a word needs to be said about the *when*. Generally, camera changes must be adequately motivated; there has to be some reason for cutting at a particular point. The audience should want to see something else. ("Give the viewers what they need to see when they need to see it.") Without proper motivation, you should avoid

the temptation to change the picture just for the sake of change. The following discussion on the timing of camera transitions applies equally to the timing of editing shots together in the postproduction process for a single-camera production.

One of the strongest motivations for cutting is to capture action. When the action starts, you need a wider view. When the talent walks to a new area, you need an establishing shot. When cutting on action, you should always try to cut *just prior to the action*—not too long before it nor immediately after it. Ideally, as soon as the action starts, the audience needs to see the wider shot. Cutting to a movement that is in progress creates a jarring effect.

In a similar vein, you usually should not cut to a camera that is in the *middle of movement*—**panning, tilting,** or **zooming.** Occasionally, it is acceptable to cut (or preferably dissolve) from one moving camera to another that is moving in the same way. For example, if a camera is panning right, a cut can be made to another camera that is also panning right at the same pace. Cutting to a camera panning left or zooming in or to a stationary camera would be very jarring. But, of course, this abrupt effect is desired in some situations.

During a talk show, the strongest motivation for cutting is when a speaker *starts to talk.* The ideal timing of the take is precisely between the two speakers—not three seconds after the second speaker has started. As a practical matter, cutting during an ad-lib program will usually involve a delay of one second or so. To counteract this, the director has to be sensitive to the body language and facial expressions of all participants (watching the off-the-air camera monitors). Who has his mouth open? Who just leaned forward? Anticipate who the next speaker is going to be. Include appropriate, judiciously spaced **reaction shots** also, particularly when someone is reacting in an animated fashion. In timing reaction shots, *do not* cut at the end of an obvious statement or during a break in the speaking; it will look too much like a cut to the wrong participant. Reaction shots are most effective in the middle of a speech.

4.3 The "Psychologist" Role

Any video production involves the work of a team of people. You, as the director, are the team captain and must motivate people to do their best work. Sometimes this involves at least listening to problems that have nothing to do with the production at hand—the illness of the camera operator's father, a child care problem that the associate director is having. Other personal problems that you must deal with are very much related to the production, in that they involve interactions among members of the cast and crew.

Familiarity

Cast and crew members (and college classmates) who work with each other over and over for a continuing series often become like *family.* This has the same advantages and disadvantages as other family situations. Individuals come to know each other well and can anticipate each other's moves and thoughts. In fact, people who **freelance** often choose to work with each other because they have developed a well-oiled working pattern.

However, like brothers and sisters, people who work together regularly get on each other's nerves and develop rivalries and incompatibilities. You should realize that this will happen occasionally and try to make sure it has positive rather than negative outcomes. A disagreement on microphone placement between the audio person and the lighting director can be healthy, because it can lead to better lighting and better sound. However, if the antipathy between the two grows to the point where the audio person purposely places a boom microphone where he or she knows it will give the lighting director problems, the feud has gone too far.

New Relationships

When the people involved with the shoot have not worked with one another before, the director's job can be even more complicated. You must mold these people into a workable whole, taking advantage of the skills and personality traits each brings to the production. If you have the opportunity to hire crew members, check their references and interview them thoroughly to make sure they are right for the project and for one another.

Initial rehearsals usually take longer when crew members are strangers (or when students first start working together), because all of them are trying to find their specific roles. Which of the camera operators should be given the complicated zooming shot? Should the audio operator use his or her own initiative in deciding how slowly to fade in the music or wait for specific instructions from the director? How much background information should the stage manager give the talent?

The best way for you to handle a new cast and crew situation is to start the rehearsal session by holding a meeting and talking through the entire program, specifying each person's role at various points. As the rehearsal proceeds, changes and discrepancies will alter these roles, but at least everyone will have had the same starting point; all people will have not only ideas about their specific roles but also a general understanding about the roles of all others.

A variation on a new situation is one in which the crew and some of the performers (e.g., the game-show host, the soap-opera regulars) are the same for each production, but others of the talent are new (e.g., the game-show contestants, an "uncle" visiting a soap-opera regular). These people must be made to feel at home so that they can perform at their best. As the director, you should welcome them and spend a little time orienting them.

Directorial Style

Your style as a director can also affect the psychological makeup of interpersonal relationships. Some directors give precise instructions, such as specifying exactly how much **headroom** (the distance between the top of a person's head and the top of the frame) a camera operator should allow or telling an actress precisely when she should wrinkle her nose. Others let cast and crew members make more decisions—the actress works out her own facial expressions and the camera operator frames the shot; the director intervenes only if something is incorrect. Either method can work. The former assures quality control, but it can antagonize creative people who like to exercise their own judgment; the latter can lead to extra creative input that enhances what the director wants to do, but it can also lead to chaos if various cast and crew members run counter to each other.

Your best bet is to be yourself—but be consistent. If you feel most comfortable letting cast and crew members make many of their own decisions, do so, but don't expect initiative one moment and then clamp down on it the next.

Working with Talent

There is a great deal of difference between working with trained **actors** and working with **performers** who have never been on television before (see Chapter 2). You must teach performers basic aspects of the medium, such as where to look and how to move. You can expect actors to understand the medium, but you must work with them on the development of the characters they portray, whereas performers will be portraying themselves.

If you have the opportunity to audition actors and decide who will be selected for various roles, you can begin building a relationship with them at the audition stage. In addition to listening to them perform as the character they might be portraying, interview them and discuss how they interpret the character and what they think they can bring to the part that would be special. Give some of your ideas about the characters' traits and see how they react.

Nervousness can be a problem for both actors and performers. There is no cure for nervousness, but it can be mitigated if the person appearing on TV has confidence. Self-confidence is an internal trait, but confidence can also be gained through knowledge of the situation, which in turn leads to comfort. If a guest on a talk show knows ahead of time that she is to enter from the left after the host says, "Our next guest," and if she can practice her entrance once or twice, she will build confidence that will show during the taping. Actors and actresses are more relaxed if they know what your expectations are. They also need time to get away from the set and "get into character" when they have a particularly dramatic scene to perform.

If it is necessary to talk to an actor or performer about some major shortcoming in his or her performance, do this in private, not in front of the entire crew. Small corrections, such as turning the head to a slightly different angle, can be handled publicly, however. Always tell a person why some change is needed, phrasing it in terms of how the change will help the overall production.

Working with Crew

A director should be able to assume that the crew members working on a production have both the *discipline* and *technique* to do the job. If any are not exhibiting one or both of these characteristics, you should have a talk with him or her, outlining expectations. If this does not work, you should try to remove the person from the crew. However, in union situations (and student situations), this may not be possible.

The director must then use psychological persuasion to motivate the person as much as possible. One tactic is to compliment the person when he or she does something well. A compliment can often motivate a person to continue the good work. Another is to involve the person in solving problems. If someone can see the difficulty he or she is causing by some form of behavior and can have a say in how the situation should be remedied, the bad behavior often disappears.

When you see a minor problem developing between crew members, nip it in the bud before it becomes major. Usually the best way is to sit the people involved down and have a frank, open discussion with them. Doing nothing and hoping the problem will go away rarely works.

Most production situations work very well, however. Cast, crew, and director develop a sense of unity and exhilaration wherein the sum of the whole is greater than any of its parts.

Discussion Questions

1. What are several reasons why marking a script is important?
2. As a director, what jobs would you most likely give to your AD?
3. Give some specific examples of when you might use a defocus effect. A wipe. A fade. A digital spin.
4. As a director, do you think you would lean toward giving precise instructions or toward letting the cast and crew members make many of their own decisions? Based on your answer, what might you

have to watch for as danger signs that your directing was becoming ineffective?

Notes

1. Several books contain good advice for directors: Ivan Cury, *Directing and Producing for Television* (Woburn, MA: Focal Press, 1998); Alan A. Armer, *Directing Television and Film*, 2nd ed. (Belmont, CA: Wadsworth, 1990); Mark Travis, *Directing Feature Films* (Studio City, CA: Michael Wiese Productions, 2002); Steven D. Katz, *Shot by Shot* (Studio City, CA: Michael Wiese Productions, 1991); and Ron Richards, *Director's Method for Film and Television* (Stoneham, MA: Focal Press, 1992).

2. For example, when a band member is shown doing the same movements over and over with constantly changing scenery, this is an example of total lack of continuity. In real life one cannot repeat the movement that quickly, especially in front of different backgrounds. But the audience expects music videos to have a different style than dramas, so such effects are easily accepted and appreciated.

3. Two of the main theorists were Russian filmmakers V. I. Pudovkin and Sergei Eisenstein. Pudovkin's ideas can be found in V. I. Pudovkin, *Film Technique and Film Acting* (New York: Grove, 1970); two sources that discuss Eisenstein's thoughts are Sergei Eisenstein, *Film Form* (New York: Harcourt, Brace & World, 1949) and *Film Sense* (New York: Harcourt, Brace & World, 1947).

CHAPTER 5

Cameras

Perhaps no other piece of equipment exemplifies video production like the video camera does. It is, in many ways, the symbol of video production, and most video work begins with raw images, captured and recorded onto tape or computer disk by the video camera.

A wide variety of cameras are available for video production, ranging in price from under $1,000 to more than $100,000. Some are intended for use exclusively in the studio, while others are designed for field use. Many cameras are designed to be adaptable to either type of production environment. All cameras, however, perform the same basic function: **transducing,** or converting physical energy in the form of light waves into electrical signals. What happens to these signals after they leave the camera will be discussed in later chapters, as this process varies according to the production situation. In studio productions, the output of one or more cameras is routed through a **switcher** (see Chapter 9) and then broadcast live or recorded onto either tape or computer media (see Chapters 10 and 13). In field work, the signal is recorded directly onto tape or other media (see Chapter 10) and then edited (see Chapter 11).

This chapter introduces the basic function and operation of the video camera and its integral lens and mounting systems. Like any piece of production equipment, the video camera is a *tool*, and using that tool to its greatest functional and creative potential requires an understanding of both *disciplines* and *techniques*, including not only how to operate the tool but the underlying principles that make the tool work. As you read this chapter, you should firmly grasp the following topics:

- Basic scanning processes and signal differences between NTSC and ATSC formats (5.1)
- The role of hue, saturation, and luminance in creating video color (5.2)
- The color video system and how it works, including how the camera produces video signals (5.2)
- Lens characteristics and principles of lens operation (5.3)
- The theory and operation of zoom lenses (5.4)
- Camera controls and how they are used (5.5)
- Camera mounting equipment and how it is used to create shots (5.6)
- Basic fields of view (camera shots) (5.7)
- Basic principles of picture composition, including framing, headroom, angle of elevation, and balance for standard definition and high definition (5.8)
- Production techniques of camera operation (5.9)

5.1 | Television Formats

As discussed in Chapter 1, **ATSC** formats are poised to replace **NTSC** television. Consequently, a growing number of cameras are designed for shooting in one or more of the ATSC formats. Some ATSC formats have higher resolution than NTSC and are thus referred to as **high-definition (HD)** formats. The NTSC format and those ATSC formats that have comparable resolution to NTSC are usually referred to as **standard-definition (SD)** formats.

Although the future clearly belongs to ATSC cameras, manufacturers are still improving NTSC cameras, offering higher quality at lower and lower prices. The rise of so-called prosumer **camcorders** (cameras with onboard videotape or disc recorders) has made high-quality equipment available at modest prices. The Canon GL-2 shown in Figure 5.1, for example, produces professional-quality pictures and can be purchased for under $2,000.

There are some minor operational differences between cameras designed for NTSC and those designed

for ATSC. The fact that many ATSC formats have higher picture quality and a different screen shape (referred to as **aspect ratio**), also changes in some ways the aesthetic principles of shooting. Overall, however, both types of cameras operate and are used in much the same way. If you learn how to operate an NTSC

Figure 5.1

The Canon GL-2. *Photo Courtesy of Canon USA. The Canon logo is a trademark of Canon Inc. All rights reserved.*

camera properly and use it to hone your shooting skills, you'll be well poised to make the jump to ATSC.

There are also differences in how NTSC and ATSC signals are created by the camera and, as you will see in later chapters, how they are channeled, selected and altered, monitored, and recorded and played back. We begin, however, with some basic principles of how *all* cameras transduce light energy into electrical signals in a process called **scanning.**

The Video Scanning Process

The video picture that you see on any television monitor—no matter what the format—is composed of a series of small, illuminating phosphors called **pixels** (short for "picture elements"). The pixels are arranged in a grid pattern made up of horizontal rows and vertical columns, as shown in Figure 5.2. As different pixels in the grid illuminate, different colors and shapes are created on the screen.

During the transducing process, a video camera produces a rapidly changing series of "still" images, each made up of thousands of pixels "drawn" elec-

tronically. These still images are called **frames,** and the actual number of pixels that make up each frame depends on the format, as you will see. The "movement" of images on the screen is an illusion caused by a phenomenon known as **persistence of vision,** in which the human eye perceives smooth movement of an image when its position is changed rapidly on the television screen.

The more pixels in each frame, the higher the **resolution,** or fineness of detail, that can be reproduced on the screen. In television, resolution is measured in **lines,** referring to the number of horizontal rows of pixels in the picture—the higher the number of lines, the greater the resolution.

The number of frames contained in each second of video is called the **frame rate,** measured in **frames per second (fps).** The higher the frame rate, generally, the "smoother" the motion appears on the screen. The usual range of frame rates is 24 to 60 fps.

There are two methods of creating the individual frames: **interlace scanning** and **progressive scanning.** In interlace scanning, as shown in Figure 5.3, each

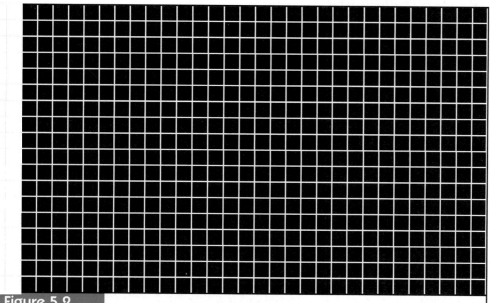

Figure 5.2

The pixels that make up a video picture are arranged in a grid pattern of horizontal rows and vertical columns. Note: For clarity, the number of pixels shown has been reduced and the size of the pixels has been enlarged.

(a)

(b)

(c)

Figure 5.3

The interlace scanning process works in the following manner: (1) each of the odd-numbered lines, from left to right and top to bottom, is scanned, creating the first field (*a*); (2) each of the even-numbered lines, left to right and top to bottom, is scanned, creating the complementary field (*b*). A completed frame is created after the two fields have been drawn (*c*). Note: For clarity, the number of lines in these illustrations has been reduced.

NTSC Format

The NTSC television format has existed largely unchanged since its inception in the 1940s. Color was added to the formerly black-and-white-only system in

Figure 5.4

In systems using progressive scanning, all lines are scanned sequentially. Note: For clarity, the number of rows in this illustration has been reduced.

frame is created by first drawing the odd-numbered lines and then the even-numbered lines. Each of these picture "halves" is called a **field;** two fields, then, make up a complete frame. Thus, an interlace scanning system made up of 30 fps actually contains 60 fields per second. Progressive scanning, on the other hand, creates an entire frame with each pass, as shown in Figure 5.4. Thus, there are no fields in progressive scanning, only frames.

Progressive scanning can create a clearer picture than interlace, all else being equal. Interlace systems also suffer from a subtle "flicker" effect caused by the fact that every other horizontal line is being displayed at a slightly different time. The advantage of interlace, however, is that it is less resource intensive, requiring less **bandwidth** than comparable progressive systems (see Chapter 10).

the 1960s, but other than that it is still as it was more than six decades ago. Although limited in terms of resolution, it has survived remarkably well. Most people are still quite satisfied watching the relatively ancient NTSC system—as long as they haven't seen high definition!

The frame rate for NTSC is 30 fps using interlace scanning. Each frame is made up of 480 lines of 640 columns—a total of 307,200 pixels. When we refer to the size of the screen grid, we usually refer to the number of columns first; thus, the NTSC picture is 640 by 480. This creates a picture that is four units wide for each three units of height, thus the aspect ratio of NTSC is 4 to 3 or 4:3.

ATSC Formats

As noted, ATSC actually consists of a number of different formats. Some ATSC formats use progressive scanning, while others use interlace. Frame rates and screen resolution also vary among the formats.

Figure 5.5 shows some of the formats available in ATSC. The formats are usually referred to using the number of lines and then either an "i" for interlace scanning or a "p" for progressive scanning. For example, "480p" refers to the format with 480 lines and progressive scanning. From among the many different formats available, the industry seems to be settling on three: 480p, 720p, and 1080i.

In addition, some formats are referred to as "24p." In this case, the number indicates not lines of resolution but frame rate, which is in this case the same frame rate traditionally used in film production. 24p cameras may be designed to work in various formats up to 1920 by 1080, and they have additional circuitry designed to duplicate the rich look created by film. Since it is less expensive to work in video than film, 24p video cameras are replacing film for movies, television dramas, and sitcoms traditionally shot on film.

You also will notice that some ATSC formats have a 4:3 aspect ratio while others have a 16:9 aspect ratio. The latter aspect ratio is wider than the 4:3 standard—closer to what you see when you watch a movie in a theater. The different aspect ratios can have an effect on how you should frame shots, as will be discussed in Section 5.8.

Signal Types—Analog and Digital

A given camera is usually designed to shoot in either NTSC or one or more ATSC formats. In some cases, a camera may be able to shoot in either NTSC or ATSC. The type of signal put out by the camera will depend on the format it is shooting.

Since NTSC was originally devised as an analog format, nearly every NTSC camera provides an analog signal output. However, most new NTSC cameras also provide digital output capability as well. Digital output provides several advantages over analog, as will be discussed in Chapters 10 and 11. The most popular form of digital video and audio output is **Firewire,** also referred to as "IEEE-1394," which allows a camera to be plugged directly into a computer or other digital device. Some cameras also have a **serial digital interface (SDI)** that provides a digital output with video and audio information.

Format	Horizontal Pixels	Vertical Pixels	Aspect Ratio	Scanning	Frame Rate
480i	640	480	4:3	Interlace	30
	704	480	16:9	Interlace	30
480p	640	480	4:3	Progressive	24, 30, or 60
	704	480	16:9	Progressive	24, 30, or 60
720p	1280	720	16:9	Progressive	24, 30, or 60
1080i	1920	1080	16:9	Interlace	30
1080p	1920	1080	16:9	Progressive	24 or 30

Figure 5.5

Popular HDTV Formats. The ATSC specification provides for several different resolutions, aspect ratios, and frame rates. The most popular ones, 480p, 720p, and 1080i, are highlighted.

ATSC is a purely digital format, so there is no need for an analog output on an ATSC camera. However, since some current HD cameras can also shoot in NTSC or at least "downconvert" to NTSC for viewing on a standard monitor, these cameras also provide analog outputs. When the day comes that NTSC television has completely vanished, however, cameras will not need to output analog signals at all. Most HD cameras are equipped with some form of SDI output. Although initial versions of IEEE-1394 are not sufficiently robust to handle HD signals, later versions likely will be.

5.2 Principles of Video Color

The video camera, as discussed in the opening of this chapter, essentially converts the light energy reflected off of objects into an electrical signal. To understand how this is accomplished, it is important to understand some principles of how colors are processed by a video camera and how humans perceive color.

Light enters a camera through the lens, which focuses it onto one or more **charge-coupled devices (CCDs).** A CCD, which is actually a computer chip, is what actually transduces the light energy into electrical energy. A camera may have a single CCD chip or three CCD chips. On three-chip cameras, each CCD chip is designed to process the color information for one of television's three **primary colors**—red, green, and blue. A device called a **beam splitter,** which is essentially a light prism, separates the incoming light into the three primary colors, directing each set of color information to the appropriate CCD. On single-chip cameras, one chip processes all color information. Three-chip cameras normally provide a much higher quality picture than single-chip cameras, but they are more expensive as well.[1]

Video cameras and video display devices (such as television monitors), like the human eye, are sensitive to three attributes of color: the color tint itself **(hue);** the vividness of that color **(saturation);** and its relative brightness **(luminance).**

Hue

Color Plate A shows the three primary colors and how any two of them can be combined (in the overlapping areas) to produce the three additional secondary colors—cyan (a turquoise formed from blue and green), magenta (blending red and blue), and yellow (the combination of red and green). These primary and secondary colors are the basic pure hues seen when a prism breaks up white light into its individual color components, or when we marvel at a rainbow, which essentially is millions of droplets of water acting as tiny prisms to create vivid primary and secondary colors.

When light waves of all three primary colors are added together in a proportion that relates to the color sensitivity of the human eye (59 percent green, 30 percent red, and 11 percent blue), the resulting effect is white. Sometimes thought of as the *absence* of color, white is actually *the presence of all colors.* The proportions are a bit off, but you can get the idea from the area in Color Plate A where the three primary colors overlap. If you still have trouble accepting this on faith, prove it by looking carefully at the individual grains of sand that make up a white sandy beach. The variety of colors that we are used to seeing in our daily lives result from the reflected combination of these primary colors.

As the proportions among the hues being combined are varied, an enormous range of colors becomes possible. For example, when red and green are added together, a range of pure hues from red to orange to yellow to green can be created. As the third primary color, blue, is added, a wide variety of browns, tans, mahoganies, beiges, ochers, maroons, sepias, and so forth are achieved. You may have experimented with this using a computer-graphics program that has the ability to mix ultrafine gradations of color and, as a result, can create literally millions of different hues.

Saturation

The intensity or vividness of a color is described in terms of its saturation. If we are dealing strictly with a red hue, the intensity of that red can range from a highly saturated vivid red, as shown in the lower right square of the left half of Color Plate B, to the less saturated pastel red shown in the upper right square. The pastel red is achieved by diluting the color with white. Another effect is achieved by diluting the vivid red with gray, producing more of a brown tone, as seen in the lower left corner.

As other hues are blended together, other color combinations result. Red and green hues combined in varying proportions with different amounts of white produce yellows. If increasing amounts of gray are used to dilute the saturation of the red and green factors in this yellow, a series of golden brown tones will result. Just as the saturation effect can be controlled on a scale leading to white, gray is on a scale of increasing darkness leading to black. Together, the hue and saturation portions of a video picture are termed the **chrominance** signal.

Luminance

The final color attribute is the luminance, or brightness of the color. As shown in Color Plate B, colors with low brightness are darker than their high brightness counterparts. The luminance of a color must not be confused with video gain, which increases (or decreases) the brightness of an *entire* picture through an amplification of the video signal, as is discussed in Section 5.3. Luminance, on the other hand, refers to the brightness of an *individual* color as displayed on the screen.

5.3 | Lens Characteristics

Possibly the most crucial element in the whole process of producing video pictures is the lens. The quality of the lens, to a large extent, can determine the quality of the picture produced by a particular camera—and, consequently, the quality of the picture seen on the home TV screen or studio monitor. A high-quality lens on a "cheap" camera can improve its output significantly, while a low-quality lens can substantially drag down the quality of even the finest camera.

From an operational standpoint, the **focal length** of a lens determines how "wide" or "narrow" the viewing range or **field of view** is, as is discussed in the following "Focal Length" section.[2] Although **fixed-focal-length lenses** were common on cameras in the early days of television, now a **zoom lens** is found on nearly every video camera. Unlike a fixed-focal-length lens, which can provide only one range of view, a zoom lens is continuously variable along a range of focal lengths.

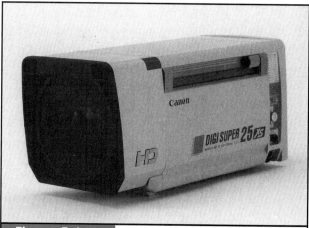

Although zoom-lens technology is constantly improving, a zoom lens is never quite as optically perfect as a fixed-focal-length lens designed for one specified viewing range. These slight deficiencies may not be noticeable in standard-definition format, but they are more likely to show up in HD. Thus, lenses designed for HD use must be manufactured even more precisely, not only because of HD's higher resolution, but because formats with 16:9 aspect ratios require the lens to provide an undistorted image across a wider horizontal field of view. (See Figure 5.6.)

Focal Length

Differing focal lengths are used primarily so that differing amounts of a scene can be included in the picture when shot from the same position. *The longer a lens is, the narrower its viewing angle will be, the less you will be able to fit into the picture, and therefore, the more magnified individual subjects will be.* Conversely, a short-focal-length lens will give you a wider viewing angle, thereby allowing you to fit more into the picture, but individual subjects will appear smaller. This law of lenses is illustrated in Figure 5.7. A long lens, or telephoto lens, therefore, can be used to obtain closer views of objects and can get a relatively close-up view of an object from a great distance. A short-focal-length lens is similar to a zoom lens

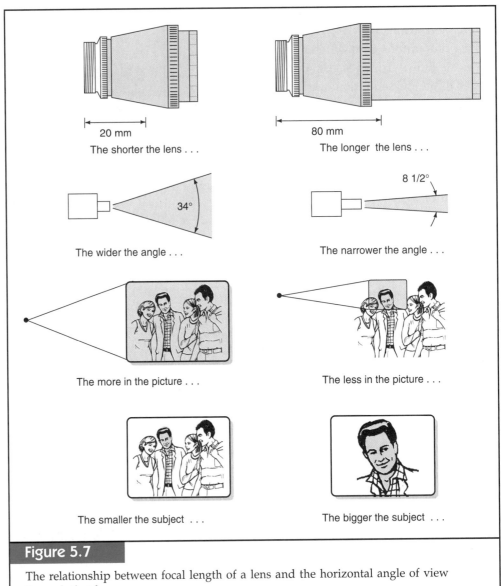

20 mm

The shorter the lens . . .

80 mm

The longer the lens . . .

34°

The wider the angle . . .

8 1/2°

The narrower the angle . . .

The more in the picture . . .

The less in the picture . . .

The smaller the subject . . .

The bigger the subject . . .

Figure 5.7

The relationship between focal length of a lens and the horizontal angle of view through that lens.

that is zoomed *out,* while a long-focal-length lens is similar to a zoom lens that is zoomed *in.*

A long lens will *compress* distance. Two objects that are far apart from each other and at a great distance from the camera will be brought closer to the camera with a long lens and, consequently, will seemingly be brought closer to each other. A common example is the baseball shot of the pitcher and batter as seen with a long telephoto lens from center field, perhaps 400 feet away. Although the pitcher and batter are about 60 feet apart, the camera shot from the long lens makes it *look* as if the two players are much closer to each other. On the home screen, they may look as if they are only 10 or 15 feet apart. Figure 5.8 shows another example of the distance compression created by a long lens. Conversely, a **short lens,** or **wide-angle lens,** will tend to increase distance and make things look farther away than they are.

Figure 5.8

The picture on the top shows the shot of a 54 mm high-magnification fixed-focal-length lens. Note the optical compression even though the children are nine feet apart. The picture on the bottom approximates a 9 mm lens. The children are still nine feet apart, but the effect of the wide-angle lens shows the actual separation. To approximate the girl's position in the earlier picture, the camera was moved much closer to her for the second shot.

Focus

A video image is in proper focus when the subject is clear and distinct, not fuzzy or blurred. On zoom lenses, the focus control is the slip ring located farthest toward the front of the lens. (See Figure 5.9.) When a camera is set up for studio use, this ring is usually adjusted by the use of a remote-control cable. The determining factor in setting proper focus is an object's distance from the camera lens. For example, if you focus on an object that is 4 feet from the camera and then the object moves 20 feet away from the camera, it is likely that you will have to refocus.

To set the focus on a zoom lens, zoom in all the way to the tightest shot possible and then adjust the focus. This is called **front focus.** Following this procedure ensures that the object will remain in focus throughout the range of the zoom lens (assuming, of course, that the distance between the object and the camera does not change). If you find after setting focus that the object goes out of focus as you zoom out, check the lens's **macro flange,** which is normally located at the point that the lens attaches to the camera, to be sure that it is not set for **macro focus** (discussed in Section 5.4). If this does not solve the problem, it is likely that there is something wrong with the lens.

The camera operator—whether in a studio or field situation—must be constantly diligent to ensure the proper focus is maintained. As cameras and objects move, there is a constantly changing distance relationship between the camera and its various subjects. Each change necessitates checking to be sure that the lens is properly focused. Precise focusing is particularly important in HD formats, as slight focusing errors will be more visible to the viewer.

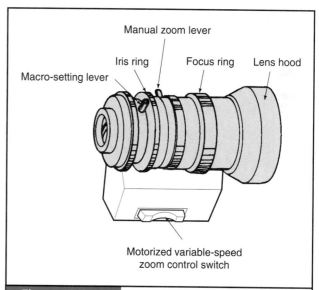

Figure 5.9

Portable camera zoom lens. In addition to the motorized variable-speed zoom control switch, adjustments on the lens include the macro lens setting, the iris (f-stop) setting, the manual zoom lever, and the focus ring.

F-stop Aperture

All camera lenses have an adjustable iris that allows the amount of light coming into the camera to be controlled. When the iris is adjusted, it opens or closes the aperture, which is made up of a series of metal "blades" that adjust the size of the lens's light opening. The aperture does not, however, affect the size of the picture the lens will pick up. Some cameras are equipped with an automatic iris, in which the camera adjusts the aperture depending on the amount of light present. Still, in many production situations, the camera operator will want to override the automatic iris control and adjust the iris manually for a variety of creative reasons.

The various sizes of aperture openings are identified by different **f-stop** numbers. The lower the f-stop number, the larger the lens opening, and the higher the f-stop number, the smaller the lens opening. (See Figure 5.10.) For instance, f-22 is typically the smallest aperture found on most television lenses. The widest

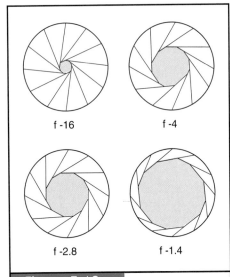

Figure 5.10

Diagrams of various f-stop openings. The basic rule to remember with iris changes is the higher the f-stop number, the smaller the opening. Each marked position on the lens represents one full f-stop, and each time the stop is changed one position, the light going into the camera is doubled or cut in half.

opening could be f-2.8, depending on the lens. In between, the numbers would range through 4, 5.6, 8, 11, and 16. The change from one stop to another represents a doubling or the cutting in half of the amount of light being allowed into the camera. It is a precise measurement, hence the need for some decimal figures.

If working under very poor lighting conditions with no option for increasing the amount of light, for example, it might be advisable to open up to f-4. On the other hand, if working under extremely bright conditions (perhaps outdoors on a sunny day), you might want to "stop down" to f-11 or f-16. The term *stop down*, which actually means closing up the iris to a higher number, may take a little getting used to, but it's the accepted phrase.

One word of warning about f-stop adjustments should be stated at this point. Generally speaking, the camera operator should not routinely think of the f-stop as a means of compensating for bad lighting. Bad lighting or uneven lighting should be handled by correcting the lighting, not by adjusting the camera.

In addition to the lens's f-stop controls, most cameras have an **automatic gain control (AGC)** that adjusts video levels to compensate for differing light levels. Other cameras have a **video output control** that allows the operator to boost the signal in low light situations. The level of boost is measured in decibels (dB), and each 6 dB increase in gain doubles the signal amplification. The manufacturer establishes the "0 dB" position as the standard level of video output for the camera under prescribed lighting conditions. Like f-stop adjustments, this control should never be thought of as a way to make a poorly lit picture better. All it can do is make the poor picture look a little brighter. Increasing the automatic gain control above 0 dB also usually makes the picture appear more grainy; the higher you set the gain, the grainier the picture.

Depth of Field

The distance between the nearest point at which objects are in focus and the farthest point at which objects are in focus in a given shot is called **depth of field.** Once the focus is set for a specific object, other objects closer to the camera will be out of focus, as will objects located farther away. Making sure that you can predict the location and range of the middle ground where objects are in focus is important in the production planning process.

Three different factors interrelate to determine the depth of field: the f-stop (the smaller the lens opening, the greater the depth of field); the distance from the subject to the camera (the greater the camera-to-subject distance, the greater the depth of field); and the focal length of the lens (the shorter the lens, the greater the depth of field). Figure 5.11 illustrates these three variables.

The manipulation of depth of field is often used for artistic effect. In some situations, such as sporting events, you might want to have a very large depth of field so that rapidly moving action will stay in focus. In an interview situation, you might want to have narrower depth of field so that the element in focus (the person being interviewed) is separated from the background. Figure 5.12 shows another artistic effect created by a narrow depth of field. The best way to increase the depth of field is simply to add light and to stop down the lens. This allows the shot to remain the same, which

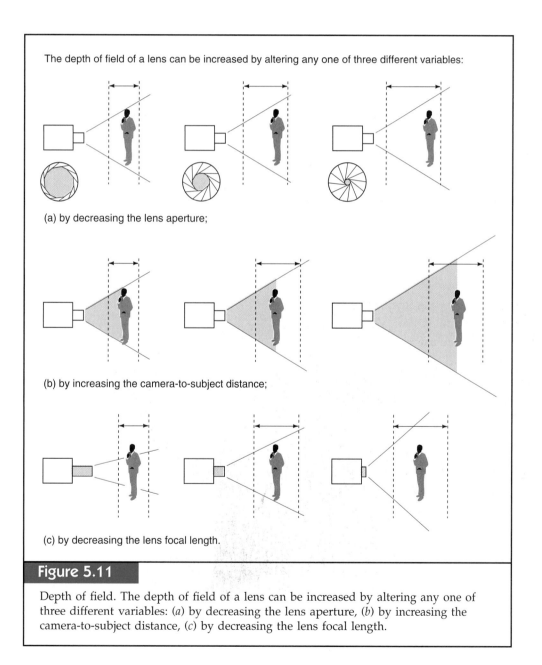

The depth of field of a lens can be increased by altering any one of three different variables:

(a) by decreasing the lens aperture;

(b) by increasing the camera-to-subject distance;

(c) by decreasing the lens focal length.

Figure 5.11

Depth of field. The depth of field of a lens can be increased by altering any one of three different variables: (*a*) by decreasing the lens aperture, (*b*) by increasing the camera-to-subject distance, (*c*) by decreasing the lens focal length.

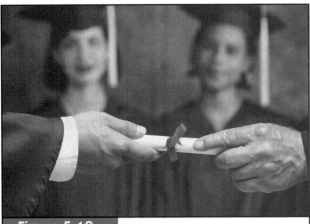

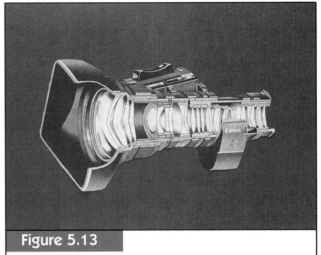

would not be the case if attempts were made to change the focal length with a zoom movement or to change the camera-to-subject distance. Similarly, depth of field can be decreased by moving the camera farther away from the subject and zooming in, or by opening up the lens. The latter technique means you will have to either reduce the amount of light on the subject or reduce the amount of light entering the camera by using a **neutral density (ND)** filter, as discussed in the next section.

Another artistic effect that relates to depth of field is called the **rack focus.** In this type of shot, the camera operator initially focuses on one object in the frame (with other objects blurred), then smoothly adjusts the focus so that *another* object in the frame comes into focus. For example, the camera may start on a tight close-up shot of a half-empty glass close to the camera with the background out of focus; the camera operator would then change to focus on a person lying on the sofa, while the foreground glass goes blurry. Such shots tend to be most dramatic when the depth of field is relatively narrow.

5.4 Production Use of the Zoom

The zoom lens allows camera operators and directors to achieve rapid and continuous adjustment of the lens focal length and, consequently, to control precisely the size and framing of shots. In addition to giving the director and camera operator a wide range of lens lengths that are immediately available, the zoom lens also facilitates very smooth on-the-air movement.

The variable-focal-length zoom lens is essentially an arrangement of gears and optical elements that allows the operator to shift these lens elements—moving them back and forth in relation to each other. (See Figure 5.13.) This achieves varying focal lengths by changing the theoretical center point of the lens. Zoom lenses vary greatly with price and manufacturer, but lenses designed for professional and industrial levels all share some of the same basic characteristics.

Lens Ratio

For many production situations, a 10-to-1 magnification ratio is sufficient. On a typical lens this would result in focal lengths ranging from 10.5 mm at the wide-angle position to 105 mm at the zoomed-in position. Figure 5.14 provides some indication of the range of shots available with a 10-to-1 zoom ratio lens. Many studio cameras are equipped with 20-to-1 lenses, while field cameras often have lenses in the range of 15-to-1. For sporting events and other outdoor productions, cameras with zoom ratios of 30-to-1 and greater are common. The use of an **extender** increases the focal

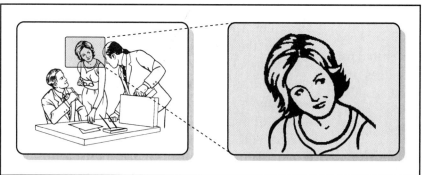

Figure 5.14

Range of a zoom lens. These two views represent the extreme focal lengths of a 10-to-1 zoom lens: *left,* zoomed "out" to the shortest focal length (widest angle); *right,* zoomed "in" to the longest focal length (narrowest angle).

length of a lens, allowing it to zoom in even closer to distant objects. A 2X extender, for example, doubles the focal length of the zoom lens at both the wide-angle and zoomed-in positions. Some extenders are placed between the zoom lens and the camera, while others are built into the zoom lens itself. On these latter types, the camera operator can select either normal or extended lens lengths.

Movement Control

Virtually all zoom lenses have a motor-driven zoom mechanism. Less expensive models may have only one or two speeds, which provides only limited artistic control. Professional lenses usually have variable-speed controls, and this ability to obtain smooth, on-the-air zoom movement gives the director and camera operator a great deal of production flexibility. It is possible to tighten up a shot on the air, going smoothly from a wide shot to a medium shot to a close-up at variable speeds. The best zoom work—smooth and precise—usually goes unnoticed to the average viewer, because it does not call attention to itself.

Generally, professional zoom lenses also will provide a manual zoom control lever that allows the operator to zoom without the aid of the motor. Most commonly, this manual control is used to perform a **snap zoom,** in which the lens is rapidly (in effect instantly) changed from one focal length to another. If you are using a camera that allows manual operation of the zoom control, it is important that you disengage the power zoom before moving the zoom lever. Serious damage can result if the manual lever is moved while the power zoom control is engaged.

Macro Focus

Under normal circumstances, most zoom lenses cannot focus on objects that are very close to the lens. For instance, it may not be possible to set focus on a small insect that is being held eight inches from the lens. However, on lenses equipped with a macro flange, it is possible to set focus on objects very close to the lens. By moving the macro-setting lever attached to the macro flange (see Figure 5.9), you can take extreme close-ups of printed material or small objects at distances of two inches or less from the lens.

5.5 Camera Controls

A number of controls on the camera body itself can be set for optimum picture quality or to achieve an artistic effect. Not all of these controls, however, are found on all cameras, and they may not be on the cameras you use at your school.

Viewfinder Visual Indicators and Controls

Although the viewfinder has no effect on the signal that is actually produced by the camera, it does provide a great deal of information about how the camera unit's controls are set. The primary purpose of the viewfinder, of course, is to show how the shot is framed on a small (usually black-and-white) video monitor that shows the camera's output. Most cameras offer brightness and contrast controls so that the operator can adjust the picture shown on the viewfinder monitor. These controls, however, have no effect on the actual output of the camera.

Modern cameras also provide a great deal of other information to the camera operator through the viewfinder. By using small LED lights around the viewfinder monitor or by superimposing information over the picture on the viewfinder monitor, cameras provide information about the current settings of the controls. For example, visual indications in the viewfinder may show how filters, white balance, and gain controls are set (see the next section, "Filters"). The viewfinder also may provide visual warnings to the operator for such problems as a low battery or insufficient lighting.

Finally, **tally lights** on the front side of the viewfinder tell the talent/subject that the camera is currently "on the air" or, in field-production situations, that the tape is rolling.

Filters

Some professional cameras designed for both studio and field use have a built-in filter system to compensate for Kelvin temperature differences between indoor and outdoor lighting (see Chapter 6). Usually located between the lens and the beam splitter, this filter component is an integral part of the camera system. Typically, a camera has a rotating disk of filters for different lighting conditions: (1) tungsten studio lamps and sunrise and sunset; (2) bright outdoor light; and (3) clouds or rain. If the camera is kept in a studio, the filter setting never needs to be changed; the studio position (which is actually no filter) is always the correct one.

But if the camera is taken outside, the filter disk should be changed to one of the outdoor filters. These are both orange to compensate for the more bluish outdoor light. The difference between the bright outdoor filter and the cloud filter is the amount of neutral density (ND) that is mixed with the orange filter. Neutral density filters are designed to limit brightness but do not adjust color. The ND #1 allows one-half the light to pass through, while ND #2 and ND #3 allow one-quarter and one-eighth, respectively. The filter for bright light has more neutral density than the one for cloudy conditions.

Sometimes other filters are part of the filter disk, or they are added to the front of the lens. For example, a **soft contrast filter** is used to create a fuzzy effect, and a **star filter** gives a star effect that radiates from bright spots on the screen.

White Balance

An important control on the camera is the one that establishes the correct color balance by electronically adjusting the red, green, and blue components of the signal so that pure white *looks* pure white. Since different types of lighting have different characteristics; some types of light may produce a bluish or reddish tint if no compensation is made. White balance adjusts for different conditions.

Depending on the camera, proper white balance can be set and maintained in several ways. An increasing number of cameras have an **automatic white balance** control that continuously tracks lighting conditions and adjusts the white balance accordingly. On low-cost and older cameras, however, automatic white balance can produce less-than-optimal results.

Some cameras have one or more **preset white balance** settings that allow the user to select a preadjusted white balance setting for specific lighting conditions. On these cameras, the presets may be labeled for the lighting situation (e.g., indoor).

Perhaps the safest way to ensure proper white balance, however, is to set it yourself. To do this, set the camera to **manual white balance** and position a pure white object in front of the camera lens. Then, press the appropriate button on the camera to set white balance. Normally, you will need to hold the button for a second or two, and the camera will give some sort of indication in the viewfinder that proper white balance is set. The disadvantage of using manual white balance, of course, is that you must constantly be aware of changes in lighting conditions and reset white balance as appropriate.

Other Controls

Some cameras have several additional controls that, while not necessarily complicated, are best suited to an individualized-study approach. Such items as the fade time control, the negative/positive selector, and the phase control selector should have clearly marked "0" or neutral positions. The beginning student should be aware of these off positions and make sure that such controls are in the safe neutral position for normal camera operations.

Camera Control Unit

A camera used in a studio environment usually has a separate **camera control unit (CCU).** The CCU is mounted in the control room, connected to the camera body by special cabling, usually a dual-shielded cable called a triax. For HD applications a fiber optic cable may be required. The CCU allows the camera to be precisely calibrated so that it will produce quality video, a process called setup. A technician usually performs this calibration, which is likely done before each production session. In addition to initial setup, the CCU also allows adjustment of the camera from the control room during the production if necessary.

Prompter

As discussed in Chapter 2, a **prompter** is a device that displays the script on a monitor in front of the camera lens. This allows talent to read the words on the script while looking at the camera. The prompter system consists of the prompter unit mounted on the camera, a computer that stores the scripts and provides the input signal for the prompter, and a controller.

Once the script is entered into the prompter computer, it can be displayed on the prompter unit. During the production, the prompter operator will use the controller to select the proper speed at which the script will scroll on the prompter. Most systems also allow the script to be "backed up" in case a scene needs to be shot again. On some systems, the computer's keyboard or mouse is used instead of a separate controller,

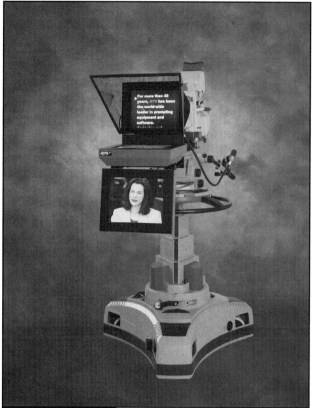

Figure 5.15

This prompting system reflects copy from a monitor onto a mirror positioned in front of the camera lens. The camera shoots through the mirror to pick up the talent's image, here displayed underneath the prompter. *Photo courtesy of QTV.*

and in other cases the talent may actually control the prompter using a foot-operated switch. (See Figure 5.15.)

5.6 | Camera Mounting and Movement

Efficient use of the camera depends on several primary factors that interact with one another during a production. The first of these is simply the *position* of the camera in relationship to a subject (or multiple subjects in wide-angle shots). The camera reveals the front, side, or top of the elements in the picture according to where it is placed. A second factor involves changing the *direction* in which the camera is aimed to reveal different subjects.

There also can be a continuing change in the *point of view* of the camera as it is moved to reveal different aspects of a subject or sequence of subjects. This movement also can involve changes in the *elevation* of the camera, especially for artistic effect. The effectiveness of these operations is very dependent on the hardware that provides movement and support for the camera.

Camera mounting equipment also makes provision for the use of ancillary devices attached to the camera, most notably a prompter, as discussed previously. In some cases, a video monitor or clock also may be attached to the camera mounting apparatus.

Camera Head Movement

Figure 5.16 shows the basic parts of a studio camera unit, including: (a) the video components of the camera itself; (b) the mounting head containing the equipment used for movement of the camera; and (c) the camera mount that controls floor movement of the entire unit.

Shot changes involving vertical and horizontal camera movement are fundamental to video production. When these kinds of movements are continuous on-the-air moves, they require a skilled operator and a suitable mounting head with which to execute them. A

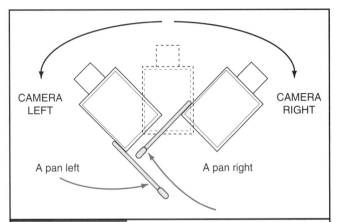

Figure 5.17

Camera panning. To pan the camera in a given direction, the panning handle must be moved in the opposite direction. Thus, to execute a "pan left," the camera operator has to move the panning handle to the right.

horizontal movement to the left or to the right is known as a **pan.** (See Figure 5.17.) When told to "pan right," the operator moves the camera lens in the direction of his or her right hand. This is the reverse of stage movements, which are given from the standpoint of the performer looking out toward an audience.

Up-and-down movements of the camera are called **tilts.** The lens end of the camera is moved up or down to view elements at different elevations of the set. (See Figure 5.18.) Both pans and tilts are accomplished by exerting pressure on the **pan handle** that projects from the right rear of the camera. Zoom and focus controls are usually located on this pan handle. In the mounting head area, there is a coupling device such as a cam or cradle assembly that is important to smoothness of motion, especially in a tilting action.

Camera Mounts

Although both pans and tilts can be accomplished by simply moving the camera head, any change of camera position, whether done as an "on-the-air" movement or simply to change the framing of a shot, is accomplished through movement of the camera mount.

The simplest and least expensive camera mount is the **tripod.** When used in a studio environment, this three-legged stand is usually fastened to a dolly base

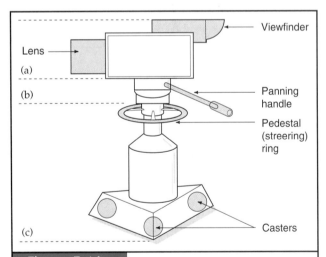

Figure 5.16

Three basic parts of the camera. (*a*) The video components of the camera itself, including the lens, viewfinder, and CCD; (*b*) the mounting head with the panning handle that controls camera movement; and (*c*) the camera mount that is the transport and support mechanism for the entire unit.

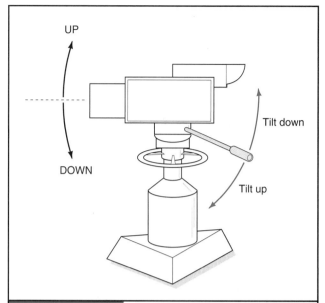

Figure 5.18

Camera tilting. In tilting the camera up or down, the camera head is pivoted through the use of the pan handle.

with three casters. The casters can either rotate freely, which facilitates quick and easy movement of the camera in all directions, or can be locked into a non-movable position, resulting in a steady camera unit.

The field model tripod, illustrated in Figure 5.19, has a crank-operated elevation adjustment that can be used to raise and lower the camera—although not smoothly enough to be used on the air. Many tripods have no adjustment for height other than the laborious process of mechanically adjusting the spread of the tripod legs. Thus, there is no way to achieve any elevation change during an actual production. The tripod, however, is lightweight, and most models are readily collapsible. This makes the tripod a desirable camera mount for most field productions.

The **pedestal mount** shown in Figure 5.20 has been the standard for studio production since the beginning of television. Its distinctive feature is the central pedestal that can be raised or lowered with the assistance of counterweights or air pressure. It also has a steering ring that controls all three casters in a synchronized manner to allow smooth on-the-air camera movements across the studio floor. This ease and steadiness in camera movement have

made the studio pedestal a must in any big studio production.

When more pronounced changes of position and elevation are called for, they are accomplished through the use of specialized mounts, such as the motorized **crane** mount (shown in Figure 5.21) and the smaller **crab dolly.** With the crane, considerable camera movement over a wide range is possible, because the motorized base has a separate driver. Inherited from the film industry, the crane is the largest and most flexible type of camera mount and comes in a variety of sizes. The camera itself is mounted on a boom arm that can be moved vertically or laterally without moving the crane base. Depending on the model, the length of the arm extension is 10 to 15 feet for studio models and much more for a few special field units. For everything from rock concerts to

Figure 5.19

Camera mounted on a camera head assembly with an adjustable tripod. *Photo courtesy of Panasonic.*

Figure 5.20

A studio camera on a pedestal mount.
Photo courtesy of Panasonic.

Figure 5.21

A large truck-mounted crane used for Olympic coverage. Such equipment is now commonplace for any large-scale outdoor concert, parade, or sporting event. *Photo courtesy of ABC Sports.*

Olympic coverage, the moving crane shot has become an indispensable part of the visual language of television.

Camera Mount Movements

One of the most obvious changes in picture framing is accomplished by moving the camera closer to or farther away from the subject. This is referred to as dollying the camera, and it produces a dolly shot. (See Figure 5.22.) While the zoom lens may have reduced the use of dolly-in and dolly-out shots, this movement still has its uses. As noted in Figure 5.8, there is a definite difference in the way the zoom lens in a wide-angle mode sees two subjects separated by 10 feet or so and the way those two subjects are seen with the lens in the high-magnification mode.

Lateral movement of the camera and its mount is known as **trucking.** A change of picture is accomplished

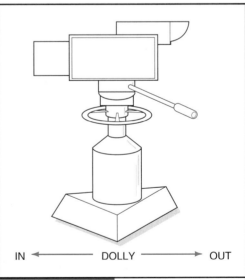

IN ←————— DOLLY ——————→ OUT

Figure 5.22

Camera dollying. In a dolly movement, the camera is simply moved closer to or farther from the subject.

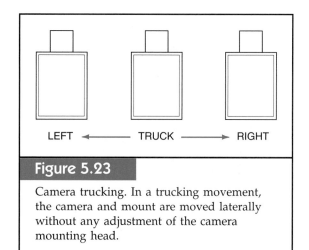

Figure 5.23

Camera trucking. In a trucking movement, the camera and mount are moved laterally without any adjustment of the camera mounting head.

as the camera trucks right or trucks left, because the camera moves sideways without panning to the right or left. (See Figure 5.23.) In the field, dollying and trucking movements normally cannot be attempted unless special tracks have been laid down to facilitate smooth, level movement. Usually, such movements are set up only for ambitious productions like high-budget dramatic programs or major sporting events.

A **follow shot** can use both the trucking and dollying techniques. Here, a camera moves with the subject and maintains a constant distance from it, while the background is seen to move past in a constantly changing panoramic sequence. An **arc shot** is another variation of a trucking movement. The camera circles around the stationary subject to reveal different aspects of the subject. (See Figure 5.24.)

Another move uses studio camera pedestals that are designed to facilitate a slight change in camera height. In this case, the word *pedestal* is used as a command verb as the camera operator is asked to "pedestal up" or "pedestal down." (See Figure 5.25.) In larger studios where crane mounts or crab dollies are used, other effective movements are also possible. **Craning,** or **booming** (up or down), involves raising or lowering the crane or boom arm. The effect is similar to a pedestal movement, except that much greater vertical distances can be covered. Another kind of motion is the **arm move.** With a large crane, the boom arm or crane can be moved left, right, up, or down or any continuing combination of these, while the base remains stationary. With both the crane and the crab mounts,

the camera operator retains control over the angle and tilt of the camera throughout all these moves.

It should be noted that all these movements are difficult to use on-air when a zoom lens is at a position of high magnification (narrow angle). The slightest unsteadiness during the camera movement is exaggerated, because the long lens, while magnifying the subject, is also magnifying the shaky camera movement. To a lesser extent, the same problem is apparent with panning and tilting movements.

Handheld Cameras

For some types of production, especially out-of-studio work, the use of handheld cameras is very common. Shoulder-supported professional units and consumer-oriented palm-sized camcorders facilitate situations where the camera *operator* becomes, in effect, the camera mount.

Since no mount is used, the camera operator is not constrained in either time (by having to pick up and move a camera mount) or space (by having to shoot only from locations where a mount can be set up). The use of a handheld camera can provide greater flexibility and thus is considered indispensable for "reality-based" television, news, sporting events, and concerts.

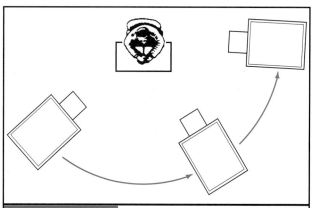

Figure 5.24

Camera arcing. This move is accomplished mainly by a maneuver of the camera mount as the camera arcs around, keeping the lens pointed at the subject. The move is much easier to make with a crab dolly than with a tripod or pedestal mount.

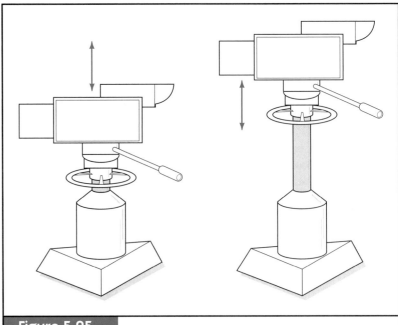

Figure 5.25

Camera pedestaling. In a pedestal movement, the entire camera and mounting head are moved straight up or down by a system of counterweights or compressed air.

However, it is important that the operator of a handheld camera be able to keep the camera *steady* and avoid shaky shots and jerky movements. Such skill usually comes from practice, not only in building arm and shoulder strength but in learning ways to "cheat," such as leaning against a wall to keep the camera steady. Body braces can help an operator keep the camera steady, and some cameras have built-in electronic **image stabilization** circuitry designed to help maintain picture stability (see Chapter 12).

Robotic Camera Control

The use of robotic camera control in news, public-affairs, and sports programs is on the rise. In these systems, the zoom, focus, and camera mount movements of one or more cameras can be controlled by a single camera operator (see Color Plate F). Sophisticated camera moves (such as a simultaneous arc shot, pedestal up, and slow zoom in) can be programmed to execute automatically during a show.

5.7 Field of View

The camera operator should be familiar with the various terms designating the size of the shot desired, or the field of view, as discussed in Chapter 4. Generally most television shots in either standard definition or high definition can be related to several basic categories, as shown in Figure 5.26.

The Long Shot (LS)

The perspective of the **long shot (LS),** also referred to as the **wide shot (WS),** is far enough away from a person that the entire body and quite a bit of the surroundings are included. Often, the facial features of a performer are not exactly distinguishable at this distance—although they will be more distinguishable in HD formats. It is also known as an establishing shot when used in the beginning of a production (or segment), because it relates those people involved in a program not only to each other but also to the setting and circumstances of that

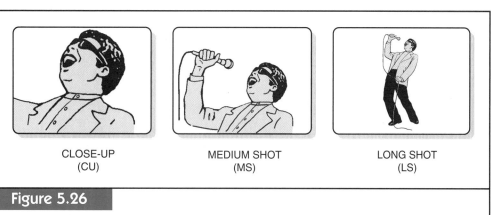

| CLOSE-UP
(CU) | MEDIUM SHOT
(MS) | LONG SHOT
(LS) |

Figure 5.26

Basic television shots. In addition to these basic shots, many other designations and modifications are possible, such as the "extreme long shot," the "medium long shot," the "medium close-up," and the "extreme close-up."

program. In drama and in other applications, these wider shots are also necessary whenever people move from one part of the set to another. It can be used as a closing shot to signal a pulling back from the action—out of the drama—as it comes to a close.

Sometimes you might want to establish a panoramic scene or cover the sweep of action with a very wide shot. If characters are so far away that they are hardly identifiable as specific individuals, the shot can be labeled an **extreme long shot (ELS** or **XLS).**

The Medium Shot (MS)

These shot designations are to some degree relative to their use and the artistic concepts of the director or camera operator. What is a long shot for one dramatic segment could be considered a **medium shot (MS)** in another situation. For the most part, however, an MS of a person includes most of the body or perhaps even two people. The MS is the basic shot in standard television production. It is used to convey much of the dialogue in drama and most of the action in talk shows, game shows, variety programs, and many other studio productions.

The Close-up (CU)

The **close-up (CU)**—with its sense of physical intimacy—can probe the individual and personal aspects of what a program is communicating. In many dramatic situations, the CU is the only way to get in-

sight into the emotional state of a person or performer. A CU shot may, of course, be used to view objects as well as people. It may be a close-up of some item that has importance to the narrative of a drama. In a commercial, it may be the product that is examined in more detail.

The **extreme close-up** shot is most often used to intensify the emotion of a dramatic situation or musical performance. When these shots are used carefully, they can add the right artistic effect at the right moment. Although the difference between the close-up and extreme close-up is open to interpretation, the essential distinction is that the *extreme* close-up normally calls attention to itself. While a close-up of a person's entire face will not normally call special attention to itself, for example, an extreme close-up of a tear rolling down that person's face will.

5.8 Picture Composition

Beyond understanding how cameras are operated and how different types of shots are identified, it is important to understand some of the aesthetic disciplines of shooting video. As we discuss the following elements of framing, headroom, lead room, depth composition, angle of elevation, balance, and aspect ratio, keep in mind that the various "rules" that have evolved as part of the grammar of the medium should be considered

WRONG   WRONG   CORRECT

Figure 5.27

Correct headroom framing. Although it is largely a matter of subjective judgment and artistic "feel," it is important that the camera operator always be aware of the headroom on every shot. Too much headroom is as bad as too little.

guidelines. As with any artistic effort, there is always room for a new approach if it communicates something to an audience. Once the rules have been mastered, they can be modified or even ignored as long as the creative person does so with a full understanding of the basic purposes of those guidelines.

Framing

Television directors have developed a simple terminology to describe the basic dimension of a shot to the camera operator. The scope of a shot is described in terms of that portion of the body that is to be cut off by the bottom edge of the picture. Thus a *thigh shot* or *chest shot* quickly communicates the desired framing of the person or persons in the picture.

Equally useful are the terms *single, two-shot,* or *three-shot,* which describe the number of people to be included in the shot. Other descriptive labels have evolved to specify certain kinds of desired shots. For example, an *over-the-shoulder shot* (O/S) might be called for in a situation when two people are facing each other in a conversation (such as a dramatic scene or an interview program). This is a shot favoring one person (who generally is facing the camera) framed by the back of the head and shoulder of the person whose back is to the camera.

Headroom

An important discipline for all camera operators is to consistently maintain an appropriate amount of **headroom.** This term refers to the space between the top of a subject's head and the top of the frame. When this

distance is not observed, the results can be distracting. (See Figure 5.27.)

It is especially important that headroom distance be uniform among all cameras on any production. A helpful guide for shot consistency is to place the eyes of subjects at the point of an imaginary line approximately one-third of the way down from the top of the picture. In close-up shots, the framing is best with the eyes slightly below the line; in wider shots, they should be slightly above the line.

Lead Room

When speakers or performers directly address the camera, they generally are centered in the frame, unless a foreground object or over-the-shoulder visual effect is to be included in the frame. When an individual in a close-up shot is speaking to another with his or her head turned toward that person, the framing is much more attractive if there is an added amount of **lead room** (talk space) in the side of the frame to which the person has turned. (See Figure 5.28.) By the same token, a distracting, crowded effect is created if the framing is such that the person's face is placed too close to the frame edge. The concept of lead room applies even more strongly to moving subjects. If a person (or animal or object, for that matter) is moving laterally across the screen, it is important to allow lead room in front. (See Figure 5.29.)

Depth Composition

The video message is transmitted by means of a two-dimensional medium. To simulate some feeling of

BAD   BETTER   BEST

Figure 5.28

Proper lead room or "talk space." The camera operator should always intuitively give additional space in the direction that the talent is looking.

depth, the director has a number of options that involve lighting, camera work, the set, and the placement of performers. One method is to make sure that the performers are separated from the set in the background both by their physical positions and by the constructive use of lighting. In this situation, it is important to portray something familiar like the interior of a room or office to provide a feeling of scale or perspective. If a plain or abstract background is used, the viewer has no yardstick against which to gauge the distance from the subject to background.

Foreground objects can add significantly to the feeling of depth. By framing some nearby objects off to one side or along the bottom of the picture, the subject in the background is placed in greater relief. Care must be taken, though, not to force an unnatural effect for its

own sake, as this will undoubtedly appear contrived to the viewer.

Whenever possible, depth composition can be achieved with the arrangement—or **blocking**—of talent. If several people appear in a scene, try to arrange them so that some are closer to the camera than others. In a two-shot, an O/S shot as a rule is preferred to a flat two-shot of a double profile. (See Figure 5.30.)

A feeling of depth also can be achieved by careful use of angles. If a shot calls for someone to sit behind a desk, the camera can get a much more interesting shot by shooting the desk and the person from an angle. (Of course, the dramatic context might call for a formal head-on shot of a character such as a judge or stern employer.)

BAD   CORRECT

Figure 5.29

Proper lead room for a moving subject. Whenever a subject is moving, the camera operator should visually anticipate the flow of movement, allowing the viewer to see where the subject is going.

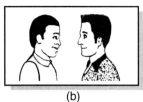

| (a) | (b) | (c) | (d) |

Figure 5.30

Depth staging. The over-the-shoulder shot (*a*) generally presents a more dynamic, interesting, and aesthetically pleasing picture than the flat double-profile two-shot (*b*). By shooting the person behind the desk from an angle (*c*), a more inviting and vigorous effect can be achieved than with a formal head-on flat shot (*d*).

Angle of Elevation

For most conventional composition, the camera should shoot at an angle relatively level to the subject. Generally speaking, try to place the camera lens at eye level with the talent. This is fairly normal when the talent is standing. When talent is seated, however, you must move the camera down so the camera is as low as the talent. To achieve this level angle, most "talk sets" (news programs, interviews, discussion shows, talk shows) are staged on a raised platform or riser. If you cannot avoid shooting down into an interview or discussion set, the steep angle can be minimized somewhat by using a longer lens setting and dollying back away from the set. The farther back you can get, the less steep the angle will be.

There are times when, for dramatic effect, you will not want to shoot the talent at a level angle. To portray an actor as being overwhelmed, submissive, or downtrodden, you will shoot the actor from a higher elevation. Shooting from a high angle implies control and dominance over the individual. On the other hand, if you want to give a character power and authority, you should shoot that actor from a low angle. By placing the viewer in the lowered position, you endow the character with force and strength.

Balance

Many beginning camera operators try to achieve a pleasing composition by striving for symmetrical balance. They try to place the most important element directly in the center of the picture and/or try to balance picture components with equal elements equidistant from the center. This kind of mechanical or symmetrical balancing can lead to very stiff, dull, formal pictures.

A more dynamic kind of composition is **asymmetrical balance,** wherein a lightweight object some distance from the center of the picture can balance a heavier object closer to the center (similar to a seesaw with a light person at the end of the board balancing a heavier person seated close to the center).

Another way to avoid centralization of picture elements is to think in terms of the **rule of thirds.** Imagine the television screen divided horizontally and vertically into thirds. If major pictorial elements are placed at the points where the lines intersect, the result is a more pleasing balance than if perfect symmetry is achieved. The rule of thirds is a good principle to follow on both 4:3 and 16:9 aspect ratio formats, as shown in Figure 5.31.

Special Considerations for the 16:9 Aspect Ratio

The basic principles of composition are the same in both standard definition and high definition. However, there are some differences in execution between the two because of the 16:9 aspect ratio of most HD formats. The wider 16:9 aspect ratio more closely mimics the natural human field of vision, and so can be particularly compelling for landscape shots and other horizontal views. Vertically oriented subjects present more of a challenge in 16:9 because shots that would look fine in 4:3 have awkward "empty" space at the sides, as shown in Figure 5.32. This problem can be remedied by framing the shot so that other elements fill these empty spaces, or by shooting the vertical object from a low angle, as shown in Figure 5.33.

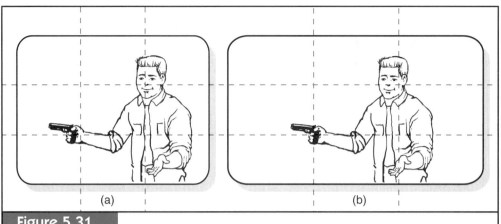

Figure 5.31

Asymmetrical balance and the rule of thirds. In either the 4:3 (*a*) or 16:9 (*b*) aspect ratio, divide the screen into thirds vertically and horizontally. Then, frame your shots so that points of interest are positioned at the intersections of these lines.

Figure 5.32

A vertically oriented shot that looks fine in 4:3 aspect ratio (*a*) can look awkward when shot in 16:9 (*b*).

Figure 5.33

To make vertically oriented shots look more pleasing in 16:9, either frame them with other elements (*a*) or shoot them from low angles (*b*).

Shooting for Multiple Aspect Ratios

In some situations, you may be shooting something that will be seen in *both* 4:3 and 16:9 aspect ratios. Particularly during the switchover from NTSC to ATSC, some television operations are simultaneously sending out both 4:3 and 16:9 pictures—4:3 for viewers with NTSC televisions and 16:9 for viewers with ATSC sets. The camera operator will shoot with a 16:9 camera, but NTSC viewers will see only the center portion of the picture, as shown in Figure 5.34.

(a)

(b)

Figure 5.34

When a shot framed in 16:9 (*a*) is converted to 4:3 (*b*), the side edges of the picture will be lost.

In these situations, you need to frame your shots so that the viewers seeing only the 4:3 aspect ratio will still see the important parts of the picture. This will likely lead to some compromises in the way you shoot, but it is something of a necessary evil. At times, for example, you will want to keep the shot wider than you normally would so that it won't matter if viewers watching in 4:3 can't see the outer edges of the frame. The good news is that HD's greater resolution will still allow the viewer to see more detail, even in a wider shot.

Other Composition Problems

There are other compositional problems to avoid, some of which may arise when cameras are used outside the studio. For example, you should be aware of the background when shooting a close-up or medium shot of talent; you should avoid framing the person so that it appears a sign, telephone pole, or plant is "growing" out of his or her head. (See Figure 5.35.)

You should also be sure that the camera is level when shooting. A misadjusted tripod (with one leg extended farther than the others, for example) will create a "tilted" camera. Consequently, the **horizon line** in your shots will not be flat, creating the impression that people and objects are about to "fall" out of frame. (See Figure 5.36.)

Figure 5.35

Poor shot composition. The sign looks like it is "growing" out of the person's head.

Figure 5.36

Tilted horizon. An improperly leveled camera mount can lead to shots in which the horizon line is not exactly horizontal, and thus people and objects appear to be "leaning."

5.9 | Production Techniques

Since cameras are used in such a wide variety of situations, it is difficult to generalize the operational procedures you should follow. Using a camera in a studio situation will be much different from using a camera in the field, for example, and production techniques for a quiz show will be much different from those used for a drama.

However, a few standard procedures will help you no matter what the production situation. The first of these is to become familiar with the camera's operational controls as much as possible *before* the production begins. Of course, the only way to learn some things is through the "trial by fire" that comes with real production, but you should take the time to familiarize yourself generally with the camera and its mounting components beforehand. Practice using the motorized zoom control, try doing a few tilts and pans, and practice focusing, for example.

You should also develop the habit of checking the camera before the production starts to make sure it is in proper working order. Here, again, true expertise will come only with experience, but it is important to "put a camera through its paces" to make sure all of its components are functioning properly. A lot of this will come from simply going through the process of familiarizing yourself with the camera, but you should do other things as well, such as checking connectors and making sure the picture controls are properly adjusted.

When using a camcorder in the field, it is a good idea to record some "test" footage before the production begins. In this way, you will check to be sure that both the camera and recorder are operating properly.

It is also a good idea to practice specific camera moves you know you will have to do during a production. Before the show, you may be given a **shot sheet** that lists the shots you will have to get during the production. If one of these, for instance, is a smooth zoom out and tilt up from the logo on the desk to the talent sitting at the desk, you can practice this move before the production begins.

Finally, once the production begins, you should stay alert and ready. If you're working in a studio environment, you likely will wear a **headset** so that you can talk with the director and other personnel through the studio **intercom** system. Be ready for the director's commands and to provide feedback if the director asks for it. In some situations, such as live talk shows, the director may occasionally ask you to look for good audience or guest reaction shots, for example.

Many specific operational procedures will be established by the production facility. In your classes, for example, the instructor will establish operational procedures for the cameras and other equipment, including what controls you should *not* operate. Learning and properly following these procedures is itself an important production technique.

Discussion Questions

1. What are the main differences between NTSC and ATSC formats in terms of resolution, scanning, and frame rate?

2. How do the three aspects of color (hue, saturation, and brightness) combine to create specific colors?

3. What are the basic aspects of lens design, and how do they affect shots?

4. How do different camera mounts affect camera shots? What types of shots are possible with each type of camera mount?

5. Discuss the basic guidelines of picture composition. Why is each guideline relevant, and how does each serve to make a better picture? What differences does a 16:9 aspect ratio make in the way shots should be composed?

Notes

1. An increasing number of cameras are using CMOS (complementary metal oxide semiconductor) imagers instead of CCDs. CMOS imagers offer lower power consumption, lower cost, higher image quality, and ultimately the development of "camera on a chip" technologies that can replace the CCDs and circuitry of a traditional camera with a single microchip.

2. Technically, the focal length of a lens is the measure from the optical center point of the lens (when it is focused at infinity) to a point where the image is in focus. Focal length is measured in either millimeters or inches (25.4 millimeters being equal to 1 inch).

CHAPTER 6

Lighting

Many *techniques* have been developed over the years to create appropriate lighting, both so there is enough light to operate the camera and so that the proper mood or reality is established for the scene. But lighting is very much a creative process, and usually there is no one right way to light a set. The techniques serve as a starting point that may then be fine-tuned.

Lighting can be dangerous and time-consuming. The *discipline* needed to think about safety cannot be overemphasized nor can the fact that lighting must be carefully planned so it can be executed as quickly as possible. Both techniques and disciplines figure heavily in this chapter as it covers the following:

- The difference between incident and reflected light (6.1)

- General illumination principles such as intensity, contrast ratio, and color temperature (6.2)

- How and when to use a light meter (6.2)

- How to accomplish creative lighting objectives such as shape, reality, mood, and focus of attention (6.3)

- The different types of lamps used in lighting instruments such as quartz, high-frequency fluorescents, and HMIs (6.4)

- The differences between spotlights and floodlights (6.4)

- The key, fill, and backlights needed for three-point lighting and their approximate ratios (6.5)

- Set lights and kicker lights (6.5)
- Principles for multicamera, cameo, silhouette, chroma key, and HDTV lighting (6.5)
- How to mount lights (6.6)
- Equipment principles used to create intensity, diffusion, shape, and color (6.7)
- The need for a light plot (6.8)
- How to set up lights (6.8)
- The importance of safety (6.9)

6.1 Types of Light: Incident and Reflected

Light exists in the form of waves that move at the speed of 186,284 miles per second. Variations in frequency of those waves account for what many living creatures perceive as differences in color. Visible light is part of a much larger electromagnetic spectrum that also includes X rays and all frequencies of the broadcast band. (See Color Plate C.)

All light that comes to our eyes is one of two different forms of the same basic light energy. When it comes *directly* from a source, such as the sun or a lightbulb, it is called **incident light.** As important as this light is, it conveys little beyond the fact that we are looking at a car headlight or a neon sign, for example. Our ability to see is largely the result of **reflected light** that has first come in contact with some material surface before it enters our field of vision. In this process it has been changed, and this now *reflected light* can tell us much about such things as an object's color, structure, and texture. The even, shiny quality of light reflected from a wooden table denotes a hard, uniform, brown surface. We can perceive the texture of heavy cloth material by the many tiny shadows created by the design of the weave.

Illumination for video production is an art that involves the proper use of lighting equipment to control the light that is reflected *from* the subject *into* the camera lens. The way in which we shape and control this reflected light determines what the TV camera perceives as a picture, and the result creates somewhat of an illusion of three dimensions on the viewing surface of a TV screen.

6.2 Technical Lighting Objectives

When the **lighting director (LD)** designs the lighting plan for any type of video production, two interacting concerns must be addressed. On one hand, important considerations grow out of specific *artistic needs* of the program. On the other hand, the LD knows that those creative aspects of lighting must coordinate with the larger context of a plan for *general illumination* **(base light)** related to the technical needs of the camera system.

The lighting plan starts with the need for all performers to be lit in a way that allows their features and person to be adequately portrayed in all locations of the set. Are there adequate light levels for performers as they face into multiple camera directions from varying set locations? Do colors, especially flesh tones, look realistic? To achieve good general illumination, the LD needs to measure the light for intensity and consistency, consider the contrast ratio of the scene, and make sure the color temperature is correct.

Intensity and Consistency

At the most basic level, a scene must have enough light so that the camera can record a picture. This is not much of a problem with modern cameras because they can record in low light levels. In fact, cameras have been designed that can "see" at night better than human beings. But the presence of light enhances the quality of the camera's picture. Most cameras used in studios operate best if they have about 100 **foot-candles (fc)** of light.[1] Foot-candles can be measured using a **light meter,** a device that visually indicates the intensity of light coming from the direction in which it is pointed. Some light meters have an analog foot-candle scale with a needle that indicates the number of foot-candles being registered. Other light meters give a digital readout of the number of foot-candles. (See Figure 6.1.)

During the lighting setup, the LD uses the light meter to make sure there are enough foot-candles for the camera to operate optimally. The LD also uses the light meter to check for balanced light within the set. For most productions, the amount of light at the left side of the set should be similar to that in the middle and at the right side. If this consistency is not maintained, the scene will look very different when the director

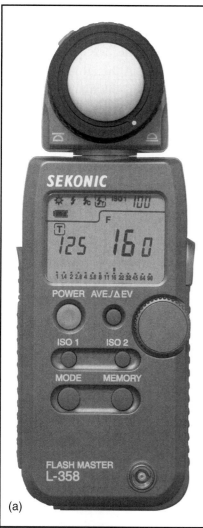

(a)

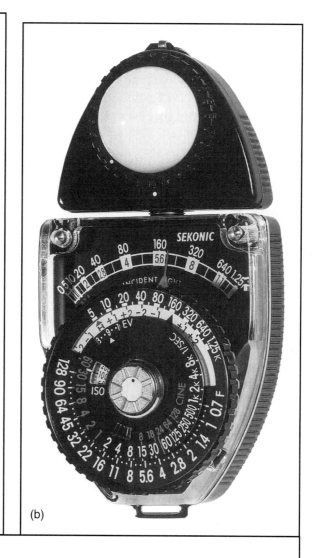

(b)

Figure 6.1

Photo *a* shows a digital readout of foot-candle levels. Photo *b* is an analog meter with a needle that points to various foot-candle readings on a scale. *Photos courtesy of Sekonic.*

switches from a camera capturing a straight-on angle to one that is pointing toward the right of the set. The LD also needs to take into account what will be photographed. Lighting should look approximately the same when a light-skinned person is on camera as when a dark-skinned person is shown. Similarly, someone walking onto the set in a bright dress should not make the lighting look different. All surfaces absorb and reflect light, but generally the darker the surface, the more light it absorbs; and the lighter the surface, the more light it reflects.

The LD checks for intensity and consistency by measuring light two different ways. *Incident* (source) light is measured by holding the meter very near the subject and pointing it directly toward the light source. This incident-light measure tells how much light *arrives* at a given point. *Reflected* light is measured by pointing the light directly at the subject from the perspective of the camera. The meter should be held close to the subject, but without casting any sort of a shadow on the subject. This reading indicates how much light is reflected *from* the surface areas *into* the camera lens. (See Figure 6.2.)

As could be expected, the two methods of measuring light produce different intensity readings. Reflected light loses strength in the process of being reflected, and the reflecting ability varies considerably. The two different meter readings are generally used for different purposes. In the primary stages of setting up lighting, the LD measures incident lighting to look for more general levels of intensity and consistency in area coverage as generated by the main source lights. The LD first adjusts the primary strengths of individual lighting instruments, and then again uses the meter from different points in the set to find *hot spots* where overlapping projection patterns have caused the intensity to exceed the average level. The members of the lighting crew can then correct the hot spots by moving lights or blocking off some of the light with various lighting accessories.

When dealing with the more subtle aspects of lighting, the LD works with the reflective qualities of the texture and color of a surface. Although only reduced amounts of the original source light are reflected back to the cameras, this is the light that really matters. A light green knitted dress might reflect 30 to 40 percent of the illumination falling on it, whereas a black knitted dress might reflect less than 10 percent. The measures of reflected light are used to fine-tune the lights and the elements of the set. One of the main considerations is contrast ratio.

Contrast Ratio

The human eye can accept a **contrast ratio** of up to 100 to 1. In other words, within your range of vision, the brightest element can be 100 times brighter than the darkest element. The eye allows you to see both. A conservative but safe figure for the standard-definition television camera would approach a ratio of 30 to 1. This means that the brightest area of a picture should not be more than 30 times as bright as the darkest area. High-definition cameras have a contrast ratio that is higher than standard definition but still not as good as the eye. This disparity between the eye and a video camera obviously means that some care must be taken in designing lighting that falls within the safe parameters of the camera.

Different elements of the set may produce large variations in the amount of reflected light bounced back to the camera. The reflected light readings tell the LD when the contrast ratio for a given camera has

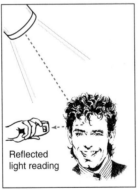

Incident light reading

Reflected light reading

Figure 6.2

Incident and reflected light readings. An incident light meter reading indicates the amount of light energy that is falling on a subject or larger surface from one general direction, possibly a single source. A reflected light reading indicates the amount of light energy being reflected from that subject or surface directly toward the camera lens.

been exceeded. The contrast ratio is determined by dividing the brightest reflected light reading by the darkest reading. For example, if the brightest spot at which the camera aims is 800 fc and the darkest spot in the picture is 20 fc, the ratio is 40 to 1; many cameras will not handle that well. If, on the other hand, the brightest spot is 450 fc and the darkest is 30 fc, the contrast ratio is an acceptable 15 to 1. Whenever the contrast ratio is too great, either the bright hot spots must be toned down or the darker areas must have more light.

As an example, take an evenly lit living room scene on a wide shot. A performer wearing a white raincoat enters and steps into a brightly lit area at the left of the shot. This sends much more light into the camera lens than was expected, and several rather drastic things immediately happen to the picture. The camera's **automatic iris** (see Chapter 5) reacts to the introduction of the very bright area by closing down. Without changing either the lighting or the camera controls, the right three-quarters of the picture will suddenly become much darker. The colors will have a muddy tone, and the set details will be obscured. The raincoat will be an out-of-focus blur, and the person's face will be a dark spot. Stated in simple terms, the acceptable range of contrast between the brightest and darkest elements of the picture has been greatly exceeded. The light level that was previously sufficient for a picture has been distorted by the introduction of an overpowering amount of light. The best solution is to have the actor wear a different coat—a gray one or a green one. If the white coat is necessary to the story, a lighting plan can be devised that will minimize light to the performer's entrance area but still allow for a small light to cover the performer's face from the close-up camera angle.

An error commonly occurs as students are learning balanced lighting techniques. Consider a picture in which the faces appear to be slightly darker than the background. In an attempt to solve the problem, the novice LD adds more light. If this light, aimed toward the dark faces, also falls on an already too brightly lit background, the problem has actually been made worse. As this additional light illuminates the background, the camera's automatic iris reacts as described in the last paragraph and attempts to compensate for the generally brighter video, and that adjustment darkens the entire picture. The faces remain dark in relationship to the brighter background. The solution to the problem is to use equipment, described later in the chapter, that provides additional light on the faces while blocking the light falling on the background. Another part of the solution could be to change the angle from which the light falls on the subjects. A higher angle would put light harmlessly on the floor.

Color Temperature

For colors to remain true throughout a scene, all lights should have the same **color temperature.** This is measured on a scale of **Kelvin (K)** degrees. What is being measured is neither heat nor brightness but the *frequency* of the light wave. One rule of thumb to remember is that the redder the light source, the lower the Kelvin temperature frequency; the bluer a source, the higher the Kelvin temperature. (See Color Plate D.) All light within one setting should be the same color temperature. A camera cannot adjust for differing temperatures, and color will not be true if the Kelvin varies widely from one light source to another.

Most studio lights register about 3,200 K. If a light is connected through a dimmer board that allows for gradual changes in applied voltage, the light-wave frequency and color temperature will decrease as the light voltage is decreased. A lighting element that produces a white light of 3,200 K when operated at full intensity will gradually become reddish as voltage is decreased and will give performers and set pieces a slight red tint. Increased voltage results in a bluish white tint. This distortion is not readily perceived by the naked eye, but the camera is very sensitive to any drop in color temperature over a few hundred degrees Kelvin. As a result, most lights used for TV production are not dimmed unless they are part of a special effect fade-out.

Color temperature is a much greater problem outdoors, where lighting cannot be as well controlled as it can in a studio. Outdoor light for many daylight situations registers about 5,500 K and is quite blue. However, red sunrises and sunsets go down to about 2,000 K, and haze and clouds also affect color temperature. If color temperature changes, video cameras must be adjusted by changing the built-in color temperature filter and/or by resetting the white balance (see Chapter 5).

If this is not done (and sometimes even when it is), shots taped at one time of day may not edit together well with shots from another time of day.

6.3 Creative Lighting Objectives

As a creative or artistic factor in video production, lighting can be said to have four main purposes: (1) to define the shape and texture of physical form and, by extension, to create a sense of depth and perspective within the elements of the set or location; (2) to imitate the quality of light that is characteristic of a situation or setting in reality; (3) to establish and enhance the psychological mood of a performance or setting; and (4) to focus attention on a single performer or aspect of the production and, thereby, to separate that subject from any feeling of relationship with setting or location.

Although this last concept usually has a specialized application, the other three purposes should be thought of as principles that can be simultaneously applied within a given production situation. The same light that gives shape to a person's features can also provide mood and at the same time relate to the setting itself (for example, a beam of sunlight coming through a window and falling on a woman's face).

Shape, Texture, and Perspective

When a light source is placed right next to a camera, the light waves reflected back into the lens are of a generally uniform quality. This effect is *flat lighting,* because the illumination has "filled" the hollows and curves that are the distinguishing features of the subject. When the light source is moved so that the beam comes from an angle, the resulting shadows "etch" the features so that the eye can perceive depth and texture. The art of creating the illusion of depth on a flat video screen is largely a matter of accentuating the illumination patterns that influence our normal process of vision.

The experienced LD knows that often the manipulation of shadows, rather than direct illumination, most effectively adds form and texture to any object. Light coming from the side or below an object will throw shadows in certain shape-defining ways.

Extreme side lighting (at right angles to the camera position) emphasizes textural quality by exaggerating shadows, making any object look more textured than it would otherwise appear.

The heightened sense of perspective necessary to the video picture is simply an application of this basic concept in the context of the entire set. Performers and foreground objects can be separated from the background when the angle and intensity of the light beam are adjusted to create a slight "highlight" effect.

Reality

Light operates on our conditioned responses in other equally important ways. We all have tuned in to the middle of a television play and watched a series of close-up shots. Either consciously or unconsciously, we are soon aware of being indoors or outdoors and of the time of day by the quality of light on the actor's face. It is probably outdoors and near noontime if the light is relatively bright and if there are definite shadows under the actor's eyebrows, nose, and chin. If the scene has been shot inside a studio, the *imitation of reality* is a product of the lighting.

Other specific shadow and lighting effects suggest certain kinds of realistic situations. Shadows of venetian blinds or prison bars cast on the rear wall of a set help to suggest a particular locale. Other *off-camera* lighting effects help to pinpoint a setting: A low-angle flickering light indicates a campfire or fireplace; a continually flashing red light indicates the presence of an emergency vehicle. Other effects help to carry forth the dramatic narrative: A shaft of light coming from under the door of a previously unoccupied room indicates the presence of an intruder; a flashlight probing around a darkened room helps reveal evidence of a burglary in progress.

Mood

Similarly, the psychological *mood* of a performance or production can be reinforced by the quality of light and its abundance or absence. Comedy is bright; therefore, bright **high-key lighting** is used to give an intense overall illumination with a fully lit background. Situation comedies and game shows rely on this kind of lighting to establish a lighthearted mood. Conversely, tragedy is communicated when the area surrounding an actor is dark or dimly lit. **Low-key lighting** refers to selective illumination that highlights only special elements of a scene. Usually the background is dark, and extreme lighting angles are used.

Specific dramatic moods may be reinforced by special effects—a flashing neon sign outside a sparsely furnished hotel room suggests a seedy part of town; lightning flashes create an eerie mood. Sometimes lighting will change within a show because the mood changes. An actor in a daytime soap opera may go through most of the day with fairly basic lighting, but for a certain shot, there may be special needs for that actor. For example, a particular scene could reveal that the character is sinister. For this revelation, a light could be placed at a low angle giving the character a foreboding, unnatural appearance. (See Figure 6.3.)

Such techniques are not limited to drama. Some of the most successful quiz programs use what appears as very general illumination of the host and participants, but in the final playoff rounds of competition, there is a dramatic change. Suddenly the background grows darker and the main lights on the participants are from a steeper angle that is almost directly above

them. The host's light gets very intense. Most of the audience is not consciously aware of the changes but feel the increased tension.

Focus of Attention

When a high contrast exists between the light on a subject and the light on the background area, the eye is drawn to the subject. The most obvious example is the use of a **follow spot,** where the light follows a performer in a musical or variety show as he or she moves from one place to another. Another variation of this technique is **limbo lighting,** where the subject is placed "in limbo" against a softly lit, nondescriptive, neutral background.

Another way to achieve focus of attention is with **cameo lighting**—the performer is lit, but the background is completely dark. (See Figure 6.4.) A **silhouette** effect—with the performers kept in darkness, but outlined against a brightly lit background—may be desired for a dance routine or other special situation. (See Figure 6.5.) A single shaft of light may be used to accent a contestant in the suspenseful climax of a game show. The host of a documentary may be accented with a strong light from the back or side. Subtle lighting highlights may be used in many other dramatic and nondramatic settings to control focus of attention.

Figure 6.3

Sinister lighting effect. Lighting from unusual angles or sources can give unnatural or symbolic effects; for example, lighting from a low angle usually results in a foreboding, sinister appearance.

Figure 6.4

Typical cameo lighting: figure against a dark background.

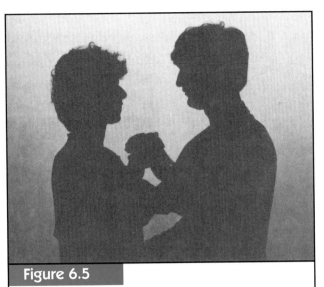

Figure 6.5

Silhouette lighting: dark figures against a light background.

So, above and beyond the necessity of using enough base light for basic illumination, the LD must also plan creative lighting to add shape, texture, and perspective; heighten the illusion of reality; create and enhance a specific mood; and focus attention.

6.4 Lighting Instruments

The actual apparatus used to light a set generally consists of a lamp (lightbulb) and a housing in which the lamp is placed. Both of these are important in determining the characteristics of the light. Different lamps are used for various situations, and housings allow for the light to be projected in varying ways.

Lamps

One type of lightbulb that is used a great deal in television lighting is the **quartz lamp,** which is also referred to as a **quartz-halogen** or **tungsten-halogen lamp.** The bulb is made of quartz glass that is filled with halogen gas and has a tungsten filament. Quartz lamps give off light that is 3,200 K, and this color temperature is consistent for most of the life of the lamp.

A newer type of lamp is the **high-frequency fluo-rescent,** also referred to as **high-speed fluorescent.**

Traditionally, fluorescent lights, such as the ones used in offices and schools, have not been satisfactory as television lights. There are many different colors of fluorescent lights—some tend toward blue while others give off a yellow tint and others are more on the green side. There is little consistency in their color temperature, and most of them do not contain much red. As a result, people lighting for television have been well advised to turn off the fluorescent lights and use only quartz lights. However, the new high-frequency fluorescent lamps can be a consistent 3,200 K color temperature.[2] They also consume very little energy because they operate through a chemical reaction that involves phosphors, and they last for about 10,000 hours as compared with 400 hours for quartz. They are becoming fairly common for television lighting.

A bulb with a totally different color temperature is an **HMI** (short for **hydrargyrum medium-arc-length iodide**). This lamp has a color temperature of 5,500 K, so it looks like outdoor light. Its main use, in fact, is to supplement light outside. However, it can also be used in a studio situation when a set is to look like it is outside—a patio, a street. Each HMI lighting instrument needs a ballast unit (a high-voltage power supply) to produce a consistent, flicker-free light. Figure 6.6 shows instruments equipped with several different types of lamps.

New lamps that are cool and use little power are constantly being developed. One is a ceramic bulb that produces 3,200 K light with only a fourth of the power required by a tungsten lamp. Another is the **high-intensity discharge (HID) lamp** that yields 5,500 K light and is more efficient than tungsten. **Light-emitting diode (LED)** technology, such as that used for computer laptop screens, also has possibilities for lamps.[3]

Sometimes studios will use a variety of lamps. High-frequency fluorescents give off a soft light while light from a tungsten bulb is more intense; so one lighting setup may incorporate a fluorescent for broad overall light, a tungsten for more specific light, and an HMI to simulate the outdoors.

Spotlights

Lamps are placed in housings that generally fall into one of two basic categories—spotlights and

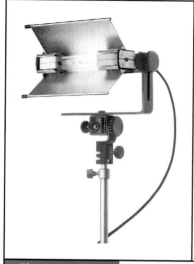

Figure 6.6

Lighting equipment with various types of lamps. *Left*, quartz lamp; *middle*, high-frequency fluorescent light; *right*, HMI. *(Left and middle) Photos courtesy of Lowel-Light Manufacturing. (Right) Photo courtesy of Mole-Richardson.*

floodlights. **Spotlights** have a controlled beam that is highly directional, can be shaped and focused to cover a rather narrow area, and casts a definite shadow. Its chief characteristic is the ability to throw a variable-sized spot of light on an area or performer. The most common form of spotlight is referred to as a **Fresnel** (pronounced without the *s*), although each manufacturer has a different name for it.[4] Although they are constructed in a number of different ways, the basic concept of spotlights is that shown in Figure 6.7.

The Fresnel type of lamp has a special structure of step lens rings to help dissipate the heat and direct the light. Another distinguishing feature is the movable assembly that allows the illuminating unit (bulb and reflector) to move back and forth between the front and rear of the instrument. With the bulb in the rear **"pinned"** position, the light rays focus in a narrow beam of high intensity, perhaps spreading no more than 10 degrees. As the bulb moves forward in the housing, the beam becomes **"spread"** and its intensity is diminished. In its full-forward spread position, the beam forms approximately a 60-degree angle. Fresnels come in different sizes that are often described by the diameter of the lens—6-inch, 8-inch, 10-inch, and so on. They also come with bulbs of different wattages,

ranging from several hundred watts to several thousand. (See Figure 6.8.)

There also are spotlights that do not have a lens on the front of them and, therefore, weigh less than the

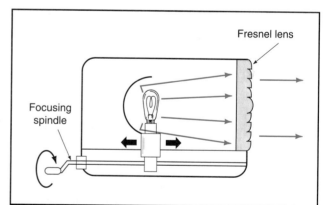

Figure 6.7

Spotlight construction. By turning the focusing handle or spindle, the bulb-reflector unit can be moved toward the lens *(right)* or back to the rear of the housing *(left)*. When in the forward position, the spotlight beam is "spread" to cover a relatively wide area. When moved to the rear of the housing, the beam is more narrowly focused, or "pinned," on a smaller area. Not all units use a spindle. Some use a lever attached to the lamp mechanism that moves it back and forth.

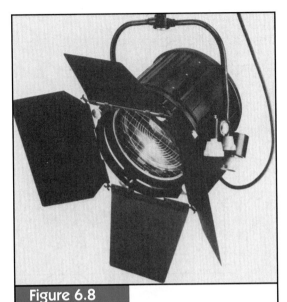

Figure 6.8

A Fresnel light. Notice particularly the lens and the barn doors. *Photo courtesy of Strand Lighting.*

regular Fresnels. However, although these open-face housings allow the lamp to be moved back and forth, they do not have the same degree of beam control as the Fresnel. Spotlights often have four movable panels extending from the front of the instrument. These are called **barn doors** and are used to block off selected areas of the projecting light beam.

The Fresnel (and, to some extent, its open-face cousin) is the workhorse of studio lighting, but occasionally other types of spotlights are used. For example, when an intense directional beam is needed, the **ellipsoidal** spotlight may be called into duty. It consists of a curved, fixed reflecting mirror at the back of the unit, a long tube, and a focusing lens. These elements enable it to project a beam that is well defined at its edge. The beam can be further shaped by movable metal shutters located inside the lamp housing behind the lens (see Figure 6.9.). At this point, where all the reflected light rays are in sharp focus, there is also a place to insert a patterned metal design cutout. The shadow of this **cucalorus** or **cookie** or **kook** is then projected to add visual interest to large, plain background surfaces. (See Figure 6.10.)

Floodlights

Floodlights have a diffused beam that produces a soft light that is spread out over a wide area and casts very little shadow. This light source softens and thereby controls the shadows that are created by the angle of the focused spotlight. To help achieve the effect of a large source area of light and the resultant easing of shadows, the floodlight does not use a lens.

The classic model for a floodlight is the one-half hollow globe structure known as a **scoop.** (See Figure 6.11.) Its large reflecting area is made of a light-diffusing material that spreads the illumination in a nonfocused scattered pattern. Floodlights built in a rectangular shape are known as **pans** or **broads.** (See Figure 6.12.) Some have controls that allow adjustment of the degree of spread. Their square shape makes possible the additional use of barn doors. When a series of pans are constructed in a continuous side-by-side row, they are called **strip lights.** (See Figure 6.13.) They are used frequently with colored **gels** in lighting the **cyclorama** (tightly stretched cloth) or other large set surfaces (see Chapter 8). Sometimes the front of a floodlight (scoop or pan) is covered with a **scrim**—a soft, spun-glass filter or other translucent piece of material that further diffuses the light.

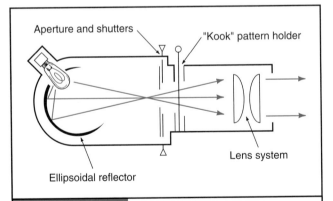

Aperture and shutters

"Kook" pattern holder

Lens system

Ellipsoidal reflector

Figure 6.9

Lens system of the ellipsoidal spotlight. Light rays are reflected from the fixed reflector and focused through the aperture. At this point, the shutters can be adjusted to shape the beam of light precisely, or cucalorus patterns may be inserted to project hard-edged shadow designs through the lens system.

Figure 6.10

Top: Ellipsoidal spotlight. *Bottom:* Example of a shadow pattern cast by a "cookie" inserted in an ellipsoidal spotlight. *(Top) Photo courtesy of Strand Lighting.*

Another type of floodlight is the **softlight.** (See Figure 6.14.) It is constructed with the bulb (or bulbs) positioned so that the light is reflected off the back of the lamp housing before leaving the housing; the reflection material diffuses the light intensity coming from the bulb. Floodlights, like spotlights, come in wattages ranging from hundreds to thousands of watts.

This brief review of lighting instruments barely suggests the scope and variety of available equipment.

Many special purpose lights exist, and manufacturers are constantly developing new lamps and housings.[5]

6.5 Fundamental Lighting Concepts

As noted previously, creative lighting is largely a matter of careful control over the effects of light and shadow. The manipulation of these two factors permits the camera to create an illusion of depth on the viewing screen and also allows for lighting under a variety of circumstances.

Three-Point Lighting

The specific techniques through which these effects are accomplished can be easily understood by examining the classic lighting setup. It is known as **three-point lighting,** because it involves the use of three different light sources—the **key light,** the **fill light,** and the **backlight.** Each has a separate effect on the subject being lit, because the three lights differ in relative angle or direction, level of intensity, and the degree to which they are either focused or diffused. Taken together, the cumulative effect is that of a balanced and an aesthetic unity—what Rembrandt called a "golden triangle" of light.

Figure 6.15 illustrates how the three sources are used in a typical situation. The effect of three-point lighting is very natural, often occurring in our usual surroundings. By modifying one or another of its three sources, it can be made to achieve the *creative purposes* of form and texture, reality, mood, and focus of attention.

It is important, however, to keep in mind that the three-point lighting model was perfected as an ideal for still photography where a *single* camera shoots the subject or subjects from only one angle. The underlying concept must be modified to apply to multiple-camera, continuous-action video production.

Key Light

The most important illumination in any lighting plan is the *key light.* It is the apparent source of the light hitting the talent and provides the majority of the light

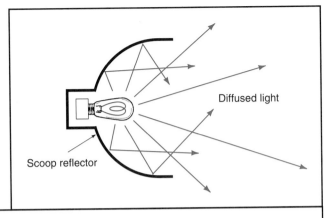

Figure 6.11

The scoop is a common source of fill light. The 14-inch and 16-inch diameters are popular sizes for most television studio applications, and the frame at the front can hold a scrim. The drawing indicates the diffused pattern of reflected light rays. *Photo courtesy of Strand Lighting.*

Figure 6.12

The *pan* shape of the reflector or the *broad* beam provided is the source of the name that describes this lighting instrument. *Left,* a floodlight that uses high-frequency fluorescent lamps; *right,* a broad with a quartz bulb and barn doors. *(Left) Photo courtesy of Lowel-Light Manufacturing. (Right) Photo courtesy of Colortran.*

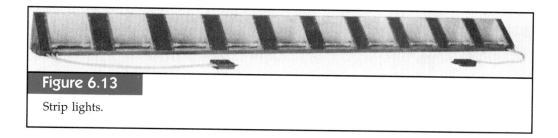

Figure 6.13

Strip lights.

that is reflected back into the camera lens. (See Figure 6.16.) Almost invariably, a spotlight is used for the key light; its strength and directional beam emphasize the contrast of light and shadow, defining the shape and texture of the subject. The use of the key light brings out the features of the face and illuminates that most dramatic feature, the eye itself.

Although more extreme angles can produce special dramatic effects, the optimum result is achieved by placing the key off to one side of the person's face, com-

Figure 6.14

Softlights. In this 8-kilowatt super-softlight, there is no direct light from the eight 1,000-watt quartz bulbs; all light is reflected by the large, curved surface. *Photo courtesy of Mole Richardson.*

ing in at an angle between 30 and 35 degrees. (If the key light is placed directly in front of the talent, the result is a flat, washed-out appearance with no shadows and no sculpting of the face.) The height of the key will depend to some extent on the talent's facial contours. It should be placed high enough to produce a slight shadow under the chin and nose, yet low enough to get the light directly into the eye sockets. (If the talent has deep-set eyes and the key light is at too steep an angle, the result is simply two dark shadows under the eyebrows.) A good rule of thumb is that the key should be placed at a 35- to 40-degree angle above the person's vision line. (If the key light is too low, it will make it difficult for the talent to read the **prompter.**)

Fill Light

To "fill in" on the dark side of the face or object being lit, some sort of *fill light* is needed. It should come in at an angle on the side opposite from the key. Ordinarily, a floodlight (such as a scoop or broad) would be used, although a spotlight in its *spread* position can be effective. In any case, a soft diffused light is desired. (See Figure 6.17.) Fill light is used simply to soften the shadows and give some illumination to the less illuminated side of the face or other object. Fill light should not be as strong or directional as key light; it should not compete in creating shadows or countering the shaping qualities of the key.

Backlight

As the name implies, *backlight* comes from behind and above the subject (not to be confused with *background light*, discussed under "Additional Light Sources"). A spotlight is used so that the light can be directed and focused like the key. The backlight falls on the person, and as a result, accentuates such features as hair, shoulders, and top surfaces of set elements. (See Figure 6.18.) This highlighting effect separates the talent from the

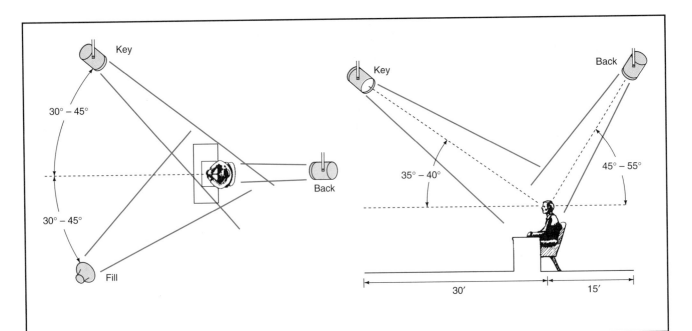

Figure 6.15

Three-point lighting. The key light and fill light should normally be placed approximately 30 to 45 degrees from a line drawn straight in front of the talent. The backlight is always behind the talent at a steeper angle than the key or fill lights.

Figure 6.16

Subject with key light only.

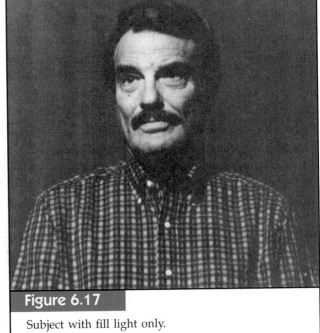

Figure 6.17

Subject with fill light only.

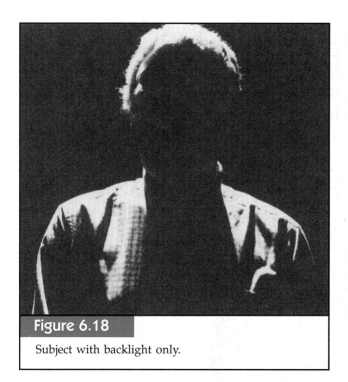

Figure 6.18

Subject with backlight only.

Figure 6.19

Subject with balanced three-point lighting (key, fill, and backlight).

background, adding to the illusion of depth within the total picture. Without adequate backlight, the talent appears flat and tends to blend in with the background.

Backlight requirements vary with the background and some characteristics of the talent. Hair color and texture are especially crucial. For example, blonds require relatively little backlight. Their natural hair color separates them from the background. On the other hand, darker tightly curled hair generally needs extra backlight because it does not reflect light well. The effect of different material in a person's clothes must also be observed.

Ratios

The key, fill, and backlight should relate to one another in terms of degree of illumination when measured for incident light at the point where the light strikes the subject. A good starting point is to have the fill light register one-half of the foot-candles of the key light and the back light register one and a half times the key. In other words, if the key light all by itself creates 100 fc of incident light, the fill light should register 50 fc by itself and the backlight should be 150 fc. When you turn on all the lights, you will *not* have a total of 300 fc (100 + 50 + 150) because when all the lights are turned on, they will overlap to give the

well-balanced lighting of the three-point technique. (See Figure 6.19.)

Once you have lit with the ratio of key = 1, fill = ½, and back = 1½, you will need to make adjustments so that the object looks right. Perhaps you will need to put a scrim over the flood you are using for the fill light because it overly washes out the shadows; or perhaps you will need to change the spotlight you are using for the backlight to one with less wattage because the person being lit is a blond.

Additional Light Sources

One of the most important additional illumination sources used in conjunction with three-point lighting is the **set light** or **background light** (not to be confused with the *backlight*). This is the major source of lighting for the background set behind the performers. In addition to helping fill in the overall picture with base light, background lighting can give form and texture to the setting, provide a sense of reality, or suggest mood. Sometimes the amount of light on the background is hard to control because the set tends to catch the wash of a lot of other lights being used for other purposes. There can suddenly be too much light if the LD has not kept an eye on the set as lights are being turned on.

In one function or another, most types of lighting instruments can be used appropriately for background lighting. Floodlights (scoops or strip lights) are often used for general illumination of a flat space. Spotlights can be used to highlight certain areas or present dramatic lighting effects (for example, strong diagonal slashes of light). And, of course, the ellipsoidal spot can be used with a variety of cucalorus patterns for various shadow effects.

Another auxiliary light often used on a set is the **kicker.** Its illumination comes from the side, usually over the camera left shoulder of the talent. (See Figure 6.20.) It can work on the side of the face without really disturbing the basic three-point effect. It is often used to create facial sculpting when people will be turning their faces to talk to each other.

Actually, in any moderately complicated lighting setup, the illumination is coming from many directions and angles. The concept of three-point lighting should be used as a guide, not as a rigid set of rules.

Multiple-Camera Lighting

One of the things that makes three-point lighting difficult for television studio production is that the same scene (which often has people or objects moving in it) is being looked at from different angles by different cameras. The neatness of a single photographic camera taking a still picture is not present.

With television's multiple-camera formats and continuous-action productions, lighting directors have found it difficult to adhere strictly to classic three-point lighting. In the talk-show format, for example, the host

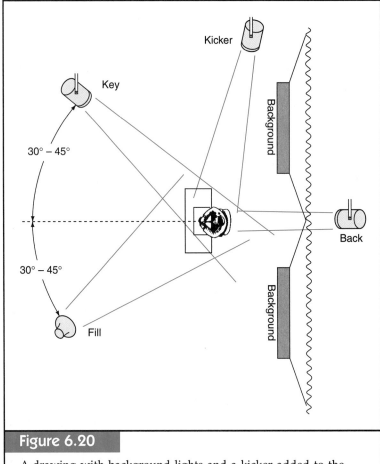

Figure 6.20

A drawing with background lights and a kicker added to the key, fill, and back.

or hostess moves to people in the audience, and the cameras must shoot from many angles. The solution to this situation is to create an overall *wash* of illumination throughout the entire set. Many soft fill lights (fewer keys) are used from all possible camera angles. This results in relatively flat lighting, but it is a workable solution.

Some situation comedies and soap operas shot with electronic multiple-camera techniques have had substantial success in overlaying the three-point lighting within a flat-lit set. Working together, the TV director and the LD select points within the scene where the actors will remain in place for a period of time. In these spots, careful three-point lighting can be used for close-ups. When portions of the scene contain physical movement, the action is picked up by the cameras on wider shots, so the flat lighting will not matter as much. Close-ups are kept to a minimum in the areas lit by flat lighting. It is a compromise, but it works fairly well.

To conserve on lights and not have too much light falling on the set when multiple cameras are in use, LDs often use one light for multiple purposes. For example, one fill light can sometimes cover several people, and a light that is used as a backlight for one person may be a key for another person, a concept that is known as **cross-keying.** (See Figure 6.21.) By the same token, a light that is a key from one camera angle might be a backlight for a different camera position, or a fill light used when a person is standing by a sofa might still be able to function as a fill when that person moves to a nearby desk.

Even though different types of lighting techniques are needed for multiple camera productions, the standard against which all lighting work is measured is three-point lighting. Lighting directors should start their multicamera lighting design by trying to incorporate as much three-point light as possible.

Lighting for Shadows

Even if you have lit a set so that most of the shots will incorporate three-point lighting and all of the set areas are evenly lit, you may find that items used for the shooting process cast unwanted shadows. The element likely to give the most trouble is a microphone **boom** (see Chapter 7). The normal position for a boom mic is

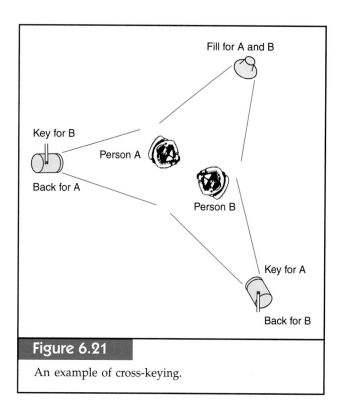

Figure 6.21

An example of cross-keying.

above the talent's head angled so it can pick up the sound from the mouth. This position is quite likely to be in the path of the key light or background light, and that light will cause the boom to cast a shadow onto the talent or the set. This shadow is particularly disturbing if the boom must be moved to capture the sound of talent walking around the set. A shadow moving across a person's face or a set piece can ruin the dramatic effect.

To correct the problem, you must first find the light causing the shadow. If you stand in the shadow and look at the microphone, you should be able to see the offending light directly behind the mic. (See Figure 6.22.) You can try turning it off, but that will probably affect other lighting considerations. You can ask the boom operator to move the mic slightly and see if the shadow then moves to a less obvious part of the set, such as an artificial leafy plant that can more easily absorb the shadow without it being noticed. A third option is to move the light slightly. Sometimes moving the key light so that it is at a slightly higher angle will cause the shadow to be cast onto the floor where, again, it will be less noticeable.

Another shadow problem often occurs with people who wear glasses. The shadow from the upper part of

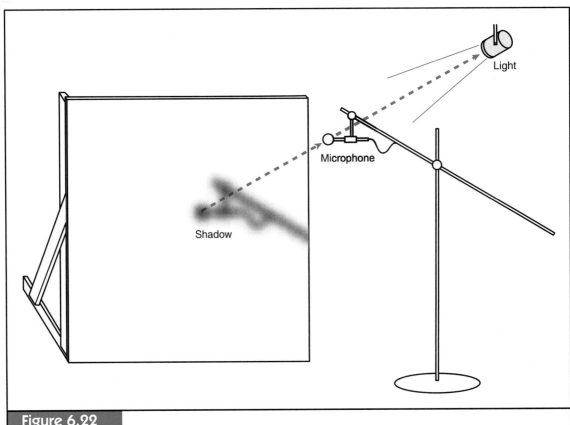

Figure 6.22

You can determine what light is causing the shadow by standing in the shadow and looking at the microphone.

the frame falls across the person's eyes, obscuring them from view. The easiest way to deal with this problem is to lower the key light so that the shadow falls on the eyebrows rather than the eyes. Lowering the light can also help prevent reflections from the glasses.

Many other objects can cause undesirable shadows. There is no way to eliminate shadows from a set—and you wouldn't want to because everything would look flat. But if the shadows are annoying, try to work with both the objects and the lights so that the shadows fall where they will not be seen.

Cameo, Silhouette, and Chroma Key Lighting

As previously mentioned, *cameo* and *silhouette* lighting can be used to focus attention. **Chroma key** (see Chapter 9) lighting is used when a background behind a

person needs to drop out of the picture so a different background can be inserted.

Cameo lighting is created by placing a spotlight directly above a person or an object. (Review Figure 6.4.) You point the light downward so that it creates a circular pool of light on the floor. The background is not lit at all. When a person stands within the pool of light, he or she is the only thing visible on the screen. This type of lighting is frequently used for commercials—the product being advertised is cameo lit so that it is the center of attraction. If the object is large, such as an automobile, or if the person is going to move, then more than one spotlight can be mounted from above, and the pools of light should overlap.

For silhouette lighting, the subject is not lit but the background is evenly lit. (Review Figure 6.5.) This is accomplished by placing the subject at some distance in front of the background. Then all the lights are placed far enough to the rear of the stage that none of the light from them hits the subject; it all falls onto the background. Although the subject is not lit, it can still be the focus of attention because it is black against a background. Silhouette lighting is often used in news broadcasts when a person is willing to talk but does not want to be seen in an identifiable way.

The most common use of chroma key lighting is for weather reports. The weathercaster stands in front of a wall painted blue (or green). When the blue background goes through the switcher, the blue drops out and the technical director inserts various weather maps instead. (See Color Plate E.) For this to work, the blue background must be uniformly lit. In other words, the same number of foot-candles must register across the entire wall. If there are bright spots or dark spots, these will not drop out to the same degree as the rest of the wall, and the inserted picture will break up or have blue bleeding through it. The best way to light the chroma key wall is with floodlights; *softlights* are particularly effective. You will, of course, have to light the weathercaster separately, using the key, fill, back principle, but you must make sure that none of this light spills onto the background. To accomplish this, have the weathercaster stand at some distance from the wall and set up the key, fill, and back lights so they are at a steeper angle than usual.

High-Definition TV Lighting

Most of the principles discussed so far apply to both **standard-definition television** and **high-definition television.** But as LDs experiment with the newer HDTV format, they do find the need for some changes. HDTV cameras need less light (as little as 14 fc) than SDTV cameras. So sets can be lit more dimly, cutting down on electricity costs and the need for air conditioning and creating greater comfort for the performers. Because HDTV has greater resolution it tends to show unimportant background items more sharply. But, because the number of foot-candles needed is low, the background can be dimly lit and the camera iris can open wide, thus creating a shallow depth of field (see Chapter 5) that draws the viewer's attention to the main action and not the background details.

Because the **aspect ratio** of HDTV is wider, it is sometimes necessary to light more of the set. For example, if two news anchors are sitting at a desk and are being shot in the 4:3 aspect ratio only, any light that is beyond their shoulders can fall off quickly. But if they are being shot with the idea that they will be broadcast in both 4:3 and 16:9 ratios, area beyond their shoulders must be lit so that it will not look muddy on the 16:9 screen.

HDTV is able to handle more *contrast* than SDTV, so a lighting director can create darker areas and brighter areas on the set. An HDTV set will be able to distinguish gradations in light and color better than an SDTV set, which is likely to lump all the dark areas into a muddy gray.

<h2>6.6   Mounting Lights</h2>

With very few exceptions, lightbulbs and their housings cannot exist by themselves. In some situations a lamp housing is simply set on the floor, but for the most part lights must be mounted or supported. Basically, this can be accomplished in two ways—by *hanging* them from above on the grid or by mounting them on a *floor stand.*

Hanging Mounts

Nearly every television studio is equipped with a lighting **grid** for mounting lights above the staging area. It comprises pipes and supporting mechanisms that place the lighting instruments in a position to produce a proper angle of illumination while leaving the studio floor uncluttered for camera and talent movement and various set elements. The grid is a rigid arrangement of pipes positioned several feet beneath the studio ceiling, and generally lighting crew members use a ladder to move the lights.

Some studios have a **batten** system upon which the lights are actually suspended. It is movable in that it raises or lowers the pipes by a counterweight system so that lights can easily be worked on from the studio floor and then raised again to ceiling height. Other studios have a **catwalk** above the grid so that crew members can access the lights by walking or crawling near the grid. Some grids are semirobotic in that the lights can be moved and adjusted through the use of a remote control.

Lighting fixtures are connected to the grid by a **C-clamp** that is attached to the light fixture's yoke and has a bolt to clamp to the grid and another bolt to allow the fixture to swivel to the right or left. (See Figure 6.23.) The clamp is always used in conjunction with an additional **safety chain** that prevents the light from falling should the clamp accidentally disconnect. The fixture can be tilted up or down with the aid of the side-tension knob.

Sometimes lights are connected to a pole and then the pole is attached vertically to the grid. The light can then be slid up or down the pole in case it needs to be raised or lowered.

Floor Stands

In many kinds of studio arrangements, the suspended lights have to be supplemented by lights mounted on **floor stands.** (See Figure 6.24.) Although too many floor stands tend to clutter the studio and get in the way of other production elements, they do represent a

Figure 6.24

A light mounted on a floor stand. *Photo courtesy of Mole Richardson.*

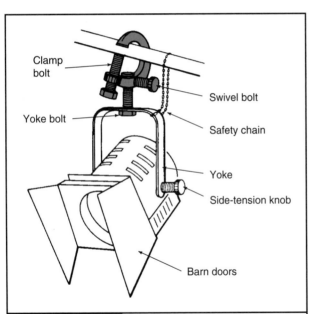

Figure 6.23

The C-clamp is the most common type of lamp hanging device. It is held in place on the pipe by tightening the clamp bolt against the pipe. There are three additional control bolts. At the bottom of the clamp unit there is the important yoke bolt that connects the yoke to the light itself. This bolt (Y-bolt or yoke bolt) should never be loosened. Instead, the swivel bolt should be loosened to allow for left and right lateral movement of the lamp. The two side-tension knobs are used for the vertical movement. A safety chain is used as illustrated or sometimes connected directly to the lamp housing.

certain degree of flexibility and simplicity of setup; and in some situations, it is simply impossible to position a light except on a floor stand.

Floor stands for studio use usually have a heavy metal base for stability or they are weighted with sandbags. They come in a variety of weights and sizes capable of handling many different types of lighting instruments. Of course, for location productions (wherever supplemental lighting is needed), the portable floor stand is indispensable.

6.7 Lighting Control Factors

To achieve the artistic and technical purposes of lighting, the LD must work within four separate yet interrelated parameters: the level of intensity, the degree of focus or diffusion, the shape of the projected beam, and the color quality.

Intensity

We have already briefly described the way that the beam from a Fresnel lamp can be spread to lessen its intensity and, at the same time, cover a much wider area. But whether a beam is focused or diffused, another factor has important implications in terms of intensity. Although it is not easily apparent to the naked eye, variations in the distance between a source light and the subject create large differences in intensity.

These differences follow the **inverse square law** that states that *as the light-to-source distance is doubled, the intensity is reduced to one-fourth of its previous strength.* And, of course, the strength is multiplied by four as the distance is cut in half.[6] It is actually a matter of an increasing surface being covered by the same amount of light energy. As a result, the power to illuminate diminishes. A light that produces 1,600 fc at a distance of 10 feet is reduced to only 400 fc at 20 feet as it covers four times the area. (See Figure 6.25.)

Intensity can also be controlled by a **dimmer board.** It is usually located some distance from the actual lighting instruments—either in a corner of the studio or in a separate control room—because it creates both heat and noise. Dimmer boards are accompanied by **patch bays** (also referred to as **patch boards**). Although this equipment will vary in size and capacity, it all functions on the same general principles.

The patch bay serves to connect numbered lights on the grid with similarly numbered cables for connection to switches in the control area, creating a **nondimmer circuit.** For rapid control of a group of lights, the cables for a number of lights can be brought through one **dimmer circuit** at the dimmer board. In fact, some dimmer boards are computer assisted so that settings can be programmed and lights can be brought up automatically—for example, one set of lights for the news anchor desk, another set for the weather area. (See Figure 6.26.) The majority of lights go through nondimmer circuits, because, as mentioned previously, any lessening of power causes a drop in color temperature that in turn produces a

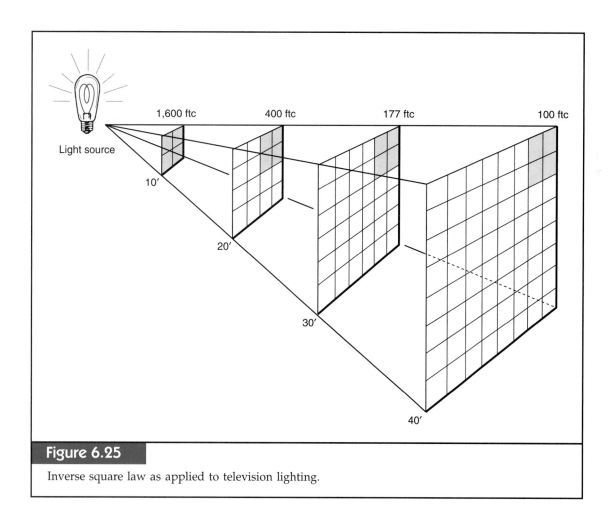

Figure 6.25

Inverse square law as applied to television lighting.

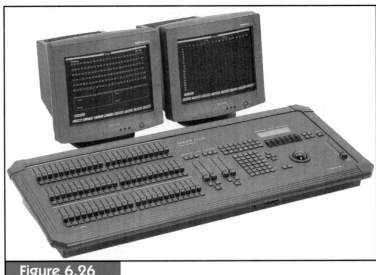

A computer-assisted dimmer board.   *Photo courtesy of Leviton Lighting Control Division.*

reddish tone. But there usually are also some dimmable circuits so lights can be faded in or out if need be during a production.

Diffusion

Diffused light is created and controlled in several ways to keep it in its proper perspective in relation to the focused key light. The primary control factor is that of adjusting intensity through some of the methods described previously. In addition, the best diffused light is achieved by using several instruments placed at differing angles.

Several devices for diffusion are also important to the LD's toolbox. The most common is a *scrim*, which is a wire mesh or spun-glass filter, shaped to fit the front of the lighting instrument. (See Figure 6.27.) It works by scattering the beam and cutting back on intensity. Scrims are used to soften a spread Fresnel light or to soften the light from a scoop or broad.

Shape

If LDs had to work with only the large raw beam projected by most instruments, their work would be difficult indeed. One of the main difficulties is controlling the overlap of multiple light sources that causes hot spots. Fortunately, a number of shaping devices can be used to modify and block parts of the beam.

The most common are *barn door* shutters that, as mentioned earlier, attach to the front of a light. (Review Figures 6.8 and 6.12.) Used in pairs or sets of four, these hinged plates can provide an adjustable edge to the beam. By moving the shutters, both the height and width of the projected light can be limited. Most assemblies can be rotated to provide maximum adjustment. In an ellipsoidal lamp, the movable shutters are inside the instrument (adjusted with outside handles) to provide an even greater definition to the projected pattern. (Review Figure 6.10.)

Sometimes the LD needs to create a small area of reduced intensity *within* a projected beam. For this a **flag** is used. Flags are rectangles of varying size made either of metal or of frames covered with black cloth. They can be hung from the lighting grid or mounted on a floor stand in a position to block out light to a specific area. (See Figure 6.28.) One use, for example, is to cast a slight shadow on the top of the head of a person with thinning hair who otherwise might appear almost bald in the bright lights of a close-up shot.

Occasionally, an added amount of light must be pinpointed at a particular area of the set. If barn doors cannot project quite as precise a pattern as needed, a

Figure 6.27

Wire mesh scrims: *top*, half scrim. Light coming from the top half of the light fixture would not be as diffuse as that coming from the bottom half. This might be used if the top half of the light is on a person and the bottom is on the set; *bottom*, full scrim. *Photos courtesy of Mole Richardson.*

Figure 6.28

A flag. Flags are used to block the light on specific areas of the performer or set. With their stands and extension arms, they provide an important final control over illumination and can provide a sharp line of shadow. *Photo courtesy of Lowel-Light Manufacturing.*

snoot can be used to do the job. Inserted in the same frame designed to hold the barn doors, the snoot, a circle that ranges in diameter from 4 to 12 inches, can reduce the spotlight's beam to a smaller, clearly defined circle without increasing the intensity of the spot.

Color

Sometimes a set or other location is simply too dull and drab for attractive pictures with sufficient color contrast. Perhaps more "warmth" from red-brown earth tones is needed. Or possibly the "cool" effect of green and blue is desired. To solve this problem, variously colored *gels* are used to add color to the setting and occasionally to the performers' clothes.

The gel is a thin transparent celluloid material and is available in a wide variety of colors. The gels can be cut to fit a specially designed holder that slides into the frame of a scoop (see Figure 6.29) or the same frame that is intended to hold the barn doors on a spotlight. Using gels to improve a scene can be tricky, however. They affect the entire shot, so although you might find that a particular green gel enhances a costume, it might be very unflattering to a person's face.

Gels are most effective for creating particular effects, such as using them with strip lights (review Figure 6.13) to color a cyclorama. A wide variety of color combinations and effects are possible. A continually changing dawn effect, for example, can be created with the background shifting from a deep violet, through various reds and pinks, to a light blue during the shooting of a scene.

6.8 Setting Up Lights

Lighting a set takes a long time. It is expensive time because it ties up a studio that could otherwise be producing programs. For that reason, lighting directors

Figure 6.29

Gel holder on a scoop. Frames that hold a gel filter in place are designed for all types of floods and spotlights. *Photo courtesy of Mole Richardson.*

try to plan as much as they can on paper before entering the studio. The main planning device is a **light plot.** This shows the major set pieces as they will be placed in the studio and then shows the various lights that will be used. A light plot usually indicates the types of lights, their use, their power, their location, and the direction of their beam. (See Figure 6.30.)

Armed with the light plot, the LD and crew members can enter a studio and set up lights efficiently without unnecessary experimentation. No doubt a few changes will need to be made, but an experienced LD who has had a conference with the director (and maybe the producer) to learn the lighting needs for a particular show can prethink the lighting situation and plot it out accurately.

When starting a lighting setup from scratch, the first thing crew members usually do is position lights so they are where they will be needed. They do this by climbing a ladder (or going out on the catwalk), undoing the C-clamp and safety chain from the grid, and moving the light to another location on the grid. Or they lower the *batten* and work on the lights at studio

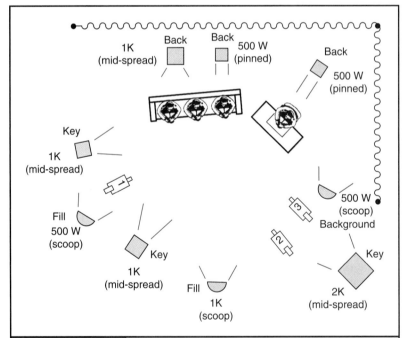

Figure 6.30

A light plot. Notice that the light icons themselves show the location and direction of the beam. Beside each light is a description of the type of light, its use, and its power.

level and then raise the batten. Many professional studios try to have enough lights that very few of them will need to be moved. With many lights on the grid, some light is probably in the right location and simply needs to be turned or tilted. Having many lights speeds up the lighting setup process and also saves wear and tear on the lights.

Once the light fixtures are in position, crew members do not turn on all lights at once. That would be very confusing. The usual procedure is to turn on the key light first and measure its intensity with a light meter and also look at the picture it is creating on a high-quality monitor. Then the key light is turned off and the fill and backlights are turned on, measured, and viewed in their turn. If someone notices something unforeseen in the monitor or if the ratio among key, fill, and back is not correct, then minor adjustments can be made. For example, you might need to tilt the key down slightly so it covers its target more accurately or move in the barn doors of the backlight so the light is more focused. Making minor adjustments is usually referred to as **trimming** the lights and is generally undertaken at the grid level by someone on a ladder. (See Figure 6.31.) Once the keys, fills, and backlights are settled, other lights such as background lights and kickers are turned on and adjusted.

Of course, once all the furniture, equipment, and performers are in place, more trimming may be needed. What do you do about the shadows under the host's eyes? Do you need to change the lighting for the chair because a yellow chair was substituted for a black chair at the last minute? How can you get rid of the boom shadow that shows when one of the actors crosses to the doorway?

Many shows do not change their lighting setup very often, so an LD may have nothing to do on a day-to-day basis except turn on the lights and make sure none of the bulbs are burned out. Often this is undertaken by another crew member—for example, the stage manager or the person who operates the robotic cameras. News shows, morning talk shows, and game shows, for example, have the same set and the same lights day after day.

Sometimes universities have preset lights because lighting takes so long; within a class period students would not have time to light a set and also produce a program. In this case a technician sets lights before the

Figure 6.31

High-tech it may not be, but this type of ladder, with one or two people to stabilize it, provides a quick and efficient way to trim lights. *Photo courtesy of Melissa Bossenmeyer.*

semester begins and groups them into the dimmer so that, for example, students can raise the first three dimmers if they want lights preset for a talk show, they can raise dimmers four through six for a news program's preset lights, and they can use dimmers seven through nine when they are using the sitcom set.

6.9 Safety Precautions and Disciplines

Lighting can be very dangerous. When working in a studio, you should always "think overhead." Are all lights, mounts, and other equipment securely fastened?

When heavy equipment is moved or repositioned overhead, is everybody warned and the area below cleared out? In addition, crew members should "think electricity." Is all equipment turned off before moving or inspecting it? Is the circuit turned off before it is plugged into an instrument? Everyone should also "think hardware." Has the item of equipment been thoroughly checked out and is it ready for use? Has everything been connected? Tightened? Tested?

Whenever a lighting assistant is moving or trimming lights, at least one person should steady the ladder from below. The person on the ladder should always carry a wrench (secured by being tied to the ladder or to the person's wrist to prevent dropping it on persons or equipment below) to tighten any lamps that may have become loose from excessive turning. When making any adjustment on any lighting instrument, the safety chain must always remain fastened, securing the light to the grid.

When changing the direction of a light, always loosen the thumb screw (swivel bolt) *first*. Do not mistake it for the bolt holding the lamp hanger to the clamp—loosening that bolt will detach the lamp from the lighting grid. When moving a light, always make certain that no people are below the working area. Be certain the power to the lamp is off. Just because no light is being emitted does not mean no power is coming through the cord. Damaged lights, burned-out bulbs, and short circuits are all potential dangers. Again, be sure the power is off at the lamp's new location before plugging it into the grid outlet. When you are moving an instrument from one location to another, the safety chain is always the last item to be unfastened, and it is the first thing to be hooked up when the instrument is repositioned.

When focusing lights, never look directly into them. A light that measures 200 fc at 30 feet may approach 100,000 fc at the source. Studio lights are bright enough to permanently damage the naked eye. Lights also create a dangerous amount of heat—a fact that should always be foremost in your mind as you are working in a studio. After being on for only a few minutes, most studio lamps are hot enough to cause serious burns. Most studio lamps have handles—use them! Lighting technicians should also be furnished with heavy-duty, heat-retardant gloves. Special caution must be used when adjusting barn doors, as they are directly in the path of the light source at only a few inches and absorb a large amount of heat.

Make sure never to touch the surface of a quartz bulb with your bare fingers (even when the bulb is cold). Always use gloves or some other cloth between your hand and the globe. A small amount of finger oil or acid on the face of the globe will interact chemically to weaken the glass envelope and can even cause it to explode. If there are lights on floor stands, take care to avoid tripping over cables and pulling over the stands.

Safety is the responsibility of everybody connected with a television production. Any unsafe situation can be avoided by using common sense and observing basic precautions. Part of the *discipline* of television production is the habit and attitude of *thinking safety*. Every crew member, whether or not part of the lighting team, should be disciplined to think in terms of avoiding or correcting hazardous conditions.

Discussion Questions

1. Assume a production situation where two people sit on a couch and talk and then one of the people moves to another area of a set and does a stand-up comedy routine. What would be your suggestions for lighting this type of situation?

2. Assume that a modern dance number is going to be taped in your school studio. The set consists of a curtain in the background and two pillars around which the performers will dance. Draw a light plot of how you might light this production.

3. As a lighting director, what steps should you go through before you start lighting the set? What are the first several things you should do when you are actually lighting the set?

4. What lighting safety precautions should you be aware of in your own studio?

Notes

1. One foot-candle (fc) is the amount of light that falls on a surface placed at a distance of one foot from an established theoretical source approximating the brightness of one candle. In many European countries light is measured in lumens or lux (approximately 10 lux = 1 fc). Twenty years ago, cameras required 200 fc to get a picture that wasn't quite as good as what modern cameras get with 70 fc.

2. Actually a high-frequency fluorescent lamp can be manufactured to be any color temperature. For example, you can place a 3,200 K bulb in the housing to shoot indoors and then simply take out the bulb and replace it with a 5,500 K bulb to shoot outside.

3. "Bright Ideas in Lights and Batteries," *TV Technology,* 26 May 2003, 44–46.

4. Augustin-Jean Fresnel was a 19th-century scientist who did important research into the nature of light and for whom the light was named.

5. To see the vast array of lighting instruments available, visit the websites of some of the major lighting equipment companies— http://www.strandlighting.com; http://www.lowel.com; http://www.mole.com; and http://www.colortran.com.

6. The inverse square law is fine for sources of light with little width, but it is not accurate for large-sized sources such as softlights. See "When the Inverse Square Law Doesn't Work," *TV Technology,* 9 February 2000, 36.

CHAPTER 7

Audio

The equipment discussed in this chapter serves as an excellent model for illustrating the basic control functions discussed in Chapter 1, Section 1.3. The microphones transduce, the outboard equipment records and plays back, the cables and connectors channel, the audio board selects and alters, and the speakers monitor.

Also, the concept of how both *disciplines* and *techniques* relate to production can be clearly applied to the field of audio. For example, knowing the steps needed to connect a microphone so that it functions through an audio console is a matter of applying several basic *techniques*. However, the care with which the operator then works to test the quality and loudness parameters of that mic for its eventual use is very much a matter of individual *discipline*.

Audio is an extremely important element of a TV program, often credited with providing 80 percent of the information. Any mistake with audio, especially the lack of sound, is readily picked up by viewers and usually leads them to change the channel to make sure their set is still working. If they get distracted with another program and don't come back, that is a lost viewer—something stations and networks definitely don't want.

People operating audio equipment must be constantly thinking ahead to their next actions. Which audio fader will you raise next to bring up the sound from the breaking news in the field? How loud should the music be over the host? How quickly will the microphone boom need to move as the talent exits?

The material in this chapter should enable you to build both audio techniques and disciplines and to understand both the technical and creative aspects of sound. It includes the following:

- The role of frequency, amplitude, and pickup patterns as they relate to microphones (7.1)
- How microphones are constructed and where they are likely to be positioned (7.1)
- Characteristics of digital outboard equipment including CD players, DAT recorders, MiniDiscs, digital carts, and computers (7.2)
- Analog recording equipment (7.2)
- Types of cables and connectors and their various uses (7.3)
- The role of a patch bay (7.3)
- How to care for cables and connectors (7.3)
- Types of audio consoles (7.4)
- Functions of typical audio consoles related to providing power, inputting, shaping, mixing, isolating, outputting, and monitoring (7.4)
- Differences between mic and line feeds (7.4)
- Types of signal processing (7.4).
- The role of faders (including the master fader) and pots (7.4)
- Why audio boards have meters (7.4)
- How speakers are used to monitor (7.5)
- How pop filters, the proximity effect, presence, perspective, the inverse square law, phase, and balance relate to effective audio production (7.6)

7.1 Microphones

Microphones are used to pick up sounds (voices, live music, etc.) and convert them into electrical audio signals, a process referred to as **transducing** (see Chapter 1). There is no single "perfect" microphone for doing this. You need to select the microphone that is best for what you are recording. A microphone that is very effective at making a male announcer's voice sound mellow might be quite ineffective for recording a flute solo. A microphone that works well in the controlled environment of a studio might not be rugged enough to take outdoors for a field shoot. A singer's favorite microphone would probably be inadequate for picking up the laughter from a sitcom audience. To take care of a variety of situations, microphone manufacturers make many different microphones that vary in such qualities as frequency response, amplitude, pickup patterns, construction, and positioning possibilities.[1]

Frequency and Amplitude

Microphones take into account the **frequency** of voice or music sound waves—the rate at which they move, measured in **hertz** (also called **cycles per second** and abbreviated **Hz**).[2] For example, if the sound waves are produced at a constant rate of 440 Hz (cycles per second), the result is the musical tone of A above middle C on the piano. Bass sounds have fewer cycles per second than treble sounds. (See Figure 7.1.) Another way

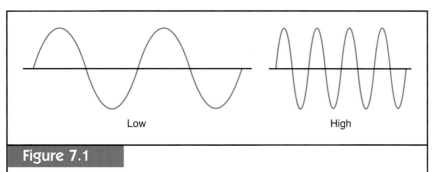

Low   High

Figure 7.1

Low-frequency sound has fewer cycles per second than high-frequency sound.

of saying this is that treble sounds have a higher frequency than bass sounds.[3] Men's voices have frequencies around 500 Hz, whereas women's voices are more likely to range at about 1,500 Hz or above. The higher the frequency, the higher the **pitch.** Humans with good hearing can discern ranges from a low rumble at 20 Hz up to a possible high of 20,000 Hz.

The main frequency of the sound is called the **fundamental,** but sounds also have a number of higher frequency **overtones.** Although these overtones (also known as **harmonics**) are produced at much lower loudness than the fundamental tone, they are very definitely picked up by the human ear. These overtones vibrate at different degrees of loudness according to the resonating qualities of each voice or musical

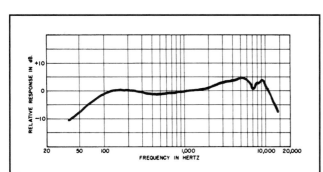

Figure 7.2

The frequency response chart gives the audio operator an accurate and quick indication of how a mic will perform at all frequency levels. The mic depicted in this chart doesn't pick up low frequencies very well, is fairly flat through the speech range, picks up quite well around 10,000 Hz, and then drops off sharply.

instrument **(timbre).** A trumpet has a different sound from a clarinet even when it is playing the same note because its overtone pattern is very different from that of a clarinet. Likewise, two women's voices sound different even though they are roughly the same frequency.

Microphones can be manufactured to pick up different ranges of frequencies, a trait referred to as their **frequency response.** Microphone manufacturers often provide charts to show frequency response characteristics so that you can choose the mic that is best for your particular application. (See Figure 7.2.) A mic that picks up all frequencies equally well is said to have a **flat** frequency response. One that picks up the human voice better than higher or lower frequencies is said to have a **speech bump** because the line rises starting at about 300 Hz and then falls off by 3,000 Hz. Some mics pick up certain frequencies better at different positions. For example, the Shure mic shown in Figure 7.3 picks up 125 Hz frequencies but not 1,000 Hz frequencies toward the back of the mic. If you are producing a discussion program, you can use mics with more limited frequency response than those used in producing a musical show where all the overtones will be particularly important.

Another element that microphones take into account is **amplitude.** Amplitude refers to the strength or volume of the sound. A 440 Hz "A" piano note played loudly will produce a higher amplitude than that same note played softly. (See Figure 7.4.) Amplitude is measured in **decibels (dB).**[4] A whisper is about 20 dB and a gunshot is about 140 dB. The range of loudness that a microphone or other equipment can handle is referred

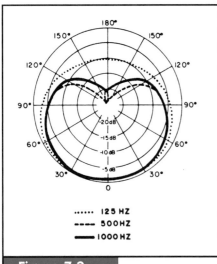

······ 125 HZ
---- 500HZ
——— 1000HZ

Figure 7.3

The different lines show the directional sensitivity of the Shure SM 58 mic at three different frequencies. The low 125 Hz sounds pick up better toward the back of the mic than do the 1,000 Hz sounds.

to as **dynamic range.** A piece of equipment with a wide dynamic range could record a whisper so it could be understood and a gun shot so it was not distorted.

Pickup Patterns

Microphones can be designed so that they pick up sound from different directions. Some are **omni-**

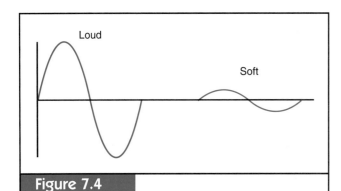

Figure 7.4

The sound represented on the left would be louder than the sound represented on the right because it has more amplitude.

directional, meaning they pick up sound from all directions. They are good for picking up crowd noises, audience reaction, and sounds from a group of people in a circle. Other mics are **cardioid,** picking up sound in a heart-shaped pattern. Cardioids are effective when you want to pick up sounds in one direction while excluding sounds from other directions. They are the most-used TV studio production mics because they pick up talent voices without picking up the background noise of cameras moving in the studio.

Some mics have very narrow pickup patterns, usually referred to as **supercardioid, hypercardioid,** or **ultracardioid.** They can pick up sound from a distance, but they have a progressively smaller pickup area than a cardioid mic. They are less likely to be used in a studio than they are in the field where circumstances, such as breaking news, prevent close miking. **Bidirectional** mics pick up sound from two sides, making them useful if two people are directly facing each other. (See Figure 7.5.)

A few mics are manufactured so that they can switch from one directionality to another, perhaps cardioid to omnidirectional. For some of these mics, you unscrew a top element that is cardioid and screw on another element that is omnidirectional. A **zoom mic,** however, contains electronics within the mic that allow you to change gradually from cardioid through to ultracardioid.

More and more television programs are recorded and distributed in **stereo** rather than **monaural.** Stereo recording can be accomplished in a number of ways.[5] For example, mics can be crossed to form an X so that they pick up sounds from the left and the right, often referred to as **cross-pair miking.** Another method, **mid-side miking,** picks up sound from the middle and the two sides. This type of miking can use three microphones (usually supercardioid), or it can use two mics—a supercardioid mic and a bidirectional mic. (See Figure 7.6.) Some single mics have multiple elements in them that imitate the various stereo miking patterns. They are not perfect, but they are simpler to set up and use than any of the mic setups already described. (See Figure 7.7.)

It is also possible to record **surround sound,** so that the final sound can come from six or eight speakers

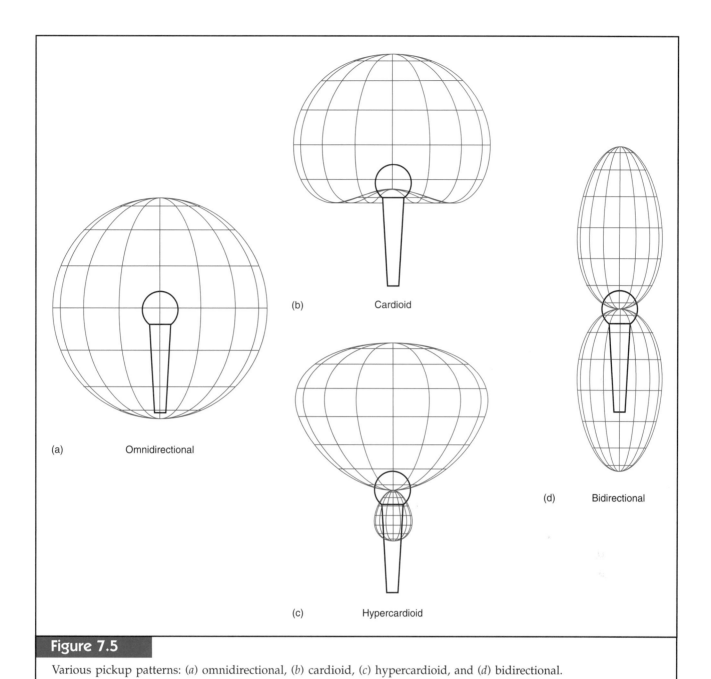

(b)   Cardioid

(a)   Omnidirectional

(d)   Bidirectional

(c)   Hypercardioid

Figure 7.5

Various pickup patterns: (*a*) omnidirectional, (*b*) cardioid, (*c*) hypercardioid, and (*d*) bidirectional.

located around the room. This sound configuration is becoming particularly popular for HDTV. Surround sound recording is quite complex[6] and usually involves setting up arrays of cardioid and supercardioid microphones pointed at different spots around the circumference of a circle. There are also single-unit surround sound mics. (See Figure 7.8.) Miking for either stereo or surround sound is complicated when it involves multiple microphones, because mics placed too close to each other tend to cancel out each other's sound. For this and other reasons, stereo and surround are often created in postproduction where the sounds can be manipulated in a more leisurely fashion.

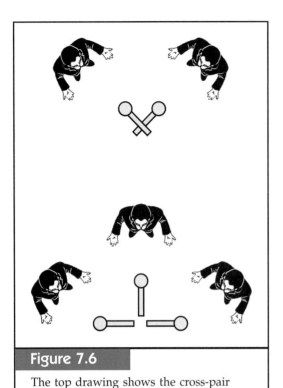

Figure 7.6

The top drawing shows the cross-pair method of stereo miking, and the bottom shows the mid-side method.

Figure 7.7

A stereo mic. This self-contained microphone includes the various elements needed to record stereo. *Photo courtesy of Audio-Technica.*

Microphone Construction

When sound is transduced by a microphone, audible sound pressure waves, with their particular frequencies and amplitudes, move through the air and come in contact with the **diaphragm** of the microphone. Some types of microphones, referred to as **dynamic** mics, contain a **magnet** and a **coil.** The sound waves cause the diaphragm to vibrate within the magnetic field, and this sets up a current in the coil. (See Figure 7.9.) In this way the sound signal is transduced into an electronic form that retains its original information. The structure of a dynamic mic makes it able to tolerate rough handling as well as temperature and humidity extremes, so it is often the choice for field production.

Other microphones, know as **condenser** mics, also have a movable diaphragm to receive sound waves. A difference lies in the condenser mic's use of an electrically charged **backplate** just behind the diaphragm. The two elements form what is called a **capacitor,** enabling the unit to generate voltage in response to sound wave pressure. (See Figure 7.10.) This structure

not only produces very high-quality sound but also allows the unit to be small. Whereas a dynamic mic can generate its own charge, this condenser unit must have a source of electricity to function. One way is to have batteries located in the handle or in a portable battery pack. Another solution is using what is called **phantom power;** a small current is sent to the mic through its cable from the audio console. Condenser microphones that have permanently charged backplates are another option. A condenser mic is not quite as durable as a dynamic mic, but it has slightly better frequency response.[7]

Another element of a mic's construction is whether it is intended to be used in a wired or wireless configuration. Both dynamic and condenser mics can be either wired or **wireless** mics. The difference is not in how

Figure 7.8

A surround sound microphone.
Photo courtesy of Holophone.

the sound is picked up but rather how it is delivered. Wired mics will have a connector that enables them to be attached to a wire that carries the signal from the mic to wherever it needs to go. (See Figure 7.11.) A wireless mic has a small antenna that sends the sound

through the air to a small receiver—sort of a miniature radio station. The receiver is then connected to the wall outlet in the studio or to a particular piece of equipment. (See Figure 7.12, bottom left.) Wireless mics are used when the talent needs to move about—a singer who also dances or a talk-show host going into the audience, for example. However, sometimes they are subject to interference from other nearby wireless devices, and water (or sweat) reduces their signal strength.

Positioning Possibilities

Microphones, be they omnidirectional or cardioid, dynamic or condenser, wired or wireless, need to be placed somewhere on the set where they can pick up sound. For some situations (interviews, musical performers) it is acceptable for the microphone to be seen, but the general convention is for the microphone to be out of sight or at least unobtrusive.

One place where TV microphones are often placed is on a performer's clothing somewhere close to the mouth. These unobtrusive **lavaliere (lav)** mics are generally condenser mics because they need to be small. (Refer to Figure 7.12, bottom left.) For optimum pickup, they are usually positioned slightly below the neck on top of a tie or blouse so they do not pick up clothes' rustling noises. The mic is usually attached to a slightly bulkier power supply (and integrated antenna if a wireless mic) that can be worn around the waist or buried in

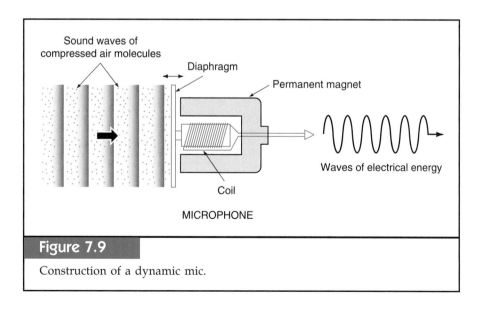

Figure 7.9

Construction of a dynamic mic.

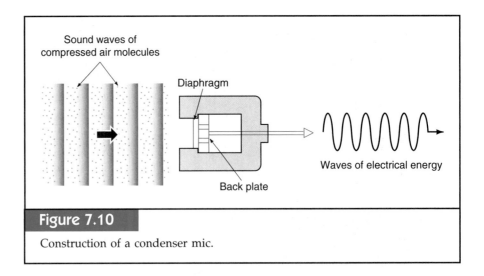

Figure 7.10

Construction of a condenser mic.

Sound waves of compressed air molecules

Diaphragm

Back plate

Waves of electrical energy

the set. This, in turn, sends a signal to the wireless receiver or is attached to more wires that deliver the signal to its next destination. It is best to put all the visible wires under the talent's clothing so they do not show and so the wires will move if the talent does. Lavalieres have the advantage of being inconspicuous, but they can only pick up the sound of one person.

Larger, more conspicuous mics (refer to Figure 7.11) are often used for situations where the viewer expects to see someone using a mic. Sometimes these mics are held by the talent and are referred to as **hand mics**—for example, a singer, a reporter interviewing someone, or a talk-show host wandering through the audience. Obviously, one mic can be used by more than one person, but the person holding the mic should know how to use it so the sound does not fade in and out because he or she moves the mic too far away from the source of the sound.

The same microphones that are handheld can be placed on stands. A talk show where people sit around a table may use a number of mics mounted on **table**

Figure 7.11

This Shure microphone is well known in professional circles as a reliable hand/stand mic with a dynamic transducing element. The mic has a pop filter on the top of it, and its sound is transmitted through wire. *Photo courtesy of Shure Bros. Inc.*

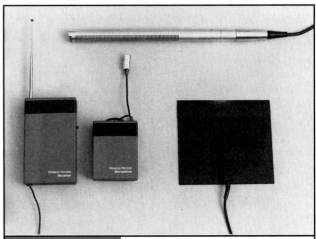

Figure 7.12

The top microphone is a shotgun mic used primarily to pick up sounds from a distance. Bottom left shows a wireless lavaliere microphone attached to its transmitter and the receiver that picks up the wireless signal through its antenna. Bottom right is a boundary (PZM) microphone.

Two or more large studio perambulator booms are often used to cover drama or variety programs. *Photo courtesy of KCET-TV, Los Angeles.*

stands. Sometimes for musical performances, a mic is placed on a **floor stand** and, after the singer performs in place, he or she removes the mic and uses it in a handheld fashion. At news conferences, mics are often placed on a stand that rests on a podium.

Sometimes these larger mics are attached to a **boom** that is moved around by a boom operator. This is particularly common for dramas and sitcoms, where actors move about but where seeing the mic might spoil suspended reality. Booms come in various sizes and with varying degrees of maneuverability. Large **perambulator** booms are motorized and can move the mic into a variety of positions—up, down, left, right, in, out. (See Figure 7.13.) Usually it takes two people to operate a perambulator—one to drive it and one to position the mic. Smaller booms, called **giraffes,** have wheels and can be operated by one person. (See Figure 7.14.) Simpler yet is the **fishpole,** a pole with a mic on the end that a person holds and moves above the heads of the people who are speaking. (See Figure 12.16 in the field production chapter.) The boom has the obvious economic disadvantage of needing to pay two people to operate it. Both it and the giraffe can use up valuable floor space. A fishpole is smaller but difficult to hold for a long period of time. All three types of booms are likely to cast unwanted shadows, but, on the positive side, they are flexible mics that can free the talent of sound responsibilities.

Sometimes mics can be mounted on set walls or the studio ceiling. The **boundary mic** (also called a **pressure zone mic** or **PZM**) is effective for this use. (Refer to Figure 7.12, bottom right.) Its flat shape enables it to pick up overall sounds, so it is often used to gather audience laughter or applause. It is also effective for talk shows where participants sit around a table.[8]

Mics can also be hung from the ceiling **grid.** However, the actors can't move from under them or the sound will fade. Sometimes, especially for sitcoms, they are hung right above a door where people often stand and talk as they are leaving. Mics can also be hidden in props on the set, but, once again, they can only be used when actors are standing still relatively close by.

If a mic must be at some distance from the actors (more likely out in the field than in a studio), a **shotgun**

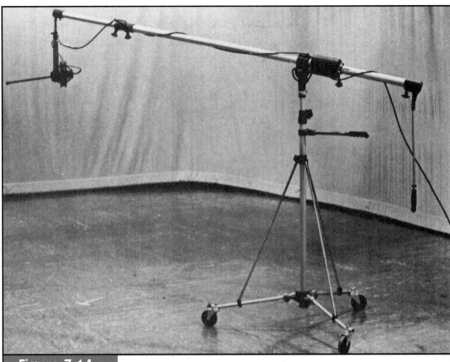

Figure 7.14

A giraffe microphone boom.

mic can be positioned on the ground or on a stand. It is a long, thin mic with a super-, ultra-, or hypercardioid pickup pattern. (Refer to Figure 7.12, top.) For a remote sports production, a sportscaster often wears a microphone that is part of a headset arrangement. In fact, for field and remote production, mics are likely to be positioned in any number of unusual places, such as the dashboard of a race car or the branch of a tree.

7.2 Outboard Equipment

In studio production the output of the microphones usually goes to the audio board to be mixed. It is usually mixed with sound from **outboard equipment** (equipment that is outside the board). Outboard equipment plays back material that has been prerecorded on some medium, such as a CD or a tape.

Most of this equipment can also record, so it may be used for **recording** the final program material. Recording audio is usually undertaken with equip-

ment that also records video, such as **videocassette recorders** and **servers.** That equipment is discussed fully in Chapter 10, so this chapter concentrates on equipment that is audio only, most of which is used for **playback** rather than to record.

Video recorders also play back such things as news packages or opening credit montages, and some productions, especially news, are likely to have both audio and video playing back from satellite and microwave feeds. But for many sound elements of TV programs, the playback comes primarily from digital or analog audio outboard equipment. You will no doubt be familiar with at least some of this equipment, having used it in your home. Professional equipment operates much like consumer equipment, but professional equipment is sturdier because it is used for many hours of the day.

Professional equipment may also provide superior sound in terms of *frequency response* and **signal-to-noise ratio (S/N).** Frequency response has already been discussed in terms of microphones. High-quality outboard equipment is capable of receiving a wide

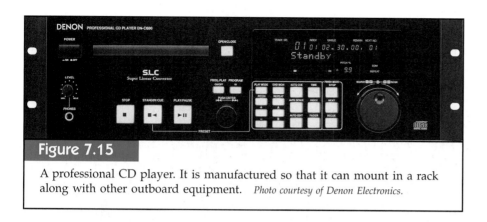

Figure 7.15

A professional CD player. It is manufactured so that it can mount in a rack along with other outboard equipment. *Photo courtesy of Denon Electronics.*

range of frequencies from very low bass sounds to high trebles. The S/N rates the amount of wanted sound that gets through a piece of equipment in relation to the unwanted noise that is not part of the original sound signal. Usually this unwanted sound comes from mechanical gears or electronic circuits. The higher the S/N, the better. Professional equipment usually has at least 60 units of signal for each unit of noise, whereas consumer equipment may have an S/N closer to 40 to 1.

Digital Equipment

Microphones need to start out as **analog** (see Chapter 1) because noises (such as the human voice, a clarinet, a falling chair) are analog—they send out waves of sounds, not 0s and 1s. But once sound is transduced into electrical energy, it can be converted to **digital.** This transformation takes place within a digital-to-analog component that can be freestanding or can be part of a microphone or some other piece of equipment such as a recorder or audio board. Most digital outboard equipment has provisions for converting from analog to digital and vice versa.

The concept of **sampling** rate is important for digital recording and playback. Sampling rate is how many times per second analog information is converted to the 0s and 1s of digital technology. The most common rates are 44.1 kHz (44,100 times per second), 48 kHz, and 96 kHz. The higher the sampling rate, the better the quality (although at some point human ears cannot perceive the difference); but material sampled at a high rate takes up more storage space than material sampled at a lower rate.

CD Players

One the most ubiquitous pieces of outboard equipment is the **CD (compact disc) player.** In fact, audio setups often have two CD players so that the audio operator can undertake quick transitions from the sound on one to the sound on the other. CDs used for professional production cue up quickly so that there is no *dead air* when going from one to the other. (See Figure 7.15.) The quality of the digital sound (which has a sampling rate of 44.1 kHz) and the small size and sturdiness of CDs make this an excellent technology for production. CDs are not indestructible, however. You should be careful not to scratch them or get fingerprints on them because, if you do, the laser within the CD player may not be able to read the data. A great deal of music is prerecorded on CDs, and there are also some excellent sound-effects CDs.

Some CD equipment records, but it is more likely to be used for postproduction in radio and music recording than in studio television production. There are two ways that it records, depending on the disc that is used. **CD-Rs** (which stands for compact disc recordable) can only record once, whereas **CD-RWs** (compact disc rewritable) can undertake repeated recording.

DAT Recorders

With **digital audiotape (DAT),** digital information is recorded onto the tape at either 44.1 or 48 kHz. A small one-eighth-inch **cassette** tape can hold several hours of material. Portable units can record in the field, and larger console units can play back the material for

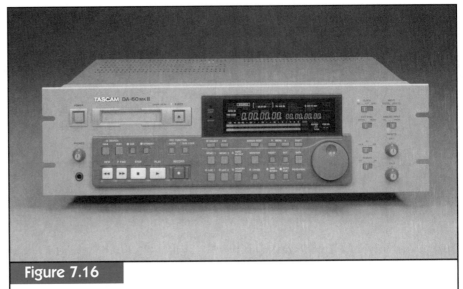

Figure 7.16

A digital audiotape (DAT) recorder. *Photo courtesy of Tascam.*

studio production. (See Figure 7.16.) Some DAT recorders use open reels rather than cassettes, but those that use cassettes are most common. Generally, DAT is used for material specially recorded for a particular program as opposed to preproduced material such as music and sound effects. DAT recorders cue easily and accurately and have visual displays that help you navigate through the tape.

MiniDisc Recorders

The **MiniDisc** is a digitally based recorder/player that records material on a two-and-a-half-inch magneto-optical disc that can be recorded on over and over. The disc holds 74 minutes of stereo 44.1 kHz sound. Again, there are portable and tabletop models,

and they have visual displays that aid cueing and other functions. (See Figure 7.17.) One of the big advantages of the MiniDisc is its editing capabilities. It is possible to edit within the recorder itself, so a reporter, for example, could record a story in the field and edit it on the way back to the studio. For television, this story would need to be accompanied by visuals, but the MiniDisc works well for an audio-based story with graphics.

Digital Carts

A **digital cart** really amounts to a computer with a great deal of storage that can hold a large number of digital audio files. (It is called a "cart" because it serves much the same function as the analog cart—discussed in the

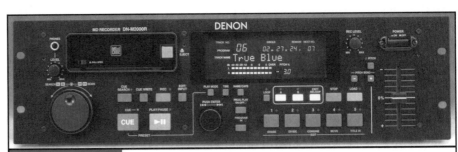

Figure 7.17

A MiniDisc recorder. *Photo courtesy of Denon Electronics.*

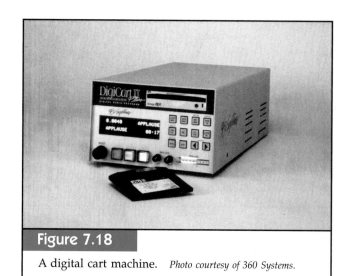

Figure 7.18

A digital cart machine. *Photo courtesy of 360 Systems.*

"Analog Equipment" section—that it has largely replaced.) Jingles, voice-overs for commercials, and the like can be produced in a digital editing system and outputted to a **zip drive.** The disc from the zip can be placed in the digital cart in order to transfer the audio files to the cart. (See Figure 7.18.) Or something (such as a voice-over for a news story or a music bridge) can be played back from a CD, DAT, or MiniDisc and transferred to a digital cart. Then the audio operator simply brings up a file and activates it when it needs to air. Or an operator can program a number of files to play one after another. This works well for short pieces that need to follow each other quickly.

Other Digital Equipment

Other audio players or recorders are found less frequently in TV studios. For example, some facilities have a digital recorder/editor called Shortcut that is used to edit audio before it goes on-air. Other facilities have **MP3 players** in case something recorded on that format needs to be played back.

Many facilities incorporate computer hard drives as part of the audio system. If the computers are used only for audio, they are sometimes referred to as **digital audio workstations (DAWs).** The primary purpose of a DAW is for editing and altering audio sounds—something that is completed prior to production using audio editing software that works similarly to the

editing software described in Chapter 11. However, once the editing is completed, the sound can be played back from the DAW through the audio board or some other piece of equipment. Sometimes computers are used for less elaborate computer software that can be used during the course of a TV production. There is, for example, software that provides copyright-cleared music and sound effects.

Analog Equipment

When TV production facilities buy new audio equipment, they invariably buy digital. But a great deal of analog audio equipment out there still gets used on a regular basis.

Most facilities still have at least one **turntable** for playing vinyl records. It comes in handy for music that is old and has not been rereleased on CD. Cueing a record is harder than cueing a CD. You must find the spot you want and back up half a turn so that the turntable has time to get up to speed when you actually want to use the sound.

Analog **cassette recorders** are also still in use. They are very inexpensive, and many people (including students) personally own them and can use them to acquire material to include within a program.

For many years the analog **cartridge recorder** was a workhorse in production centers. The analog cartridge recorder uses cartridges that fit into the player and contain a continuous loop of tape that can be of short or long duration. When something is recorded on a cart, the machine places an inaudible cue tone on the tape that enables the tape to cue itself accurately to the beginning of the recorded segment. Many studios had a rack of carts for short material that was played often and needed to be cued up quickly (station IDs, program theme music, commercial copy). As already mentioned, analog carts have been largely replaced by digital carts.

The very first analog tape recorders were **reel-to-reel.** The tape was not on a cassette or cartridge or computer-based disc but rather on a single reel that had to be manually threaded past the tape-recorder heads onto a take-up reel. Needless to say, digital technologies have enabled playback and recording to come a long way.

7.3 | Cables and Connectors

Cables and connectors are wires and metal joints used for channeling—moving sound from one place to another. Sound can also move through the airwaves in a *wireless* manner. The sound from someone's lips is "channeled" to the microphone through the air. As already mentioned, wireless mics send the signal from a small antenna to a nearby receiver. Signals from the television station antenna travel through airwaves, as do signals from a satellite.

But within a TV studio, where distances are short and most equipment stays in the same place, channeling is generally done through cables. Both the cables and the equipment have connectors so that sound can be channeled a number of ways. For example, most microphones have a connector at the end so that the mic can be connected to a cable with a similar connector. This cable has a connector at the other end that can plug into the audio board or, if preferred, into some other piece of equipment such as a tape recorder.

In reality, cables rarely go directly from microphones in the studio to the audio board in the control room—the studio floor would be cluttered with wires. More often the mic cables plug into connectors placed in the studio walls near where the talent will be speaking. Sometimes they plug into a **snake**, which is a box of connectors that can be moved about the studio; it has a cable that goes to the studio wall. Then wires go inside the walls to the area of the audio console where, once again, a connector is used to send the signal into the board. Wires from the various pieces of outboard equipment can also be attached to the board with cables and connectors.

Types of Cables

Most cables used for TV production consist of copper wires encased in plastic sheathing. Occasionally **fiber optics** (thin strands made of glass) are used during the production process, but they are more likely to be used for distribution of signals, particularly in cable TV systems. Fiber can carry much more information than copper in much less space, so it may be used more widely with HDTV than it currently is with SDTV.

Cables that hold copper wires can be either balanced or unbalanced. **Balanced cables** have three wires—two

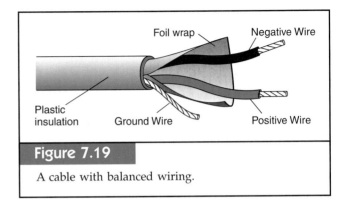

Foil wrap Negative Wire
Plastic insulation Ground Wire Positive Wire

Figure 7.19

A cable with balanced wiring.

to carry the signal and one to act as a ground. (See Figure 7.19.) **Unbalanced cables** have just two wires—one carries the signal, and the other carries part of the signal and also acts as a ground. Balanced cables are higher quality (and more expensive) than unbalanced cables because they are less susceptible to the electronic interference caused by, for example, a vacuum cleaner or power tool. Generally, professional studios use balanced systems while unbalanced cables are found in consumer gear.

Types of Connectors

A variety of connectors are used for studio, field, and remote production. (See Figure 7.20.) One commonly found in the studio is the **XLR connector.** It has three conductors so is compatible with the three wires of balanced cables. With the aid of a **guide pin,** the prongs of the male **plug** fit into the female **jack** so that they are tightly connected. The only way to unlock them is to press on the connector lock. Generally male plugs are on the end of cable, and female jacks are on equipment.

Digital audio often uses a **BNC connector,** which was previously used for video and is of high quality. Another type of connector is the **phone connector.** The **sleeve** and **tip** of the male plug fit into the female jack. A **miniphone connector** is similar to a phone connector except that it is smaller. Male **RCA connectors** have a prong surrounded by an outer sleeve that fits into the female jack.

There are a variety of connectors because each has a different purpose. As already alluded to, XLR connectors are used in professional situations because they are part of a balanced system. However, they are large and bulky, so they are not really suitable for most consumer gear, which is more likely to employ miniphone connectors.

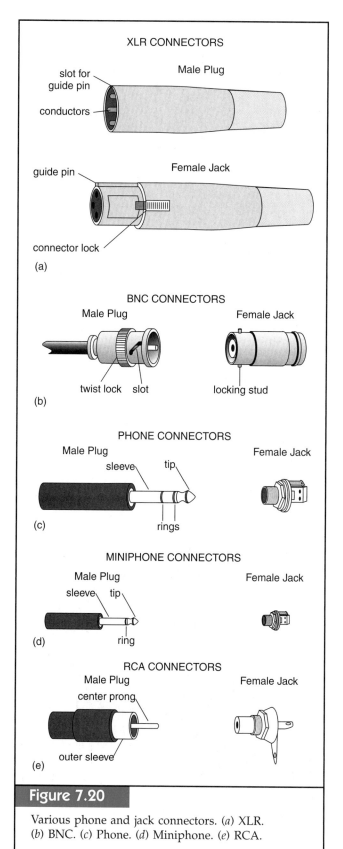

Figure 7.20

Various phone and jack connectors. (*a*) XLR.
(*b*) BNC. (*c*) Phone. (*d*) Miniphone. (*e*) RCA.

RCA connectors are versatile in that they are used for both professional and consumer applications and also for both audio and video (although not at the same time). Both phone and miniphone connectors can carry either mono or stereo sound. If the connector has one ring, it can carry only mono; if it has two rings, it is capable of transporting stereo. For the XLR, BNC, and RCA connectors, one connector can carry only mono. Two connectors are needed to handle stereo, one for the right channel and one for the left.

Sometimes two pieces of equipment that need to be connected may have different connectors. For example, a DAT with a miniphone may need to connect to a VTR with an RCA connection. Other times the equipment may have a male plug but the end of the cable also has a male plug and the two cannot connect. To solve these types of problems there are **adapters;** for example, the female end is a miniphone and the male end is an RCA, or both ends of the adapter are female RCA. Figure 7.21 shows an array of adapters.

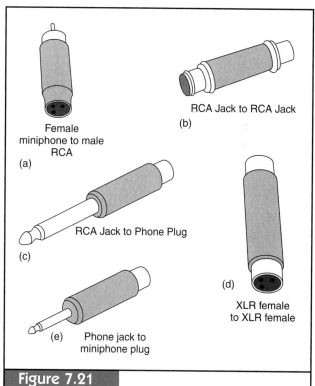

Figure 7.21

An array of adapters. (*a*) Female miniphone jack to male RCA plug. (*b*) RCA jack to RCA jack. (*c*) RCA jack to phone plug. (*d*) XLR jack to XLR jack. (*e*) Phone jack to miniphone plug.

Patch Bays

Sometimes the wires from mics and outboard equipment go to a **patch bay,** and from the patch bay wires go to a variety of places, such as different inputs on the audio board, an audiotape recorder, a videotape recorder, and the station transmitter.

Patch bays are boxes that usually consist of a large number of *phone jacks.* One row of jacks is for sounds coming from equipment, and another row is for sounds going to equipment. Each piece of equipment is wired to the back of a particular jack.

Some equipment is wired both for a signal to come in and a signal to go out in order to allow for flexibility. For example, sometimes you may want to send the sound from the DAT to the VTR; other times you may want to send the VTR audio to the DAT. When a signal needs to go from one place to another, you simply use a cable (usually called a **patch cord**) with male phone plugs at each end to transfer the audio from the top row to the bottom row. Figure 7.22 shows a patch bay with a patch cord going from the DAT to the VTR.

If you do not put in a patch cord, the sound goes from whatever is on the top row to whatever is on the bottom row. That is because this connection is **normaled.** So if the DAT is not patched into something else (such as the VTR), its sound will go to channel 4 of the audio board—the place it *normally* goes.

In some TV facilities, actual patch bays are giving way to virtual patch bays. Computer software allows properly connected audio signals from any source to be sent to any other source with the click of a mouse.

Care of Cables and Connectors

Cables and connectors must be handled very carefully because they can be easily damaged. In fact, they are the parts of the audio system that are most likely to give you trouble. The tiny wires of cables can be easily broken, and these broken wires are particularly difficult to find because they are inside the plastic casing. To prevent this breakage, cable should be neatly coiled after it is used. One effective coiling technique is to string the cable on the floor in a figure-eight pattern and then fold the two halves together. When cable is coiled properly, it should look like the cable in Figure 7.23. It takes *discipline* to do this neatly and correctly at the end of a long production, but it pays off in the long run.

You should never pull on the cable when you are disconnecting it; use the connector instead. But treat the connector gently; don't force it, because the prongs can bend or break, rendering it ineffective or, worse yet, intermittent.

This is a patch cord with male phone plugs on each end

Figure 7.22

In this patch bay, the digital cart is normaled to channel 1 on the audio board; one CD player is normaled to channel 2; and the other CD player is normaled to channel 3. The DAT is normaled to channel 4, but in this illustration it is patched so that it will go to VTR 1.

Figure 7.23

This is how cable should look when it is coiled properly. The two ends are connected to keep dust out of the connectors. *Photo courtesy of Melissa Bossenmeyer.*

| Audio Consoles

It seems obvious now that the ability to blend and **select** a number of sound sources and to control separately the volume levels of each would be a primary requisite for any type of audio production. History tells us, however, that early radio studios had only one microphone and that volume control was accomplished by placing people and musicians closer or farther away from one mic. Fortunately, engineers developed the **audio console** (also called the **audio board**), which allows a number of audio sources to be fed into this one piece of equipment.

Types of Consoles

Audio consoles come in many configurations from very basic to very complex. Basic ones are usually used for live and live-on-tape audio work. (See Figure 7.24.) More complex ones are used for postproduction editions and complicated production such as recording musical bands. (See Figure 7.25.) TV stations usually try for something in the middle. (See Figure 7.26.) Basic consoles often do not have enough knobs and buttons to fulfill all the needs of a TV facility. But complex (expensive) boards with extensive capabilities can have too many features. When you are working in a TV facility, you rarely have time to change a large number of settings. In fact, a large number of controls can impede you because something is invariably set in the wrong position for what you want and you have to troubleshoot through an array of controls to correct the problem. However, some TV recording facilities cannot afford a number of boards, so they opt for a more complicated board that can be used for a variety of applications.

Another difference with audio consoles is that some are analog (refer back to Figure 7.24), and some are digital. (See Figure 7.27.) Digital boards, which obviously were developed after analog boards, have been designed to minimize the amount of time someone who has operated an analog board needs to learn the digital board. So digital boards operate in much the same way as analog boards. The digital boards are, of course, more computer based; and although most of them have actual levers, buttons, and knobs similar to analog boards, they also have LCD computer screens where functions can be changed with the click of a mouse or some other control. For this reason digital boards can take up less space than analog boards. Analog boards need to have buttons and knobs for many functions just in case they are needed. With digital boards, things that are likely to be used less often or things that can be set ahead of time are relegated to the computer and brought up only when needed. Some analog boards have digital elements to them. For example, you can save settings in a computer and then recall them for a program a week or two later. Digital boards can, of course, also allow you to do this.

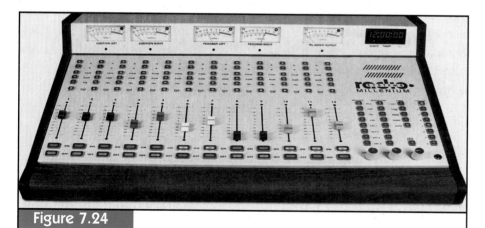

Figure 7.24

A simple basic board such as might be used by a disc jockey at a club or by a radio station. *Photo courtesy of Radio Systems.*

Figure 7.25

A much more complex board that might be used for mixing music or a movie soundtrack.   *Photo courtesy of Solid State Logic.*

In addition, some boards are mono and some are stereo, with stereo being more common. Some stereo boards duplicate everything for the left and right channel while others have stereo controls so that the left and right channels can travel together through the board.

The Basic Console

To explain how a board works, we have "designed" a generic board that illustrates common board features. (See Figure 7.28.) Refer to it frequently as we discuss the various functions of the board. For simplicity, we have designed this console to look like a very basic analog monaural board. But the functions it performs

are the same as those for digital and/or stereo, and we will discuss features that are beyond the basic ones depicted here.

In all probability we will discuss a number of features your board does not have and will not mention some that it does have. Also, controls will be in different positions on our make-believe board than on yours. The only way to truly understand the operation of an audio console is to work with it. But once you have mastered one board, it is easy to transfer your skills to another board because they all operate using the same principles.

Our generic console is what is called an *8 in, 4 out* board. It has the capacity to manipulate eight different

A console that is marketed as a good board for TV station live broadcasting. It has many of the features discussed in this section. *Photo courtesy of Wheatstone.*

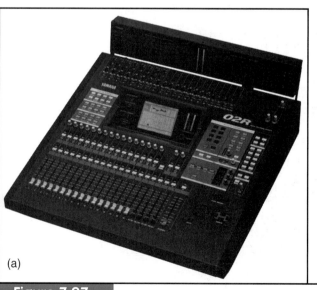

(a)

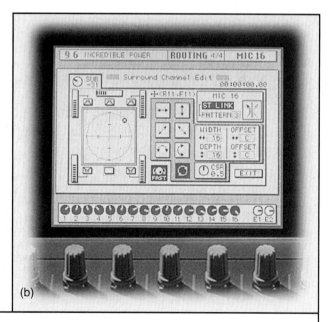

(b)

This Yamaha 02R digital audio console (*a*) contains a screen that displays a number of control settings and other operational information. For example, the screen shown in (*b*) is used to preset conditions for creating surround sound. These settings can be stored in the computer for later recall. *Photo courtesy of Yamaha.*

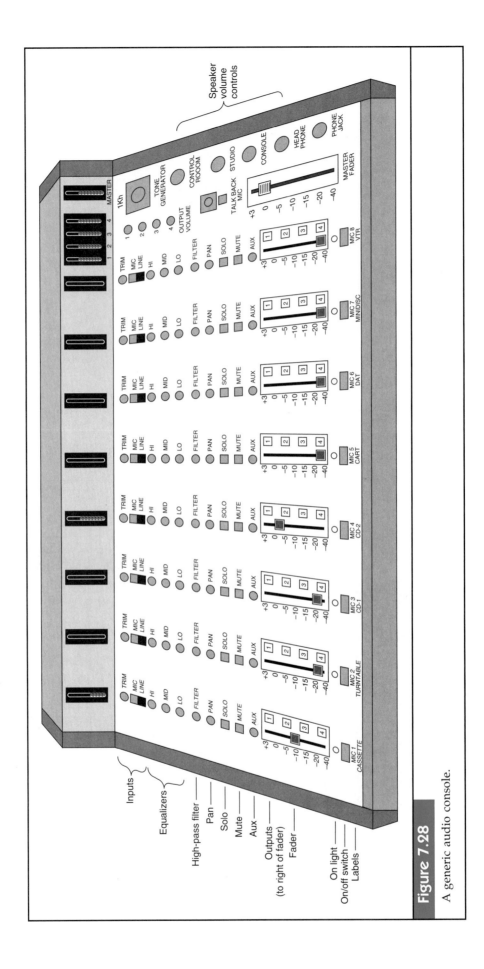

Figure 7.28

A generic audio console.

sounds at the same time. (You can actually wire in 16 sounds, as we will see a little later, but you can't play them all at the same time.) Whatever you bring into the board can be sent to four different places as it leaves the board. Even this basic board may look a bit intimidating to you because of all its knobs and buttons. But if you look at it carefully you will see a great deal of duplication. Each input channel has the same controls, and they all work the same.

Board Functions

Generally speaking, an audio console enables its operator to bring a number of different sounds into the board, alter their characteristics if desired, mix them together, adjust their volume, and then send them on to their next destination. To explain how the board works, we look next at its basic functions related to providing power, inputting, shaping, mixing, isolating, outputting, and monitoring.

Providing Power

At the very basic level, you need to be able to turn the console on. Most boards have a master power switch that is often in an inconspicuous place such as the back of the board (that's where the one on our generic board is hiding) so that someone does not accidentally turn it off while operating other controls.

Often there are on-off switches for each channel such as those at the bottom of Figure 7.28. If you are not using a channel, it is best not to have it turned on because some sound may accidentally come through. Some boards have two large buttons, one for on and one for off. We have designed our board with one button that toggles on and off. A small red light above the button lights up when the channel is on.

Another aspect of power is that some boards have a switch that can send *phantom power* to condenser mics, as mentioned previously. We don't have that switch on our generic board, but phantom power provides a good example of why a digital board can be smaller than an analog board. An analog board would need to have a phantom power switch for each channel, just in case that channel was used for a condenser mic. A digital board would not need a switch. Phantom power could be selected on the computer screen for the particular channel that needed it. Once the power was

activated, it would not need to be changed during the production.

Inputting

As mentioned previously, our sample console has eight input channels, enough to illustrate board principles. Most boards have more—inputs from telephones, satellite feeds, field locations, and so on. Note that all the inputs can be used for microphones *or* for some piece of outboard equipment (a situation that will be explained shortly). We have labeled the channels (it is a very good idea to label the board to whatever extent possible) indicating the use of each. We have arranged our board with the idea that we will generally use the first two or three positions for microphones and the rest for outboard equipment that we use frequently. We are assuming we don't use our analog cassette or turntable much anymore and for some programs we can make do with one CD player, but we use our digital cart, DAT, MiniDisc, and VTR playback frequently.

At the top of the board you see the area for indicating whether the sound on the channel will be a mic or outboard (line) equipment. The sound that comes from a microphone is very weak. To be heard it must be **amplified** a number of times as it is channeled through a system. Audio boards have amplifiers built into them that boost the microphone signal. The outboard sounds coming into a board also need to be amplified but not as much as the sound from a mic. Therefore, the board routes mic sound through more amplification than it does sound from other equipment. The mic and line equipment plug in on the back of the board and the person connecting them should make sure never to plug a mic into a line input or vice versa because doing so will make the audio unusable and can damage equipment—and ears.

Boards allow the operator to designate whether the sound to be used for a particular channel is a **mic feed** or a **line feed.** On our board we have a pad for making this selection. Not all outboard equipment (or mics) needs to be amplified the same amount, so a pot (sometimes referred to as **trim**) can be used to fine-tune the amplification.

The input channel cannot be used for the mic feed and the line feed at the same time. However, the operator can switch back and forth between the mic and line position during a production. If, for example, the production requires eight mics, then the audio operator should make sure the person on mic 8 does not speak right before a VTR roll-in so that there is time to change the mic/line pad on channel 8 to accommodate both mic and VTR needs. Another solution would be to use a *patch bay* to temporarily change where one of the inputs goes. If, for some reason, you had to use mic 8 and the VTR at the same time, you could patch the VTR into channel 5. Some digital boards have patch bay software built into them.

To help with the operation of the inputs, some consoles have *remote controls* for outboard equipment. By using them, the operator can start or stop tape recorders, CD players, and other equipment without having to stretch to reach them.

Shaping

Shaping, often referred to as **signal processing,** is a process of **altering** the tonal characteristics of sound, usually to eliminate flaws or create special effects. Often the goal of an audio operator is to reproduce the same quality and dimension that existed in an original sound pressure wave—replicating the natural sound as we would hear it without electronic intervention. A related goal is that of creating an enhanced version of that original sound so that it sounds like the tone the listener *expects* to hear in a given program situation. The problem of turning natural sound into electronically reproduced sound is that the equipment used and the physical conditions of the recording location strongly affect the quality of the sound. For example, if the microphone does not produce *overtones* well or if the tape recorder has a low *signal-to-noise ratio*, the audio will not sound like it originally did.

Sometimes sound needs to be changed to fit the creative needs of a TV program. You might want to change a voice recording so that the voice sounds like it is coming from an answering machine or emanating from a cave. These are all situations that can be helped by signal processing.

We have placed just a few samples of shaping capabilities on our TV studio board. These controls are more prevalent on boards used for post-production because, when you are altering sounds, it takes experimentation to get it right. With fast-paced studio productions there usually isn't much time for experimentation, and the studio environment is such that the sound can be controlled so that it does not contain many flaws.

But we have included a bit of **equalization**[9] on our board that enables us to alter the frequencies of sound. The equalizer unit in this board handles high, mid-level, and low frequencies separately so that we can emphasize or de-emphasize ranges. For example, if we wanted to give someone's voice a deeper sound, we might turn the knob for low frequencies so that they are maximized, leave the knob for midfrequencies in the center position, and adjust the high-frequency knob slightly to lessen these frequencies.

We have also included a high pass **filter.** Filters deal with frequencies also, either cutting out a certain band of frequencies or allowing a certain band to pass through. A high pass filter allows high frequencies to pass through so it is good for blocking low-frequency rumbles that are sometimes picked up from power lines.

Another control we have put on our board is a **pan knob.** It controls the amount of each channel that is going to the right speaker and the amount going to the left speaker. Some boards are able to control for surround sound, but because that is quite complex it is better suited to digital boards that can encompass small gradations of control.

Sometimes boards have signal processing equipment that deals with *amplitude*. For example, they will have **compressors**[10] that reduce dynamic range by compressing the distance between the lowest and highest volume levels, in effect raising the lowest levels to bring them up close to the loudest levels the system can handle. They also have **limiters** that do not allow the signal to go beyond a certain volume.

There is signal processing for time control. For example, **digital delay** holds what a person is saying for several seconds before it is sent to the transmitter. This is so the sound can be stopped if a person says something that is not fit for air. Its most useful application would be during a live talk show. **Reverberation** gives sound a bit of a bounce or echo in case, for example, you want something recorded in a studio to sound like it was recorded in a cathedral. In fact, some digital boards have a library of sound environments, such as a large auditorium or closet, that already have the appropriate signal processing levels set to produce that environment.

Although these shaping processes (and many more) can be incorporated within audio boards, they can also be performed by a variety of "black boxes" that have been created for special effects. If a particular board does not have a particular effect, it is easy to find hardware or software to fill the gap.

Mixing

A major purpose of an audio console is to mix several sounds together—voice and music, two sound effects, four people talking. This is accomplished through **faders** (positioned near the bottom of the board) that control the volume (sometimes referred to as the **gain**) of the sound for each particular channel. The 0 dB[11] position is usually the optimum area for sound, but, of course, the reason you have the faders is so you can vary the gain. If someone with a loud voice is speaking into mic 1, you would want to set the volume lower than you would for talent with a soft voice. Some boards do not have faders that move up and down. Rather they have knobs you turn to the right to increase the volume. These knobs are referred to as **pots** (short for potentiometers).

When you are operating the board during a production, you often need to bring a particular fader up to **fade in** a sound and take it down to **fade out** a sound. Or you may do a **crossfade,** where you bring one sound in slowly while you take another out slowly. For example, if you are doing a crossfade from music on CD player 1 to music on CD player 2, you would gradually bring channel 3's fader down while raising channel 4's fader. The other main type of audio transition is called a **segue.** This is an abrupt change from one sound to another. For effect's sake, you might want to move abruptly from the middle of a piece of music to a voice statement coming from a MiniDisc. You would lower channel 4's fader quickly while raising channel 7's fader.

As previously mentioned, some consoles allow you to set levels for a particular program and then memorize them within the board software. You can do this during rehearsal for a complicated program and then use them during actual recording. Or you can set them for a repeating program that has a set audio pattern. Sometimes these settings are combined with motorized faders that allow for very smooth transitions.

Isolating

Sometimes you do not want to hear all the sounds coming from the board. You may want to hear one particular sound so that you can, for example, properly equalize it. Pushing the **solo** button on one particular channel allows you to hear just that channel's sound. On the other hand, a **mute** button allows you to hear all the sounds except the one from the channel with the mute button pushed.

It is possible to mute or solo several channels at once, and on some boards it is possible to group solo or mute buttons so they all go on or off at once. For example, you might want to group all the talent mics so you can mute them quickly whenever a commercial break occurs. Our board just has simple solo and mute buttons for each channel, so if we wanted to mute several channels at once, we would have to push all the relevant buttons.

Some boards, usually those that do not have a function called solo, have a **cue button** (also sometimes called **audition**). This is used when you want to get something ready but you don't want it to record. For example, before production begins you can listen to the DAT so you can cue it to the point where you want it to start and then bring it in later in the program.

Outputting

If you look next to the faders, you will see four buttons numbered one through four.[12] These buttons determine where the sound goes once it leaves the board. This is really a function of how the engineer wires the board.

In a TV studio, you want one of the outputs to go to the VTR so that the sound can be recorded with the picture. You might want another output to go into the studio for when talent needs to hear program audio. Perhaps you want to send one output to the DAT so you can have an audio-only recording of the program. Or you might want the sound to go to the patch bay so that it can be sent other places, if desired. The signal can go to all four places at the same time; you simply push the buttons for the designations you want. Each channel has its own selection of outputs because you might want to send only part of the sound to a particular place. For example, if you are making a DAT, you might want to record only the voices coming through the mics, but not the music from the CD.

The **master fader** at the right end of the board controls the sound for the whole board. If it is down, nothing will come through the console. If something unusual happens and you want to lose all sound, a quick way is to take down the master fader. On the other hand, and far more likely, if you are not getting any sound out of the console, chances are you have not raised the master fader (or faders if the board is stereo or surround).

A more complicated concept is that of **submastering.** If you have many sources coming into a large console (perhaps a 24 in board), you may want to group some of them together so you can raise one fader to activate all of them. For example, if you have four mics over the violin section of an orchestra, you will probably want to activate all of them at once. You can use a **group assign switch** to assign the four channels for the violin mics to one submaster fader. Likewise, you could assign the microphones covering the percussion section to another submaster. These submaster faders are used to mix groups of sounds and come before the master fader.

Many boards have an **auxiliary send** feature, such as that located above the input faders on our board. This, too, is a type of output. Using the aux send feature you can send the sound to external equipment, such as a stand-alone compressor, which can alter the sound and then send it back again into the board. Aux send can also be used to send the program audio to another source, such as the boom operator's headphone or the talent's IFB.

Some consoles include a **mix-minus** module. This is used to send all of the program sound except that being recorded. One use is for vocalists. All the instrumental music is sent to the singer's earphone, and he or she then sings and records the vocal. Mix-minus is also used when reporters, located at some distance from each other, are all reporting on the same story and need to hear what everyone else is saying without the annoyance of hearing their own voice (probably with an echo).

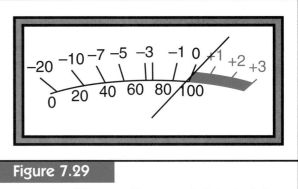

Figure 7.29

An analog VU meter. The top scale is in decibels, and the bottom scale is in percentages.

Monitoring

Obviously, you want to know that sound is getting from the inputs to the outputs of the console in an acceptable manner. The **volume unit (VU) meter**[13] provides a visual description of volume levels and the degrees of difference among the ongoing level changes. Some VU meters, such as the one in Figure 7.29, have a needle-sized pointer that is in constant motion as it indicates differing intensities of volume. On other equipment, including our sample board, the meter consists of a column of **light emitting diodes (LED).** The effect is a bar of light that grows and shrinks to indicate ongoing changes in volume level.

On VU meters that have a needle, this needle should **peak** (reach the high point of its swing) at the "0" position (refer again to Figure 7.29). On LED meters, the color of the lights usually changes from green to red at the point where the signal should peak. It is very important for an audio operator to pay attention to the peaking point because, as the amplification of the signal is increased beyond this point, not all frequencies are equally amplified. With analog sound this results in **distortion.** Digital sound that is too loud for the equipment often disappears, or **clips.** When levels drop below an acceptable minimum, they are not processed by the system and are lost.

We have equipped our board with a meter for each input channel, a meter for each of the four output channels, and a meter for the master fader. The regular procedure we envision for our generic board would be that the master volume would be set at 0, which, if the board is properly engineered, should register right before the lights change from green to red on the master meter when the tone generator is turned on.

The **tone generator,** located upper right on the generic board, is used to calibrate sound levels throughout the system. It creates a steady tone at 1 kHz. If the master fader is at 0 and the tone generator is turned on, then the volume controls for the four outputs (the pots above the master fader) can all be set so that these outputs are at the same level—the last green LED. In this way, sound will be consistent as it moves from one place to another. For example, when the tone on output 1 has been set, then that tone can be sent to the VTR so that the VTR VU meter can be set the same. In that way the sound coming from the audio board will be the same volume as it goes into and comes out of the VTR. Once you have calibrated all the equipment, you should not move the master fader or the output pots because doing so will upset the consistency of volumes from one place to another.

It is possible that you will not want to set all the outputs the same. You might, for example, want to send the sound to the DAT at a lower volume level than what you send to the VTR.

Meters give you a visual representation of the sound, but they do not let you actually hear it. To hear sound created within the board you need amplification and speakers. Speakers are generally stand-alone pieces of equipment located in the studio or control room (see the next section), but the console itself may contain a tiny speaker that can be used for cueing material. It is also usually possible to hear the sound through a headphone plugged into the board. Being able to use the console speaker or headphones is particularly helpful before production begins when people in the control room want to be able to communicate with each other and concentrate on their jobs without the annoying noises of tapes rewinding or the same part of some CD being played over and over. If a board has a talkback mic (located above the master fader on our board), the audio operator can use it to talk through the studio speaker and communicate with crew and talent about mic levels.

The volume controls for all the speakers—control room, studio, console, headphone—are on the console (far right on Figure 7.28). These volume levels are not set with the tone generator and are not tied to any meters. Those volumes are independent and do not affect the recording level. Any number of students have been tricked by turning the control room monitor up loud while having the program levels low. They think they are recording good sound, but in reality the only sound that is loud enough is that in the control room. One way to prevent such a problem (in addition to setting the volumes correctly in the first place) is to keep a wary eye on the meters during production.

7.5 | Speakers

As previously mentioned, a common way of **monitoring** sound is to listen to it on a speaker. A speaker, like a microphone, is a transducer except that instead of turning sound energy into an electrical energy it turns an electrical signal into audible sound. Television facilities usually have a number of speakers. There may be a speaker in the studio, and there is always at least one speaker in the control room called a **program monitor.** It provides a high-quality reproduction of the sound coming from the audio board and going to a recorder or out over the air. In addition, there may be another speaker, called an **air monitor,** through which you can hear the sound as it is broadcast over the air for a live feed. Individual pieces of equipment, such as the VTR, often have their own speakers so that the operators can hear what they are playing.

If the sound you are creating is stereo, there will be two speakers—one for the right channel and one for the left. Make sure the speakers are positioned so that they give you an accurate sound reproduction. The general rule for speaker placement is that the distance between the speakers should be the same as the distance from the speaker to the listener.

7.6 | Tips for Recording Good Sound

Because sound conveys so much of the information provided by a TV program, it needs to be understandable and appropriate. Recording good sound is not easy. You cannot simply place a microphone near the sound source and hope for the best. You must take the discipline to plan how the sound will be recorded and then follow through on that plan.

To record good sound, start by selecting the most appropriate microphone. How many people are you miking? If just one, you will probably want a cardioid. Is there any chance the mic might be handled roughly? If so, use a dynamic mic. Mics are very individual, so even though two microphones have the same specifications, one brand might work better for a particular performer than another. For example, sometimes a particular mic will make Talent A's s's hiss or p's pop while Talent B will sound fine with the same mic. If this happens, try a different mic for Talent A or put a **pop filter** over the front of the mic. This is a ball-shaped accessory made out of metal or foam; the mics in Figure 7.11 have pop filters on them.

Many cardioid mics are subject to a **proximity effect.** As the sound gets close to the mic (about two or three inches away), the mic boosts the bass frequencies. Some men particularly like this effect because it makes their voices sound deeper.[14] Try to avoid having talent change microphones in the middle of a production. Because each mic has an individual sound, the talent's voice quality will change when he or she starts using a new mic, destroying the aural **continuity** of the production.

Also think through the method of positioning the mic carefully. The best position is 6 to 12 inches from the person's mouth, but that is not always possible. Often compromises need to be made, especially with mics on booms, because of shadow problems with the lighting or because of the height of the camera shot. If the camera has a wide shot and the mic should not show in the picture, you should keep the mic as low as possible and point it toward the mouth. Sometimes you have to be creative with positioning. For example, if you are using a fishpole and the camera has a long shot, you might need to try placing the mic near the talent's feet and pointing it upward toward the mouth.

One easy method to ensure good sound pickup is to insist on checking the sound carefully during setup and rehearsal. Have the talent speak into the mic as they will speak during the program—not the usual "Testing 1, 2, 3" routine. If it is a talk show, have each person say a few things as they might say them for the show. If your talent is going to sit up straight and clearly enunciate "Testing 1, 2, 3" for the test and then slouch and mumble during the show, it is better to know this ahead of time than to try to compensate during the actual production. Have each person talk separately so you can set the optimum volume level for each ahead of time. This doesn't mean you won't have to make changes during the program, but you will be starting at a better point.

You want to make sure that your sound has both presence and perspective. **Presence** relates to sound that is loud and clear and sounds like it is coming from the person's mouth. You do not want sound that is **off-mic**—that sounds as if it is coming from behind the person or off to the side. This is usually a matter of placing the mic near enough to the person's mouth. (See Figure 7.30.) You may also want to minimize the amount of sound you pick up that has bounced off a wall, creating an echo-type effect. (See Figure 7.31.)

Perspective is the relationship between the picture and the sound. The sound should be what the viewer expects. If a person is being shown in the distance in a long shot, the sound should be different than if the person is seen in a close-up. The best way to achieve proper perspective is to move the mic closer to or farther away from the person. The farther the mic is from the sound source, the farther the audience will perceive the sound source to be. For this reason, you should not use a lav mic if what you are recording calls for perspective changes, because a lav mic attached to a person will always remain at the same distance.

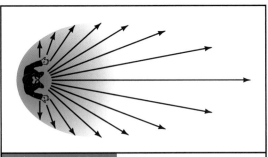

Figure 7.30

The sound pressure waves of the human voice begin to decline in intensity beyond a 45-degree angle from those projected directly to the front of the speaker.

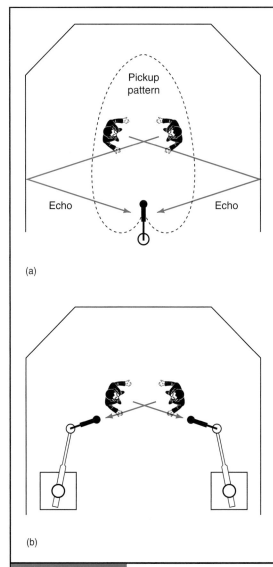

(a)

(b)

Figure 7.31

(*a*) Incorrect placement of directional mic between two performers. Although the two actors are standing "in the pattern" of the directional mic, their voices will be picked up with a hollow "off-mic" quality because they are not facing toward the mic; they are directing their voices away from the microphone. (*b*) Correct placement of directional mics. To achieve optimum presence from two actors facing each other, it is necessary to use two directional microphones—a separate mic placed directly in the vocal path of each actor.

The distance that a mic is placed from the talent must take into account the **inverse square law.** This is the same principle that was discussed in Chapter 6 in relation to lighting. In terms of sound it means that *as the microphone-to-source distance is doubled, the loudness is reduced to one-fourth of its previous strength.* Therefore, if you have an audio source (voice) giving you a constant level of sound at a distance of one foot from the microphone, and then you move the mic back to a distance of two feet, the strength of the sound pressure (loudness) hitting the microphone will be only one-quarter of what it was when the mic was one foot from the source. If you again double the distance and place the mic four feet from the source, it will again reduce the loudness level to one-quarter of what it was at two feet so that the level is now ¹⁄₁₆th of what it had been at a distance of one foot. If you are working with a relatively short source-to-mic position, such as you might have for a talk show, any distance change can be crucial. This is all the more reason to check the sound levels carefully before you start recording a program. Also don't be confused by the sound you *hear* with your ears. You may hear people just fine when you stand four feet away, but that doesn't mean the mic will pick up the sound as well as you hear it.

Have the discipline to think ahead to problems that might occur. Are any of the performers going to move during the program? If so, make sure they have enough mic cable to make the move comfortably. You should have spare microphone batteries nearby. Some audio operators use redundancy. They mic the performer with two microphones so that if one goes bad the other can quickly be put into operation. You usually don't want to have both mics operating at the same time, however, because that can create a phase problem.

Phase problems arise when you place microphones too close together so that they are picking up the same sound source. Their similar waveforms tend to cancel each other out when they get to the audio console. The result is disappearing sound or sound that goes in and out. To prevent this problem, you should obey the **three-to-one rule** that states that if two singers (or other performers) are standing (or sitting) side by side, each working at a distance of one foot from their respective mics, then the two mics must

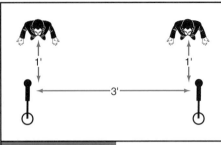

Figure 7.32

The three-to-one rule. If the microphones are one foot from the sound source, they should be at least three feet away from each other to prevent phase problems.

be at least three feet apart. (See Figure 7.32.) If source-to-mic distance is increased, mic separation must similarly be increased. A further application is that if a person wearing a lavaliere mic walks over to a boom mic, one of the mics must be turned down.

Anyone operating an audio board must pay careful attention to **balance.** This is the relationship of one sound to another. The most common balance problem is that the music is too loud and drowns out the voice. This is fairly easy to fix simply by lowering the volume of the music. Harder to balance are the voice levels of different talent. If one person speaks very loudly and another is soft-spoken, the audio operator should attempt to balance their levels. Sometimes this is simply a matter of having one fader higher than another, but often the position of the mics needs to be changed. If one mic is being used, it can be cheated toward the soft-spoken person; if two mics are being used, the soft-spoken person's mic can be placed a little closer to the mouth, taking into account the inverse square law.

Recording good sound requires great discipline on the part of the audio operator because it is very easy for sound to become unintelligible. That is why boom operators or audio console operators often wear headsets—so they can concentrate on the quality of the sound they are recording and also listen for unwanted sounds, such as clothing rustle. Some sound operators close their eyes during rehearsal and recording so that they are not aware of the picture and can become totally absorbed in the sound.

Discussion Questions

1. Name at least one piece of audio equipment in your facility that does each of the following: transducing, channeling, selecting, recording, monitoring.

2. If you were the audio operator for a TV studio-based game show, what kind of mic do you think you would use for the host? Cardioid or omnidirectional? Dynamic or condenser? Flat frequency response or with a speech bump? Lavaliere, hand-held, stand, boom? Would you use balanced or unbalanced cable? What type of connectors would you use? Justify your answers.

3. If the sound from the CD player is not getting through the audio board but the sound from the microphone is, what troubleshooting could you do to get the CD sound operating properly?

4. Define proximity effect, presence, perspective, and phase and tell what you would need to do to make sure you are handling these four aspects of sound properly.

Notes

1. Other characteristics of microphones are also important, such as impedance and sensitivity. Impedance cuts down on the amount of sound that gets through and is expressed in ohms. Low-impedance mics of 600 ohms or less are used in professional situations because they impede the sound very little and are therefore good quality. High-impedance mics (10,000 ohms and higher) are used for consumer equipment. Because they impede sound, they cannot have cables longer than about six feet. Sensitivity refers to a mic's efficiency—ability to create an output.

2. The term *cycles per second (cps)* was the first term used as the basic unit of measure for sound pressure waves and electromagnetic waves. Now, engineering terminology has for the most part replaced the term *cycles per second* with the term *hertz* (abbreviated Hz), in honor of Heinrich Hertz, who first demonstrated the existence of electromagnetic waves.

3. Waves can also be discussed in terms of their wavelength. The distance between the peaks is the wavelength. Lower frequency sounds, because they are more spread out, have longer wavelengths than higher pitch sounds.

4. A decibel is actually $\frac{1}{10}$th of a larger unit, the Bel, named for Alexander Graham Bell of telephone fame.

5. The simplest way to record stereo is to take the *monaural* signal from one microphone and send it to both the left and right

channels of the stereo equipment. This is not true stereo, however, and does not allow for effects, such as the sound of an airplane that moves across the screen. For a method called split-pair miking you place mics several feet from each other to pick up sounds much as the ear does. For more on stereo miking, see "Two Ears, Two Mics: Stereo Miking for TV," *TV Technology*, 24 March 1999, 58.

6. For information on how to mic for surround, see "A Look at Surround Microphone Techniques," *TV Technology*, 27 June 2001, 36.

7. There are dual-element microphones with both dynamic and condenser mic elements mounted side by side so that the audio operator can switch from one to the other if the need arises. See "Audio-Technica AE2500 Dual-Element Mic," *Mix*, June 2003, 106.

8. "Boundary Microphones," *Sound and Video Contractor*, April 2003, 58.

9. Equalization is undertaken two ways—graphic equalization and parametric equalization. The graphic equalization divides the frequency response range into separate bands that can then be altered. The controls on the equalizer form a graph of what fre-quencies are emphasized and which are de-emphasized. The parametric equalizer can control individual frequencies as well as a band of frequencies.

10. This term *compressor* should not be confused with compression technology used with video. It is a term that predates the new use of the word *compression*.

11. Zero decibels has been calibrated to be a level that equipment can handle without distortion or clipping. Sound down from 0 has been marked with minuses, while sound above 0 is indicated with pluses. Some boards use percentages rather than decibels, with 100 percent being equal to 0 decibels.

12. Most boards have more than four outputs, especially if they are used for stereo or the surround sound that is likely to accompany HDTV.

13. There is also a meter called a peak program meter (PPM) that measures loudness peaks. It reacts more quickly to overmodulation than a VU meter.

14. "Cardioid-Carrying Member," *Mix*, March 2003, 122.

CHAPTER 8

Graphics and Sets

Graphics and sets are the two major pictorial elements that are a part of television production. Graphics include lettering and artwork, normally displayed on-screen to supplement the images captured on-camera. A news anchor's name, for example, can be shown on a graphic with simple lettering. More-advanced graphics might include the map of a war zone, a chart showing how tax money is spent, or even a moving graphic of a working piston engine or blood flowing through arteries. A wide variety of set designs are also possible, from the simplicity of a single folding chair and a curtain for background to an entire re-creation of a classroom, corporate office, or apartment.

The *disciplines* of using pictorial elements include understanding and applying appropriate design principles. It is also important to have a clear understanding of *what* you want to convey to the viewer and *how* you will do it. The *techniques* of graphics include understanding your particular graphics system as well as a more general knowledge of the types of equipment and graphics effects available. Some of the techniques needed for sets require the skill of a carpenter or painter, but others are simple tasks that anyone can master with a little practice. This chapter covers graphics and sets by emphasizing the following topics:

- The informational and emotional aspects of pictorial elements (8.1)
- Different types of graphics equipment and the functions they perform (8.2)
- Aesthetic considerations in using television graphics (8.3)

- Techniques for using non-computer-generated graphics (8.4)

- The purpose of sets (8.5)

- The possibilities for virtual sets (8.6)

- How physical sets are designed, constructed, assembled, and stored (8.7)

- Differences among permanent sets, removable sets, and cycs and drapes (8.7)

- Elements to consider concerning furniture, set dressing, and props (8.8)

- How sets relate to other aspects of production (8.9)

8.1 Pictorial Functions

One of the major reasons for using graphics and sets is to convey a wide range of *information* to the viewer without disrupting the overall flow of a program. During a baseball game, for example, a graphic in the upper-left corner constantly shows the current status of the game (score, team batting, number of balls, strikes, and outs, and runners on base), while supplemental graphics show information about particular players. The lower-screen **crawl** showing news headlines has become a fixture on cable news channels like MSNBC and CNN. (See Figure 8.1.)

Sets, too, convey information to the viewer, although in a less direct way. A well-designed set made to represent the inside of a church tells the viewer that the scene is happening inside a church yet does not call attention to itself. In the same way, the set for a news program should provide an inviting, pleasant, and functional background without distracting from the message provided by the news anchors.

Beyond informational functions, graphics and sets also play *emotional* or *psychological* functions. Many subtle messages can be conveyed by the total production design, and the pictorial elements—graphics, sets, props, and furniture—combine to give an "image" or "feel" to the program. In a news program, do you want the image of an advanced technological communications center or of a working newsroom? In a religious program, do you want the image of a traditional church service or of an avant-garde contemporary movement?

The emotional function of design also includes creating and maintaining a style or **continuity** for the program. This style should carry through to all the pictorial elements used in the production; each pictorial element should look like it *belongs* with every other element. In some cases, for instance, a station has a news bureau in another city, and thus part of the newscast originates from the set located there. These "satellite" sets should match the main set, exhibiting similar style cues such as color and decoration. Maintaining this type of consistency is especially important in designing graphic elements; watch an evening newscast and notice how the various graphic elements seem to fit

Figure 8.1

A graphic "crawl" of news information has become a common feature on cable news stations. *Photo courtesy of CNN.*

together with one another and convey a sense of professionalism and trust.

Every pictorial design, then, should serve both an *informational* function and an *emotional* function. The set should not only tell us what time of day it is but also give us a hint as to what is going to happen this day. The graphic should not only give us information but also emphasize how important the information is.

8.2 Graphics Equipment

For many years most TV graphics consisted of "title cards" made by applying rub-on or stick-on letters to sheets of cardboard that were then placed in front of the camera. If a chart or graph was needed, an artist drew it by hand. Although on-camera graphics are still used on occasion (see Section 8.4), today nearly all television graphics are created with computers.

Creating Graphics with Computers

In the past, the functions of character generation and graphics generation were performed by separate pieces of equipment. In other words, to create lettering on the screen you used a device called a **character generator (CG),** and to create pictures and other artwork you used a **graphics generator** or **paintbox.** Today, however, these functions have been for the most part combined into a single unit, usually run by a person called the **graphics operator.**[1]

Nearly all graphics systems use a normal—or somewhat modified—personal computer as their starting point. In fact, many graphics systems consist only of software designed to be installed and run on standard PC computers.[2] Chyron's Duet, for example, is a graphics system and **digital video effects (DVE)** unit based on a PC running the Windows operating system. (See Figure 8.2.) Designed to be adaptable to various **standard-definition** and **high-definition** formats, the Duet also can run software designed by other companies. Adobe

Figure 8.2

Chyron's Duet graphics system uses the Lyric user interface to perform a variety of graphics functions. *Photo courtesy of Chyron Corporation. All rights reserved.*

Photoshop, a software program originally designed for print-based graphic artists, also has become an important tool for creating television graphics. And, as you will see in Chapter 11, most nonlinear editing systems have graphics software built in, allowing an editor to create graphics and seamlessly edit them into a program.

Working with Text

If you have used a word-processing or desktop-publishing program on a computer, you are familiar with the basic concept of how you can work with text in a television graphics system. (See Figure 8.3.) With these systems, you basically type text on the computer screen, and it is then output as either a standard-definition or high-definition television signal. Alternately, you may create text-based graphics in a program such as Photoshop and then **import,** or bring them into, the graphics system.

Graphics systems allow you to choose from a wide variety of text sizes and lettering styles, or **fonts.** You also can produce many special effects such as boldface, italics, drop shadow, outline, and multicolor lettering.

Graphics systems normally operate with a "screen" or "page" metaphor—information is typed in and saved as various screens or pages for later recall. With the push of a button, the graphics operator can move to the next page, go back to the last page, or even skip to a completely new page. In a television newscast, for instance, the anchor's name might be on one page and the name of a reporter on another page. During the show, the graphics operator can easily move from page to page.

Text can be **keyed** with a switcher over other video information (see Chapter 9) or be displayed **full screen,** as shown in Figure 8.4. You also can perform

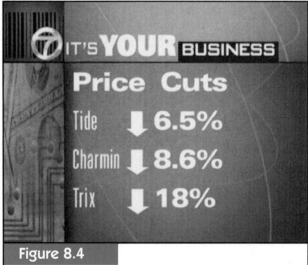

Figure 8.4

Graphics can be keyed over a portion of the frame or used as full screens. The top photo shows a key of the anchor's name and station logo over a shot of the anchor reading a tease. The bottom photo shows a full-screen graphic of consumer information.
Photos courtesy of WXYZ-TV, Detroit.

Figure 8.3

A character generator can be operated with a keyboard and mouse.

special effects with text, such as **rolling,** which moves the text up or down the screen (often used for closing credits); and crawling, which, as discussed previously, moves the text horizontally across the screen in a single line. Other special effects can make text elements spin or fly across the screen. **Animations,** in which the lettering can, for example, appear to "melt" or stretch, can also be created with graphics systems.

Working with Graphics

More-sophisticated graphics such as pictures, maps, and diagrams also can be created and combined with text elements. To input information, the graphics operator can use the keyboard or mouse, or a **graphics tablet** that allows him or her to actually "draw" electronically on a pad using a **digitizing pen.** (See Figure 8.5.)

Graphics operators may produce artwork from scratch or they may start with an existing frame of video or a print-based graphic element such as a photograph. Here again, programs like Adobe *Photoshop* are often used as a starting point for creating and manipu-

lating various graphic elements that can then be imported into the graphics system. Figure 8.6(a), for example, shows a graphic in Photoshop designed to be keyed over video to identify a television reporter. Here, Photoshop's "layers" feature allows different elements of a graphic to be moved and manipulated separately from one another, as shown in Figure 8.6(b). Similarly Color Plate G shows an example of how individual elements of existing video can be combined to create a sophisticated graphic.

As with text, the graphics system can perform many functions on pictures and other graphic elements, including resizing, rotating, changing colors, and creating animations. Advanced systems can capture multiple frames of video, then be used to "paint" effects onto the video. For example, you could capture a shot of a car driving down the street, then use the graphics system to change the color of the car.

Storing and Recalling Graphics

Graphics of any type created on a computer exist in **digital** form, which means they can be stored on

Figure 8.5

A graphics tablet and digitizing pen are basic tools for the electronic artist.

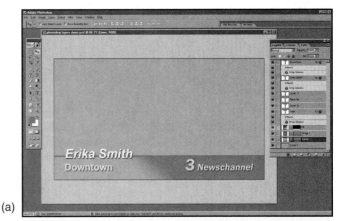

(a)

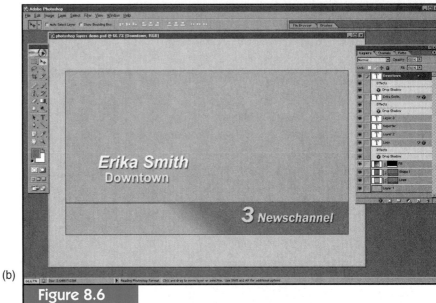

(b)

Figure 8.6

Adobe *Photoshop* used to create a text-based graphic (*a*). The program's layers feature allows individual elements to be moved and manipulated without disturbing other elements (*b*). *Adobe product screen shot reprinted with permission from Adobe Systems Incorporated.*

computer-based media such as hard disks, optical disks, and **video servers** (see Chapter 10). The graphics system can be configured to save projects to one or more of these media.

Most graphics systems incorporate **electronic still store** (ESS) features, meaning individual graphics and frames of video can be stored, indexed, and easily retrieved. For example, a graphics operator might capture a video frame of a face shot of each member of a basketball team, then add graphic and text elements such as a team logo and the player's name and number. Then, the graphics operator can assign a specific name or number to each graphic and later be able to instantly call up the desired frame. Many television stations use ESS units to store over-the-shoulder graphics for their newscasts. (See Figure 8.7.) These graphics are usually indexed by number ("1000" for the automobile accident graphic, "1001" for the city council graphic, for instance) and can be easily called up and reused as appropriate.

Figure 8.7

Over-the-shoulder graphics, such as this one indicating "Your World Tonight," can be stored, indexed, and recalled using an electronic still store (ESS) unit. *Photo Courtesy WXYZ-TV, Detroit.*

8.3 | Graphic Aesthetics

The overall goal of graphic design for television is that the information displayed on-screen should be easy to read and pleasing to the eye. In this regard, TV graphics people adhere to some of the same principles as graphic designers working in print or other media.

However, the television screen is a unique medium: Its resolution (even in high-definition formats) is much lower than print, and it is subject to temporal limitations—namely, that any graphic image will only be on the screen for a limited amount of time. Consequently, television graphics have to convey the intended information quickly, clearly, and with little or no distraction.

Graphic Design

The creation of sophisticated animations or complex still graphic images "from scratch" takes quite a bit of artistic talent in addition to technical skills and aesthetic understanding. Not everyone can create these types of graphics effectively, no matter how much training he or she may have had. For that reason, this section concentrates on the effective presentation of graphic elements where text is the predominant feature. For the design of these types of graphics, artistic ability can help, but it is not crucial. Instead, it is merely necessary to follow some basic design principles, namely structure, contrast, and readability.

Structure

If there is one primary rule about the preparation of television graphics, it is this: *Keep it simple.* As noted, the television screen is relatively low resolution, and any one graphic won't be on the screen a very long time. Therefore, there is no room (or time) for unnecessary elements, and the message of the graphic must be easy to grasp. The information on the screen needs to be structured effectively to help the viewer immediately understand the message being conveyed.

Only a limited amount of information can be on the television screen at any given time. Go beyond a certain point, and the viewer becomes overwhelmed and frustrated. If you have a lot of information to get across, think about how that information can be pared down to its essential elements, or—if necessary—divide the information into more than one screen. Then, present the information in an effectively structured way.

Figure 8.8 (which is also repeated in color as Color Plate E) shows a screen from CNN Headline News. No

Figure 8.8

This screen shot from CNN Headline News shows several different graphic elements conveying separate information. *Photo courtesy of CNN.*

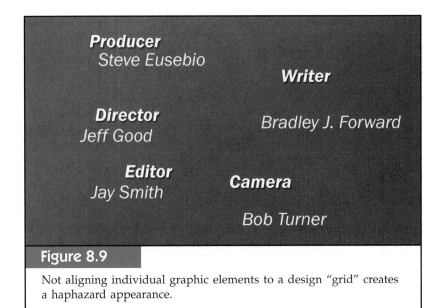

Figure 8.9

Not aligning individual graphic elements to a design "grid" creates a haphazard appearance.

fewer than six separate graphic elements are conveying information at the same time. However, the presentation of the information is relatively clear, as the screen is structured so that certain *kinds* of information are always found in the same place. For example, viewers quickly learn always to look for weather information in the bottom-left part of the screen and sports scores at the bottom right. This consistency of structural presentation makes a lot of information readily available and easy to understand.

One way to achieve structure is to use a *grid design*. In a grid design, you align the elements of the page to form a coherent design. Elements are not placed haphazardly, but as part of a unified and aligned structure. In Figure 8.8, notice that the white bar with the time on it, the news headline, and the sports scoreboard are all placed flush against an imaginary vertical line about one-third of the way across the screen. This same imaginary line also forms the opening in the lower left for the weather information and provides the separation between the anchor's body and the story summary on the left. You can also discern an imaginary horizontal line located about a third of the way up the screen. The time bar and the weather information are aligned to this line, which also separates the anchor and the main story summary from information not directly related to the current story. Thus, this grid structure helps organize the information effectively, making it easy for

viewers to discern individual pieces of information. Figure 8.9, on the other hand, shows an example of a poor design structure where there is no discernable grid and the individual elements just seem to "float around" independently of one another.

You may also be noticing that thirds of the screen are important to graphic design. Just as discussed in Chapter 5 in regard to the composition of camera shots, the **rule of thirds** applies to graphics as well.

In nontext pictorial elements, simplicity of structure is also crucial. This is particularly true with maps. Usually maps prepared for print applications cannot be used on television because such maps normally contain detail information (such as tiny roads, city names, and mileage markers) that cannot be deciphered on the television screen. When creating maps for television, use only outlines of countries or natural geographical bodies and a few key labels or key locations. (See Figure 8.10.) Remember, we need to make it easy for the viewer to *quickly* discern the main point of the graphic—any extraneous information makes figuring out the graphic more difficult.

Contrast

Contrast helps the viewer separate individual elements in a graphic from one another. It is usually achieved by using contrasting colors—black text on a light blue background, for example. Graphics with

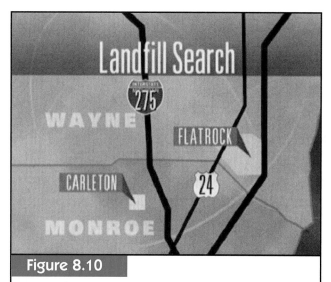

Figure 8.10

Maps designed for use on television must be simple, presenting only the minimum amount of information necessary to convey the message, in this case the location of two landfill sites. *Photo courtesy of WXYZ-TV, Detroit.*

good contrast are pleasing to the eye and provide visual interest, making the viewer *want* to pay attention to the information.

Selecting good colors to provide contrast requires recalling some of the information about **hue, saturation,** and **brightness** presented in Chapter 5. **Hue** is the actual color base itself (red, green, purple, etc.); **saturation** refers to the strength or intensity of a color, how far removed it is from a neutral or gray shade; and **luminance** (brightness) indicates where the color would fall on a scale from light (white) to dark (black).

Generally, colors with the same level of brightness or saturation provide poor contrast, as shown in Color Plate B. Two different hues (say, red and blue) will contrast best if you also use differing levels of saturation and brightness. A dark brownish red will contrast better against a brilliant green than against a dark brownish green.

In fact, contrasting saturations of the same hue (for example, a vivid chartreuse and a grayish olive green) provide considerable contrast. And even contrasting brightness or lightness of the same hue and saturation (for example, a light pink and a dark rose) provides essential contrast and legibility.

With most graphics generators, thousands or even millions of colors are available. Take time to experiment with your system and see what combinations of hues, saturation, and brightness work best for your purpose. Video engineers like to have just a little white and a little black in a picture for reference points. Thus, a good graphic would be one that has two or three shades of brightness plus a little white and black for sparkle and interest.

Referring again to Color Plate E, notice how the use of contrasting colors works with the grid design to provide separation between individual elements and an overall pleasing design. The black and vivid red text contrasts well with the white background in the time bar, as does the white and bright yellow text in the news headline and weather areas against the darker background. The black background of the sports scoreboard provides contrast not only from the white and yellow text within, but also from the other colors on the page.

Readability

Text is the most important element in television graphic design as it is what conveys most of the information in a typical graphic. Therefore, proper use of text is essential to good design.

As you probably know from using computer-based word processors or desktop publishing programs, there are literally thousands of different fonts available. Only a small percentage of these, however, are suitable for television work.

Lettering used in television should be bold, thick, and well defined, with a sharp, firm contour. As illustrated in Figure 8.11, some styles of lettering have **serifs,** small extensions on the tips of letters. In printed text, these extensions help guide the eye from one letter to the next and one word to the next, helping ease eyestrain. But because of television's lower resolution (especially in standard definition), serifs often disappear on screen. Consequently, you should avoid lettering styles with serifs or make sure the serifs show up properly on the screen. Serif fonts are not completely out of the question for television graphics, but you will notice that the overwhelming majority of fonts you see on television are non-serif.

One mistake that beginning graphics operators make is using too many different font styles or font

Figure 8.11

These two text examples show the difference between serif and non-serif type. Serifs are the small protrusions on the ends of letters, as indicated by the circled portion of the letter *f*.

styles that are inappropriate. Generally, you should use only one or two different font styles on a television graphic. Use more than that, and the graphic will quickly take on a "ransom note" effect, as shown in Figure 8.12. Notice that in Figure 8.8 there are only one or two different font styles, all of them non-serif.

You should also resist the temptation to use so-called novelty fonts—lettering designed to convey a sort of "fun" or playful image. Some examples of novelty fonts are lettering that looks like it was drawn by hand, or lettering that appears to be printed on a child's building blocks. These fonts needlessly call attention to themselves and are generally hard to read.

Font effects also should be used with caution. Most graphics equipment provides a nearly limitless arsenal of shadow, coloring, and scaling effects. The use of drop shadow or a subtle outline effect can help lettering stand out from its background, but again you should use good judgment. If the effect will not make the graphic more visually appealing or easier to read, you shouldn't use it.

Figure 8.12

An undesirable "ransom note" effect is created by using too many different font styles on a single graphic.

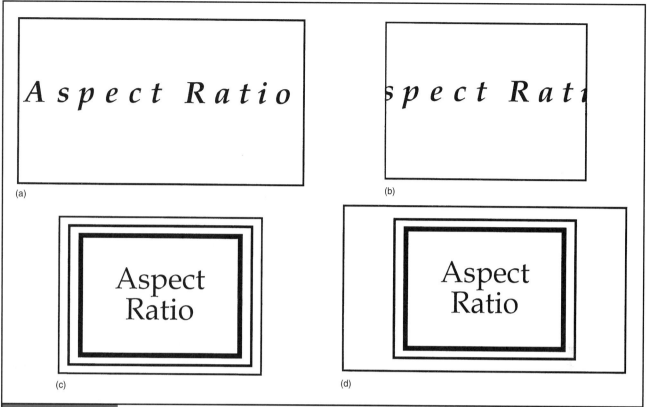

(a)

(b)

(c)

(d)

Figure 8.13

When graphics designed for one aspect ratio are viewed in a different aspect ratio, problems can result. Illustration (a) shows a graphic produced for use in 16:9, while (b) shows that graphic viewed on a 4:3 television screen (only the text "pect Rat" will be visible). Similarly, a graphic produced for a 4:3 aspect ratio will have extra space on the vertical edges of the screen, as shown in (c) and (d).

Aspect Ratios

As discussed in Chapter 5, standard-definition and high-definition television systems have different **aspect ratios,** the ratio of width to height. In the standard-definition format, the aspect ratio is 4:3, while in most high-definition formats the ratio is 16:9. Graphics that are created for use on television, of course, must conform to the format's aspect ratio.

Graphics computers designed for use with only standard definition automatically produce graphics in the proper ratio, while graphics computers that are compatible with high definition can be set to the appropriate aspect ratio. During the transition from standard definition to high definition, however, producing graphics will be an additional challenge because they will have to look good in *both* formats. This leads to what some people jokingly call the "pect rat" problem,

as shown in Figure 8.13, when graphics designed for one aspect ratio are viewed in a different aspect ratio. The best advice is to design your graphics for the ratio in which they will most often be viewed; there is really no simple solution to the problems created by multiple aspect ratios.

8.4 Other Graphics

Sometimes it is necessary to use graphics that are not created by a computer—an award-winning photograph, a map of the world that you want to show in its entirety and then zoom in on Egypt, a page from an old manuscript. These types of graphics must be shot using a camera, but you can do several things to be sure that they will look good on television.

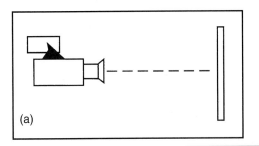

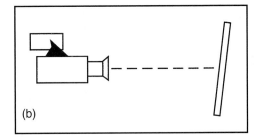

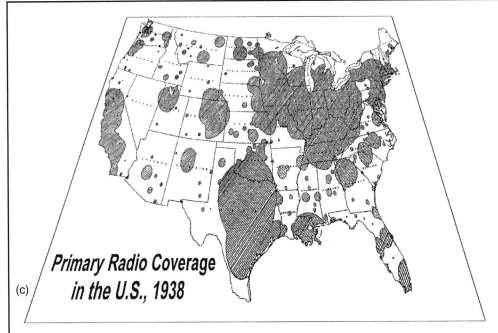

Primary Radio Coverage in the U.S., 1938

Figure 8.14

When shooting graphics on-camera, always be sure the shooting angle is perpendicular to the surface of the graphic (*a*). If the angle is not perpendicular, as shown in (*b*), the resulting image will be distorted in a keystone effect (*c*).

Using Out-of-Aspect Graphics

Most times, you will find that the item you want to shoot is not in the proper aspect ratio for your production. The manuscript page will almost invariably be too tall, or the map will be too wide. However, you can still use an "improperly" shaped graphic on television by employing one or more of the following techniques: showing only part of the graphic; tilting the camera from the top to bottom or panning from the left to right side of the graphic; or mounting the graphic on a larger board that is the proper aspect ratio and showing borders around it.

Keystoning and Essential Area

No matter how you shoot a graphic, you should be sure that the shooting angle is exactly perpendicular to the surface of the graphic. As shown in Figure 8.14, if the angle is not perpendicular, the result will be **keystoning,** in which the appearance of the original graphic will be distorted. Of course, you can intentionally shoot off-angle if you wish to achieve keystoning for creative effect, but normally you should avoid this type of image distortion.

It is also important to keep in mind **essential area** when shooting graphics on camera. From the time you

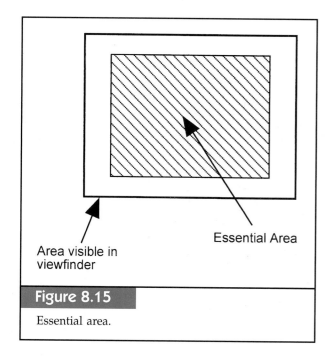

Area visible in
viewfinder

Essential Area

Figure 8.15

Essential area.

look at a graphic through the camera's viewfinder to the time it reaches the home viewer's set, up to 30 percent of the picture area around the outer edge of the screen may be lost. These losses occur due to alignment differences in studio monitors and television sets, the transmission of the picture from the television tower to the home set, and other electronic factors. Because of this, you should always keep crucial graphic information within the essential area, which is the area left after cropping 25 to 30 percent from around the edges of the screen, as shown in Figure 8.15. Although digital transmission means that less of the signal will be lost in this manner in high-definition formats, it is still an issue to keep in mind.

Many graphics computers automatically keep graphics within the essential area, and a number of cameras and studio monitors have markings on the screen to show the essential— "safe"—area. By keeping all of your important graphic information within the essential area of the screen, you can be sure that it will not be cut off on the home viewer's set.

8.5 Basics of Sets

Most studio productions need some sort of set. For some programs, such as sitcoms, the set is essential to create a locale and give actors some of the needed

elements for interaction. For others, such as dance programs, the set adds interest to the background and foreground and establishes a tone. For a news program the set creates interest but also has functional elements that allow videotape to appear beside the anchors and storm patterns to be seen behind the weathercaster.

Although most sets are made from physical materials, such as metal, plastic, or wood, some organizations use **virtual sets** that are "built" in a computer and do not actually exist. Sometimes a set may be partially virtual and partially physical.

8.6 Virtual Sets

When a virtual set is used, the performers are shot against a blank background and the set is inserted electronically. The procedure resembles **chroma keying** discussed in Chapter 9, but it is more to be sophisticated and complex. A virtual set can be three-dimensional, with articles placed in front of and behind the actors. Its perspective changes as the camera moves so that set pieces can look natural and consistent from any angle.

A wide variety of basic sets are available as software programs from a number of companies that have entered the virtual set business.[3] Many of these sets can be customized (colors changed, logos added) by using techniques similar to those used for graphics or other computer applications. Some of the software requires that the production be shot against a blue screen. As the show is being taped or aired, the blue drops out and the computer-generated set replaces it. For other systems, the action takes place in front of a portable gray screen. The blue comes from a ring of blue lights that attach around the camera lens and project onto the screen. The color bounces back directly into the camera lens at a carefully controlled angle that allows for a keying effect. Each camera is equipped with a tracking mechanism that communicates positional data to the virtual set computer program in order to generate the correct set position. A computer interface controls switching from one camera to another.

Sometimes only part of a set is virtual. For example, the walls of a set may be real, but the ceiling is

Figure 8.16

A virtual set. The table is real but all the other set elements are computer generated. *Photo courtesy of Orad.*

Figure 8.17

This is a permanent news set for CBS, New York, that was built by an independent company, Broadcast Design International, Inc. The company designs and builds more than 30 projects a year, so it behooves it to have the latest software and equipment. *Photo courtesy of Broadcast Design International, Inc., Carlsbad, CA.*

added virtually for the few shots where the camera shoots with an upward angle. (See Figure 8.16.) Virtual elements are often used for advertised products—for example, a sign for Coke that appears behind first base on your TV set even though it isn't really there at the ball park.

The virtual set concept is fairly new and has not become hugely successful. It requires a substantial initial financial investment, and, if the system crashes, there suddenly is no set at all. A show involving an audience would find it awkward to use a virtual set because the audience wouldn't see any background. But virtual sets work well for a small studio that produces a lot of different programs that all need different sets, and they are effective for abstract material, such as music videos, with numerous background changes.

8.7 Physical Sets

The physical sets that are made of plastic, wood, metal, and other materials are still the most common. Designing, constructing, assembling, and storing them is a study in and of itself. It requires carpentry, metalworking, and artistic skills beyond the scope of this book. All we can do is touch on some of the basic elements

students are likely to encounter in their universities and in their jobs after they graduate.[4]

Permanent Sets

Many modern-day production facilities place a set in a studio and leave it there for a long time. For example, a TV station or network that produces news every day would find it cumbersome and inefficient to put the news set up and down each day. Rather, the production facility obtains a set and leaves it in the studio day after day. (See Figure 8.17.) These sets need to be durable and can be constructed of heavy, structurally sound elements because they will not be moved. If a station produces little besides news, it probably will not have a crew of people who build and install sets. The station instead hires an outside company that might build sets for a number of purposes—other TV stations, movies, amusement parks, restaurants—to build and install a new set when it needs one. (See Figure 8.18.) These companies use computer programs to design the sets, and often some of their equipment interacts with the computer programs. For example, a saw can be

This large scene shop undertakes work for a large number of entertainment companies and events. It includes woodworking, metalworking, painting, sculpturing, prop construction, and so on.   *Photo courtesy of Lexington Scenery and Props, Sun Valley, CA.*

connected to computer information so that it saws wood to the exact measurements designed for the set.[5] (See Figure 8.19.)

Many types of recurring productions, such as talk shows and game shows, use these semipermanent sets. Sitcoms and soap operas also have some rather permanent sets where a lot of action takes place in many episodes, but occasionally they need special temporary sets for some particular twist of the plot.

Universities may have a permanent set, especially if they produce a regular newscast. Although a university may not have enough money to hire a company to build a set, they can sometimes obtain hand-me-down news sets from a local station that has decided to change to a new set and is willing to donate its old set to the university. But usually, in a college, sets are put up and taken down to fit the needs of varying student productions.

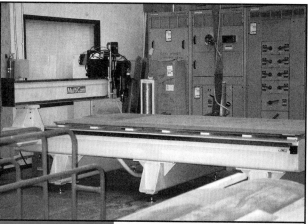

Figure 8.19

This is a computer-operated machine that takes dimensions for sets that are designed with a computer program and then activates dimensions to cut material (wood, metal, foam) to the appropriate size needed for the set piece.   *Photo courtesy of Lexington Scenery and Props, Sun Valley, CA.*

Removable Sets

Sets that need to be changed often must also be carefully designed. Computer programs are a great asset to design, but, as a student, you may not have access to them. Instead, you can draw a **floor plan** of your studio. (See Figure 8.20.) A typical studio staging floor plan includes the placement of all set pieces and the exact location of all stage props and furniture. It is important that all flats and furniture be drawn to exact scale; otherwise the director's shooting angles, the talent's movement, and the lighting design will all be off.

A floor plan should be prepared with as much detail and precision as possible.

Sets meant to be removed need to be of lighter-weight material than permanent sets and need to be constructed in small enough pieces that people can carry them. One of the basic set units for such a purpose is the **flat.** It is a cross-braced wood or metal frame faced with either canvas (which is lightweight but too flimsy for repeated heavy use) or thin pressed board or plywood (which will take more abuse, although it is heavier to work with). The layout for a

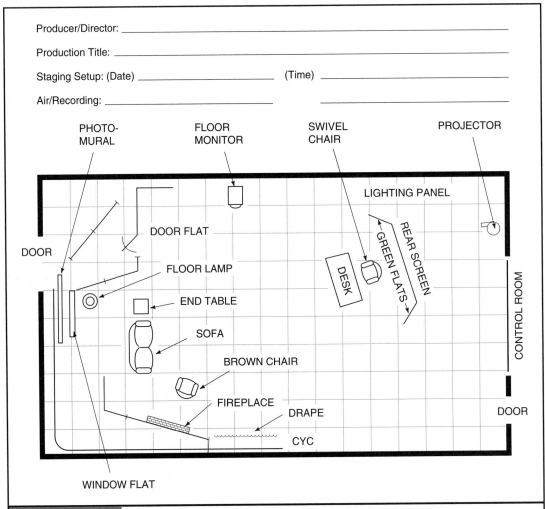

| Producer/Director: |
| Production Title: |
| Staging Setup: (Date) _____ (Time) _____ |
| Air/Recording: |

PHOTO-MURAL · FLOOR MONITOR · SWIVEL CHAIR · PROJECTOR · LIGHTING PANEL · DOOR FLAT · DOOR · REAR SCREEN · GREEN FLATS · DESK · CONTROL ROOM · FLOOR LAMP · END TABLE · SOFA · BROWN CHAIR · FIREPLACE · DRAPE · DOOR · CYC · WINDOW FLAT

Figure 8.20

Sample staging floor plan. In this floor plan, the squares on the floor correspond to three-foot tiles actually laid on the studio floor. In other floor plans, a lighting grid or pipe battens might be superimposed over the studio layout.

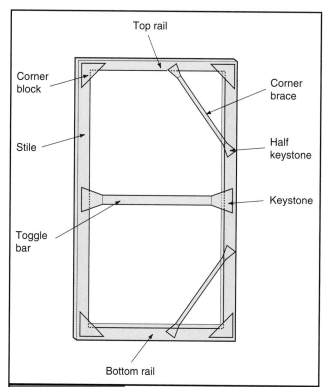

Figure 8.21

Construction of an ordinary flat. Standard construction of a simple flat consists of a frame made of $^3/_4''$ by 3" plywood strips with $^1/_4''$ plywood for the corner blocks and keystones. The front of the frame is typically covered with canvas or with plywood (or pressed hardboard). If a solid wooden front covering is used, then the corner braces will not be needed.

(Figure labels: Top rail, Corner block, Corner brace, Stile, Half keystone, Keystone, Toggle bar, Bottom rail)

standard flat is shown in Figure 8.21. Common heights are 10 feet for larger studios with very high ceilings and 8 feet for smaller studios with lower ceilings. Widths are seldom broader than five feet (the width that one person can comfortably handle with arms outstretched). Often the fronts of flats are painted to look like whatever is needed for the production—a storefront, a child's bedroom, a garden. (See Figure 8.22.) In addition to standard flats, studios use other rigid but lightweight materials, such as foam and corrugated feather board, to construct removable scenic elements. (See Figure 8.23.)

Sometimes it is necessary to construct something more substantial even though it is going to be temporary. For example, a flat with a door through which

people are going to enter and exit must be quite strong so that it looks realistic and doesn't wobble (or fall down) when someone slams it. Stairways, platforms, and such require heavy bracing and sturdy framing for the amount of abuse and wear to which they will be subjected. (See Figure 8.24.)

Constructing and setting up removable sets can be difficult. Usually they are constructed somewhere away from the studio, such as a nearby scene shop, where the necessary tools are available. Students in university TV courses sometimes avail themselves of the same facilities used to construct sets for theater productions. At a specified time, shortly before production, the set must be brought to the studio and assembled for use. Flats need to be braced in some way so they do not fall over. One of the most common braces is a **jack,** which is a hinged triangle usually made of wood. When the flat is in place, the jack is swung out behind the flat at a right angle and held in place with stage weights or **sandbags.** (See Figure 8.25.) When flats or other set pieces must be joined together, it is usually done with power tools that can be used to shoot staples or removable nails through one piece of scenery and into another.

After the sets are used, they are usually stored away somewhere because they can be used, with a

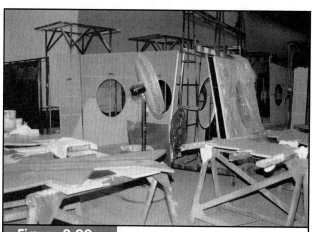

Figure 8.22

Flats that have been painted and are sitting on racks to dry. Note that very little of the flat touches the rack. *Photo courtesy of Lexington Scenery and Props, Sun Valley, CA.*

few modifications, for another show. For example, a flat that was used as a storefront can be repainted to look like a garden rather than starting from scratch and building a whole new flat. In many small stations and educational institutions, scenery storage can be a serious problem. There is never enough room to house everything that is needed, and scenery storage always seems to be one area that suffers the most. Flats and other narrow units are usually stored in racks, which are simple frames designed to hold a number of flats in an upright position. Each rack can be designed and labeled to hold similarly matched scenic units (for example, living-room flats, office flats, green-speckled flats, log-cabin flats, etc.).

Sets constructed for standard-definition television have been able to be rather shoddy looking. Scratches or chipped paint or fake books looked fine because the camera did not pick up imperfections. However, this is changing for some high-definition programs. Because of the sharper resolution, elements of the set that are going to be in sharp focus during production must be constructed to more accurately depict details and must be stored carefully so they are not damaged.

Cloth Backgrounds

Some studios use cloth backdrops, either **cycloramas (cycs)** or drapes. These can be instead of or in addition to physical sets. Cycs are made of canvas, duck, or gauze (depending on the desired texture and reflectance quality desired) and are generally designed to be stretched taut over piping and weighted down. They give a smooth limbo background, or they can be painted to fit a particular need. A neutral gray is preferable. Seams should be vertical, not horizontal. (See Figure 8.26.)

Drapes, which are usually of a heavier material and often darker, can be either pulled taut or pleated, depending on the desired effect. Darker, low-reflectance drapes are effective backing for **cameo lighting** (see Chapter 6). Drapes are usually used in smaller widths than a cyc and can ordinarily be easily rigged or hung for specific applications. A cyc, on the other hand, is often permanently mounted, covering two or even three walls of a studio.

Figure 8.23

A scenery element being carved from foam.
Photo courtesy of Lexington Scenery and Props, Sun Valley, CA.

8.8 | Furniture, Set Dressings, and Props

Most of the time a set will also consist of furniture—the chairs for talk-show guests, the podium for a game-show host, the porch swing for a soap opera. Sometimes these elements need to be specially constructed, but often they can be bought at used-furniture stores or borrowed from someone's apartment. Several types of furniture create problems on TV, however.

One is the *swinging swivel chair*, in which guests vent their nervous energy by rotating back and forth. Another is the *precarious perch*, in which talent must sit uncomfortably on top of a high, hard stool. And a

(a)

(b)

Figure 8.24

Two approaches to designing part of an airplane to be used as a removable but sturdy set piece. The first (*a*) shows a metal frame to be used to construct the fuselage. The second (*b*) is a section of an airplane fuselage that shows construction that is typical of specialized set pieces. *Photo* (a) *courtesy of Lexington Scenery and Props, Sun Valley, CA. Photo* (b) *courtesy of Universal Studios, Universal City, CA.*

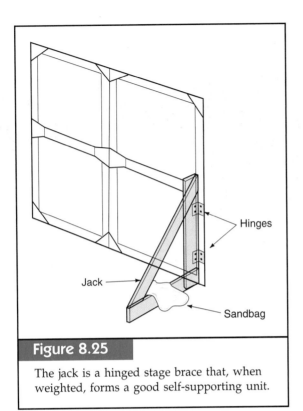

Figure 8.25

The jack is a hinged stage brace that, when weighted, forms a good self-supporting unit.

Figure 8.26

A canvas backdrop painted to serve as a street-front scene. *Photo courtesy of Universal Studios, Universal City, CA.*

third is the *talent swallower,* overstuffed chairs and sofas that are so plush and soft that the person sinks down so far the director is left with nothing but a shot of the knees.

You must also take set dressings and props into account when designing and constructing sets. A **prop** is something that is actually used during the production—the toy the clown gives to a child, the vase someone throws in anger, the book someone reads. **Set dressings** are not actually used but add to the interest or atmosphere of the production—toys that indicate that children live in the house, a vase of wilted flowers, books that litter the sofa. Again, you may need to construct some of these from scratch while others are readily available—sometimes set dressings and props can be rented from a furniture store.

If props need to be in a precise place, their location is often marked in some way (a piece of tape on the floor, an inconspicuous chalk mark on a sofa). In that way they can quickly be placed in their proper position after they have been used and moved during a rehearsal.

Props and other small items can be stored on deep shelves in the storage area. It is important that each shelf and/or cubicle be clearly labeled: "telephones," "dishes," "bottles," and so on. Even furniture and large stage props can be stored in multitiered shelves. Large overstuffed chairs, sofas, and heavy tables can be stored on the floor level; medium-sized chairs and tables can be stored on another level (four to five feet off the floor); and lightweight chairs and stools and small appliances can be stored on a third level (perhaps seven to eight feet above the floor).

All set elements must be considered well ahead of the production date. This is similar to the preproduction discipline needed for other aspects of production. How long will it take to build and paint the flats? Will the furniture clash with the artwork hung on the walls? Are the colors of the game-show set bright enough? What types of magazines would the lead character be likely to have on the coffee table?

8.9 Sets and Other Production Elements

The whole set assembly process must take into account other aspects of the production such as camera movements, mic placement, lighting, and talent movement.

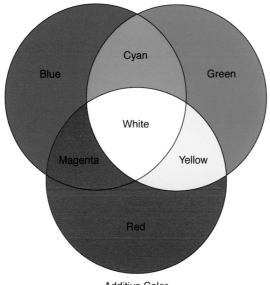

Additive Color

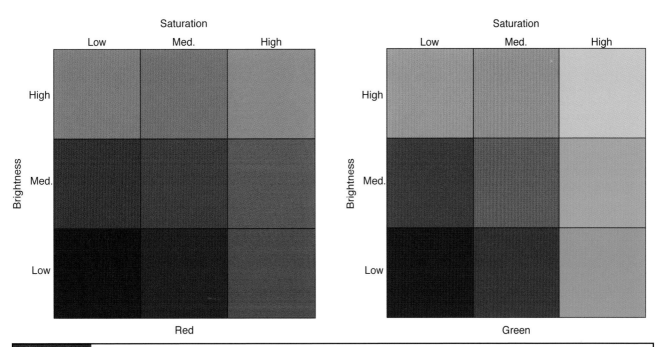

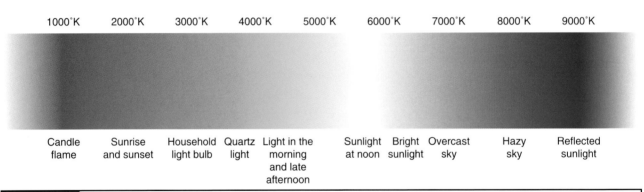

Visible light

Long-range military communications | AM radio | Shortwave | TV | Microwaves | Infrared rays | Ultraviolet rays | X rays | Gamma rays | Cosmic rays

Visible light

Plate C

Visible light is just a small part of the electromagnetic spectrum. The human eye perceives this part of the spectrum as various colors ranging from reds, through oranges, yellows, greens, and blues to purples.

1000°K 2000°K 3000°K 4000°K 5000°K 6000°K 7000°K 8000°K 9000°K

Candle flame | Sunrise and sunset | Household light bulb | Quartz light | Light in the morning and late afternoon | Sunlight at noon | Bright sunlight | Overcast sky | Hazy sky | Reflected sunlight

Plate D

This chart shows the color temperature of some common light sources.

(a)

(b)

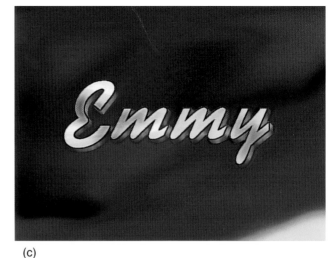

(c)

(d)

The process of animating this promotional graphic for the *Entertainment Tonight* program starts with the individual elements pictured here in examples (*a*) the basic ET logo, (*b*) the Emmy statue, and (*c*) the word *Emmy* (along with the additional word *special*). Each visual is taken from a storage disc or is specially designed on the day of production. When needed, each visual is then put on a line from the computer and fed to the switcher in the control room. A typical assembly would start with the live camera shot of anchor Mary Hart. Then, individually or grouped as with example (*d*), the visual elements come whizzing into the picture (along with sound effects) to complete the final graphic effect (*e*). *Courtesy of Entertainment Tonight.*

(e)

Readying everything for production involves cooperation from many crew members.

Camera Movement

No matter what the set looks like, there must be provision for adequate camera movement. Several cameras will have to have free access from different angles in the setting. This usually poses no problems with settings that have few set units and very little furniture. A talk show with a desk and several chairs set against a cyc is easy for cameras to move around in. What creates problems are elaborate realistic settings with windows and doors and a great deal of furniture. For this reason, sets are usually constructed as just two-walled or three-walled sets. The open wall (the missing side of the set) is used for camera access. In three-walled sets, the walls do not have to be set at exactly 90 degrees; they can be left open at oblique angles so that the camera can have even more access. In some sets (occasionally a four-walled set may have to be used), it is possible to position cameras behind the flats or other scenic elements and shoot through a window, a doorway, a hole in the bookcase, or other camouflaged openings.

Microphone Placement

The setting also has to have provision for adequate microphone placement and movement. Although wireless microphones are increasingly used in studio drama scenes, soap operas, and situation comedies, there are many times when staging must be concerned with wired microphones. Sometimes microphone connectors are built into sets, particularly news desks where they can be easily hidden. Many productions use some sort of **perambulator, giraffe,** or **fishpole.** These mic holders can create shadow problems on the set (see Chapters 6 and 7).

If the lighting has not been carefully worked out with the precise boom placement in mind, there will be a strong possibility of unwanted shadows against the set. This could be more of a problem in a setting with a plain background than in a busy set that may make a shadow less noticeable. In most cases, however, either the mic boom or the lighting instrument will have to be repositioned somewhat, or the light will have to be barn-doored off the boom.

Lighting Instruments

Other lighting problems can be caused by certain kinds of set arrangements (see Chapter 6). Occasionally, pillars or other foreground set pieces may be blocking crucial front lighting from a certain angle. Sometimes a strong **key light** may throw a very distracting shadow on a close-up shot of some small object; or if the talent is lighted too closely to the set, the key light may throw too much illumination on the set. One of the most common problems, however, is the blocking of the **backlight** by a flat or other set element. If the flat is too high for the studio (a 10-foot flat might be too high if the studio has a low ceiling), if the flat is out too far into the studio from the backlight, or if the talent is standing too close to the flat, it is going to be difficult to hit the talent with the backlight. (See Figure 8.27.) In this

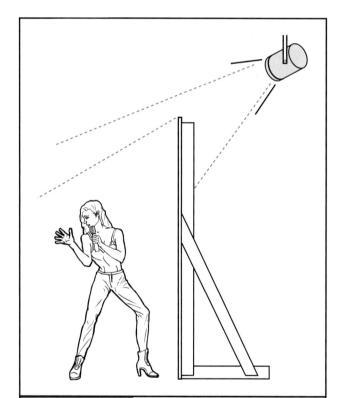

Figure 8.27

Backlighting problems with a scenic flat. In this kind of situation, either the backlight will have to be mounted higher, the light will have to be repositioned closer to the flat, the flat will have to be moved back (closer to the backlight), or the talent will have to move forward, farther away from the flat.

case, something—the backlight, the flat, or the talent—will have to be moved.

To minimize the problems between sets and lighting and make for ease of operation, large set pieces are put up before lights are positioned. However, furniture and set dressings are not put into place. This allows the lighting people to light according to the general placement of the sets without having to maneuver their ladders around pieces of furniture. Once the lighting ladders are put away, the set is dressed. Some minor lighting changes may then be made, but these adjustments can usually be made from the floor or with the aid of a small stepladder.

Talent Movement

Finally, the setting has to consider all anticipated movement by the talent. How much action is required? Will several people be moving in the same direction simultaneously? How much space is needed for certain movement (a fight in a bar)? Is the set large enough to accommodate all the talent moves without the cameras being in danger of shooting off the set? Is there plenty of room for all entrances and exits? Will the talent be forced to maneuver so close to the set walls that part of their lighting will be cut off? Or, if the performers work too close to the set, will they cast unwanted shadows?

Sets are an integral part of most productions. Whether they are virtual, permanent, or removable, they must be given careful consideration and they must blend appropriately in style and structure with the overall program.

Discussion Questions

1. What types of computer graphics systems does your school have? Do you have ESS capability? Are these capabilities achieved by one machine or more? What kinds of graphics effects discussed in this chapter could you do in your school's studio?

2. You are producing a historical documentary, and the local museum has a very fragile 500-year-old book that you need to shoot. The museum will not let you remove the book from the museum, and it can be very gently handled only by a museum employee wearing gloves. What plans can you make to get shots of the individual pages in the book, which include maps, scientific drawings, and ornate text?

3. Come up with a list of virtual sets that it would be wise for your school to have. Why did you select these particular sets? How could you modify them so you could use them more often?

4. Think through a basic talk show. What background set pieces would you want? Furniture? Set dressing?

Notes

1. Sometimes this person is called a CG operator because that was the original designation when lettering came from character generators only.

2. For more detail on graphics software, see "Graphics and Animation Leap Forward," *TV Technology*, 9 June 2003, 22–28.

3. Some of the companies offering virtual set software are Photron USA (http://www.photron.com), Orad (http://www.orad.co.il), FOR-A (http://hydra.ro), Accom (http://www.accom.com), and Produzione TV (http://www.produzionetv.rai.it). See "Virtual Sets Get Real," *TV Technology*, 23 July 2003, 14–15.

4. For a full discussion of scenery construction and use, consult any good theater stagecraft text or manual, such as Paul Carter, *Backstage Handbook* (Louisville, KY: Broadway Press, 1994); or Jay Michael Gillette, *Theatrical Design and Production* (Mountain View, CA: Mayfield Publishing Co., 1987).

5. Autocad and 3D Studio Max are two of the programs used. In addition to helping with the design of the set, some computer programs allow you to "enter" a set and look at it from a number of different angles and also keep track of the supplies needed to construct the set, the cost, and what has been finished and still needs to be completed. When equipment for constructing a set can be tied to the design software, the software is said to be CAD/CAM (computer-assisted design/computer-assisted manufacturing).

CHAPTER 9

Video Switchers

It's no exaggeration to call the switcher the "heart" or "nerve center" of a modern video production facility. More than any other piece of equipment, the switcher is central to the creation of video programs of all types, and it is literally the connecting point for most other pieces of video equipment in a studio. Although switchers are also used in **postproduction** editing facilities, as you will see in Chapter 11, this chapter concentrates on the operation of the switcher in a studio production environment. The general operation of the switcher is the same in either situation.

The video switcher serves a number of different functions. First and foremost, it is an *editing* device that facilitates the time-ordered sequencing of inputs within a live or live-to-tape video production. To do this, the switcher serves a *channeling* or routing function as it selects a video source from all the available inputs, such as cameras, videotape machines, remote feeds, **graphics generators,** and computer-generated graphics. The switcher also functions as a *selecting and altering* component that can combine two or more visual sources in a number of different ways. Through the use of **digital video effects (DVE),** a switcher can become a **special effects generator (SEG)** with the capability of altering the appearance of video inputs.

The continuing conversion of television signals and equipment to **digital** is affecting switchers as well. Increasingly, switchers function fully in the digital domain, inputting and outputting digital **bitstreams,** performing digital effects, and even "talking to" other digital equipment such as **video servers, videotape recorders,** and computers. For the most part, however, this chapter does not differentiate between **analog** and digital switchers. Operationally, they are essentially the same, at least when it comes to the basic techniques described in this chapter. For the most part, it makes no difference to the switcher operator whether the signals coming into and going out of the switcher are analog or digital.

Despite the wide range of switcher types and levels of complexity, a few basic principles of design, function, and operation are common to all units. Once you understand these essential principles, you can more confidently approach the operation of the advanced switcher units found in professional production environments. This chapter is designed to help you understand these essential principles and the basic operation of video switchers.

The *disciplines* of switchers include understanding how they are connected to other equipment and the basic concepts of their design. This understanding will make the *techniques* of achieving various effects using a switcher much easier to grasp. This chapter covers the following topics:

- The basic configuration and design concepts of switchers (9.1)

- The types of buses found on switchers (9.2)

- The function of various buses found on switchers (9.2)

- Basic operating concepts of a typical switcher, including performing cuts, dissolves, wipes, and other effects (9.2–9.3)

- Advanced functions of switchers, including digital effects and the control of external equipment (9.4)

- Commands given by the director to the technical director operating the switcher (9.5)

9.1 Basic Types of Switchers

Figure 9.1 shows a simplified block diagram of how a switcher might be connected in a typical studio. As you can see, several video sources are connected as inputs to the switcher—in this case there are three cameras, two videotape recorders, and a graphics generator, which is used to put words and graphics on-screen. Usually all video sources in a studio will be run through the switcher, and in advanced settings these might include several cameras, tape machines, satellite feeds, digital storage devices, and various graphic computers.

The switcher shown in Figure 9.1 has two outputs. The **program line** is the main output—the one that goes over the air or is recorded to tape. A **program monitor** allows studio personnel to see the video signal that is being put out by the switcher. The **preview** line is a separate output that is used to set up video effects before they are put on the air. For example, you might want to see what a graphic placed over a camera shot looks like before it is actually put on the air; a **preview monitor** allows you to do this. In more-advanced facilities, a number of preview lines and monitors may be available to set up particular special effects.

Monitoring Multiple Signals

Video monitors in the control room are essential to the proper use of the switcher as well as for camera operations. Even a moderate-sized studio may contain up to a dozen different monitors, each performing an important individual function. Each studio camera, graphics generator, and video recorder, for example, will have a small (7- to 10-inch) individual monitor. In a live broadcasting situation, an **air monitor** always shows the actual broadcast picture, which is received over the air from the transmitter or other source.[1]

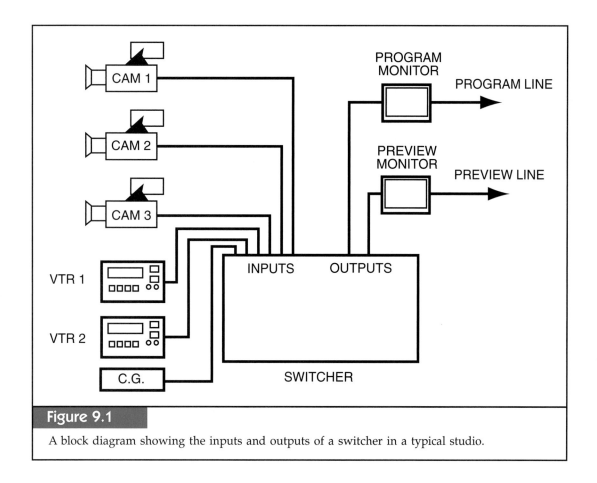

Figure 9.1

A block diagram showing the inputs and outputs of a switcher in a typical studio.

In an increasing number of production environments, both **standard-definition** and **high-definition** signals are being handled simultaneously. As discussed in Chapter 5, high-definition television formats use a 16:9 **aspect ratio,** meaning the screen is wider than standard definition. A number of switchers have the capability to process both 4:3 and 16:9 aspect ratio pictures simultaneously, or to convert one aspect ratio to another. This usually means even more monitors in the control room, as you must be able to see what the picture looks like in 4:3 *and* 16:9.

Even the depth and weight of monitors are changing. Traditionally, monitors have been very deep and heavy, because they have a very large, deep glass tube inside with an **electron gun** in back that shoots electrons to the front, making the phosphors on the screen glow. This process in essence re-creates the scanning sequence that produced the original image, as **transduced** by a camera, for example. It also makes for monitors that are large, heavy, and fragile. But several new technologies allow monitors to be much thinner

and lighter. One is **liquid crystal display (LCD),** made up of two transparent pads with crystal molecules between them that light up according to the voltage applied to them. The other technology is **plasma** screens, which are made up of two glass panels with gas between them. The gas activates colored dots according to the pattern of voltages applied to it. Although some purists prefer the picture of the traditional tube monitor, the newer technologies are continually improving and becoming a greater presence in production environments.

Digital technology is also making it possible for one monitor to display several different inputs at the same time. For example, instead of using four 10-inch monitors to show the shots of the three cameras in the studio and the graphics generator, these inputs could be combined onto one large monitor. Each input could be shown on a different quadrant of the screen, as shown in Figure 9.2. The large monitor takes up less space than the four individual ones, and it can be programmed to display different inputs as needed.

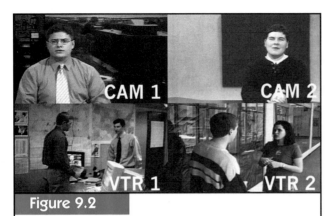

Figure 9.2

Digital monitors allow the inputs of four separate monitors to be combined into different quadrants of a single screen.

Portable and Computer-Based Switchers

Increasing digitization also has allowed switchers to be made smaller. Some manufacturers are now making so-called portable switchers, which can be transported and set up with relative ease. Creation Technologies' PIXBOX system even has the monitor functions built in to an onboard computer screen, as shown in Figure 9.3.

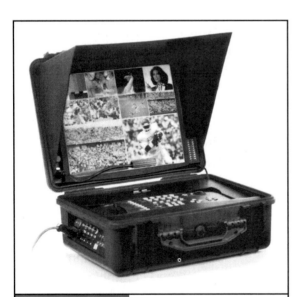

Figure 9.3

Creation Technologies' PIXBOX portable switcher includes a built-in computer screen that can function as several different studio monitors. *Photo Courtesy of Creation Technologies.*

When not in use, the switcher can be folded into a box about the size of a suitcase.

Another unique approach is NewTek's Video-Toaster, which the company calls a "TV studio-in-a-box." Based on a personal computer running a Windows operating system, the VideoToaster includes a switcher, digital effects, and graphics capabilities. Instead of physically pushing buttons, you operate the VideoToaster by "pressing" virtual buttons on a computer screen with your mouse. The VideoToaster's screen is set up to look like a traditional switcher, adding monitoring functions as well. Again, the system works much like any other switcher; you just interact with virtual buttons and controls instead of real ones.

Master Control and Routing Switchers

Less-sophisticated switchers are found in the **master control** area of television stations, where they are used to select various video sources such as network feeds, commercials, and studio output. Even simpler units, known as **routing switchers,** are used to distribute video sources within a studio. For example, a simple routing switcher may be used to select which video input is viewed on a particular studio monitor.

9.2 Basic Switcher Design

A video switcher, especially one as elaborate as the one shown in Figure 9.4, can be an intimidating-looking piece of equipment. There can be literally hundreds of buttons, dozens of knobs, several LED display readouts, and numerous other controls. It is well beyond the scope of this chapter to equip you to competently operate such an advanced switcher, but a number of design and operation principles are common to *all* switchers. Once you gain a basic understanding of how switchers are designed and the essential elements of how they are operated, then practice on simpler switchers, you will eventually be prepared to tackle advanced units. At that point, the sea of buttons, knobs, and levers will make a lot more sense to you and indeed will become familiar tools that you'll use routinely to achieve your production goals.

Figure 9.4

A high-end switcher's vast array of knobs, buttons, and other controls can be quite intimidating. However, it is not difficult to master any switcher once you've learned the basic operational techniques of a simple unit. *Photo Courtesy of Thomson Grass Valley.*

Buses

The main operational feature of any switcher is the rows of switches called **buses** or **banks.**[2] Each bus has one button for each video input, and additional buttons for other functions. Figure 9.5 shows a bus for the sample switcher shown in Figure 9.1. In addition to the video inputs, this sample bus also shows a **black** button used to select a fully synchronized black signal. Only one signal source per bus can be pressed down at a time since the buttons are mutually canceling—when one

button is pushed, the previously depressed button is automatically released. Therefore, each bus can have just one signal punched into it at any given moment.[3]

The number of buses, their functions, and their design vary from switcher to switcher. However, a few types of buses are common to most switchers. The first of these is the **program bus,** which selects the video input that will be put out over the program line. If we were to consider the sample bus shown in Figure 9.5 as the switcher's program bus, we could select video outputs by pressing the appropriate button on this bus. For example, if we want to have camera 1's output go over the program line, we would press the "Cam 1" button. To change the shot to camera 2, we would press the "Cam 2" button. The "Cam 1" button would then deselect, and camera 2's output would be seen on the program line. Changing from one shot to another is called performing a **transition.** The simplest type of transition, as just illustrated, is the **cut,** which instantaneously replaces one picture with another.

Using the Preset Bus

To perform a transition other than a cut, we need to add one or more additional buses and have a method to gradually move between the buses. This is because any transition other than a cut will have a certain duration, or speed at which it occurs. Thus, we need to have a way of controlling that duration, in effect determining how long the transition will take. Cuts, which happen instantaneously, effectively have no duration.

Figure 9.6 shows a new bus added to our sample switcher and a **fader bar** we use to transition from one bus selection to the other. The program bus still determines the video source that is going out over the program line, but now we use the **preset bus** to select the *next* video input. The preset bus also normally has its own video monitor, meaning that the operator can

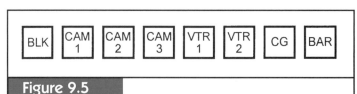

Figure 9.5

A bus as it might appear on the switcher illustrated in Figure 9.1

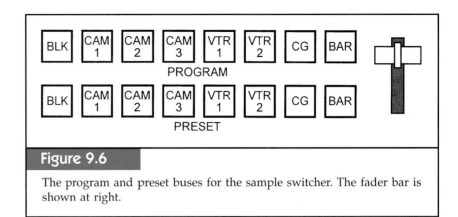

Figure 9.6

The program and preset buses for the sample switcher. The fader bar is shown at right.

see (preview) the input selected on the preset bus before it is actually put on the air.

The use of two or more separate buses allows us to perform transitions such as **dissolves**—in which one picture gradually fades into another—**wipes,** and advanced effects; the specific transition is determined by selecting the appropriate controls elsewhere on the switcher. Wipes and advanced effects are discussed later in this chapter, but for now let's assume that we want to perform a dissolve.

The simplest type of dissolve is a **fade-in** from black signal to a video input, commonly used at the beginning of a program. For example, let's say we want

to begin on black signal, then fade in to camera 1. We set up our buses as shown in Figure 9.7(a): We place the fader bar in the fully downward position, select "Black" on the program bus, and "Cam 1" on the preset bus. As set up in this manner, we will see black signal over the program line. When we move the fader bar upward, the input selected on the preset bus gradually fades in, eventually completely replacing the original signal on the program bus. At completion, as shown in Figure 9.7(b), "Cam 1" is selected on the program bus, and camera 1's signal is now seen on the program line. The speed at which we move the fader bar determines the duration of the dissolve between buses.

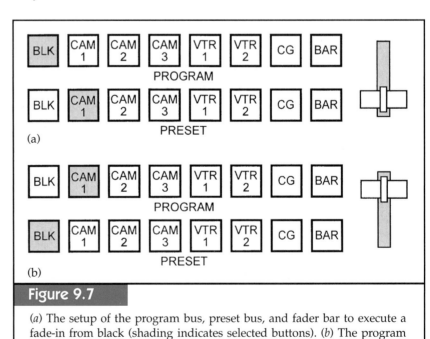

Figure 9.7

(*a*) The setup of the program bus, preset bus, and fader bar to execute a fade-in from black (shading indicates selected buttons). (*b*) The program bus, preset bus, and fader bar after execution of the fade-in from black.

We can still perform cuts by simply pressing other buttons on the program bus. For example, we could cut to camera 2, then camera 3, then back to camera 1 by appropriately pressing the buttons on the program bus. If, in the middle of the program, we want to dissolve from camera 2 to camera 3, we simply press "Cam 3" on the preset bus ("Cam 2" will already be selected on the program bus, since it is currently on-air), then move the fader bar back down to perform the dissolve.

It is important to point out that on switchers that use preset buses, the *physical* position of the fader bar does not correspond to which bus is selected. For example, just because the fader bar is in the down position, it does not mean that the preset bus selection is currently on-air. The program bus is *always* on-air, and moving the fader bar—whether down to up or up to down—always replaces the program bus input with the preset bus input. It also—as you can see in Figure 9.7(b)—replaces the preset bus selection with the previous selection on the program bus. Thus, the fader bar essentially "flip-flops" the program and preset bus selections.

We can **fade out** to black at the end of the program much like we performed the fade-in from black. To do this, we would simply select "Black" on the preset bus, then move the fader bar to its opposite position. On our program monitor, we would see the picture gradually fade to black, the duration of the fade determined by how quickly we moved the fader bar.

If in the process of performing a dissolve between video inputs we simply stop the fader bar at its midpoint, we end up with a **superimposition,** or **super.** This is simply two pictures that are blended together. You have probably seen this effect in live musical performances, where, for instance, a close-up of a guitar player's hand is blended with a wider shot. We can "hold" the super as long as we wish by simply leaving the fader bar at midpoint.

Wipes

In making a transition between two consecutive pictures, there are times when neither the cut nor the dissolve is suitable. An example might be if you want to draw special attention to a picture or series of pictures. The wipe transition often accomplishes this

perfectly—by letting the viewer see portions of both pictures as the separation line moves through the screen. Used excessively, the wipe calls attention to itself as a gimmick, but when used with discretion, it can become an important part of your visual vocabulary.

Many switchers have dozens of patterned wipe designs—ranging from the traditional vertical line moving horizontally across the screen (or the horizontal line moving vertically down the screen) to diagonals, diamonds, circles, and boxes, to the jagged shark-tooth effect, which is the cliché of the late-night horror-movie show. Most switchers also have at least some capability to create and manipulate the borders, or edges, that appear between wipe effects. These borders can be made different colors and thicknesses and also can be set as either "hard" (creating a sharp delineation between the border and the video) or "soft" (where the border fades into the video).

Wipe transitions are performed just like dissolves; it is, as noted in the previous section, simply a matter of selecting a wipe instead of a dissolve by pressing the appropriate button on the switcher, as will be discussed later.

Just as dissolves can be halted at midpoint to create superimpositions, wipes also can be halted at midpoint to create a number of effects. One common application of a "suspended" wipe transition, the **split screen,** combines two pictures with either a horizontal or vertical (or occasionally diagonal) line separating the screen into two distinct areas—with a different picture (from separate cameras or other video sources) in each part of the screen, as shown in Figure 9.8. By positioning the fader bar, the relative sizes of the two pictures can be adjusted.

It also is possible to create a **corner insert,** which places the inserted camera picture in any quadrant of the screen, as shown in Figure 9.9 Again, the exact size and proportion of the corner insert can be adjusted by using the fader bar. Another useful special effect is the **spotlight,** which enables the operator to dim the entire screen except for one circle of light that can be shaped, changed in size, and positioned anywhere on the screen with a joystick.

Figure 9.8

A split-screen effect between two cameras produced using a wipe halted at midpoint.

Keys

We have already discussed how a suspended dissolve can create a superimposition that blends two separate video sources. A key effect also blends two or more sources but actually "cuts out" part of one source and replaces it with another source.[4] In this way, both sources are able to maintain their brightness level, unlike the superimposition that actually weakens the level of both sources. Keys are most often used to place

Figure 9.9

A corner insert effect produced using a wipe transition halted at midpoint.

lettering or graphics "over" a video signal; in reality, the switcher "cuts a hole" in the video signal and inserts the lettering (from a separate video source) into it. Figure 9.10 illustrates the difference between a super and a key.

The example shown on the right in Figure 9.10 is called a **self key** (also known as a **luminance key** or **internal key**) because the dominant brightness level of the lettering cuts its own electronic pattern in the background picture. However, in many such effects, a wipe pattern is used to create the outline shape, and a third source is used as an input to fill the hole with another picture. Another version of this three-source effect, known as an **auto key** or **external key,** uses one video source to establish the external shape of a letter or figure—in effect, stamping out an image much like a stencil might cut out a shape. The key effect then uses a third source to fill in the picture and color of the "stenciled-out" part of the design.

Keys can be created in a manner similar to dissolves and wipes. For example, you could select a "key" effect on one of the buses, then set up the appropriate video inputs. Some switchers have one or more dedicated **key buses** that are used to select key backgrounds and overlays. Switchers equipped with **downstream keyers** actually perform the key effect *after* the signal has gone through all other effects, thus saving other buses for more-advanced effects.

Chroma key is a process in which a specific color—rather than a graphic design or pattern—is used as the electronic key to cut out part of the picture. Any color can be designated as the key color; however, blue or green is most often used because it is farthest from any skin tones. Wherever the foreground or key camera detects the designated **hue** (and **brightness**) in its picture, that video information is discarded and background picture signals are supplied from a second source such as a graphics unit, camera, or VTR.

Probably the most common example of this process is seen nightly on the local weathercast. The studio camera has a shot of the weathercaster standing in front of a blue background (but not wearing any blue item of clothing), as shown in Figure 9.11(a). Through the switcher, this picture is combined with the computer-generated local or national weather map that includes cloud movement and other animated

Figure 9.10

Two monitors illustrate the difference between a super and a key. The left-hand monitor shows white lettering from a graphics generator supered over the woman's face. The brightness level of each source is diminished as the two pictures are "blended" together. The right-hand monitor shows the same lettering keyed over the woman's face. In this case both sources maintain their brightness levels—the lettering is in effect cutting a hole in the picture of the woman's face.

effects. As seen on the home set in Figure 9.11(b), the result gives the impression that the weathercaster is standing in front of a map. Much of the effect's success, of course, depends on the weathercaster's skill in pointing out specific areas on the blank wall through the use of monitors not seen by the audience.

Although the use of chroma key is widespread, it is not without potential difficulties. The electronic equipment has to be adjusted delicately; lighting of the color background of the key camera has to be perfectly even. Considerable attention must be given to selection of costumes and scenery. Slight problems in any of these areas lead to troubles such as "tearing" of the foreground image, an obvious border around the foreground figure, discoloration, or indistinct contours. Many of these drawbacks have been overcome by newer systems, such as Ultimatte,[5] which has supplanted or replaced chroma key in most major professional studios. These advanced systems don't actually cut out the part of the picture colored blue or green but rather blend the second video source with the first. The level of blending is determined by the intensity of the background color—this makes it possible, for example, to use smoke effects or translucent objects in the foreground video source.

Mix and Preview Buses

Many switchers have additional buses, called **mix buses** or **mix/effects** (**M/E**) buses, to facilitate dissolves, wipes, and other effects. Mix buses are actually sets of two buses on which transitions or effects can be set up in advance, then selected on the program bus. The necessity of such buses becomes apparent when you think about the limitations of the sample program/preset bus switcher we have been using as an example. Using this switcher, there is no way to go directly from a shot on camera 3 to a corner insert effect or split-screen effect using cameras 1 and 2. Our only choice would be to start on camera 3, select camera 2 on the program bus, then quickly set

(a)

(b)

Figure 9.11

(*a*) Like most weathercasters, KABC-TV's Johnny Mountain actually works against a blank blue or green screen. The orientation of hand movements and visuals is done through the use of monitors to his left and right. (*b*) The computer-generated map and other animated effects are chroma-keyed through the switcher to produce the visual effect seen on the televised picture. *Photos courtesy of KABC-TV.*

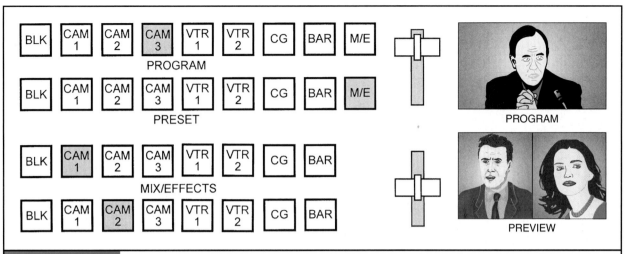

Figure 9.12

The use of a mix/effects bus to set up a split-screen effect. A mix/effects bus has been added to the sample switcher, along with buttons to select the mix/effects bus on the program and preset buses. Selecting the mix/effects bus on the preset bus as shown allows the operator to see the effect on the preset monitor before it airs.

up the corner effect on-air; we would have no way of setting up the effect before it went out on-air. Obviously, this would look sloppy and would be confusing to the viewer.

Mix buses not only allow us to set up effects in advance, then seamlessly put them on the air, they also allow us to see what the effect will look like before it is put on the air. This is normally accomplished through the use of one or more preview lines, discussed at the beginning of this chapter. On these preview lines (connected to video monitors), we can see an effect without putting it on the air. Depending on the switcher, each mix bus may have its own preview line, or the preview function may be facilitated by using a **preview bus** that allows us to select the input(s) we want to preview. On some switchers, the preset and preview buses are combined into a single bus—thus the input selected there will replace the input currently on the program bus when we move the fader bar, and we will be able to preview that input before putting it on the air.

Figure 9.12 shows a mix bus added to our sample switcher and the various buses set up to prepare for a split-screen effect. Camera 3 is on the air now, as its input is selected on the program bus, and we can see it on the program monitor. The effect is ready to go on

the M/E bus, as we have selected camera 1 on the top row, camera 2 on the bottom row, and moved the M/E bus's fader bar to a midpoint position. Although not shown in the diagram, we have selected a horizontal wipe transition for the M/E bus. We have selected "M/E" (mix/effects) on the preset/preview bus, because the next thing we want to see on-air is the effect from the M/E bus. This also allows us to see what the effect will look like on the preview monitor.

When we're ready, we can put the effect on the air by pressing the "M/E" button on the program bus, cutting from camera 3 to the split-screen effect as shown in Figure 9.13. The program monitor now shows the effect from the M/E bus, and the preview monitor still shows it as well since we have not taken the effect off the preset/preview bus.

If we want to dissolve to the split-screen effect instead of cut, we can do so by selecting a dissolve transition between the program and preset/preview buses, then moving the main fader bar to its opposite position, as shown in Figure 9.14. By comparing 9.13 and 9.14, you see that the end result is much the same, with the exception that the fader bar is now in the opposite position and the program and preset/preview buses have "flip-flopped" in Figure 9.14. We now see the input from camera 3 on the preview monitor. There was

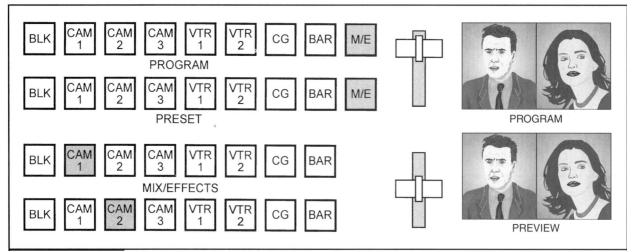

Figure 9.13

The use of a mix/effects bus to set up a split-screen effect. Selecting mix/effects on the program bus puts the split-screen effect on-air.

no flip-flop in Figure 9.13 because we selected the M/E input directly on the program bus.

9.3 Operational Techniques of Video Switchers

Now that we have discussed some of the general principles of how video switchers are designed and operated, we can move on to some actual operational examples. To do this, we will use a relatively simple production switcher, as shown in Figure 9.15. It is similar in its basic design to switchers you might find in a variety of production environments.

Switcher Overview

A careful look at Figure 9.15 shows that this particular switcher uses a program and combined preset/preview bus design, similar to our sample switcher discussed in the last section. It also has a key bus, located above the

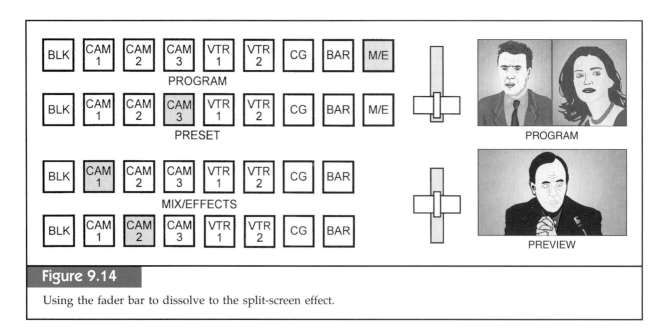

Figure 9.14

Using the fader bar to dissolve to the split-screen effect.

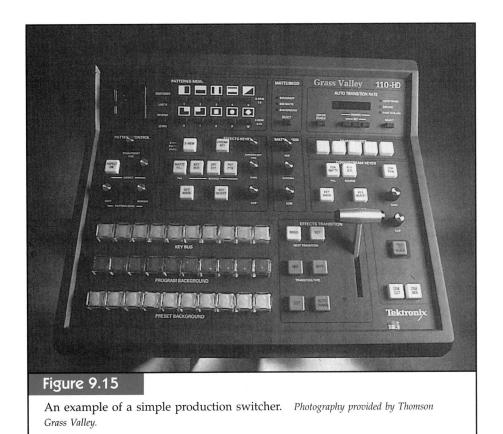

Figure 9.15

An example of a simple production switcher. *Photography provided by Thomson Grass Valley.*

program bus. The switcher can accept up to eight video inputs in addition to black and color bars; you will notice that each bus, then, has a total of 10 buttons. To the immediate right of the three buses is the fader bar, along with several controls for selecting transition type. The downstream keyer controls wrap around the fader bar, above it and to the right. In the middle of the switcher above the key bus are controls for performing other types of key effects, as well as controls for creating background colors.

The wipe controls are located in the upper-left corner of the switcher, including a joystick to position "spotlight" and other wipes. Finally, at the upper right of the switcher are the auto transition controls, which allow the operator to set the switcher to perform automatic transitions of a desired length.

Performing Dissolves

Let's follow an example of a simple dissolve from camera 1 to camera 2. We would first go to the transition section shown at the right-hand side of Figure 9.16 and press the "mix" button just above transition type, be-

cause with a dissolve we will be mixing two signals together. We also press the background ("bkgd") button above the next transition section of the effects transition group of controls. (We will look at this in more detail later.) Next, with the fader lever in the upper position, we press the camera 1 button on the upper program bank and the camera 2 button on the lower

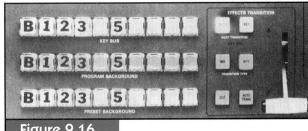

Figure 9.16

Operating buses of the sample switcher. The "transition control section" is composed of the individual buttons on each bank for input selection and the fader arm for dissolves and effects. *Photography provided by Thomson Grass Valley.*

preset bank. The camera 1 button on the program bank will glow brightly with what is called *high tally;* this reinforces what our program monitor tells us—that we are feeding a camera 1 signal on the program line. The camera 2 button on the preset bank glows with a softer intensity called a *low tally;* this indicates that camera 2 is selected to be the next camera on the air.

Fader Movement

As we begin to move the fader downward, we will see a green arrow glow at the place where the fader arm will be when we have completed the dissolve to camera 2. (This reinforcement of the direction of our lever move is important in more complex operations.) As we continue the fader movement downward, both the camera 1 and the camera 2 buttons glow brightly as both cameras are seen briefly on the program monitor (a momentary superimposition) during the dissolve.

As the dissolve is completed and the fader lever makes contact at the lower position, we have put camera 2 on the air, and we see camera 2 on the program line monitor. The upper program bank now shows its camera 2 button glowing brightly (high tally); on the lower preset bank, the camera 1 button (the camera from which we have just dissolved) is now glowing dimly (low tally).

Automatic Transitions

If we want a dissolve lasting exactly two seconds, we can use the automatic transition feature of the switcher and not use the fader levers at all. We start out by having the program and preset buses set up exactly as in the beginning of the previous example, with the fader bar in the upper position. (Remember, we could just as well have started with it in the lower position.) We then use the auto transition rate controls at the upper right-hand corner of the unit. (See Figure 9.17.) In this case, we will assume that we are working in a video format using 30 frames per second, and so we would set the transition rate to 60 frames.

In this same group of controls, we would use the "select" button to move the indicator light to the "auto trans" position. The mix button for the "transition type" and the "bkgd" button for the next transition are still pressed. (See Figure 9.16.) By pressing the "auto trans" button, we achieve a perfect two-second dissolve from camera 1 to camera 2. The fader bar is

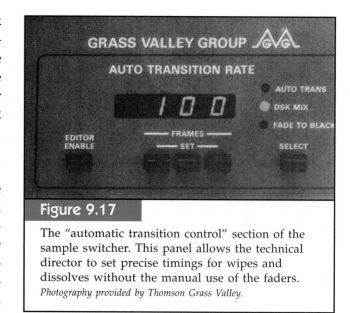

Figure 9.17

The "automatic transition control" section of the sample switcher. This panel allows the technical director to set precise timings for wipes and dissolves without the manual use of the faders.
Photography provided by Thomson Grass Valley.

not moved, although it can be used to override the automatic dissolve at any time.

For an instantaneous cut between cameras 1 and 2, we would only have had to press the "cut" button (right next to the auto trans button) instead of the auto trans button itself.

Execution of the Wipe Transition

The method of handling the patterned wipe transition is not too difficult once you understand the basics of the dissolve transition. We first need to push the "wipe" button for transition type next to the fader bar (see Figure 9.16), canceling the "mix" transition button. On the pattern control section of the switcher (see Figure 9.18), the "select" button (under the pattern with a confirming light) determines the basic shape of the wipe. Keep in mind that the new video from the preset camera will appear in the *white* area of the pattern shown on the button. With the center circle wipe (the fourth wipe from the left in the bottom row of patterns), the new picture will emerge on the screen as a circle in the middle of the picture; its image will be widened by the movement of the fader bar.

Selecting the "reverse" button causes the *black* area of the pattern to represent the new input. Other controls allow for changes in position and shape of the circle or other selected design. You also can adjust the appearance of the edge of the wipe and the width of

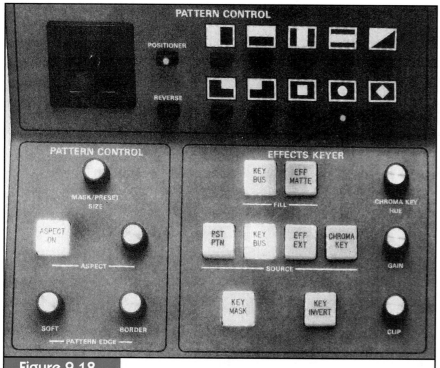

The "pattern control" section of the sample switcher. The pattern control buttons allow the switcher operator to select specific patterns for wipes and inserts. It also has controls that can further position and shape the patterns.   *Photography provided by Thomson Grass Valley.*

the border between the two video source pictures. The auto transition feature discussed previously can be used for the execution of wipes as well as for dissolves.

Keyed Special Effects with Two and Three Sources

Let's say that we are going to use a key over camera 1 at the beginning of a program. To do this, we press *black* ("B") on the program bus, camera 1 on the preset bank, and button 5 (for titles from the graphics generator) on the key bus (refer back to Figure 9.16). In this case, camera 1 is the preset background, and the graphics generator will be the key source. The fader arm can be in either the upper or lower position to start.

The two next transition buttons in the effects transition area allow us to select the source bus or buses used in the next transition or effect. In this case, we press both the "bkgd" (background) and "key" buttons, because when we come up from black, we are going to fade to a key consisting of two images—the

preset background from camera 1 and, keyed over it, the lettering originating from the graphics generator on the key bus 5 position.

In the effects keyer section (see Figure 9.18), we must press both "key bus" buttons, because the key bus will be both the source and the fill of the effect. (If we were preparing a three-source key, we would punch up different sources for the source and for the fill.)

Once the selections have been punched up on the preset background bank (camera 1) and on the key bus bank (the graphics generator), the preview monitor will display the key effect of those two sources. Because the difference in brightness between the lettering and the background is always a matter of delicate balance, a look at the preview monitor will now tell us just what adjustments must be made. The "clip" knob sets the brightness threshold for the key source video that allows the letters to "cut" the electronic hole, and the "gain" knob sets the sharpness of the key effect itself. After viewing the result of these adjustments, we are ready to fade up on our key effect by moving the fader bar to its opposite position. The key effect is brought up on the line, and we see the results on the program monitor.

9.4 Advanced Switcher Functions

Like most other components used in video production, switchers are becoming increasingly sophisticated, with additional capabilities and automated control. Still, the basic operating functions remain the same, as discussed in the first three sections of this chapter.

Digital Effects

Transitions such as dissolves and wipes, and keying functions found on nearly all switchers are obviously quite useful to video production. However, these effects are also limited in that they cannot make any significant changes to the switcher inputs. These effects merely arrange the inputs in different ways, revealing only part of them, perhaps, as in the case of an external key, or replacing one input with another by performing a gradual dissolve. No significant changes can be made to the inputs themselves.

As an example of this limitation, consider the corner insert effect originally shown in Figure 9.9 and repeated in Figure 9.19(a). The end result looks fine, but getting there requires some rather awkward camera work. The switcher's box wipe effect cannot "squeeze" or move camera 2's shot in any way—it can only reveal that portion of the shot where the box is positioned. Consequently, the shot on camera 2 must be framed so that the person's head is quite small and positioned in the upper-right portion of the screen, as shown in Figure 9.19(b). The operator of camera 2 must frame the shot so that the person's head will be positioned exactly where the box cutout is, as shown in Figure 9.19(a).

By using DVE effects, however, we *can* actually "squeeze" a normally framed shot into a corner of the screen, as shown in Figure 9.19(c). Thus, the operator of camera 2 could frame the shot normally, as shown in Figure 9.19(d). This would make it easier to cut from the shot on camera 2 to the effect shown in Figure 9.19(c).

Or the switcher operator could set up a "live" DVE effect that would actually squeeze the full-frame shot from camera 2 into the corner in real time.

This is the essence of digital video effects. They actually allow the inputs of the switcher to be manipulated—stretched, bent, colored, flipped, spun around, and so on. Digital manipulation creates nearly limitless possibilities, not only for transitions, but for creating other types of effects as well.

DVE Transitions

DVE functions can take transitions well beyond the capabilities of traditional dissolves and wipes. For example, in a **push-off** transition, the second picture actually seems to "push" the first picture off the screen, as shown in Figure 9.20(a). Although this particular example shows the push moving left to right, the transition can actually move in any direction—vertical, horizontal, or at an angle. Another type of DVE transition can actually "peel away" one picture to reveal another one, as shown in Figure 9.20(b). Here again, the example shown is but one of nearly limitless possibilities: The picture can peel away from any direction we want.

In other DVE transitions, a picture can spin and appear to fly off the screen, as shown in Figure 9.20(c), or "melt" away, as shown in Figure 9.20(d). Once again, the effects are open to nearly infinite adjustment to suit your particular desires.

The main thing to notice about these DVE transitions is that they are different from traditional wipes because they can actually *change* the video that is coming into the switcher. They create transitions by bending, stretching, flipping, and moving the video images.

Other DVE Effects

DVE functions also allow us to change the way video looks without actually performing a transition. For example, Figure 9.21(a) shows a mosaic effect, where the picture is given a tiled look. You may have seen this effect used to obscure the face of someone who does not wish to be identified. **Posterization,** shown in Figure 9.21(b) can be used to create something of a cartoonlike effect, reducing the number of colors in the picture and creating greater levels of contrast.

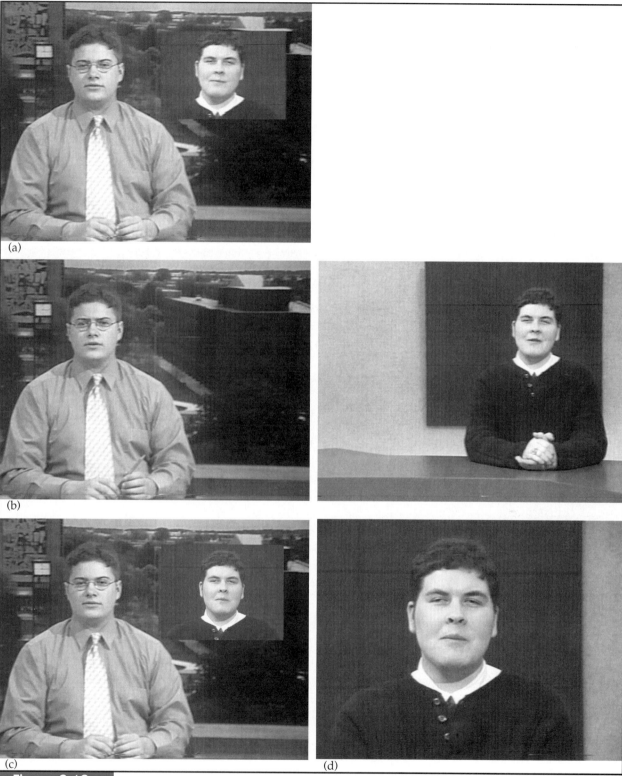

Figure 9.19

(*a*) The corner insert effect originally shown in Figure 9.9. (*b*) The individual camera shots required to produce the corner insert effect on a switcher without DVE capability (camera 1 on the left, camera 2 on the right). (*c*) The corner insert effect produced using DVE. (*d*) The camera 2 shot for creating the corner effect using DVE.

Figure 9.20

Some examples of DVE transitions. For each transition, the leftmost frame shows the beginning shot, and the rightmost frame shows the ending shot. The two middle frames show midpoints of the transition. (*a*) A left-to-right push. (*b*) A "peel" transition. (*c*) A transition where the first shot zooms back and then slides out of the frame. (*d*) A "melt" effect.

One of the digital switcher effects most often seen is **continuous image compression,** which enables the switcher operator to compress the full-frame picture down to the size of a tiny circle, square, or other shape (at any speed, to any size) and—with a joystick—to place the shrunken image anywhere on the screen. **Image expansion** allows the operator to take any segment of the video frame and enlarge it. Another effect is **image stretching,** where any portion of the picture can be expanded or compressed in any direction; ratios can be altered, and graphics can be shaped to fit the picture. This can be used to change the perspective of the picture, as shown in Figure 9.21(c).

Digital video effects also allow us to combine several different inputs into a single picture, such as a cube effect where each side of the cube is actually a different video input. The cube can even be made to spin, change sizes, or bounce off the screen if we wish. Similarly, we can create different types of **layering** effects where various video inputs are placed over top of one another, as shown in Figure 9.21(d).

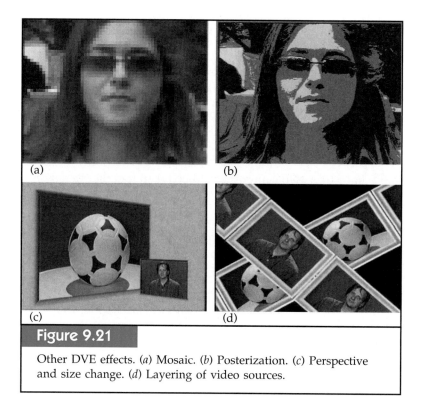

Figure 9.21

Other DVE effects. (*a*) Mosaic. (*b*) Posterization. (*c*) Perspective and size change. (*d*) Layering of video sources.

Increasingly, digital video effects are built into production switchers, especially high-end ones. However, DVE units are also available as separate pieces, which are normally designed to integrate closely with the switcher unit.

Advanced Control

High-end switchers can be set up to actually *control* other studio equipment. For example, some switchers have the ability to not only take the video output from a tape machine but actually to *play* the tape machine. Similarly, switchers can control external DVE units by triggering when and how the DVE effect is executed and also can manipulate graphics generators and other graphics equipment.

Advanced switchers also allow the user to automate complex switching functions and switcher setup, saving the settings to computer disk and then recalling them. In this way, an operator can program complex switching functions and then have them execute with the touch of a single button. With proper planning, this allows very complex switching operations to be performed in real time during a live broadcast with much less chance of error.

9.5 Video Production Commands

In discussing directing (see Chapter 4), we stressed the difference between commands of *preparation* and commands of *execution*. Nowhere is this distinction more important than in giving commands to the **technical director**, the person who operates the switcher in a studio environment.[6] The preparation and execution of the various transitions and effects involve different amounts of switcher operation time. A straight take (cut) is ready instantly, but a dissolve to a chroma key effect requires a number of operations, done in a precise order. The commands of preparation must allow for sufficient lead time. Such commands, given over the intercom system, allow camera, VTR, and graphics operators time for their own preparations.

One helpful rule is that the command of preparation for any straight take is "ready." The preparation for any dissolve, super, fade, or special transition or effect that involves getting something set or prepared on another bus uses the command "prepare." (A few directors prefer to use the command "set up.") Although some directors use the term "stand by" as a preparation for both takes and dissolves, this can be confusing to the crew. The use of correct terminology immediately lets the technical director know whether to simply get ready to push a button on the same bus or to prepare or set up another camera or effect on another bus. The command sequence for a direct take from camera 1 to camera 2 is stated by the director as follows:

(Preparation): "Ready camera 2" (or simply "Ready 2").

(Execution): "Take 2."

The word *ready* lets the technical director know only to place a finger on the camera 2 button on the program bus.

No matter how rushed the director may be or how fast-paced the program, the director should never skimp on the commands of preparation. If occasionally the director does not have time to give full commands, some abbreviation could be used:

(Preparation): "Ready 2."

(Execution): "Take it" (or simply "Take").

If time is so short that even this much preparation is impossible (for example, shooting a game show, fast-paced panel discussion, or football game), the command of preparation still must be given priority:

(Preparation): "Two."

(Execution): "Take."

When such abbreviated commands are used successfully, it is usually in a situation where the director and the crew have worked together for an extended period of time. Even so, most directors will return to the safer, more complete commands when time allows.

A dissolve requires a different-sounding command of preparation to allow the technical director time to prepare for a more complex series of actions. Assuming you already have camera 1 on the program line, the correct commands for a dissolve would be:

(Preparation): "Prepare a dissolve to 2" (or "Prepare 2" or "Set up 2").

(Execution): "Dissolve to 2."

For a super, the actions are the same, so the commands are much the same:

(Preparation): "Prepare to super 2 over 1" (or) "Set up 2" (implying that camera 1 stays on the air).

(Execution): "Super camera 2 over 1" (or just "Super 2").

We depart slightly from the basic pattern whenever two cameras are to be taken together in a super, key, or DVE effect. Although these effects may involve a movement of the control levers and other switcher components to set them up, the movement is not one of program execution. As previously outlined, the command of execution is "take"—calling only for the technical director to press the line mix output button or take bar. For this reason, the voice procedure in the case of a 2-camera DVE effect should be as follows:

(Preparation): "Ready to take 2 and 3 in effect."

(Execution): "Take effect" (or "Take 2 and 3").

The repetition of camera numbers in the command is optional, but it does reinforce the intent of the command.

Much of the discipline necessary for keeping a program under control comes from this pattern of preparation followed by execution. The technical director must be able to depend on this sequence. The pattern is broken when a complicated effect that must be set up in advance is called for. A complicated effect, for example, might need to be preset several shots before its use. In this situation, after the command of preparation that acknowledges the time delay in execution, there may be several intervening commands. Then a new command of preparation is issued before the execution command for the key. The command of preparation must be given far enough in advance so that the technical director has a chance to do the preset at a time most convenient during the ongoing program. The director keeps an eye on the preview monitor to see when the effect is ready. The commands might be as follows:

(Advance preparation): "We're about to wrap, so preview your effect of camera 2 and full screen on the CG."

(Ongoing shots in the program continue): "Ready 1, take 1 . . . etc."

(Immediate preparation): "Now set up a dissolve to the effect of camera 2 and full screen."

(Execution of the key): "Dissolve to the effect."

Similarly, any command to preview and adjust—say, a corner wipe or an insert—in the coverage of a live event may be given well in advance of its eventual use on the air. There may be several intervening ad-libbed shots. This can be thought of as a non-time-specific command. For example:

(Advance preparation): "Preview a top-left corner insert, camera 3, of runner off first base, within camera 2."

(Intervening shots ad-libbed): "Ready 4, take 4, . . . etc."

(Adjustment of preparation): "Tighten the framing on camera 3 insert."

(Intervening shots ad-libbed): "Ready 1, take 1, . . . etc."

(Immediate preparation): "OK. Now, ready to take corner insert."

(Execution of the effect): "Take effect."

One final note: Fades to and from black are handled in a manner very similar to the dissolve. Because a sync black picture has such a definite connotation of separation and/or conclusion, many directors reserve the term "fade" for use as a command only to dissolve to or from black. This serves as a safeguard to protect against any inadvertent dissolve to full-screen black.

As switchers have become more complex, the numerous visual options available to the director have placed many demands on the technical director. The director is obligated to use the clearest of command language, which in turn must be based on an operational understanding of what is involved in achieving execution of those commands. Beyond common courtesy, there is a very practical aspect to this. Ill-timed and poorly stated commands simply cannot be executed within the time framework that the director may have in mind. Such a disparity can have serious side effects, especially with live programming.

Discussion Questions

1. Evaluate the switcher in your school's studio. Is it a special-effects-generating switcher? Does it have a downstream keyer? How many inputs does it have? What kinds of effects can it perform?

2. Why has the key replaced the superimposition in most video production situations? Can you think of a program in which you've seen a superimposition?

3. How does the use of buses on switchers help simplify operation? Can you think of a more logical way to lay out a switcher?

4. Explain the difference between a split-screen effect created on a non-DVE switcher and a similar effect using a special-effects-generating switcher. Do you think a viewer at home would notice the difference?

Notes

1. The video monitors used in studio environments are distinguished from regular television receivers in that these monitors are usually high-quality units with the ability to reproduce fine detail. They receive a direct unmodulated video signal, as opposed to a modulated radio frequency signal. Thus, there is no audio and no channel selection capability.

2. Technically speaking, the line and its connectors that run under each row of buttons are termed the bus, and the row of buttons is called the bank; however, in common usage, the two terms are interchangeable.

3. On most switchers, a selected button does not *stay* depressed but simply lights up to show it is selected. So the way to tell which button is selected on a bus is not to look for a button that is physically pressed down but to look for the button that is lighted.

4. Occasionally the word *matte* is associated with the key process. The term was derived from the traditional film technique that printed or "matted" inserts within the larger film frame.

5. Ultimatte is a trademark of the Ultimatte Corporation.

6. The term "technical director" is derived from professional situations where the person given that title has a much larger engineering responsibility to supervise the entire technical staff and to operate the switcher only at the latter part of the production effort. There are circumstances when a person may function only as the switcher operator and is usually then known as the "switcher."

Video Recording and Playback

The ability to record and play back video signals is crucial to nearly any video production. The majority of programming on network television is broadcast from a recording, and most of what isn't relies at least in part on **roll-ins,** or recorded segments (see Chapter 12). Thus, we need ways of recording and playing back high-quality video signals (along with their associated audio signals). Intertwined with the recording and playing back of video signals are the basic control functions of **channeling,** moving the signal to and from the recording device (and other equipment), and **monitoring,** making sure the recorded signal is as true to the original as possible.

Video signals, whether in **analog** or **digital** form, have several unique characteristics that can make these functions a bit more complicated than you might expect. Certainly, compared with audio signals (see Chapter 7), channeling, monitoring, and recording and playing back video signals require much more complex technical equipment. Consider the fact that the technology to record *audio* existed for several decades before the advent of the first *video* recorder. Indeed, when Ampex introduced the first commercial **videotape recorder (VTR)** in 1956, it sparked a revolution in television production.

Now digitization, along with the digital channeling and storage of video signals, is creating another revolution, which holds the possibility of bringing even greater changes than those brought by tape. As video exists increasingly in digital form, it can seamlessly interface with computers, and—even more important—computers and computer equipment can be used to perform basic control functions. You have already seen how digital technology is changing other video production components such as cameras, **switchers,** and **DVE** units. In the same way, digitization is changing how video signals are recorded and played back, as tape machines are being replaced by **video servers,** powerful computers with large storage capacity. The chief advantage of such servers is that they are **nonlinear,** meaning you can access anything stored on them nearly instantly, without having to fast-forward or rewind as you do with tape. When we combine video servers with computer **network** interconnections, we allow any number of people in a production facility to simultaneously access and manipulate the video information.

But the day when every station and production facility has gone all digital and "tapeless" is still a ways off. For that reason, a significant portion of this chapter concentrates on the function and operation of VTRs, which are likely to be prevalent for at least the near future. However, this chapter begins with a discussion of some technical aspects of video (in analog and digital form) and their impact on how video is stored and distributed.

There are both important *disciplines* and *techniques* to the operation of video storage and distribution equipment. The *disciplines* include an understanding of how video is recorded, digitized, and distributed, while *techniques* include specific operating and maintenance procedures. This chapter includes the following topics:

- The basic components and special attributes of video signals (10.1)

- The advantages of digital signals over analog signals, and the basic methods of converting analog information into digital video (10.2)

- The importance of compression in digital video, and the major methods of compression (10.2)

- The basic design and operation of digital video servers, including the concepts of ingesting and asset management (10.3)

- Other digital-based storage options for video, including optical media and memory cards (10.3)

- Principles of videotape recording, and the function of various videotape tracks (10.4)

- The basic layout and operation of typical videotape recorder operational controls (10.5)

- Basic procedures for operating and maintaining videotape equipment (10.6)

10.1 Video Signal Basics

For the purposes of a discussion about channeling, monitoring, and recording and playback, we can divide video signals into three main types: **analog NTSC, digital** NTSC, and digital **ATSC.** Analog NTSC video signals are becoming increasingly rare in production facilities, but they are still out there, especially in university environments where the money to upgrade to digital equipment is often hard to come by. Analog NTSC signals usually travel over **coaxial cable** and are stored only on videotape.[1] Digital signals (both NTSC and ATSC) can travel over computer network connections or coaxial cable and can be stored on either videotape, video servers, or other digital media (see Chapter 13).

In Chapter 5, the three color components (**hue, saturation,** and **luminance**) that make up a video signal

Figure 10.1

The rear connection deck of a Panasonic AJ-D580 (D-5) VCR shows the connections necessary to receive, record, convert, and output a wide range of digital and analog signal combinations, including those using the multiple-pin connectors that match disk units and digital formats.
Photo courtesy of Panasonic.

were discussed. There are a number of different ways to channel and store a video signal, based on different ways of handling these individual color components.

A **composite** signal combines the **chrominance** (which, you should remember, includes hue and saturation information) and the luminance (brightness) information. This method's chief advantage is that all the video information can be carried as a single signal, yet it also suffers quality degradation because of interference between the chrominance and luminance information.

In a **component** system the chrominance and luminance information are kept separated and distributed as distinct signals. While maintaining a higher quality because there is no interference between chrominance and luminance information, a component system requires the distribution of at least two separate signals. Many component systems, in fact, use *two* chrominance signals and the luminance signal, requiring three separate signals.[2] In digital systems, as

you will see in Section 10.2, this is not much of a problem because the distinct signals can still travel over a single connection (in other words, you only need one wire). However, in analog component systems each signal must have its own separate wire, although these wires may be molded together into a single cable unit with individual connectors on each end. It is common for storage and other equipment to facilitate *both* composite and component video signals, as shown in Figure 10.1.

Another method of distributing video also should be acknowledged, although it is normally not used for carrying video information within production facilities or television stations. When converted to a **radio frequency (RF)** signal, the video and audio signals are combined onto a **carrier wave** that can then transmit the signal through the air. This is how television stations broadcast television signals, and also how cable television signals enter the home. Videotape recorders, especially units designed for consumer use, usually offer an RF output so that you can watch (and listen to) a tape by plugging it into the VHF antenna jack of a television set tuned to channel 3 or 4. However, because it combines all video information along with audio information, it causes much greater signal degradation than either component or composite distribution.

Special Attributes of the Video Signal

Although video signals can be stored and distributed through wires in a manner similar to audio signals, word-processing files, or even electricity, it is important to point out some unique attributes of the video signal. These attributes, as you will see in the following sections, have a substantial impact on how video storage and distribution systems must be designed and operated.

The first factor is that the video signal—whether **standard definition** or **high definition**—contains a tremendous amount of information. You know, for instance, that more than 300,000 individual pieces of information correspond to the **pixels** on a standard-definition television screen. A 1080i high-definition picture contains more than 2 *million* pixels of information. This means that a video signal requires a lot of storage space.

The second factor relates to the first in that the video signal is *constantly changing*—meaning that *new* information must be moved quickly. Typically, a new **frame** of video is being drawn at least 30 times a second, if not more. Thus, systems for channeling and storing video signals must have high **bandwidth,** meaning they can handle a large amount of information at one time. Bandwidth is—metaphorically speaking—equivalent to the size of a pipe. A large-diameter pipe, for example, can carry more (water, oil, sludge) than a small pipe, and thus a large-bandwidth system can carry more information than a small-bandwidth system. Although bandwidth is a consideration for both analog and digital signal channeling, you will see it most often in dealing with digital information.

Finally, the video signal requires great precision in order to operate properly. A standard-definition videotape recorder, for example, must *precisely* record 30 frames of video per second; even a slight deviance can create an unusable picture. Whereas an analog audiocassette can be played in a machine that runs at the wrong speed (the music will just sound too fast or too

slow), a videotape player that runs at the wrong speed is practically useless. Thus, methods of storing and distributing video signals—analog or digital—must operate precisely and accurately.

It is imperative that the scanning sequence in the camera and other video components be precisely synchronized at every stage of a video signal's journey through the **switcher** to all other recording and editing equipment in a production facility, as well as to the home receiving set. A series of specialized pulses—generated independently of the color and luminance portion of the video signal—are used for this purpose. The **vertical sync pulse** coordinates the start of each new frame or field, while the **horizontal sync pulse** coordinates the scanning of individual lines within a frame or field. The timing and frequency of these pulses depends on what type of signal (NTSC or one of the ATSC formats) is being used, but the point is that all components in a video system must be synchronized to one another.

Time Code

Time code provides an accurate *address system* that assigns each frame of video a unique numeric designation. Developed by the Society of Motion Picture and Television Engineers (SMPTE), time code gives each frame of video an eight-digit address in the format hours: minutes: seconds: frames, as shown in Figure 10.2.

Time code is used with both digital and analog systems, and with both NTSC and ATSC formats. Time code consists of electronic signal pulses recorded using a **time code generator.** How these pulses are recorded depends on the application.

There are three ways to record time code on tape. The first method records the time code pulses in the **vertical interval** sections of the tape, which are essentially

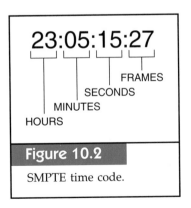

Figure 10.2

SMPTE time code.

the spaces between frames. Called **vertical interval time code (VITC),** this type of time code must be recorded at the same time as the video information. The second type of time code, **longitudinal time code (LTC),** is recorded onto an unused audio channel or cue track of the tape. The advantage of LTC is that it can be added *after* the video has already been recorded, a process often called **striping.** The third method, used only with digital formats, embeds the time code in a designated area of the digital **bitstream.** This allows video information to be moved among compatible servers and tape systems seamlessly without losing time code information.

Most high-end video equipment has time code generators and **time code readers** built in. For instance, high-end cameras can record time code as they record video; this time code can then be read by playback and recording equipment. The time code generator is normally set to **record run** mode, which means the time code "clock" runs only while the camera is recording. For example, if you stop the camera at time code 00:05:35:15, then begin recording again 20 minutes later, the time code will resume at 00:05:35:16. In **free run** mode, the time code continues to increment even if the camera is not recording. In this mode, if the camera stops recording at time code 00:05:35:15, then resumes recording exactly 20 minutes later, the time code on tape will pick up at 00:25:35:15. Free-run time code is often used to set the time code to the time of day, allowing the footage to be identified by the precise time it was shot.

Time code also can be set to either **drop-frame** or **non-drop-frame** mode. In drop-frame mode, the time code periodically "skips" a frame number to compensate for the fact that NTSC color video runs at 29.97 frames per second and not exactly 30 frames per second. This allows the time code to be time-accurate, meaning that one hour of time-coded video is exactly one hour long. Non-drop frame does not skip frame numbers, and thus one hour of non-drop-frame time code video is actually one hour plus 3.6 seconds long. In time-critical applications, drop-frame time code is usually the preferred type, for obvious reasons.

Control and Diagnostic Components

A number of components in a typical studio are designed to monitor and ensure signal integrity. The installation and operation of these devices is typically an engineering function, and so it is beyond the scope of this chapter to address those issues. However, it is important for you to understand that these components exist, and to know what they are used for. A number of additional components that are used exclusively for analog video signals are discussed later in this section.

Control Components

As discussed, it is crucial that all pieces of equipment in a studio be synchronized to one another. The **sync generator** creates the vertical sync pulse that becomes the reference point for all other equipment in a production facility. Thus, video recorders, switchers, and other equipment have a "sync" or "genlock" connector to read the sync generator's signal (in the recorder shown in Figure 10.1 the connection is located in the "Input" section on the lower half of the back panel). Since the other pieces of equipment synchronize themselves to the sync generator's signal, it is said to provide "studio sync" or "house sync."

A **frame synchronizer** is used to synchronize outside video sources to the sync generator. For example, an external satellite feed will likely not be perfectly matched with studio sync. In effect, the frame synchronizer digitally "holds" each frame of video from the external source briefly, then outputs it at the proper time to match studio sync.

A **color bar generator** sends a standardized pattern of colored bars through the switcher. This signal is then used to calibrate cameras, video recorders, monitors, and other studio components. The **color bars** also are usually recorded onto the beginning of video recordings so that the playback machine can be set to match the color levels set at the time of the recording.

Diagnostic Components

Chapter 9 discussed the use of video **monitors** in studios to check the picture of various video sources. In many cases, however, it is not enough to merely look at a video signal on a television monitor. To be sure that the signal is properly adjusted at various points in the signal flow, it is necessary to use a **waveform monitor** and **vectorscope,** which are sometimes combined into one unit. In many cases, this adjustment will involve internal calibration of a component (such as a switcher) so that it outputs a properly adjusted video signal. This type of calibration, usually done by a studio engineer, is probably done only at certain intervals (a period of weeks or months, perhaps). However, as discussed in Chapter 5, cameras used in a studio have a **camera control unit (CCU)** for adjusting their output. Such devices are normally adjusted on a daily basis, if not more often.

The art (or, perhaps more accurately, *science*) of properly adjusting a video signal using a waveform monitor and vectorscope is best learned through hands-on practice with direct instruction. The type of equipment in a given production facility will determine to a great extent how the video signals are diagnosed and adjusted (see Figure 10.3).

One more advantage brought by the rise of digital is that many monitoring and adjustment procedures can be automated. For example, a computer can continuously monitor the video signal and then make adjustments to other pieces of equipment as necessary to maintain signal integrity. In other cases, signals can be monitored remotely, perhaps from a computer in the station engineer's home.

Analog Video Control Components

Although digital distribution of video signals is rapidly replacing analog, it is still important to be familiar with some basic control equipment used in analog signal flow. In general, analog video signals differ from digital signals in that they are constantly subject to quality degradation. Whenever an analog signal is channeled, recorded, or played back, it is subject to a potential loss of quality. For that reason, the channeling of analog video signals involves several pieces of ancillary equipment designed to lessen this loss of quality.

Distribution amplifiers (DAs) are used to amplify analog video signals and allow them to "branch off" to more than one location. For example, if you wished to channel the output of a switcher to several different

Figure 10.3

The Leader LV5700 digital video monitor provides access to a vectorscope, waveform monitor, and the actual video signal simultaneously. *Photo Courtesy of Leader Instruments Corporation.*

VTRs, you would use a DA. Similarly, a **process amplifier** takes the video signal—color, brightness, and synchronizing information—from the switcher and stabilizes the levels, amplifies the signal, and removes unwanted interference, often called **noise.** A **time-base corrector** is used to repair synchronization problems from the analog output of videotape machines.

10.2 Digital Video Signals

As you know from Chapter 1, any digital signal is nothing more than a **bitstream,** or a series of "on" and "off" pulses. A digital video bitstream can thus be channeled, manipulated, and stored just like any other piece of computer data, be it a word-processing file, an e-mail message, or a digitized sound. However, given video's high storage and bandwidth requirements, equipment for digital video work is normally specifically designed for handling video data.

A digital video bitstream may represent an NTSC signal, an ATSC standard-definition signal, or an ATSC high-definition signal. For the purposes of our discussion, there is little fundamental difference among the three, with the exception that the high-definition signal will have greater storage and bandwidth requirements. Also, NTSC may be converted between analog and digital forms more than once as it moves through the production process, depending on the production facility. For example, a studio may be equipped with analog NTSC cameras that send an analog signal to a digital switcher, which performs **digital video effects** on the signal and then outputs it again as an analog signal. An ATSC signal, on the other hand, will *stay* digital from beginning to end.

The main advantage of an all-digital system is that digital distribution of video signals can be completely **transparent,** meaning that there is no loss of signal quality as the bitstream travels from point to point. In fact, the quality of the signal is determined at its point of origin (as the analog visual information is **transduced** to digital data by a camera, for instance) and then can maintain that pure quality throughout the production processes. Analog signals, as discussed, are subject to quality degradation whenever they are stored or channeled.

Converting Between Analog and Digital

Some video sources, such as a graphic or a sophisticated animation created on a computer, start out in digital form and remain in digital form for channeling and storage. However, most other sources of video come from a camera, and as we know from Chapter 5, a camera transduces the analog light signal into a video signal. Thus, in the case of a digital camera, the information is converted from analog to digital. This process involves **sampling** and **quantization.**

Sampling refers to the process of literally sampling the analog signal and converting its value to digital form, as discussed in Chapter 1. The higher the **sampling rate** (meaning the more frequently the analog signal is sampled), the more accurately the digital output will reflect the original analog information. In component video systems with two chrominance signals, the sampling rate is normally stated as a ratio, such as 4:2:2. This means that for every four times the luminance signal is sampled, each chrominance signal is sampled twice. On a 4:1:1 system, each chrominance signal is sampled only once for four samples of the luminance signal. The higher the sampling rate, the higher the quality of the digital signal produced. All else being equal, then, 4:2:2 sampling yields better results than 4:1:1. However, greater sampling rates also require greater bandwidth and larger storage capacity. As a compromise, some systems use a 4:2:0 sampling rate, which alternates between the two chrominance signals, sampling one of them twice for each four samples of the luminance signal.

Quantization is how many **bits** the sampled digital signal is forced into. As discussed in Chapter 1, a bit (short for "binary digit") is an individual digital pulse that can have a value of either 0 or 1. The greater the number of bits, the higher the quality. The two most common quantizations for digital video are 8-bit and 10-bit, with 10-bit allowing higher-quality pictures. Here again, however, the higher quantization level leads to greater bandwidth and storage demands.[3]

Compression

To ease the demands on digital equipment, video data is usually made more compact through the use of

An example of a video shot in which much of the information is redundant and could thus be compressed. The subject in the frame is standing in front of a plain white wall.

compression. Several different compression schemes are available, and each is normally designed for a particular use. In general, however, all compression systems work by analyzing the visual information in a picture and then either rearranging it into a more compact form and/or discarding information that is not needed. Compression systems are termed **lossless** if they do not lessen picture quality, or **lossy** if they do. In practice, all useful compression systems cause some degradation of picture quality, although it may not be noticeable to most viewers. **Compression ratio** refers to the size of the original signal as compared with the compressed signal. The higher the compression ratio, the smaller the compressed file as compared with the original. For example, a 16:1 compression ratio will create a signal that requires less bandwidth than a signal created with a 4:1 compression ratio.

The goal of compression is to reach a suitable compromise between picture quality and required bandwidth. To do that, compression systems reduce the **data rate** of the digital video signal, meaning that less information is being sent at a time. Data rate is usually referred to in megabytes per second, or Mb/s. The lower the data rate, the less bandwidth that is required. As a starting point, consider that an uncompressed standard-definition signal has a data rate of about 270 Mb/s, while a high-definition signal will be around 1,500 Mb/s. Compression systems can significantly reduce these data rates.

The actual compression of digital video signals is performed by an **encoder.** The encoder may be a separate unit, or may be built in to a camera, server, or other piece of equipment. At the other end of the signal path, a **decoder** converts the compressed digital data into a viewable picture. A **codec** (coder-decoder) is a device that can perform both functions.

A given compression system may use either **intraframe compression, interframe compression,** or a combination of both. Intraframe compression analyzes each individual frame of video as an independent entity. For example, if a woman is standing in front of a plain white background (see Figure 10.4), the compression system might replace all of the individual bits of information that convey the whiteness of the background with a single representation of the white color. Greatly simplified, it is equivalent to the difference between saying, "This pixel is white, this pixel is white, this pixel is white, this pixel is white," and so on, and simply saying, "All these pixels are white." Intraframe compression also might merge subtle color differences (shades) if they are likely to be imperceptible to the average viewer.

Interframe compression, on the other hand, analyzes groups of frames, ignoring redundant information that doesn't change from frame to frame. For example, suppose that the woman in front of the white wall in Figure 10.4 is standing almost completely still, moving only her lips, eyes, and head slightly as she talks. From frame to frame of video, most of the picture is not changing. Thus, an interframe compression system would only continue to save the information that *is changing* from frame to frame—the movement of the lips, eyes, and head. The information that doesn't change (the plain white background and perhaps the woman's upper body) would only need to be saved once. It is the same idea as if you sent someone a 1,000-page printed document and then needed to change the name "Zach Smith" to "Zack Smith" on 10 of the pages. You wouldn't need to send all 1,000 pages again, only the 10 that you changed.

Compression methods that use both interframe and intraframe compression tend to achieve much higher compression ratios than those using only intraframe compression. However, interframe compression can cause problems for editing, as will be discussed in Chapter 11.

Motion-JPEG

The **Motion-JPEG (M-JPEG)** compression system is an outgrowth of the JPEG (Joint Photographic Experts Group) compression scheme for still pictures. You likely have already had experience with JPEG still images, as it is a popular format for saving the graphics used on Web pages.

M-JPEG uses only intraframe compression, so in theory it is well suited to editing. However, the trade-off is that M-JPEG compression has a low compression ratio. Also, several manufacturers have independently developed their own versions of M-JPEG, and thus there are compatibility issues. Although M-JPEG was the first compression system designed for moving pictures, it has for the most part been supplanted by other systems.

MPEG-1

MPEG-1 is named after the Moving Pictures Experts Group, a consortium formed after the development of JPEG to work on a more efficient compression system for moving pictures. MPEG-1 is designed to record VHS-quality standard-definition video onto CDs. It has also found use for delivering video on the Internet, as will be discussed in Chapter 13. However, MPEG-1 is not suitable for higher-quality video production.

MPEG-2

MPEG-2 is the most important and widely used compression scheme for digital television. Introduced three years after MPEG-1, MPEG-2's important place in digital television was cemented when it was selected as the compression standard for ATSC television.

Like ATSC, MPEG-2 doesn't actually define a single standard but rather a series of standards. These standards are arranged into six "profiles" and four "levels," creating the potential for 24 different compression iterations. However, at this point only 12 of the standards have actually been defined. These are shown in Figure 10.5. For each profile, the sampling rate, maximum picture resolution, and data rate are given. Each profile also lists the shorthand usually used to refer to it; for example, "4:2:2P@ML" refers to the 4:2:2 profile at the main level.

The profiles are intended to provide different levels of what MPEG calls "tools" for various video applications. Moving left to right along the bottom of the chart in Figure 10.5, higher-level profiles offer more potential "tools" for compressing signals. However, the equipment for encoding and decoding these higher-level profiles also becomes progressively more expensive. For example, the "simple" profile provides a limited set of tools that can be implemented with relatively inexpensive equipment. Video capture systems for home computers, for example, often use the main level of the simple profile (ML@MP). The "main" profile provides for the channeling and storage of finished productions, those that require no further editing. The "4:2:2" profile is designed for video signals that require further editing (see Chapter 11).

Within each profile are four levels, indicating different grades of picture resolution. The "low" profile is roughly equivalent to the picture quality produced by a VHS standard-definition tape recording, the "main" profile is equivalent to professional standard-definition television, and the "High-1440" and "High" levels are for high-definition quality.

PROFILES						
LEVELS	SIMPLE	MAIN	4:2:2	SNR SCALABLE	SPATIAL SCALABLE	HIGH
HIGH		4:2:0 1920 x 1152 80 Mb/s MP@HL				4:2:0, 4:2:2 1920 x 1152 100 Mb/s HP@HL
HIGH-1440		4:2:0 1440 x 1152 60 Mb/s MP@H14L			4:2:0 1440 x 1152 60 Mb/s SSP@H14L	4:2:0, 4:2:2 1440 x 1152 80 Mb/s HP@H14L
MAIN	4:2:0 720 x 576 15 Mb/s SP@ML	4:2:0 720 x 576 15 Mb/s MP@ML	4:2:2 720 x 608 15 Mb/s 4:2:2P@ML	4:2:0 720 x 576 15 Mb/s SNRP@ML		4:2:0, 4:2:2 720 x 576 20 Mb/s HP@ML
LOW		4:2:0 352 x 288 4 Mb/s MP@LL		4:2:0 352 x 288 4 Mb/s SNRP@LL		

Figure 10.5

This chart shows MPEG-2 profiles and levels, along with the sampling rate, maximum picture resolution, and data rate for each.

MPEG-4

A still newer compression scheme is **MPEG-4,** designed for delivering interactive multimedia content. It is not intended as a replacement for MPEG-1 or MPEG-2 but will likely find use in the creation of video games, virtual reality, and Internet-based video applications (see Chapter 13).

DV

The **DV compression** format is probably the second most-important compression technology for television production. It uses only intraframe compression and so is very well suited to editing. DV also provides for a number of different standards, including the 25 Mb/s 4:1:1 sampled and 50 Mb/s 4:2:2 sampled standard-definition formats, and 100 Mb/s formats for standard and high definition. Versions of the DV compression scheme are used in several digital tape formats.

10.3 Video Servers and Other Tapeless Storage Systems

You can grasp the general idea of a video server if you think of it as a very large computer hard disk drive. Although most video servers are specially designed to input, store, and output digital video, they perform the same basic function as the hard drive in your computer: storing digital data.

Putting Video on Servers

The main advantage of servers over tape, as discussed previously, is that they are nonlinear. Servers allow you to access the exact piece of video you want almost instantaneously. The determining factor in *how fast* you can get what you want from a video server is often how well you've kept track of what's recorded on it. Increasingly, video production professionals are concerned with **asset management,** the process of cataloguing and using video on servers in the most efficient manner possible.

For example, consider a local television station whose production department shoots footage of a local charity event to use in a public service announcement. Once that video is placed on the server, it becomes, in essence, *an asset* that can be made available to a number of different entities. For example, as shown in Figure 10.6, the news department may wish to edit together some of the footage to use in a story in that evening's nightly newscast. Later that day, the production department could access the footage to edit the public service announcement. The station might also make some footage of the event available over its Internet site (see Chapter 13). The other important capability video servers offer is the potential to do all of these things *at the same time.* If the footage only existed on tape, it could only be used by one person at a time, unless, of course, you took the time to make extra copies of the tape.

A valuable aid to asset management is the use of **metadata,** which allows additional information to be recorded with the video. For example, you can give the video footage a title and/or description ("Footage of the United Way celebrity dinner"), note the date it was shot, who shot it, and even what equipment was used. Later, the footage can be accessed easily by searching for one or more of these parameters.

Getting video on a server can still be rather time-consuming, although technology is making the job go faster. The process of putting video on a server is called **ingesting,** and it can happen in a number of different ways. One way is to record the video in real time, meaning that you essentially hook the output of the camcorder to the input of the server and play the tape. This is the only option for analog standard-definition video, as it must be **digitized** in order to be recorded onto the server. The disadvantage of this method is that it must happen in real time: If you have an hour of tape, it will take you an hour to record it on the server. Of course, if you're producing a live or "live-to-tape" program, the use of real-time recording is not a disadvantage; you can simply record the program directly onto the server instead of recording first to tape.

Another way to get video on the server is by using compressed data streams. DV and MPEG-2 systems,

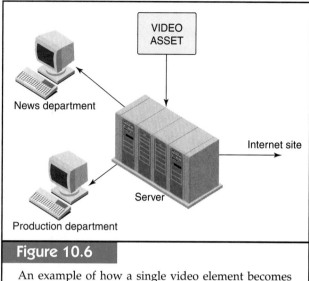

Figure 10.6

An example of how a single video element becomes an asset and can thus be used simultaneously by different people in a video production facility.

for example, can ingest video footage at four times speed, meaning that an hour of footage would take only 15 minutes to record. It is likely this speed will increase in the future as bandwidth improves and compression becomes more efficient.

Finally, video that is already in digital form on another server can be copied as a file transfer. This works the same way as if you copied your class notes from your home computer to a floppy disk. Video on servers exists essentially as very large data files, so these files can be copied from one connected server to another rather easily.

Using Servers

An ever-increasing number of video servers are available, offering a wide variety of functions, quality levels, and storage capacities. Some servers are designed specifically for use with one compression system, while others can use a variety of types. More expensive systems also have the capability to simultaneously input and output multiple bitstreams, meaning that video can be going into and coming out of the system at the same time. An increasing number of servers are also designed to simultaneously work with standard-definition and high-definition formats.

Most servers consist of two main parts: a record/play unit with a computer interface that allows the

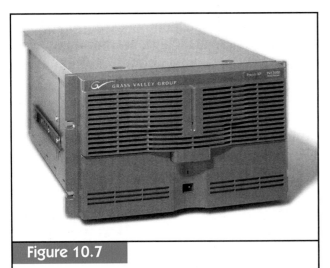

Figure 10.7

A video server disk drive unit. *Photo courtesy of Thomson Grass Valley.*

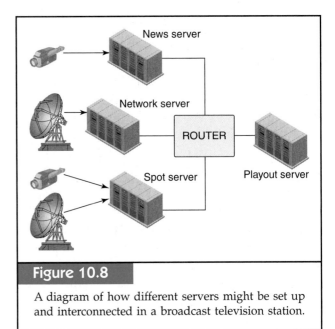

Figure 10.8

A diagram of how different servers might be set up and interconnected in a broadcast television station.

operator to access and manipulate video information and an array of disk drives used to actually store the data. (See Figure 10.7.) Some servers, however, come only as storage units. These types use some other piece of equipment (such as a switcher) as an external controller. One popular method of providing the storage and speed capacity required to work with digital video is **RAID (Redundant Array of Independent Disks).** RAID uses a group of hard disks wired and controlled as if they were one large, very fast hard disk.

Servers can be connected together (and to other video components) using a network system. The faster the network system—meaning the higher the bandwidth—the better. One network system that has become popular for video storage is called **fibre channel;** it allows data transfer speeds of up to 200 Mb/s. **Routers** allow the digital signal from one source to be sent to a number of different locations. Such systems allow servers to share digital bitstreams and to move digital data from place to place within a production facility or across long distances.

Figure 10.8 shows how a local television station might use a series of servers to meet its needs. The news department would have its own server, networked to allow different news department personnel to access information on it. Footage shot in the field would be ingested into the server, then would be available for editing into **roll-ins.** The finished roll-ins would then be fed to the station's main **playout** server.

Commercials would be stored on a **spot server** (named for commercial "spots") and would be transferred to the playout server when it was close to the time they would air. Commercials would be ingested into the spot server over a satellite connection (for national commercials), or directly from the production department (for locally produced commercials). Much of this processing of data could be automated; the servers could be programmed to exchange the relevant data files at appropriate times. Programming from the broadcast network would be ingested via satellite and stored on a dedicated server until it was time for it to air. At that point, it would be transferred to the playout server. Live network programming, of course, could still be aired by the station; this programming would simply come directly from satellite and bypass the server systems.

Other Tapeless Storage Systems

Other nonlinear storage systems are available besides traditional hard-disk-based servers. For example, as discussed in Chapter 5, some camcorders come with a hard disk drive instead of a tape recorder. Other manufacturers make camcorders equipped with memory cards or optical-disk recorders, similar to a home CD-ROM or DVD.

The traditional impediment to these types of systems has been cost. It is still generally cheaper

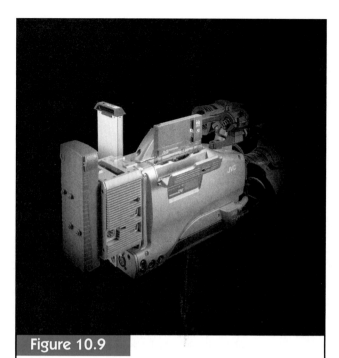

to record field footage to tape than to a hard disk, memory card, or optical disk, but the gap is quickly narrowing. JVC's GY-DV5000U camcorder, for example, can record up to 24 hours of audio and video onto a Compact Flash memory card. (See Figure 10.9.) These nonlinear storage options offer the additional advantage of being able to more closely integrate with servers. For example, using a hard-disk recording unit, a camera operator could shoot footage and then simply remove the disk unit and plug it into a central server. The footage would then be available for editing nearly instantaneously.

10.4 Principles of Videotape Recording

Despite the significant advantages of video servers and other tapeless systems, videotape technology is likely to remain an important part of video production, at least for the near term. For one thing, videotape is still a more cost-effective storage solution in many cases.

There is also nearly a half-century worth of video production that has been recorded onto various types of videotape; to access this vast library of information, we still need videotape players. Thus, although the future clearly belongs to tapeless technologies, for now it is important to understand videotape recording as well.

The development of videotape recording was based on the technology that had already been used for sound. Namely, sound energy can be made to align particles of iron oxide on a tape through the action of a magnetic **recording head** passing in contact along the tape. As shown in Figure 10.10, these alignment patterns (which are invisible to the naked eye) are actually an electromagnetic "memory" of the original information. When the tape is moved past the magnetic head in **playback** mode, this action reproduces the original **frequencies** and **amplitudes** that were recorded (or, in the case of digital, the original pattern of "on" and "off" pulses), and the resulting signal can be amplified and transduced into pictures and sound.

This simple configuration, however, in which a single stationary head records information laterally along the tape, would not be able to handle the massive amount of information required to reproduce a video signal. For such a system to work, it would have to either use *very wide* tape or move the tape *extremely quickly* past the head, neither of which would be feasible.

Helical-Scan Videotape Recording

An alternative—and decidedly more practical—way to record and play back video information on tape is to use a **helical scan** system. In this system, two or more playback/record heads are mounted on a tilted drum, as shown in Figure 10.11. During recording or playback, this drum spins rapidly, allowing the heads to move at an angle to the tape. As the tape is drawn past the spinning heads, they record (or play back) information in successive parallel slanted tracks across the tape, as shown in Figure 10.12. For this reason, helical scan is often referred to as **slant-track recording.**

To make helical scan systems work, the tape must be partially wrapped around the spinning head drum. The configuration used in VHS tape recorders, as shown in Figure 10.13, is typical of other systems.

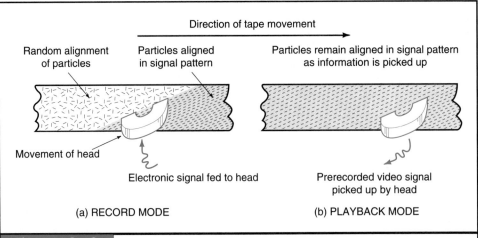

Direction of tape movement →

Random alignment
of particles

Particles aligned
in signal pattern

Particles remain aligned in signal pattern
as information is picked up

Movement of head

Electronic signal fed to head

Prerecorded video signal
picked up by head

(a) RECORD MODE

(b) PLAYBACK MODE

Figure 10.10

Video recording and playback heads. (*a*) Record Mode. The electronic video signals sent to the record head activate the magnetized head to align the iron oxide particles on the tape to retain a permanent (until erased) pattern of the recorded electronic video signal. (*b*) Playback Mode. The prerecorded video signals on the videotape generate a small amount of electrical current in the playback head that duplicates the original video signal.

When the tape is inserted into the machine, movable roller posts pull the tape out from the cassette and wind it around the head drum. As the tape records (or plays back), it follows the path created by the roller posts. This allows the tape heads to maintain contact with the surface of the tape for a longer period of time as the tape moves past, creating longer recording tracks.

Videotape Track Functions

Many different tape formats are in use, and these formats use many different track

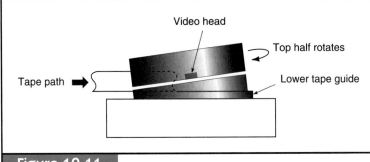

Video head

Top half rotates

Tape path →

Lower tape guide

Figure 10.11

Helical-scan videocassette drum assembly. The playback/record heads are attached to the rotating top half of the tilted head assembly.

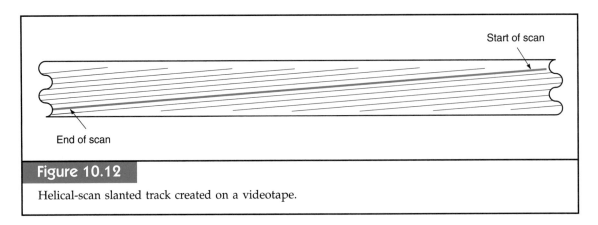

Start of scan

End of scan

Figure 10.12

Helical-scan slanted track created on a videotape.

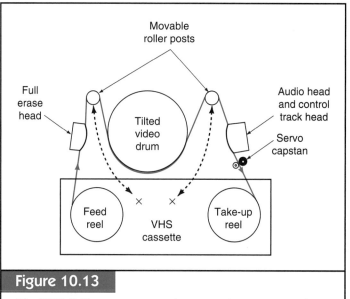

Figure 10.13

The VHS "M" wrap system of transporting tape past the head drum after it has been pulled from the cassette. The "M" refers to the shape of the tape's path, as shown.

configurations. In fact, the only generalizations that can be made about *all* videotape formats are that they use helical scan tracks to record video information and that they have one or more additional tracks available for audio and other information. Figure 10.14 shows a summary of popular analog and digital tape formats in use today. The chart also shows the tape width used, whether the format is component or composite, and—for

Format	Date Introduced	Analog/Digital	Tape Width	Component/Composite	Sampling Rate
U-Matic	1971	Analog	3/4-inch	Composite	N/A
VHS	1976	Analog	1/2-inch	Composite	N/A
Type C	1978	Analog	1-inch	Composite	N/A
Betacam SP	1986	Analog	1/2-inch	Component	N/A
D-1	1986	Digital	19 mm	Component	4:2:2
M-II	1986	Analog	1/2-inch	Component	N/A
S-VHS	1987	Analog	1/2-inch	Component	N/A
D-2	1988	Digital	19 mm	Composite	N/A
Hi-8	1989	Analog	8 mm	Component	N/A
D-3	1991	Digital	1/2-inch	Composite	N/A
D-5	1992	Digital	1/2-inch	Component	4:2:2
D-6	1993	Digital	1/2-inch	Component	4:2:2
Digital Betacam/SX	1993	Digital	1/2-inch	Component	4:2:2
Digital-S (D-9)	1995	Digital	1/2-inch	Component	4:2:2
DV	1995	Digital	1/4-inch	Component	4:1:1
DVCAM	1995	Digital	1/4-inch	Component	4:1:1
DVCPRO (D-7)	1995	Digital	1/4-inch	Component	4:1:1*
HDCAM	1997	Digital	1/4-inch	Component	3:1:1

* 4:2:2 for DVCPRO50 and DVCPROHD versions

Figure 10.14

Popular analog and digital videotape formats.

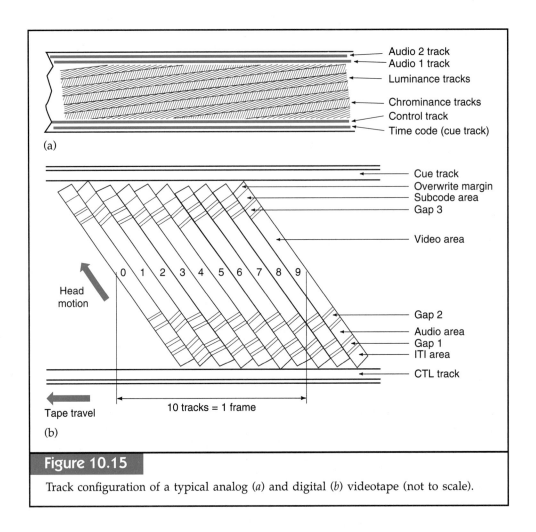

Audio 2 track
Audio 1 track
Luminance tracks
Chrominance tracks
Control track
Time code (cue track)

(a)

Cue track
Overwrite margin
Subcode area
Gap 3

Video area

0 1 2 3 4 5 6 7 8 9

Head motion

Gap 2
Audio area
Gap 1
ITI area

CTL track

Tape travel

10 tracks = 1 frame

(b)

Figure 10.15

Track configuration of a typical analog (*a*) and digital (*b*) videotape (not to scale).

digital systems—the sampling rate. You will note that although some analog formats are still in use, the last new analog format came out more than 15 years ago. Clearly, digital formats are the trend in videotape recording.

Although it is beyond the scope of this chapter to show the track configurations of all tape formats, it is certainly necessary to understand generally how video information and other information are recorded on tape. For that reason, this section looks at the general track configurations for analog and digital recording formats.

Figure 10.15 shows the track configurations for a typical analog and a typical digital tape format. In this particular case, the analog format is Betacam, and the digital format is DVCPRO (which, along with DV-CAM, is a popular variant of the DV tape format), but that is not important. What is important is looking generally at what is recorded on *all* videotape formats and the methods of doing so.

In every tape format, the majority of space will be taken up by recorded video information. Somewhere around 80 percent of the tape area likely will be used to record the video. This is logical, given video's previously discussed resource requirements. In analog formats, the video information is normally carried on a series of slanted tracks known collectively as the **video track.** Since the analog format shown in Figure 10.15(a) is a component format, you will note that the video track is actually made up of separate chrominance and luminance tracks. In digital formats, the chrominance and luminance information are recorded into the same area; however, the information remains discrete, and the separate elements can be extracted on playback.

Audio information in analog formats is typically recorded onto separate **longitudinal tracks** that run parallel to the tape edges (similar to the sound recording example discussed at the beginning of this section). The heads that record and play back this information remain stationary as the tape is drawn past them, as shown previously in Figure 10.10. The format in Figure 10.15(a) has two separate longitudinal audio tracks. Some analog formats record audio along with video on slanted tracks in a process called **audio frequency modulation (AFM),** which allows higher-quality audio than most longitudinal recording. The downside to AFM recording, however, is that it does not allow the audio information to be edited without disturbing the video information. VHS tapes with hi-fi (stereo) audio record this way.

In digital formats, the audio is often recorded along with the video on slanted tracks. Again, since it is digital, the information can be "mixed" and yet still remains discrete. Digital audio is often recorded by the use of **pulse code modulation (PCM),** which samples the analog audio signal and records it in digital form. Unlike AFM, PCM audio is separate from the video, so it can be edited easily. DVCPRO can be configured to record either two or four channels of PCM audio. However, because it is not possible to "scan" the PCM audio when a DVCPRO tape machine is in "search" mode, audio information can be duplicated on the longitudinal cue track.

Earlier sections have described how various video components are synchronized by means of synchronization pulses. When video information is recorded, these synchronization pulses are recorded onto the **control track** of the tape. During the playback of recorded videotape programs, the machine reads the signals and uses them to regulate the speed of the tape and the video head wheel to maintain proper synchronization. It does this by feeding the synchronization information to the **servo capstan,** the device that actually pulls the tape through the machine (as shown in Figure 10.13).

The **subcode** areas of the digital tape are used to record time code information (as discussed in Section 10.1), while the **insert track information** area provides signals used for automated functions, editing, and audio dubbing. The gap and overwrite areas are used to keep the different types of information separate. The final track shown on the analog tape is the **cue track,** the name of which is derived from a time when it was used for verbal editing cues. Today, it is most often used to record time code.

Generational Losses in Analog Videotape

When a copy of an analog videotape is made, the quality of that copy is not as good as the original. The reason for this loss of quality is that it is impossible to make an *exact* copy of an analog video signal on tape. For instance, if you start with an original recording—called a **master**—and make a copy (called a **dub**) of it, the copy will not look quite as good as the master, although it may take a trained eye to see the difference. If you then make a copy of that copy, the resulting tape will look even worse. Each copy made in this manner is called a **generation,** and the quality of each succeeding generation is diminished. The amount of generational loss depends on the videotape format (home VHS tapes deteriorate noticeably after only a single generation, for example), but in general you should be sure not to work with copies of videotapes when it isn't necessary.

The advent of digital tape formats has greatly lessened generational losses caused by videotape copying. In theory it is possible to copy many generations while maintaining the quality of the original. This is one reason that manufacturers have been concentrating on digital videotape formats over the past two decades.

10.5 Video Recorder Operation and Controls

The setup and operation of any videotape machine involves the use of components that generally fall under three headings: connectors, control mechanisms, and visual indicators. The arrangement, appearance, and even terminology may vary with the manufacturer, but once you know what to look for, these basic components can be identified on any video recorder.

First, since videotape machines work in conjunction with other electronic units (cameras, microphones, other recorders, speakers, monitors, editing equipment, etc.), as a primary step, you must be able to make these hookups accurately and quickly. Second, you must learn how to manipulate the collection of knobs, switches, and buttons that are used to start, stop, or change the basic audio and video functions of record, playback, and editing. Third, you must be able to monitor and understand those things that tell whether the machine is operating the way you want it to—informational feedback provided by items such as monitors, lights, and meters.

Connections

In a studio where equipment and its related cables are permanently in place, the connection process takes place primarily at the patch bays, where labeled receptacles indicate the sources and termination points of feeds. Often the camera, VTR, and other pieces of equipment are semipermanently connected, so you, as an operator, do not need to deal with the connections unless you do not obtain proper picture and sound.

However, much of the small-format video for educational and industrial purposes—and much remote production—involves a temporary "lash-up" of video recorders, cameras, mics, monitors, and associated gear in out-of-studio field locations. Whether in the studio or in the field, the operational linking of components will be most efficiently accomplished when three interacting factors are kept in mind:

1. The nature and purpose of all signal feeds
2. The direction and pathway of all signal flow
3. The structure of the connective hardware

If you know what your signal is supposed to do, it is easier to know where it should be going and how you are going to connect it to get it there.

Signal Flow

The first thing to keep in mind when making any connection is simply whether you are dealing with an *input* or an *output*. Does the receptacle into which you are putting one end of a cable represent the signal output of a component? If so, with that connection made, the other end of the cable obviously becomes the new output of the signal—and as a result goes into an input

receptacle to continue the movement of the signal. Incorrect connections not only cause operational delay but also can cause serious damage to equipment.

Signal Levels

One of the main principles involved in the connection process is understanding the different compositions and strengths of analog signals that you must deal with in making those hookups. In addition to differentiating audio from video feeds, you must realize that some lines, such as RF and digital signals, carry both audio and video.

The basic concept of amplification differences was introduced when discussing audio in Chapter 7. The same principle applies to how the video recorder handles audio and video. The recorder has a provision for the input of an external microphone ("mic in"). This low-level signal is then amplified to **line level** within the machine before being recorded on tape. However, previously amplified signals (an audio recorder, for example) are to be plugged only into "line" audio inputs. If these are plugged into a "mic" input, you will get a distortion from the double amplification.

Connecting Hardware

Connective hardware for audio and video equipment involves a wide variety of receptacles and matching plugs. For example, line video may utilize a BNC, S-Video, or RCA plug. Audio is usually handled by a phone plug, miniplug, or RCA plug (see Chapter 7). With low-impedance mic lines, a three-pin XLR connector is quite common. Figure 10.16 shows the most commonly used video-connecting hardware. The F-type connector (which may be either a "push-on" or screw type) is used to make RF connections of both video and audio. It is the connector you most likely use for the cable TV service in your home. Both the RCA plug and the BNC connector are used to connect video, although the former is usually used only in low-end applications. In a professional environment, you are more likely to use a BNC connector. The S-Video is a four-connector plug that provides separate luminance and chrominance signals. Of course, digitized video and audio also can be connected using a wide variety of computer cabling, such as the **Firewire** connector shown.

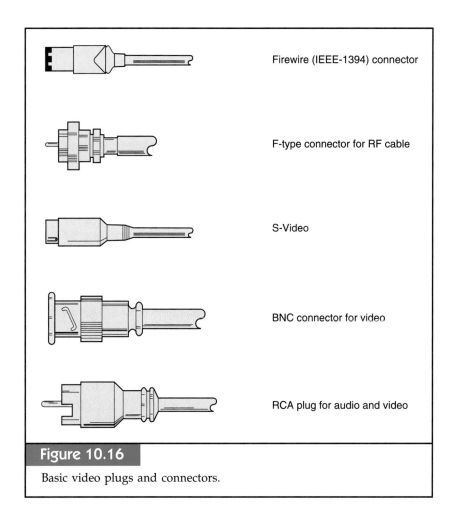

Figure 10.16

Basic video plugs and connectors.

Firewire (IEEE-1394) connector

F-type connector for RF cable

S-Video

BNC connector for video

RCA plug for audio and video

Because of all the differences in plugs and receptacles, the connecting process is greatly aided with a good supply of adapter plugs or cables with different connectors at the two ends. With a variety of these on hand, you can quickly connect a number of components. Caution and common sense, of course, should always be exercised when making such connections; you need to make sure that the connector you're adapting to is designed to use the *type of signal* you'll be connecting.

Controls

Regardless of the age or simplicity of design, the transport (tape movement) functions on all video recorders will have 8 to 10 basic controls. Normal-speed playback is accomplished by activating the control labeled "play." On many machines the recording mode is initiated by pressing play simultaneously with the "record" button; on other machines, just pressing record starts that function.

The "pause" control stops either the record or playback function and halts the movement of the tape. When pausing in record mode, you will continue to see whatever signal was being shown on the tape machine's monitor. When pausing in playback mode, you will see a "freeze-frame" picture. Pressing the pause button again will cause the previous function to resume.[4] You should be cautious about leaving a videotape recorder in pause mode for long periods of time, however, as it can cause wear on the tape and **head clogs,** in which small particles from the tape become lodged in the head and prevent proper recording and playback. The "stop" button differs from pause in that it actually releases tension on the tape, preventing damage to the tape or heads.

To get the tape quickly from one point to another, fast-forward and rewind controls are used. This is usually referred to as **search** mode. On some units, these two modes will produce a somewhat recognizable picture for visual search purposes as well as speeded-up sound. Many VTRs also will have variable-speed controls that facilitate slow or sped-up motion, either forward or backward. A **jog/shuttle knob** allows you to either rapidly search through a tape forward or backward or actually move the tape manually frame by frame by spinning the knob.

The "audio dub" (audio edit) control puts the audio record head into the record mode without activating the video record heads, making possible short audio-only edits or the addition of a whole new audio track.

Tracking and Skew

The path of the tape around the video drum is crucial to the playback of a proper picture. Bands of picture distortion sometimes result when a tape recorded on one machine is played back on another with a slightly different horizontal alignment. This problem can usually be corrected by an adjustment of the **tracking control.** The normal operating setting as determined by the factory is located at the top point (12 o'clock position) on the dial. The slight "click" you feel when passing this point is known as a *detent* position. After any tracking adjustment is made, the knob should be returned to this position for each new recording or playback.

Most professional units have an additional control for the tape transport called **skew.** When the top third of the picture appears to bend to the left or the right, it is usually caused by an incorrect amount of tension on the tape as it passes around the video drum. This is adjusted by means of the skew control knob. Keep in mind that this is a problem on the playback machine, not on the machine on which you are editing or dubbing. As with the tracking control, the knob should always be returned to the detent position before that same machine is used for a subsequent recording or playback.

Selector Switches

As discussed previously, most video recorders are designed to function with a variety of different types of inputs, such as a camera, the tuner in a receiver/monitor, or a studio line feed. There must, therefore, be an **input selector switch** that differentiates between the various levels and/or sync sources of these inputs. On

some machines, another switch separately controls the use of internal or external sync sources. The internal sync position allows the recorder to strip off any incoming sync signal and use the synchronization pulse from the machine itself during the recording process.

The **remote/local switch** determines whether the machine responds to controls on the front panel of the machine or to an external controller. When in "remote" position, you can activate the machine's functions (playback, search, record, etc.) from an external editing controller or computer. When in "local" position, the machine will respond only to front-panel commands.

Recording Tabs

One important control element is not located on the videotape machine but on the tape itself. Most formats provide a **recording tab** designed to prevent accidental erasure of a tape. When the tab is either broken off (in the case of a VHS tape) or switched to record-inhibit position, a VTR will not record on the tape. A sensor located inside the machine determines the position (or absence) of the record tab when the tape is put in the machine. You should become familiar with the location of the record tabs for the tape format you use in your classes.

Visual Indicators and Meters

Although they vary from machine to machine, there are a number of controls that group together in operational units and directly relate to a visual readout, starting with the light that indicates when the power on/off switch is activated.

The **VU meters** are used to monitor the level of audio signals being played or recorded. Before recording, you should use an audio reference tone to set the audio level to 0 dB. On many machines, you must first put the unit into "record pause" mode (by pressing the play, record, and pause buttons simultaneously) before the VU meters will register incoming audio. During recording and playback, you should monitor the audio level on the VU meters and adjust levels if necessary.

On many machines, the VU meters also are used to monitor tracking. To show tracking level on the VU meter, you usually move a "meter select" switch to the "tracking" position. After adjusting the tracking, you can return the meter to audio monitoring by moving the switch back to "audio."

VU meters can be either analog or LED. Analog units have moving "needles" that indicate the setting of audio or tracking. LED units indicate readout with rows of small LED lights.

Automatic Gain Control

Most portable recorders have an **automatic gain control (AGC)** option for audio. When this is switched on, the AGC serves as a limiter that keeps incoming audio feeds within a range that does not exceed the capabilities of the recorder. However, the AGC will often automatically boost the "noise" of the line signal when there is momentarily no other incoming signal (a pause in the voice or music source), thereby recording an amplified hiss. The AGC selector switch allows you to defeat this feature.

Most machines reflect their recording and editing functions with additional video control switches and indicators. A **video control** knob adjusts the level of incoming video, and a related AGC off-on switch allows for automatic gain control of the video signal. These are usually grouped with the video VU meter.

Warning Indicators

An increasing number of portable recorders include warning lights and status indicators that provide several types of important feedback to the operator. Sometimes these are on the body of the camcorder, and sometimes indications appear in the camera viewfinder. On some machines, a *pause mode* light serves as a reminder that the heads are continuing to scan the tape. There are also lights that indicate the condition of the battery, the presence of moisture that is dangerous to the circuitry ("auto off"), a tape supply warning light that lets you know you are coming to the end of your videotape, and a *servo lamp* that warns of improper tape transport.

Counters and Location Indicators

Almost all recorders have some sort of counter or other component that allows an operator to locate predetermined points on a recorded tape. On lower-end consumer models, there may only be a three- or four-digit readout that counts the revolutions of the take-up reel. Since the circumference of the tape on each reel

changes as the reels unwind and wind, the operator must keep in mind that a given number of revolutions will indicate different amounts of tape footage, depending on how far you are into the program. The real-time counters found on higher-end consumer and professional VTRs are far more useful.

Most consumer-level VCRs have a zero-point reset button that, on rewind, brings the tape back to the zero point and comes to an automatic stop. A somewhat more complex memory control permits the quick location of a series of selected points with the tape in the fast-forward mode.

10.6 Video Recorder Performance and Maintenance

The key to successful operation of any videotape recorder is *familiarity* and *practice*. Instructions and specific controls will, of course, vary significantly from machine to machine. Become familiar with the ones to which you have access. Make certain you have taken full advantage of the instructions and directions for the particular models with which you will be working. Especially, follow the recommended care and maintenance instructions. This is particularly important for routine cleaning of the video heads. And then practice. Become familiar with the recorder. Under the guidance of a trained technician or instructor, work with the machine; experiment with it; find out what it will and will not do. Only then can you have the confidence and discipline to handle any video-recording and playback assignment given to you.

A major part of your professional discipline will be care and respect for all production equipment. Everyone will benefit if you follow a few common rules of preventative maintenance.

1. Videotape recorders require a constantly renewed supply of clean, cool, dry air. Heat, moisture, and cigarette smoke are damaging to all electronic equipment, especially VTRs. Never place books, cassette cases, or papers on top of the recorder; doing so seriously inhibits the flow of air. Liquid

containers should be kept away from video recorders.

2. Place a dust cover on the machine when it is not in use, but only after the unit has had time to cool off.

3. When a video recorder is moved, be extremely careful not to bump or jar the unit. Delicate components are easily damaged by slight shocks. Do not attempt to operate a recorder immediately after it has been moved from a cold to a warm environment.

4. Videotape should not be left in the recorder when the unit is not in use. Tapes should be rewound and properly stored in a cool, dry place.

5. Keep the recorder and tapes at a distance from other equipment that may be generating strong magnetic fields, as these can erase the information on the tapes.

6. As the videotape operator, always allow yourself time to think carefully through all connecting and patching procedures as well as the basic disciplines of machine operation. The time spent always pays off later in time saved.

Discussion Questions

1. What are the basic attributes of video signals? How do these attributes affect how video information is channeled, monitored, recorded, and played back?

2. What are the basic methods of converting analog to digital video? What do the concepts of sampling and quantization mean, and how do they affect the quality of the resulting digital video signal?

3. Discuss the five major compression methods. What are the advantages and disadvantages of each? How prevalent is each method in the industry?

4. Discuss the concepts of asset management and metadata in relation to digital video storage. How does metadata aid asset management?

5. Name and describe the various tracks recorded onto videotape. What is the function of each track?

Notes

1. In the 1970s, a system of recording analog video onto discs was developed for home use. This LaserDisc system featured better picture quality than VHS tape, but it was not recordable and so never caught on with home users. Also, some companies developed analog disc systems for recording video effects and editing. However, in practice, nearly all of these systems have been replaced by superior digital-based equipment.

2. Another type of component signal, RGB, separates the red, blue, and green color information of video signals, using three separate wires. RGB signals are sometimes used on computer systems.

3. Interestingly, the human eye is much more forgiving than the human ear when it comes to quantizing an analog signal. While 8-bit quantization (and certainly 10-bit) can produce a visually "flawless" picture, to produce the same perceived quality level of audio it takes at least 16 bits, and perhaps as many as 24.

4. On some machines, you press the "play" button again to release the pause mode and continue playing the tape.

CHAPTER 11

Editing

Reduced to its most basic definition, editing is the process of combining video and audio elements from various sources into a coherent whole. For example, you may have one videotape that has footage of the mayor waving to a crowd and then walking into his office and another that has an interview with the mayor in which he talks about his bid for reelection. Through editing, you can combine these video and audio sources, discarding material you don't need.

Using a switcher in a studio production situation, as discussed in Chapter 9, can be thought of as a form of *real-time* editing. Here, too, you are selecting various sources of video (cameras, satellite feeds, graphics, etc.) at appropriate times to create a coherent production. **Postproduction** editing, however, is usually a more deliberative process in which much more time is taken in selecting and combining various sources of video. As its name implies, postproduction editing takes place *after* the video material has been gathered. A postproduction editor may take many hours to create a finished product that is only a few minutes in length.

Two basic editing processes can be used in postproduction editing. **Linear editing** uses videotape both as the source of the footage to be used and as the recording medium. In essence, linear editing is recording from one videotape onto another. In **nonlinear editing,** all of the video footage is stored in digital form on a **random access** medium (such as a hard drive), then edited using a computer.

Nonlinear editing offers the random access to stored information described in Chapter 10, and it also overcomes many of the temporal limitations of linear editing, as you will see. Nonlinear systems such as the one shown in Figure 11.1 have been rapidly replacing tape-based systems. However, many tape-based editing systems are still in use and likely will be for some time. For that reason, this chapter discusses linear editing as well.

The *disciplines* of editing include thorough planning before the editing even begins and attention to aesthetic considerations. The *techniques* of editing, while differing according to the equipment being used, still involve general practices that are addressed in this chapter as it covers the following:

- Types of editing situations, including the difference between on-line and off-line editing (11.1)
- The importance of planning and making decisions about editing *before* entering the editing suite (11.2)
- The basic process of nonlinear editing, including capturing, editing, and outputting (11.3)
- The difference between assemble and insert editing (11.4)
- The basic processes of linear editing (11.4)
- The importance of understanding editing aesthetics, including continuity and ethical considerations (11.5)

11.1 | Editing Basics

As discussed, editing differs from studio production switching in that it is largely a postproduction process. There are, however, several different types of situations in which editing is used, each calling for a specific technique.

Editing Situations

Editing can be used in conjunction with studio-based production. The daytime "soaps" and some prime-time situation comedies are shot using a multiple-camera technique. Such a program is recorded while the director calls the shots as if it were a live production, and the output is recorded to tape or a **video server.** At the same time, each camera is *slaved* to its own recorder, which records everything that camera shoots during the production. Then, if a problem occurs during the production that involves a poor shot or a switching mistake, it can be corrected by editing in shots from one of the slaved cameras. For example, if the director calls for camera 1 but the **technical director** accidentally takes camera 2, the correct shot

from camera 1 can be edited in afterward. If one of the performers flubs a line, it might be possible to edit in the correct line from a dress rehearsal (if it was taped), or additional **pickup shots** might be recorded at the

Figure 11.1

Computer-based nonlinear editing systems like this Avid are rapidly replacing linear tape-based systems. © *2004 Avid Technology, Inc. All rights reserved. Avid is a registered trademark of Avid Technology, Inc. Image is provided courtesy of Avid Technology, Inc.*

end of the production. Correcting and improving shots and sound from the "live" studio-based production in this way is called **sweetening.**

Editing is also used in single-camera production situations such as dramas, commercials, rock videos, and documentaries. In these projects, camera footage usually includes multiple takes of individual segments, often shot out of sequence and at different locations. The editing process, then, essentially starts from scratch, assembling the program from these diverse video elements. This type of editing—on a much less sophisticated scale—is also used in news-gathering situations, as a videojournalist shoots the various parts of a news story (such as interviews, reporter stand-ups, and footage), then edits them together into a coherent story called a **package.** These packages, which are edited onto tape or a video server, are then used as part of the live production of the nightly newscast.

The newscast itself is produced in a manner similar to studio-based productions described in this section's first paragraph, and the recorded packages are played during the show as **roll-ins** (see Chapter 12). For example, the news anchor will say, "Joe Smith has the story about the mayor's visit to France," and then the package of the mayor's visit will be played. Shows like *Entertainment Tonight* and *60 Minutes* use the same technique.

Off-line and On-line Editing

The terms **off-line** editing and **on-line** editing used to have definite and discrete meanings. However, due in large part to the advent of low-cost, high-quality videotape recording formats and—later—computer-based nonlinear editing systems, their definitions are now somewhat blurred. To make clear what the terms *originally* meant and what they have actually come to mean, it is necessary to look at a bit of history.

In the early days of electronic videotape editing, it was common practice to make copies of the tapes containing raw footage and other material to be edited. These copies would then be used to edit a **rough cut,** a basic representation of what the finished program was supposed to look like. This was called off-line editing. Then, once the rough cut was exactly the way it was supposed to be, the original tapes would be used to create an edited **master** that would look (and sound) just like the rough cut, but at a higher quality. This was called on-line editing. The point were that the original tapes would not be subject to the wear (and possible damage) caused by a lot of editing "experimentation" and other work leading up to the finished product.

In most cases, off-line and on-line editing were done on separate equipment as well. A production house, for example, might have a dedicated off-line editing suite for rough cutting and a dedicated on-line editing suite for creating edited masters. The equipment in the off-line suite would normally be of a lower quality than the equipment in the on-line suite.

Today, the most commonly used definitions of off-line and on-line are based on these same concepts. If the *purpose* of the editing is to create a rough cut and not a finished product, it is generally called off-line editing. If the purpose is to create a finished product, it is generally called on-line editing. What has changed is that often the on-line and off-line editing are both done on the same equipment. For example, with nonlinear editing equipment, the editor might first create a rough cut using video that has been **captured,** or recorded onto the computer, at a lower quality (see Section 11.3), and later create the edited master using the same equipment but recapturing the video at higher quality. Or, if the finished product doesn't *need* to be of the highest technical quality (for example, a video to be shown only over the Internet), both the off-line and on-line work might be done using equipment that would only be good enough for off-line broadcast work.

On occasion, you will hear people make distinctions between on-line and off-line work that are not based on the purpose of the editing. Some people, for example, use "off-line" to refer to any equipment that is lower quality than "on-line." Others might refer to the *quality* of the finished product, saying that work produced for the Internet is "off-line" and work produced for broadcast-quality is "on-line." For our discussions, however, we use the purpose of the editing as the criteria for distinguishing the two terms: If the purpose is to create a rough cut, that's off-line editing; if the purpose is to create a finished product, that's on-line editing.

Title Class Project 1								
TC: Non-Drop Frame								
001	Footage1	V A1	C		01:05:15:00	01:05:25:00	00:00:10:00	00:00:20:00
002	Interview1	V A1	C		05:10:10:28	05:10:42:28	00:00:20:15	00:00:52:15
002	Interview1	V A1	D	015	05:10:10:13	05:10:10:28	00:00:20:00	00:00:20:15
003	Footage1	V A1	C		01:10:10:15	01:10:20:20	00:00:52:15	00:01:02:20

Figure 11.2

A sample portion of a printed edit decision list. At the top, you see the title of the project, and the time code mode (in this case, non-drop frame). From left to right, the columns are: (1) the event number, (2) the tape that the footage comes from; (3) the edit mode (all of the edits shown are video and audio channel 1); (4) the transition type (C = cut, D = dissolve); (5) the length of the transition (shown only in event 2); (6) the begin time on the playback deck; (7) the end time on the playback deck; (8) the begin time on the record deck; and (9) the end time on the record deck.

Edit Decision Lists

The transition from off-line to on-line mode is greatly facilitated by the creation of an **edit decision list (EDL).** As shown in Figure 11.2, the EDL keeps a record of each edit, including what tape the shot originally came from, where the shot is on the tape, and how long the edited shot is. It also shows transitions and which video and audio channels were edited. Once created in off-line mode, the EDL can be fed into the on-line system, allowing the editor to automate the production of the completed product.

Although they originated with tape-based linear editing, EDLs are also used in nonlinear editing. In these cases, the EDL won't necessarily keep track of which tape the shot was on, but of the shot's location on a video server or other storage device. EDLs can be created and used by both computer-based edit controllers (see Section 11.4) and nonlinear editing programs. In fact, you might do the off-line editing using a linear editing system, then transfer the EDL to a high-end nonlinear system to do the on-line work. An EDL may also be used to reedit a **standard-definition** program in **high definition.** For EDLs to work properly, however, all of the different tapes, servers, and other systems must identify footage using **time code,** which was discussed in Chapter 10.

Compression

The use of **compression** to make video signals less resource-intensive was discussed at length in Chap-

ter 10. However, at this point it is necessary to address some additional compression factors that bear directly on editing.

You will remember that the two main types of compression are **intraframe compression,** in which each **frame** of video is treated as a discrete unit, and **interframe compression,** in which frames are analyzed in groups, discarding information that doesn't change from frame to frame (such as the plain white background behind a person). Some compression systems, such as M-JPEG and DV, use only intraframe compression, while others, such as MPEG-1 and MPEG-2, use both intraframe *and* interframe compression.

Interframe compression systems can make the video signal more compact because most of the video frames they send are not complete. Consider a group of 30 frames of video of a person standing in front of a white wall. For the first frame of this video, the compression system will create the entire frame, containing all of the information in the original signal. These frames are called *intracoded,* or "I," frames. However, the next several frames are not likely to be complete; instead they will contain only the portions of the frame that changed from the I frame (such as the person's moving lips and eyes). These frames are called *predicted,* or "P," frames, and they are created by essentially predicting what the picture will contain based on previous frames. There are also *bidirectional,* or "B," frames, which are predicted by looking at both previous and succeeding frames. In a group of 10 frames, then, there may be only two or so complete I frames, containing all of the information needed to create the frame.

If you think about this for a moment, you will be able to see how it could cause problems for editing. Since we get a complete frame only once every, say, 5 or 10 frames, we cannot perform frame-accurate editing. Instead of making an edit at time code 01:05:06:11, for example, we might have to make it at 01:05:06:18 because that's where the nearest I frame is. In some cases, that might not be a big problem, but if we require pinpoint editing at a precise frame, it could be.

That is why formats that do not use interframe compression, such as DV, are often preferred for editing. However, some MPEG-2 systems can actually create extra I frames on command if necessary. In other words, if the editor wanted to edit at precisely 01:05:06:11 and there was no I frame there, the system could create one. Also, MPEG profiles can be adapted so that more I frames are available to facilitate editing, but this of course comes at the price of a lower **compression ratio**. Interframe compression does not make precise-frame editing impossible by any means, but you need to be aware of the potential challenges it can create.

11.2 Editing Preparation

The process of editing preparation should begin long before you sit down at an editing system to put together a program. Taking time to properly *prepare* for the editing process will pay off once the actual editing begins, and the extra time you spend in the preediting phase is likely to be more than made up for by the time you will save during editing. And, since editing time—either off-line or on-line, linear or nonlinear—is expensive, good preparation reaps financial rewards as well. In fact, you should begin preparing for editing before the first shot is recorded, and each step in the production process should be taken with the editing process in mind.

Whether it is to be edited using linear or nonlinear equipment, most footage is initially shot or recorded onto videotape. Although an increasing number of products record directly onto computer disk or memory card, tape is still by far the most common method of acquiring and storing video. For that reason, the remainder of this chapter assumes that video footage is being acquired using tape. Although there are a wide variety of tape formats as discussed in Chapter 10, the basic process of gathering video and editing is the same no matter what format is being used. Of course, it is usually best to shoot your video using a format that is compatible with your editing system; otherwise, you will have to make a copy of your tape in the proper tape format and thus lose some quality from the original.

Shooting

The old adage "Shoot to edit" is a good admonition to keep in mind. To this end, you should follow not only the aesthetic rules discussed in Chapter 5 but also the directing methods discussed in Chapter 4. All tapes should be clearly and logically labeled to facilitate later use. Since most field tapes are less than an hour long, it is also frequently a good idea to set the time code hour to a different number for each tape. For example, the first tape could begin with time code 01:00:00:00, the second with 02:00:00:00, and so on. This can help speed the review and editing process, because the editor will immediately know that any shot with a time code reading of 02 hours must be on tape 2.

Review

Once all of the footage has been shot, you should critically and systematically examine the material. During the review phase, you should assemble a **shot log** that lists all of the shots on each tape. To facilitate review (and keep the original tapes from being damaged), you might make a VHS dub of all of the footage using a **time code burn-in,** as shown in Figure 11.3. This will allow you to see the time code points for all shots on a regular VHS recorder.

Decision Making

As part of the review process, you also will begin to make decisions about how the footage will be edited. This includes picking shots and deciding which takes of particular scenes will be used in the finished product. Although some final shot selection decisions will have to wait until editing actually begins, during the review and decision-making phases you will begin to

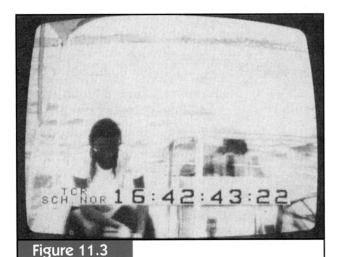

Figure 11.3

A dubbed VHS tape with time code burn-in shows the time code addressing from the original tapes.

11.3 Nonlinear Editing

An ever-growing number of nonlinear editing systems are available, ranging in price from a couple of hundred dollars to tens of thousands of dollars. The most popular nonlinear editing systems are the those made by Avid and Media 100 and the software-based Apple *Final Cut Pro* and Adobe *Premiere*.[1] At the most basic level, however, all systems are really nothing more than computers with specialized hardware to input and output video and audio, and specialized software (and sometimes hardware) to perform the editing functions. Some programs are designed around Macintosh computers (see Figure 11.4), while others are for Windows-based PCs.

The basic variables among nonlinear systems have to do with speed, quality of output, formats of video, graphics, audio accepted, input options, storage capacity, and sophistication and quality of special effects. Not surprisingly, the more features, speed, and quality you desire, the more you will have to pay for a nonlinear system. The $200 system that turns your home

assemble a preliminary EDL by hand, noting which shots will be used along with time code points. Selecting the shots to be used is especially important when using nonlinear editing, as this will determine which portions of the tape you will capture, as discussed in the next section.

Figure 11.4

Apple's *Final Cut Pro* is a software-based nonlinear editing system designed for Macintosh computers.   *Screen shot courtesy Apple Computer, Inc.*

computer into a nonlinear video editor may be fine for putting together wedding videos, but to do professional quality work you'll need something better. Systems designed for high-definition work, not surprisingly, are the most expensive.

Since such a wide variety of systems are available, and since each system has its own particular operating methods, this section discusses nonlinear editing in general terms, incorporating a few specific examples from a Media 100 editing system as an example. The only way to *really* learn how to use any nonlinear editing system is to study the manual and devote many hours to hands-on practice. This section gives you a running start.

File Management

Since the central element of a nonlinear editing system is a computer, considerations relating to managing data files are extremely important to the editing process. Before you begin editing, most nonlinear systems require you to create a "project" file that will hold the general information about the project you're working on. As you work on the project, you will create other files to save data contained in **bins** and **timelines** (as discussed later in this section). The bin, timeline, and other files are normally "associated" with a project file, meaning that when you open the project file later, the other files will automatically open along with it.

It is extremely important—especially in academic settings where several different people will likely be using the same machines—that you are careful about how and where you save your data files. Your school may have specific rules for naming files, but it is always a good idea to give all files descriptive names—containing your last name if possible. For example, the name "Foust Assignment 1 project" tells you (and others) a lot more about what the data are than a name like "My test 1." You also need to be aware of *where* you're saving your files—on what disk drive and in what folder. Again, your school may have specific guidelines for you to follow.

Since storage space is likely to be at a premium—especially in academic settings—you might have to move your data files off the machine during the times you're not editing. This can be accomplished by transferring the files over a **network** to a central server computer or by copying them onto removable media such as optical discs.

It is also important to make sure your data are backed up, or copied to another location. If you have a project that you've devoted many hours to and you experience a hard-disk crash or other mishap, you can lose all of your work. For that reason, you should save your data files frequently and be sure to make regular backups.

Raw Material—Capturing and Digitizing

Before any editing can take place on a nonlinear system, the raw material that will make up the completed presentation must be captured, or brought into, the computer. In the case of analog video, this process also involves **digitizing** (converting the analog signals to digital signals), which occurs as part of the capture process. The bulk of captured material is likely to be video footage, although graphics, animations, and audio files also can be brought into the computer as well.

As noted, most video footage is still gathered on tape, although with time an increasing percentage of video footage will be shot on nonlinear media such as hard disks. Individual pieces of captured information are called **clips,** which appear as icons on the computer screen. The individual clips are stored in a window called a bin.[2] (See Figure 11.5.)

To select footage to be captured, the editor designates an **in point** and **out point** on the tape, representing the beginning and end times of the clip. Using time code can help automate the capture process, but if your equipment doesn't have it, you can still designate clips using control-track numbers. Figure 11.6, for example, shows three clips to be captured from a section of videotape. For the first clip, the in point is 00:00:30:00 and the out point is 00:00:36:00.

You normally don't capture all of the footage you have available; doing so would be a waste of time and hard-disk space. Instead, as part of the edit-preparation process you should have compiled a list of the footage you'll need to complete your project. There is no point, for example, in taking time to capture footage of takes where talent flubbed lines or the lighting was wrong.

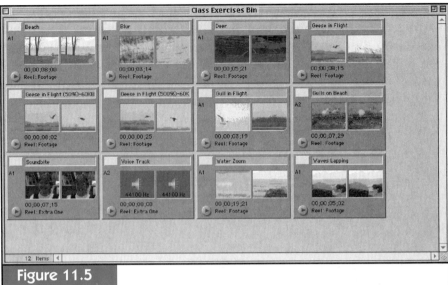

A bin window contains various clips to be used in an editing project.
Screen shot courtesy Media 100, Inc.

Working from your list, then, you will only digitize the portions of the tape that are likely to be used in the project. You also can choose the quality level of the captured audio and video signals. When doing off-line editing, for example, it is likely you will capture at a lower quality level.

Most nonlinear editors allow you to keep track of where your captured footage came from. In other words, you make note of the particular tape that each shot was originally recorded on. This is particularly valuable if for some reason you have to go back and recapture a shot—you'll be able to tell exactly which tape it came from and, if you're using time code, exactly where on the tape it is.

Video and audio can be captured in three basic ways: (1) as an analog signal, (2) as a compressed or uncompressed digital signal, or (3) as a file transfer. The choices are similar to ways to **ingest** video onto servers discussed in Chapter 10, and, in fact, the basic idea is the same—we just use the term "ingest" for servers and "capture" (or **import**) for nonlinear editors.

Capturing Analog Signals

To capture analog signals, you simply connect the video and audio outputs of a videotape machine (either the one on the camera or a separate unit) to the in-

puts of the nonlinear editing system. This method can be used for either analog or digital **standard-definition** signals, and in fact is the *only* choice for analog signals.

Nonlinear systems have a screen interface that allows you to oversee the capture process (see Figure 11.7). In most cases, this interface lets you actually control the tape machine from the computer, meaning you can use the on-screen buttons to cue up the parts of the tape you want to digitize. If your system does not offer this option, you will have to operate the transport controls on the recorder itself. This method of capturing video takes place in real time, meaning that if you have an hour of footage to digitize, it will take you at least an hour. In practice, it is likely to take much longer than that once you count the process of cueing up various parts of the tapes.

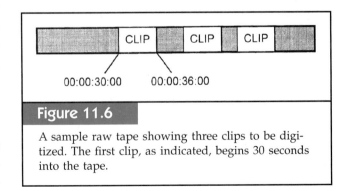

A sample raw tape showing three clips to be digitized. The first clip, as indicated, begins 30 seconds into the tape.

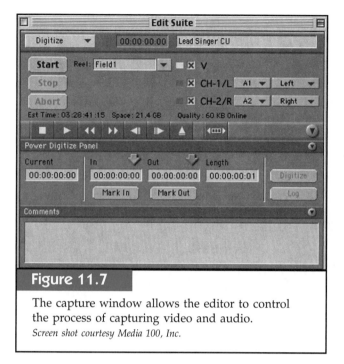

Figure 11.7

The capture window allows the editor to control the process of capturing video and audio.
Screen shot courtesy Media 100, Inc.

Capturing Digital Signals

If your video footage has been shot in a digital format, either standard definition or high definition, you can capture the data in digital form. To do this, you connect the digital output of the recorder (again, either the one on the camera itself or a separate unit) to the digital input of the nonlinear editor. This connection might be a **Firewire** (IEEE-1394), **serial digital interface (SDI)**, or some other type of connection. Depending on the system, you may be capturing compressed or uncompressed data.

As you are transferring digital bitstreams into the computer, the control interface will work the same way. You will use the computer to cue up the parts of the tape you want to capture. Some digital formats, as discussed in Chapter 10, allow four times speed digitizing, meaning you can digitize an hour of tape in 15 minutes.

Either analog or digital capture can be automated by the use of a **batch capture** function. Batch capture works by taking a "list" of begin and end points for clips and then capturing them all at once in a single pass of the tape. The list can either be created by going through the tape and marking the begin and end points as it plays, or by importing a text file into the nonlinear editor. Batch digitize saves the "start and stop" time of alternately marking, then capturing clips one by one, but it still can be time-consuming. The advantage, however, is that once you have started the batch digitize process, you don't have to do anything other than wait for the computer to finish. It's a good idea, though, to not stray too far from the computer as you're waiting, since systems can hang up or crash.

Batch capture also allows an editor to initially capture clips at low quality and work in off-line mode on creating a rough cut of the project. Once the rough cut is finished, the nonlinear editing system can recapture the clips at higher quality for on-line editing. In fact, once the clips have been recaptured, the nonlinear editing system can automatically apply the new, higher-quality footage to what the editor has already assembled. The actual on-line portion of the editing process, then, becomes less a reediting of the rough cut than simply converting the rough cut to master quality.

File Transfers

A third method of getting video footage into the nonlinear editing computer is by doing file transfers. If the video or audio you need to use is already on a server in your production facility, you can copy it to your computer's hard drive. This method is by far the fastest, but it requires that the video or audio already be stored on a server. It also can be used if your footage has been recorded on a computer disk or memory card as part of the camcorder. Either way, copying the information is usually accomplished by dragging file or folder icons from the server's folder to your local hard drive's folder.

Editing—Clips and Timelines

Once all of the video clips, audio clips, and other media have been brought into the nonlinear editing system, you are ready to begin editing. The user interface of a typical nonlinear editing system consists of three main parts: the bin, which, as discussed, holds the individual media clips; the **clip window,** which is used to manipulate clips; and the timeline, which is where individual clips are edited together (see Figure 11.8).

Additional windows can be opened to perform other types of operations, such as audio equalization, graphic design, and transitions. The editor also can choose to have more than one bin or timeline as well. The use of multiple bins allows an editor to organize

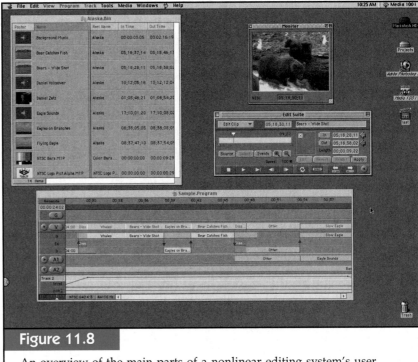

Figure 11.8

An overview of the main parts of a nonlinear editing system's user interface. At upper left is the bin, at upper right is the clip window, and below is the timeline.   *Screen shot courtesy Media 100, Inc.*

an editing project either according to individual media (audio, video, and graphics) or according to parts of a program. Having more than one timeline allows the editor to simultaneously edit more than one version of a program—perhaps one program is being edited with a soundtrack in English while another is being edited with a Spanish soundtrack, for example.

In addition to video clips, the bin will contain other types of media files, such as audio clips, transitions, and special effects. If you want to create a sophisticated graphic in a program like Adobe *PhotoShop*, for example, you could import the finished graphic into the bin. Double-clicking the mouse on an individual clip in a bin causes the clip to be displayed in the clip window, which allows the editor to make changes to the clip (see Figure 11.9). The length of a clip can be changed by dragging in-point or out-point locators, which correspond to the beginning and end of the clip, respectively. In points and out points also can be changed using the keyboard to type in a specific time code address.

In this way, individual clips can be precisely edited, a process called **trimming.** An important advan-

tage of nonlinear, however, is that even if a clip is shortened, it can be restored later to its original length. The editor also can apply special effects such as color correction or slow motion to a clip. In these cases, depending on the sophistication of the nonlinear system, the effects may be instantly applied or may have to be slowly "computed" in a process called **rendering.** When the editor has finished manipulating the clip, the new version of it is saved in the bin.

To begin editing, the editor simply drags a clip from a bin onto the timeline, then drags and places subsequent clips in the same manner. Alternately, on some editing systems you click a button or select a menu command to add a clip to the timeline. Clips that contain video and audio will appear in the appropriate channels on the program line; a clip that is audio only will only appear in an audio channel. Figure 11.10 shows an edited project consisting of three video clips with sound and a voice track in the second audio channel.

At any time in the editing process, you can play the entire program or only a portion of it. The downward-pointing white triangle with the vertical line attached

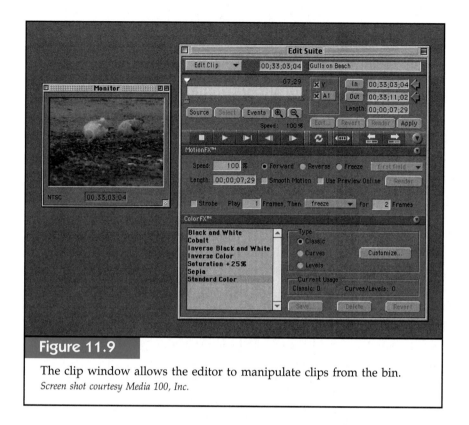

Figure 11.9

The clip window allows the editor to manipulate clips from the bin.
Screen shot courtesy Media 100, Inc.

indicates where in the timeline you are playing. To play just a portion of the program, you drag the triangle to the place you want to begin. As you drag it, you will see the program play in fast motion on the monitor. The timeline window also can be adjusted for how much of the program you want to see by dragging the scale indicator (the upward-pointing white triangle in the bottom left of the window). The timeline window shown in Figure 11.10 is set to show three-second increments across the top of the time scale. If you wanted to perform editing functions in precise detail, you could set the timeline to show a much smaller portion of the program by dragging the scale indicator to the left. Alternately, dragging it to the right will allow us to see *more* of the program. It is important to point out that these changes only affect how you *view* the program clips in the timeline window; it doesn't actually change the length of the clips or the program itself.

Clips on which the video and audio were captured together are said to be *synchronized,* meaning they are locked together. The "Deer," "Waves Lapping," and "Beach" clips shown in Figure 11.10 are synchronized. Normally you want clips to be synchronized in this way; the person's lip movements should match the audio of his or her

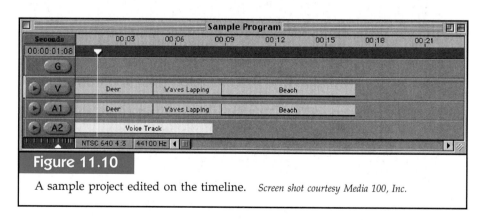

Figure 11.10

A sample project edited on the timeline. *Screen shot courtesy Media 100, Inc.*

voice, for example. However, at times you may want to unsynchronize the audio—if you wanted to remove the audio portion of a clip but leave the video, for example. To do this, you simply click on the clip in the timeline and select a menu command to unsynchronize it.[3] The clip's audio and video indicators in the timeline will change color to show that they are no longer synchronized, and then you can simply click on the audio portion of the clip and press the "delete" key to remove it. The clip still exists in its full form in the bin window; if you want to get the audio back you can simply recopy the clip from the bin to the timeline. Alternately, you could simply select the "Undo" menu item to "take back" the removal of the audio.

Clips in the timeline can be manipulated by dragging them with the mouse. Clicking near the edge of a clip will expand or contract it; clicking the left side of the clip changes the in point, while clicking the right side changes the out point. Normally, you change the in or out points of *both* the video and audio portions of a given clip in this way; however, if you want to change the in or out point of only one of the elements, you can do so. In the case of the Media 100, you simply

hold down the "Control" key on the keyboard as you drag the end of the clip—only the portion you're dragging (video or audio) will change.

You can use this technique to create a **split edit,** one in which the audio and video portions of a shot change at different times. For example, say you wanted to hear the sound of the waves lapping clip for a second before you actually *see* the shot of the waves lapping. You would simply move the out point of the audio portion of the "Deer" clip back one second, and move the video portion of the "Waves Lapping" clip ahead one second. This would create two "L-shaped" clips, as shown in Figure 11.11(a). The clips could then be dragged together to create the split edit, as shown in Figure 11.11(b). When you play back this sequence, you will hear the sound of the waves lapping for one second before you see the waves lapping shot.

As alluded to in the beginning of this chapter, one of nonlinear editing's great advantages is its ability to overcome the temporal limitations of linear editing. For example, imagine that you had edited the program shown in Figure 11.12(a), consisting of 10 shots with a

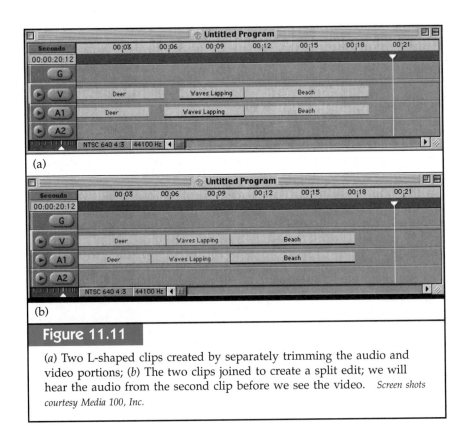

(a)

(b)

Figure 11.11

(*a*) Two L-shaped clips created by separately trimming the audio and video portions; (*b*) The two clips joined to create a split edit; we will hear the audio from the second clip before we see the video. *Screen shots courtesy Media 100, Inc.*

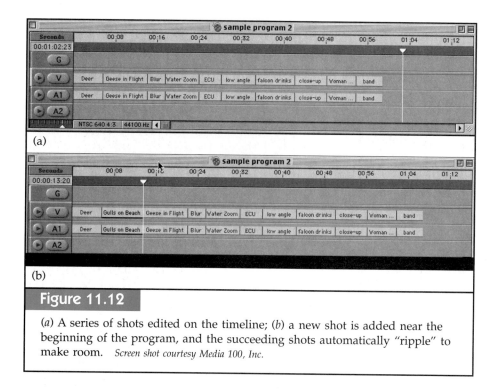

(a)

(b)

Figure 11.12

(*a*) A series of shots edited on the timeline; (*b*) a new shot is added near the beginning of the program, and the succeeding shots automatically "ripple" to make room. *Screen shot courtesy Media 100, Inc.*

total length of approximately one minute. Now, suppose you had forgotten to put a shot ("Gulls on Beach") between the first and second shots in the program—you still need all of the other shots to be the same length, but you need to add the new shot. With linear editing, your only choice would be to edit in the new shot and then reedit all of the other shots that come after that—there is no way that you can "stretch" the tape and just insert the new shot. With nonlinear editing, however, you *can* actually "create" time in the middle of a presentation, and it is remarkably easy to do so. You simply select the

new clip in the bin and then tell the editing software to insert it between the first and second clips. The editing software automatically "ripples" the clips following the new one, as shown in Figure 11.12(b).

To perform a transition other than a cut, the editor overlaps video clips in two separate video channels, as shown in Figure 11.13. On the Media 100, the overlap area represents the duration of the transition, although some nonlinear editors do not require you to overlap clips in this way. By bringing up the transition dialog box, you can select the type of transition you want—

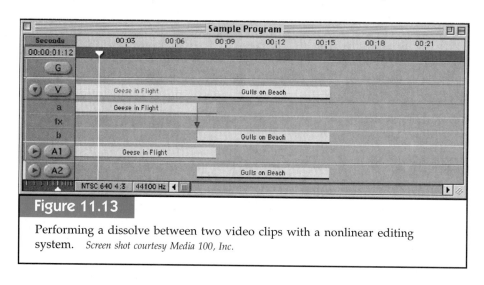

Figure 11.13

Performing a dissolve between two video clips with a nonlinear editing system. *Screen shot courtesy Media 100, Inc.*

dissolves, wipes, DVE effects. Nonlinear editing systems normally have a variety of transitions available, similar to those discussed in Chapter 9. Depending on the type of transition and the sophistication of the nonlinear system, the transition may have to render or may be immediately viewable.

Most nonlinear editing systems also have onboard graphics and titling capabilities. Using the title editor, you can make full-screen graphics, or graphics that can be keyed over video.

Output

A "finished" nonlinear editing presentation initially exists only as a series of digital data bits inside the computer's memory. Depending on the application, the finished presentation can be dubbed onto tape, or recorded onto a video server. Alternately, the program can be recorded onto an optical disc, or saved as a **streaming** file for use on the Internet (see Chapter 13). If the nonlinear editing was conducted as an off-line session, the most important output might be the computer-generated EDL, which then will be transferred to the on-line editing system.

Dubs to tape are made by simply playing the completed program with a tape machine attached to the nonlinear system's outputs. Some systems can be set up to automatically create and play back color bars, audio tones, slates, countdowns, and black signal before making the actual dub of the program. "Recordings" to a video server or other digital media are usually made by copying the finished data files.

11.4 | Linear Editing

Although there are many different configurations of linear editing systems, they all consist of at least three elements: a playback tape machine, a record tape machine, and an **edit controller** that operates the two tape machines in synchronization. (See Figure 11.14.) The edit controller allows the editor to perform basic videotape recorder functions such as playback, record, fast-forward, rewind, and search on each machine that is part of the editing system. The editor also uses the edit controller to set in and out points that designate the beginning and end of edits and to select the type of edit to be performed.

Figure 11.14

A typical edit controller for linear editing.

Once an edit has been prepared, the controller then synchronizes the playback and record machines and carries out the edit on the record machine. It synchronizes the machines by performing a **preroll**, which backs up each machine a few seconds before the edit point, then plays back the machines in unison to be sure they are running at exactly the same speed when the edit begins. At the conclusion of an edit, the edit controller stops all machines and normally recues them to the end of the edit.

Edit controllers vary widely in sophistication and capability. Most have digital time readouts that allow the editor to cue tapes and determine the length of edits. On systems without time code, these counters numerically display **control track** pulses, while on time code systems they display the actual time code addresses. More-sophisticated edit controllers also can control switchers, **DVE** units, and other devices.

Linear Editing Configurations

The most basic editing system, consisting of a playback machine, a record machine, and an edit controller, is called a **cuts-only** system. As its name implies, this type of system is capable only of editing cut transitions between shots.

To perform other types of transitions, you must use an **A/B roll** or **multiple-source** editing system. This type of system uses more than one playback machine, then allows the editor to perform transitions between footage on the playback machines. Another way to perform advanced transitions is by using a digital recording machine with **preread** function, in which the recorder actually plays back the footage on its tape while simultaneously adding footage from the playback machine.

Several peripheral pieces of equipment may also be included in an editing system. The most basic of these is one or more video monitors that allow the editor to view the footage on the various tape machines. Similarly, audio monitors are used to listen to audio sources. In a multiple-source system, a switcher, DVE unit, and graphics unit may be used to create more-sophisticated editing effects, and each of these components may have its own video monitor. An audio mixer may be used to more precisely control the level and equalization of audio sources, which may include CD players, cart machines, and cassette tape players.

A final variable among editing systems is tape format. Normally, all the machines in an editing system are the same format, although in **interformat** editing systems there may be a mixture of formats. For example, an edit system may record onto Digital Betacam but allow both Digital Betacam and DVCPRO source tapes.

Types of Tape Edits

Audio or video information can be recorded onto tape during an edit session in two basic ways. The first of

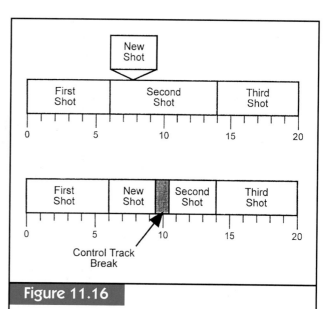

Figure 11.16

Assemble editing a shot in the middle of a completed program causes a break in the control track, and all shots after the break have to be reedited.

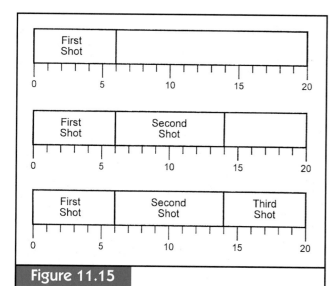

Figure 11.15

Assemble editing is useful for editing a series of shots one after the other.

these, called **assemble editing,** records all tape elements (video, all audio channels, and control track), essentially wiping out any previous material recorded on the tape. Assemble editing is useful for simple editing functions, such as placing a series of shots one after the other, as shown in Figure 11.15. However, since it records *all* tape elements, it cannot be used to edit a shot in the middle of a presentation because it will cause a break in the control track, as shown in Figure 11.16. Obviously, assemble editing cannot be used to change an individual element (video or audio channel 1, for example) in a presentation.

More-advanced editing functions require the use of **insert editing,** which allows the editor to select individual elements (video and/or specific audio channels) to record. Since it does not disturb the control track, insert editing can be used in the middle of an edited presentation. Insert editing gives the editor much more capability than assemble editing, and for that reason it is the kind of editing most often used. However, before you can perform insert editing, you have to have the control track already on the record tape. If you want to begin insert editing on a blank tape, you must first **black** the tape by recording the control track (and usually a black sync signal) onto it. If you have

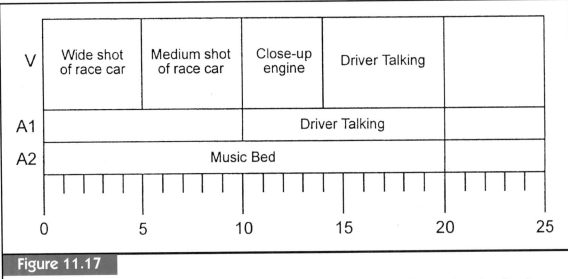

Figure 11.17

A visual representation of the completed program, showing video, audio channel 1, and audio channel 2 tracks in timeline form.

already used assemble editing to lay shots on the tape, you can then go back and use insert editing to change individual shots.

Linear Editing Techniques

Despite the wide diversity of edit controllers and tape machines, the basic techniques of tape-based editing remain the same. This section uses a simple editing example to illustrate some of these techniques.

Suppose that you have a raw tape with various footage on it. You want to rearrange this footage into the completed form shown on the edit master tape in Figure 11.17. The finished program begins with a five-second wide shot of the race car, then a 5-second medium shot of the race car. Next, there is a 10-second interview clip in which the driver talks about the race car; the first 4 seconds of the interview clip are covered with a close-up shot of the car's engine (in other words, we hear the driver talking for 4 seconds before we *see* him). Throughout the entire program, we have a music bed.

This program can be completed in several ways, but for our example we will build its basic structure using assemble editing, then complete it using insert editing. The first step is to perform a **cold edit** at the very beginning of the edit master tape. This is accomplished by simply pressing the "record" and "play" buttons on the recorder and letting the tape record

black sync signal for at least 10 seconds. This is done because we need to have space for the edit controller to preroll the first edit. If we simply tried to do an edit at the very beginning of the edit master tape, the recorder would "run into" the beginning of the tape while attempting to preroll, and the edit controller would abort the edit. The 10-second black recording at the beginning of the tape will provide sufficient space for the preroll (which is normally set to between 3 and 7 seconds, depending on the edit controller).

Now, we are ready to begin building the program. First, we will use the edit controller to cue the edit master tape to 10 seconds; then we will press the "set in" button on the edit controller to tell the machine that we want the first shot to begin at that point.[4] Next, we use the edit controller to cue the raw tape to the wide shot of the car. Again, we will use the set in button to set the beginning of the shot on the raw tape. Finally, we will tell the edit controller that we want to perform an assemble edit by selecting "assemble" under edit type.

We are now ready to perform the first edit. In this case, it will be an **open-ended edit** because we have not set an out point to designate the end of the edit. When we press the "edit" button on the edit controller, it will preroll both the player and recorder to five seconds before their respective in points, and stop the machines momentarily.[5] Then, it will roll both machines

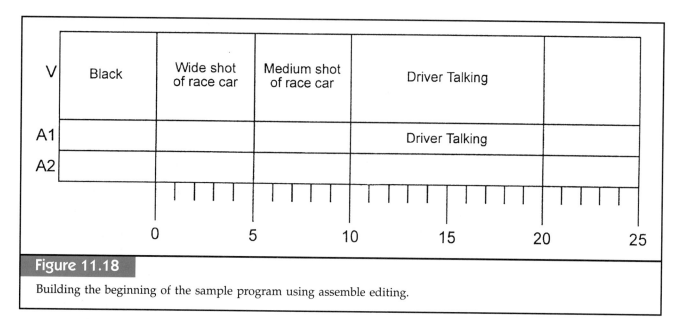

V	Black	Wide shot of race car	Medium shot of race car	Driver Talking	
A1				Driver Talking	
A2					

0   5   10   15   20   25

Building the beginning of the sample program using assemble editing.

in unison, and when we reach the in point of the record tape we will see the shot of the race car appear on the record monitor. When we have at least five seconds of the shot recorded, we will press the "all stop" button to stop both machines; the edit controller will then recue both machines to the point when we pushed the "all stop" button.[6] We are now ready to recue the machines, set in points, and do our next edit.

After similarly assemble-editing the next two shots, we end up with a program as illustrated in Figure 11.18. Now, we need to make two insert edits to complete the project. The first of these will be a video-only edit for approximately the first 4 seconds of the sound bite. We want the shot of the engine to end after the driver says, "This car has the most powerful engine of any car on the track." We will use the edit controller to cue the recorder to the beginning of the sound bite, cue the player to the shot of the engine, and set in points on both machines. Since we want the engine shot to end after the driver says "any car on the track," we will use the edit controller's shuttle/search knob to cue the record tape to just after the word *track*, then set an out point on the recorder. This tells the edit controller to end the edit at this point. Out points can be set on either the record machine or the playback machine, depending on the situation. In this instance, the critical ending point (the word *track*) is on the recorder, so we set the out point on the recorder. Finally, we will select only "video" under edit type, as we do not want to record any audio.

We are now ready to perform the edit, but in this situation we may want to "test" the edit to make sure it works as planned. Edit controllers allow us to do this through the use of a **preview** function, which rolls the machines through the edit-preparation process, then shows what the edit will look like without actually recording it. When we press the "preview" button on the edit controller, both machines will preroll, then play. If we watch and listen to the record monitor, we will see the engine shot inserted, but the machine will not actually perform the edit. If something is wrong with the edit (if the engine shot ends on the word *car*, for example), we can reset the in or out points. We can do this by just recueing the recorder to the proper location, then pressing "set out" again, or by trimming the existing edit. Trimming increments an existing in or out point frame by frame, normally by pressing a "+" or "−" button on the edit controller. If we press the "+" button 10 times, for example, the out point will be moved 10 frames later. Once we are satisfied with what we see, we will perform the edit by pressing the "edit" button. If we wish, we can look at an edit just completed by using the **review** function. We will complete the project by doing an audio channel 2 insert edit to add the music track under the entire program.

This is the basic process of linear editing: cueing tapes, setting in and out points, and designating the type of edit. More-advanced controllers allow greater usability and functionality, such as the ability to set in and out points numerically on a keypad, or to perform transition effects on multiple-source systems.

11.5 Editing Aesthetics

A finished television program, be it a live talk show, a sitcom, a game show, a documentary, or a news program, should create for the viewer an uninterrupted sense of visual and aural progression. This consistent and unobtrusive "flow," as discussed in Chapter 4, is called **continuity,** and it is a function of several aesthetic considerations. In fact, many television professionals say the best edits are the ones the home viewer doesn't even *notice*.

Continuity allows you to create a sense of uninterrupted flow not only in real-time productions such as talk shows and live sports programs but in programs where time and/or space are fluid. For example, a documentary may contain footage shot over a period of days, months, or even years, and in several different locations. In a television drama, we may want to create the impression that the actor puts on his jacket, leaves his house, gets in his car, and drives away as one continuous action, despite the fact the scene was in reality shot in several different "takes" over a period of several hours. In that same drama, we may at another time want to smoothly travel to another time or place—10 years ago or a city located hundreds of miles away. Skillful editing can make all of these actions unobtrusive and *believable* to the viewer.

Regardless of how you are editing, whether linear, nonlinear, or in real time using a switcher, achieving continuity is as much a function of the shots you have available as how they are put together. Indeed, the degree of continuity you are able to achieve is often determined in the preproduction and editing-preparation stages of a project. This is, once again, another reason that *planning* is so important in television production.

Of course, continuity considerations are often violated for special effect, especially in music videos and commercials, where smooth flow is abandoned for attention-grabbing, disjointed editing. Here, too, however, it is important that the loss of continuity serves a creative purpose and is appropriate to the production in question. It is usually not appropriate, for example, to violate continuity in a documentary or a live studio production. Still, television production is a creative endeavor, so principles of continuity should be considered guidelines and not necessarily rules.

When to Edit—Information and Action

In general, you should change from one shot to another only when there is a specific *reason* for doing so. Broadly, these reasons fit into two categories: **cutting for information** or **cutting on action.** Cutting for information means that the second shot reveals information that the first shot did not. For example, we may cut from the medium shot of the show host holding the book to a close-up of the book so that the viewer can see the title of the book or the detail of the artwork on the book's cover. (See Figure 11.19.) During a discussion show, we would want to cut from the shot of the host to a shot of a particular guest when that guest starts talking. If what the guest says elicits an enthusiastic round of applause from the audience, we might want to cut to a wide shot of the audience.

It is important *not* to make a video edit if that edit does not reveal any significant information. For example, cutting from the medium shot in Figure 11.20(a) to the slightly tighter medium shot from a similar angle in Figure 11.20(b) serves no real purpose. We are not giving the viewer any new information of significance, so it is best not to make the cut.

The transition to high-definition formats will make frequent cutting among shots less critical to visual storytelling. HDTV's increased picture resolution means that you can show all the detail of a standard-definition close-up shot (and more) in an HDTV medium or wide shot. For example, consider a baseball game in which the pitcher is preparing to pitch to a batter as a runner leads off from first base. In a standard-definition production, the director would have to cut among at least three cameras to follow the action: a camera to show a medium shot of the runner on first base, a camera to show a close-up of the pitcher watching the runner and preparing to pitch, and a camera to show a wide shot of the pitcher and batter as the ball is delivered to home plate. These three different camera shots are needed because standard-definition's lower resolution does not allow great detail to be seen in medium and wide shots. The camera

(a)　(b)

Figure 11.19

Editing for information. Start with the medium shot (*a*), and when the host holds up the book, cut to a close-up of the book's cover (*b*).

showing the runner on first could zoom out to show the pitcher as well, but there would be no way to see the concentration on the pitcher's face or the movement of his eyes from home plate, to the runner on first, and back to home plate.

With HDTV's greater resolution, however, a camera could get a shot of both the runner and the pitcher while maintaining enough picture detail to see the emotion on the pitcher's and the runner's faces. Thus, there would be no need to cut to the extra shot. In fact,

(a)　(b)

Figure 11.20

If no significant new information will be revealed by an edit, it should not be made. The shot shown in (*b*), for example, reveals no information not already shown in (*a*).

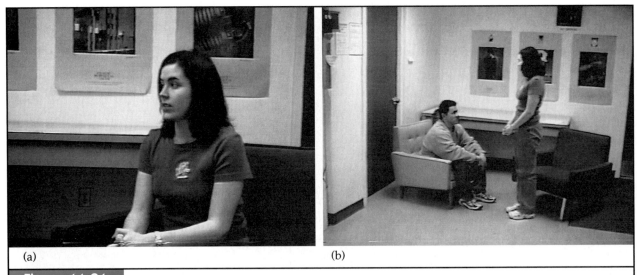

(a)   (b)

Figure 11.21

Cutting on action from shot (*a*) to shot (*b*) as the actress rises from her chair.

an HDTV camera positioned near the third-base dugout could shoot the runner, pitcher, and batter in one wide shot while maintaining nearly all the detail we would see in three standard-definition shots.

Cutting on action means the edit is triggered by an action of a subject in the picture. For example, if the actress is about to rise from her chair, we could cut from a medium shot of her to a wider shot, as shown in Figure 11.21. Similarly, if we are on a medium shot of a police officer questioning a witness to a crime and a gunshot rings out, the police officer is likely to spring to attention and perhaps draw his gun. This would be an appropriate place to cut to a tighter shot of the police officer as he turns his head in the direction of the gunshot, then perhaps cut to a wide shot of a suspect scurrying away down the alley.

It is important to note that the action not only triggers the edit, it also provides the temporal *point* for the edit. The edit, then, should take place just before the action occurs, or in some cases just after. Either way, the edit point needs to be in *very close temporal proximity* to the action. Cutting to the second shot in Figure 11.21 two seconds after that actress actually gets up, for example, destroys the logical sense of making the cut created by the action.

Pacing refers to the overall speed at which shot changes are made in a production. A fast-paced pro-

duction, for example, will have a lot of edits, and individual shots will be on the screen for only a short period of time. There is no "right" number of edits to make in a production, nor is there a set time between edits; the most important thing is that the pacing is appropriate to the particular production, and that the individual edits themselves are motivated by logical information and action cues. A music video, for example, is likely to have a much faster pace than a documentary. It also is important not to simply edit formulaically, such as changing pictures every three seconds. This can give an impersonal, automated feel to a presentation. Instead, edits should be made at appropriate points—the end of a sentence on the narration track in a documentary, for example, or on the beats of the music.

Jump Cuts

One of the goals of continuity in editing is creating the notion in the mind of the viewer that he or she is watching action occurring in real time, even if it is not. Perhaps the most glaring violation of continuity is the **jump cut,** in which a person or object changes in two successive shots. For example, if you edit a shot of a person typing at a computer immediately after a shot of that same person standing, as in Figure 11.22(a), you

Figure 11.22

(*a*) A jump cut; (*b*) using a cutaway shot prevents jump cuts; (*c*) changing angle or type of shot can also prevent jump cuts.

have created a jump cut. Such an edit creates confusion for the viewer, as it is physically impossible for a person to instantly go from standing to sitting at a computer.

A jump cut also can occur in less glaring forms. For example, if you cut from a shot of a man sitting on a chair with his left leg crossed over his right leg to another shot in which his *right leg* is now crossed over his *left leg*, this is in effect a jump cut. Similarly, it is a jump cut if a person's clothes change from one shot to the next or if an object sitting on a table is gone in the next shot. Many of these types of problems can be so minor that they go unnoticed; still, every effort should be

made to avoid them. If you watch movies or television dramas very closely, you can usually see a number of minor (and sometimes major) jump cuts like these.

As you might guess, jump cuts such as those just described are a much greater problem in postproduction editing than in live editing. Laws of physics prohibit someone from changing position from one shot to the next in a live production. Still, many people consider it a jump cut when an edit such as the one in Figure 11.20 is made. The person has not changed position, but the effect is so jarring that in actuality it seems as if the camera itself has "jumped."

Jump cuts can be avoided by using **cutaway** shots, in which a shot that does not include the person or object in question is inserted between the two shots. In the computer example, you could put a shot of the person to whom the subject is speaking between the two shots, as shown in Figure 11.22(b). Jumps also can be avoided by changing angles or shot type. You could in this way effectively cut from the shot of the person standing to a close-up of the person's hands on the computer keyboard to the medium shot of the person at the computer, as shown in Figure 11.22(c). Even though the first edit is technically a jump cut, the dramatic effect created by cutting to the close-up shot masks the violation of continuity for the viewer.

Another way to avoid jump cuts is to allow subjects to leave or enter the frame. In the preceding example, if we started by showing a shot of the person walking and allowed him to walk *out of the frame*, we could then cut to the shot of him sitting at the computer. Since the person actually leaves the picture (if only for a brief moment), our next shot will not create a jump cut. Similarly, if we cut from a shot of the person standing away from the computer, then cut to a shot of the computer and allow the person to walk *into* the picture, sit down, and start typing, we have not created a jump cut.

Axis of Conversation/Axis of Action

The **axis of conversation** is an imaginary line drawn between two people who are facing each other. In shooting such a conversation, all camera positions should be kept on one side or the other of the line. Doing so maintains consistent *screen direction,* the direction in which a person (or object) is facing. As shown in the first three frames of Figure 11.23, this maintains the effect that the two people are actually talking *to* each other. In editing shots in this sequence, you would make sure that the man was *always facing right* and the woman was *always facing left.* By **crossing the line,** or moving to the other side of the axis of conversation, you disrupt the consistency of screen direction, as shown in the last frame of Figure 11.23. It is important to note that there is no universally *correct* side of the axis of conversation from which to shoot; the point is that once you've selected one side or the other you should stay there.

(a)

(b)

(c)

(d)

Figure 11.23

Maintaining consistent screen direction for two people. The last shot shows the disorienting effect of violating consistency of screen direction.

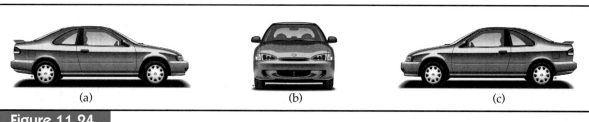

Figure 11.24

A neutral shot (*b*) can be used between two opposing direction shots (*a*) and (*c*).

Similarly, the **axis of action** applies to moving persons or objects. If you are shooting shots of a car, once you've established that the car is moving in a particular direction (left to right, for example), you should only edit shots in which the car is moving in that same direction. Editing from a shot in which the car moves left to right to one in which it moves right to left creates a jarring effect and violates continuity. If you must edit together shots in which the car changes direction, you can insert a **neutral shot**—or head-on shot—between the two shots, as shown in Figure 11.24.

Transitions

The majority of edits are simply cuts, where one picture is instantaneously replaced by another on-screen. The reason for this widespread use is that the cut is the only transition effect that does not normally call attention to itself (unless it is a jump cut or other continuity violation). However, other transitions can and should be used in appropriate situations. The dissolve is most often used to indicate the passage of time, such as dissolving from a World War II photograph of a soldier to a contemporary shot of the same person. Dissolves also can be used to visually *connect* two images; changing from a shot of the soldier riding on a train to a shot of his wife back home holding his picture connects the two images more forcefully than a cut. A dissolve to or from black, usually referred to as a **fade,** indicates a strong separation. It is usually used to end a particular sequence or go to a commercial.

Wipes and special effects such as page turns call even greater attention to themselves, and thus they should not be used when subtle transitions are needed. These transitions can be used to create interest and ac-tion in a presentation, however, and are often used (and many would say used *too much*) in commercials. In general, if you do not have a specific creative reason for using a dissolve, wipe, or special effect, you should just use a cut.

Ethics of Editing

The ability to edit sound and pictures gives the editor tremendous power to shape what the audience sees. Editing can be used to distort reality (such as by instantly transporting the viewer through space or time), create illusions, and—at its most extreme—create alternative realities (such as computer-generated animations). However, this tremendous power carries with it an *ethical responsibility* not to mislead the audience in inappropriate ways.

This ethical responsibility is most important when producing nonfiction programs, such as news, news features, and documentaries. Although a viewer expects and accepts the distortion of reality in entertainment programming, a viewer does not expect distortion in programs that claim to present reality. Common techniques used in the production of entertainment programming such as staging events, giving cues to actors, and editing to create illusions *should not* be used in nonfiction programs. Such programs should be a reflection of reality, and—as much as possible—the production and editing process should not interfere with or distort this reality.

It also is unethical to use editing to create false impressions in nonfiction programming. This includes editing sound bites so that the person seems to say something he or she really didn't. It also includes editing together shots that do not belong together to create an inaccurate impression (such as following a sound bite from a politician with raucous applause from the audience when the audience didn't respond that way).

The evolving new technologies of video editing still give the producers of nonfiction programs tremendous new capabilities and artistic possibilities. It is important to remember, however, that these capabilities should not be used to mislead the audience.

Discussion Questions

1. Envision an editing project you might do for this class, such as a 30-second commercial or a two-minute news story. Would it be easier to complete this project using linear or nonlinear editing? Why?
2. If you were to begin shooting a video project tomorrow, what things would you do in the preediting stages to help facilitate the editing process?
3. If your school uses nonlinear editing systems, locate some of the video data files on the computer. How does their size compare with other types of computer files such as word-processing files or graphics files?
4. If your school uses linear editing systems, how would you describe them? Are they cuts only or A/B roll? Do the machines use preread?

Notes

1. You can find more information about these systems at their respective websites: http://www.avid.com, http://www.media100.com, http://www.apple.com/finalcutpro, and http://www.adobe.com/products/premiere/main.html.
2. On some systems, the bin may be referred to as a "library" or a "browser."
3. On some systems, you may click on a small "padlock" icon to sync or unsync clip components.
4. Depending on the editing system, edit point set buttons may be called "edit in," "in point," or "in" as well.
5. Depending on the editing system, this button may be called "perform," "auto edit," or "edit start."
6. Depending on the editing system, this button may be called "edit stop" or "stop."

CHAPTER 12

Field Production

Most of what we have discussed in previous chapters has dealt with *live* or *live-on-tape multicamera* productions shot in a studio environment. However, many productions are shot totally or partially in out-of-studio locations with one camera. Many dramas and documentaries are shot entirely on location and then edited. For other productions, such as news and public affairs, the material that is shot is edited and used as a **roll-in** for a program that is assembled as a studio shoot. The technique of shooting single camera is often called **film-style shooting,** because most motion pictures are shot with one camera that takes shots one by one from all the various angles employed in multiple-camera shoots. If the shooting is done for news, it is usually called **electronic news gathering (ENG).** A more generic term is **field production,** because the shooting takes place in the field rather than in a studio.

Studio production and field production have numerous similarities, mainly because much of the same equipment is used. A microphone is a microphone whether it is on a game-show set or at the scene of a fire. Pictures should be focused and well composed, and talent should avoid annoying mannerisms, whether in the studio or in the field. And yet, there are many differences in both techniques and disciplines that are caused, to some degree, by the lack of control that exists outside of the studio.

This chapter concentrates on single-camera field production, looking at the similarities and differences between it and studio production, and then covers highlights of remote truck production.

It is organized in a manner that is similar to the rest of the book[1] and covers the following topics:

- Reasons for a greater need for discipline in the field (12.1)
- Different cast and crew members needed in the field as well as varying tasks that are undertaken on location (12.2)
- The organizational duties a producer must perform to ensure a smooth production (12.3)
- How to direct on location (12.4)
- How cameras are used in the field (12.5)
- Lighting for both indoor and outdoor locations (12.6)
- Handling audio problems in the field (12.7)
- The lesser role that graphics and sets play in many field shoots (12.8)
- Functions of the recording part of the camcorder (12.9)
- The greater role editing plays in single-camera shooting (12.10)
- How remote truck production is similar to and different from both studio and field production (12.11)

12.1 Introduction

Single-camera field production is younger than multi-camera studio production, mainly because the original TV equipment was too bulky to be easily taken outside the studio. However, with the introduction of the three-fourths-inch U-matic format in the early 1970s, cameras and recorders ventured out of the studio, first to cover news and then to produce other forms of programming.

Field production, like its studio-based sister, requires both *technique* and *discipline*. It involves the development of a professional attitude and knowledge of equipment and aesthetics. (See Chapter 1.)

Techniques

One of the reasons techniques are so important is that miles away from "home base," you cannot turn to the instructor or technician when you have a problem such as no picture in the viewfinder. This means that all crew members must know how to operate the equipment well. You and other crew members must also be well grounded in aesthetics, because you cannot see the finished product as you are taping the individual shots. You must be able to visualize how the shots will cut together.

Disciplines

In some ways, field production requires more discipline than studio work because you cannot easily return for a forgotten item. You must plan very thoroughly for all eventualities and expect the unexpected. You can find yourself working in undesirable conditions such as inclement weather or a mosquito-infested swamp rather than the pleasantly air-conditioned or heated studio environment. Teamwork, combined with a cooperative spirit, is a *must*. People are usually together for longer periods of time in the field than they are in the studio, especially if they commute back and forth together or stay in one location for several days. The tendency to "get on each other's nerves" must be overcome.

12.2 Cast and Crew

One of the reasons that techniques are so important for field production is that crew members may need to undertake a variety of duties so that all the little things

(a)   (b)

Figure 12.1

Crew configurations differ depending on the taping situation. For the first taping (*a*) only two crew members were needed because the footage was being shot silent to go with music during the opening credits. The director told the children what to do and the camera operator taped the material. For the second taping (*b*), which was much more complicated, five people attended—the producer, who was coordinating with the people running the children's art workshop; the director; the audio operator; the camera operator; and a combination lighting person and script supervisor.

that need to be done actually are accomplished. A reason that discipline is important is that crews are usually smaller for field productions, so it is hard to cover for anyone who is undependable.

Crew Size

One reason crews are smaller is that much less gear is involved. Only one camera is used, eliminating the need for all but one **camera operator.** With a **camcorder** configuration, this person doubles as the **videotape operator.** No one is needed to operate a **switcher;** the camera picture goes directly to the **VTR** because there is no need to cut between two or more cameras. **Prompters,** because they are bulky, are not normally taken to shoots (although there are portable prompters that hook up to laptops). Graphics are generally added during postproduction, not during shooting.

Because there is no control room, the **director** is on the location set in the midst of all the action, thus eliminating the need for a **stage manager.** Because timing is usually not crucial for scenes that are later going to be edited, an **associate director** can also be superfluous at a field shoot. However, there is often a person called a **script supervisor**[2] who keeps notes and watches for

continuity problems so that what is shot can be effectively edited.

Some crews, especially for news, are as small as two people—one to operate the camcorder and another to hold the mic and interview people, thus serving as producer-director-talent-script supervisor-audio operator. In fact, some "crews" are only one person—the camcorder has a large viewfinder that pivots so that the operator can see the image while interviewing someone in front of the camera. Or the crew of one can shoot the footage and then add narration over the pictures later. Other shoots have larger crews that include a producer, a director, an audio operator, a camera-videotape operator, a lighting director, a script supervisor, and a production assistant or two to handle any other miscellaneous duties. (See Figure 12.1.) Whatever the size of the crew, each individual member of the shoot should have a *clear idea* of his or her responsibilities—but with the understanding that flexible working arrangements may find each one helping out with other jobs.

Cleanup

One of the absolute essentials that crew members on a field shoot must handle carefully is *cleanup.* If a crew member carelessly leaves a mic cable on the floor of the studio, someone else will probably find it later and put it away. But if a mic cable is left in the middle of a park, it will quickly disappear. Everything must be conscientiously disassembled, coiled, stowed away, and neatly packed—in part as a courtesy to the next people who use the equipment and in part because such care adds to the life of the equipment. Cleanup requires discipline. It is not glamorous work, but it must be done.

Cast Considerations

Most of what applies to talent in a studio production is also true for a location shoot (see Chapter 2). Sincerity and proper projection are important to any television performer. Constantly scratching your ear will be as distracting in front of the local courthouse as it will be in front of a studio talk-show set. However, in many ways, performing at a field site is more difficult than being on camera in a studio. For starters, there probably will be no prompter, which means you must handle your own notes or script and know your lines and material well. Because there also are fewer crew members, fewer people are available to help out with talent requests.

Nonsequential Shooting

One of the hardest parts of film-style shooting, though, is that scenes are shot out of order. This can create *continuity* problems and difficulties for performers. Sometimes it is necessary for an actor to *switch emotions* on and off for the convenience of a shooting schedule. Often two scenes will be shot back to back because they are at the same location, but the emotional content of the two shots may be diametrically opposed. For example, an actor might be called upon to portray the emotion felt about the death of a friend two days before the death has been acted out.

Even within one scene, lines are sometimes shot out of order. When actors' close-ups are shot, they deliver their lines often without benefit of cues and other lines in the rest of the scene. Frequently, the characters they are supposedly talking to are not even on the set. They may find themselves professing passionate love—to a camera.

Because innumerable shots are taken of one scene, actors must perform the same in each take so that the material can be edited together. This means they must follow **blocking** very precisely. They cannot walk beside the sofa in the long shot and behind it in the close-up, because doing so would cause a continuity problem. Of course, many professional actors have learned to perform well nonsequentially. But crew members must let them have their "space" so that they can build up to the required emotions.

Taping out of order is a problem for talent in nondramatic shoots also. Because the camera is on the guest during an interview, the interviewer's face will not be seen. This means that after the interview has been completed, shots must be taped of the interviewer asking the questions over again. This is often very difficult if you are the interviewer. You must sit there and earnestly ask questions of a camera lens—because the person being interviewed has already departed. (See Figure 12.2.)

This brings up a related *ethical* problem that reporters, in particular, must face. How much can the wording of the questions change between what was asked during the actual interview and what is asked on the shots recorded later? The answer should be, "Not much." If the question is changed significantly, the guest's answer may take on an entirely different meaning. Networks and stations have policies regarding the need to keep the questions the same. One way to do this is to have someone on the crew jot down the exact wording of the questions that are asked while they are being asked. Of course, the interviewer can also replay the camera footage so that he or she can phrase the questions the same as the original questions.

Sometimes even more difficult than asking questions after the fact is the need to react after the fact. In almost all single-camera interviews, shots of the interviewer listening and reacting need to be recorded—usually after the guest has departed—so that they can be edited into the interview to prevent **jump cuts.** This requires the interviewer/reporter to just sit there looking at an empty chair and smiling or frowning every once in a while; this is a difficult acting job, especially for novices. People tend to break up into laughter or to exaggerate movements such as nods of the head.

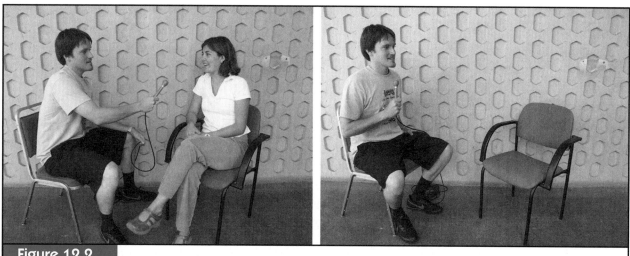

Figure 12.2

Reporters and interviewers often have to tape reaction shots after the interviewed guest has departed. (*Left*) During the interview, the single camera would have been behind the male interviewer, focusing on the female guest answering questions. (*Right*) After the guest has departed, the camera should be repositioned to shoot the interviewer repeating the same questions for later editing.   *Photos courtesy of Melissa Bossenmeyer.*

12.3 | Producing

As with studio shoots, **producers** are the people in charge of the *overall organization* of a field shoot (see Chapter 2). They may not be in charge of the overall program but rather just the segment of it that is shot at a particular location. In this capacity, the field producer makes sure the segment finishes *on time* and *on budget*.

Scripting

The same forms of **scripts** can be used for field shooting as for studio shooting—**film-style scripts, two-column scripts, rundowns, outlines,** and **storyboards** (see Chapter 3). For most types of field production, the script is absolutely essential before planning or production can take place. More than one student production team has found that all of those great ideas they thought of back in the studio just seemed to disappear into thin air once they arrived at the shooting location. The very *act* of putting things down on paper is an important test of the feasibility of the operational plan.

There are times in field production, however, when it is appropriate not to use any script at all. The most obvious example is when covering breaking

news stories. But even then, you can undertake some research ahead of time. Newspeople usually keep track of the number of crimes that have been committed in a certain area, the backgrounds of the major political figures, the actions being taken by the local city council, and similar items. This material can be incorporated into what is reported from the scene.

Location Logistics

Producing a location shoot is similar to producing a studio program in that all elements must be in the right place at the right time. However, this is usually much more complex for a field shoot because everything is out of its usual habitat. Equipment logistics, travel arrangements, power supplies, and coordination of props and talent all involve extraordinary consideration.

Selecting a Location

One of the crucial initial steps a producer must undertake is to make sure someone selects and surveys the production location. For large dramatic productions requiring many locations, a person given the title of **location scout** will undertake the job of finding, visiting, and winnowing down the possible production sites. The location scout might find 10 homes where a

1940s murder mystery could be shot. But some might be a great distance from where other scenes are being shot, some might be in noisy locations, and some may not have an appropriate-looking porch. The location person will narrow down the choices and present them to the producer and/or director. At this point, most directors and some producers like to visit the potential sites to make the final selection. Having the camera operator along to give input on these location-scouting trips can also prove invaluable.

Surveying a Location

For other types of programs you know approximately where you will be doing the shoot, and you go mainly to see the lay of the land. If, for example, you are interviewing a doctor about a new medical breakthrough, you will want to shoot at the hospital where the instruments used for the procedure will be available. You go there ahead of time to see how large the room you will be shooting in is, to find out where the electrical plugs are, to determine how you can best cut out background noise, and so on.

Fast-breaking news stories are another matter. Obviously, it may not be possible to check out the location for these ahead of time. However, some places where news is likely to occur, such as the city council chambers or the police station, can be "cased" ahead of time and notes made so that crews that need to go there have some idea of what they will face.

If you shoot in a studio regularly, you are aware of the location of power outlets, the types of curtains and set pieces available, the location of lighting instruments, and other similar information. With each field shoot, these elements are different. That is why it is *essential* that the area be scouted ahead of time. If the only available plugs are out in the hallway and you have not brought extension cords for your lights, you will be faced with a major production problem. When you go to a location, it is wise to have a list of things you want to check. A general *checklist* is shown in Figure 12.3, but elements specific to each production need to be discerned.

One of the first things you should do as part of a location survey is obtain the name of a person who is in charge—someone who gives you the permission to shoot at any particular facility, someone you can contact when you arrive with equipment, and someone to turn to quickly when any unexpected problems

crop up. Who has the keys? Whom do you contact when you trip a circuit breaker? You may wish to draw up a floor plan of the location and take digital still or moving camera shots to share with other crew members and to remind you of important details as you plan specific shots.

If you are shooting outdoors, or if you are shooting indoors with any natural light, you will want to scout the location at the *same time of day* that you will be doing the shoot so that you can see exactly what you will have to deal with in terms of sunlight, shadows, and windows.

What about possible interruptions and conflicts? Do scheduled events at the location conflict with the shoot? Will airplanes be taking off? If you are shooting on campus, for example, will the end of a class period send large numbers of people walking through the shot? What about those campus chimes? Make note of these items so that you are not in the middle of a take when any of these distractions occur. Listen for continuous extraneous noises, such as an air conditioner or telephones ringing, which will interfere with your audio. Try to obtain permission to turn them off while you are shooting. If you cannot, plan to work with more directional and less sensitive mics closer to the talent.

Substituting for a Location

Some productions require shots that will be in difficult or expensive locations—an airplane that has crashed on a remote mountainside, a koala bear asleep in a tree. Sometimes these shots can be obtained from prerecorded material. Most professional producers turn to commercial companies that supply **stock footage** for a fee. News departments carefully index their old news stories on computers and file most of what they shoot for possible later use.

Students who cannot afford professional stock footage should first examine the resources of their own university. Sometimes a former student will have shot the local area from a helicopter, and this footage is made available for future student shoots. Large companies that turn out numerous public relations films often allow use of footage if you give them a credit.

Budgeting

Budgeting for field production work is very similar to budgeting for studio productions, in that budgets

LOCATION SURVEY CHECKLIST

Type of material being shot_____

Time of shooting_____

Potential location of shooting_____

Principal contact person_____

Contact Information_____

Camera:

Where can the camera be placed?
What, if anything, is needed in the way of camera mounting devices or platforms?
What, if anything, is needed in the way of special lenses?
Will any objects interfere with the camera shots? If so, how can this situation be corrected?
If shooting is going to last several days, where is a secure place to store cameras and other equipment?

Lighting:

What types of lights will be needed?
Where can the lights be placed?
What light stands or particular light holders will be needed?
What, if any, special lighting accessories will be needed?
How can any problems regarding mixing indoor and outdoor lighting be solved?
In what ways will the sun's position at different times of day affect the shooting?
What kinds of problems are shadows likely to cause?

Power:

Is enough power available or will a generator be needed?
Where is the circuit breaker box?
Who can be contacted if a circuit blows?
Which circuits can be used and how many watts can be run on them?
How many, if any, extension cords will be needed?
What power outlets can be used?

Sound:

Are there background noises that may interfere with audio? If so, how can they be corrected?
Where can the microphones and cable be placed?
Are any particular microphone holders or stands needed?
What types of microphones should be used?
How much microphone cable will be needed?

General:

Where is parking available?
Where are the nearest restrooms?
Where are the nearest places to obtain food?
If passes are needed to enter the premises, how can they be obtained?

Figure 12.3

A location checklist is very useful when looking over an area that might be used for a production.

EQUIPMENT RENTAL FIGURES

Prosumer digital camcorder	$250 per day
S-VHS or Hi-8 camcorder	75 per day
HDTV professional camcorder	1500 per day
Tripod and Head	75 per day
Monitor	40 per day
Portable Light Kit with Four Lights	60 per day
HMI Light	50 per day
Microphone	15 per day
Portable Audio Mixer	35 per day
Walkie Talkie System	15 per day
Nonlinear Editing	35 per hour
Graphics Generation	25 per hour
Audio Recording or Editing	35 per hour

Figure 12.4

These are approximate costs for renting equipment and facilities.

include **above-the-line** and **below-the-line** categories (see Chapter 3). The main variation is that different equipment will be used and a greater emphasis will be placed on editing. Figure 12.4 gives you some equipment rental figures to help you budget for field shooting.[3]

Conceptualization and Preproduction Planning

Before most programs or segments of programs are taped on location, you should conceive them in their entirety. How each individual shot is planned and executed depends on how it will be used in the final edited program. In other words, both planning and camera work must be carried out with the eventual editing process in mind.

To aid in this process, video producers have developed a number of different forms. Some of the same paperwork used for studio production is used for field production. For example, you should ask performers to sign **performance releases,** and you should clear any music and other **copyrighted** material that is going to be used for the final edited production (see Chapter 3). However, because field productions usually involve a variety of locations and their inherent

uncertainties, producers must examine the scripts very carefully to determine production needs and schedules.

Breakdown Sheets

If you are planning to shoot a complex production that involves a number of individual scenes shot in different locations, **breakdown sheets** are indispensable. They list—for each scene to be shot—a synopsis of the scene, the location, the people who will be needed, the props, and any special considerations. (See Figure 12.5.)

As previously mentioned, program material in extensive field productions is almost always shot out of order, so you use your breakdown sheets to juggle your production shooting and determine the order in which scenes will be shot. Usually the primary element for determining shooting order is *location;* all scenes occurring in the park will be shot at one time, even though they will be interspersed at various points throughout the program. However, sometimes the primary element for determining shooting order is the talent; if someone who is crucial to the production can only work one day, all the shots involving that person will have to be shot on that one day, even though this means traveling all over town. On rare occasions, shooting order may be determined by a prop; if you need to rent a vintage automobile, you might want to shoot all scenes with it on one day so that you can cut down on rental fees.

Sometimes it is wise to make lists of props, costumes, cast members, and so forth from these breakdown sheets. These lists are similar to what you might make for a studio shoot (see Chapter 3), but usually you need more lists because the elements needed for a field shoot are more complex. For example, one list might include all the locales that the location scout needs to find; other lists might include all the animals or all the automobiles needed. Studio productions usually do not include these elements.

Shooting Schedule

Once you have assembled all the breakdown sheets in order, you can develop a **shooting schedule.** This lists everything that is to be shot during each day, giving the description, the cast, and the location. It is used throughout the shooting and, of course, must be revised if production gets behind schedule. (See Figure 12.6.)

```
                        BREAKDOWN SHEET

Program: _PARK MINI-DOC_____

Location: _Park with a slide & swing_____

Segment Number: _3_____

Synopsis: _Mary Ellen talks of the need for greater____

           _safety standards for playground equipment___
```

Cast	Props	Equipment
Mary Ellen Thomas	Jump rope	Camcorder
Jason	Tricycle	Reflector
Tiffany		Mike & cable

Crew	Special Needs	Comments
Tom	Mike cable must be	Should be shot at a
Susan	able to reach the slide	time when children
Tasha		are there

Figure 12.5

The breakdown sheet lists all the talent, crew, facilities, and other elements needed for every scene.

```
                        SHOOTING SCHEDULE

  Program: _PARK MINI-DOC_____
```

Date	Time	Description	Cast	Location
4/20	1:00	Mary Ellen discusses playground equipment and safety needs (seg 3)	Mary Ellen Thomas Jason Sorkin Tiffany Barr	Alcove Park
4/20	2:30	Mary Ellen discusses need for flowers (seg 7)	Mary Ellen Thomas Mr. Hamilton	Patterson Park
4/22	11:00	Interview with park supervisor (seg 2)	Mary Ellen Thomas Dr. Belling	Dr. Belling's office, Park building
4/22	1:00	Interview with park planners (seg 9)	Mary Ellen Thomas Mr. Loomis Mrs. Robbins	Planning offices, Park building

Figure 12.6

A shooting schedule is indispensable for coordinating location shoots on a major production.

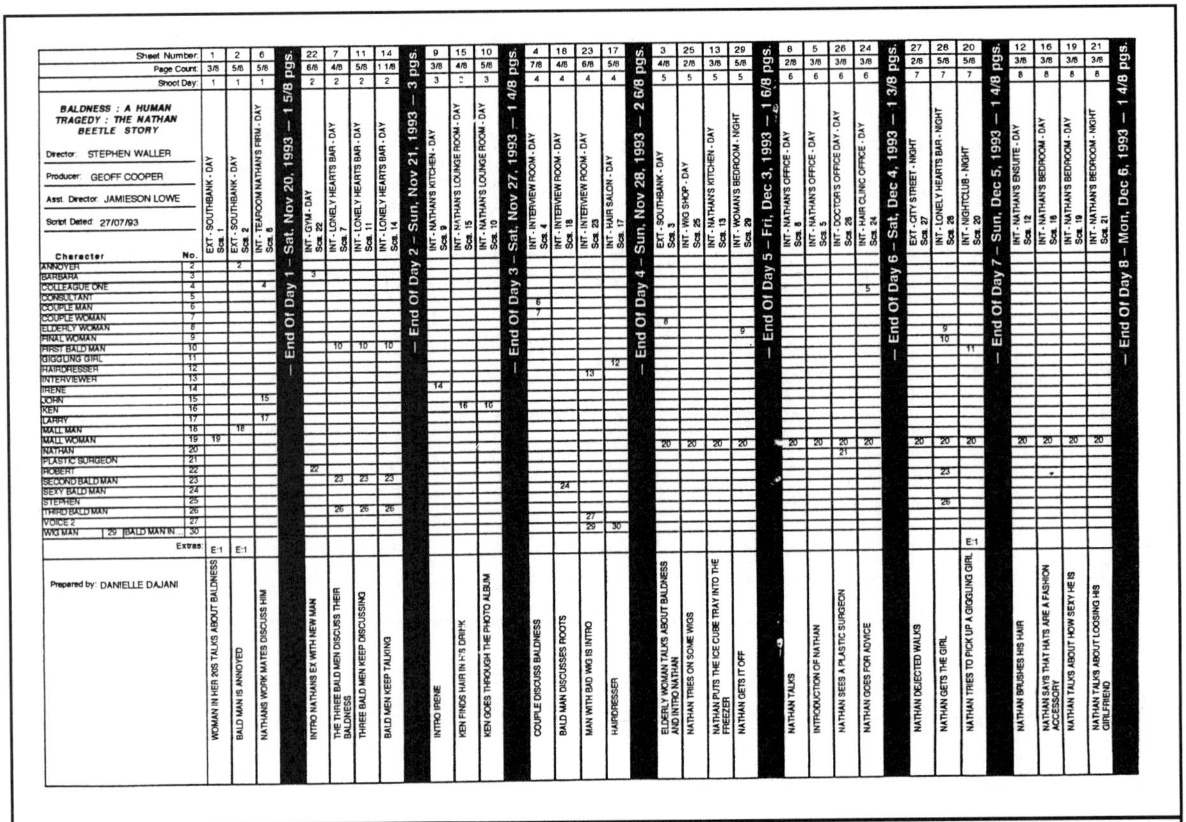

Figure 12.7

This computer-generated stripboard was produced using the program Movie Magic. *Computer work courtesy of Stephen Waller.*

Stripboards

Many producers (or their assistants) use **stripboards** to aid them with their shooting plans. Sometimes these are actual boards that can hold long strips of paper indicating the locations and characters needed each day. Computers are now heavily employed for all forms of preproduction paperwork, including stripboards. Figure 12.7 shows a stripboard made with the aid of a computer program. When the production needs to be reorganized because some scene didn't get shot, the strips can be moved around by clicking on them with a mouse and dragging them elsewhere. Strips of the old-fashioned paper stripboard can also be easily moved, making stripboards a very flexible production-planning device.

In addition, you can devise your own lists, forms, schedules, or drawings to help conceptualize and organize your material. Like the major multiple-camera studio production, every hour spent in preproduction planning and scripting will save countless hours of valuable crew time on the shoot. Careful script preparation and preproduction are perhaps the most crucial *disciplines* involved in single-camera field production.

12.4 Directing

Directing in the field is quite different from directing in the studio, mainly because the director is on the set rather than in the control room. However, a director's duties during preproduction are similar to those for a studio shoot—becoming familiar with the script and planning for equipment, cast, and crew (see Chapter 2). In addition, the director is usually quite involved with finding locations.

Rehearsals

Rehearsing for a field shoot should involve the same procedures as rehearsing for a studio program (see Chapter 4). However, because the amount of time you can use a remote facility is often limited (you can't interrupt the work on a factory floor or monopolize the merry-go-round in a park), you often do not have the luxury of rehearsal in the field—which suggests that you substitute other creative alternatives. Can you at least have a **dry run** with the primary talent to familiarize them with the actual location? How about rehearsing in a substitute location such as a large hall or your living room?

Production Processes

On the day of production, many events occur that have nothing in common with studio production. First, the equipment must be packed and taken somewhere. You, as the director, must make sure that all crew members *double-check* that everything needed is packed and in working order. If you are planning to tape and you get to a location site without any videotape, you are in big trouble.

Laying Bars

The taping procedure itself is quite different from that in a studio. If a camera has a **color bar generator,** at least 30 seconds of **color bars** should be recorded on the tape before anything else. This is to allow you or the editor time to adjust controls that will enable the tape to be played back with proper color balance during the editing sessions.

Slating

Each shot needs to be slated. As soon as the VCR is up to speed, one of the crew members (often the script supervisor or a production assistant) should hold a cardboard sign, small chalkboard, or professionally prepared **slate** in front of the camera. This should indicate the scene number, take number, director's name, and description of the shot.

The *scene number* should be the same as that on the script, and the *take number* is the number of times that same material has been shot—take 1 for the first attempt, take 2 for the second, and so on. While this written slate is being taped, the person holding it should

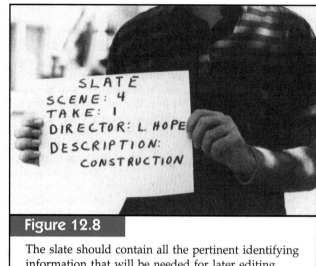

Figure 12.8

The slate should contain all the pertinent identifying information that will be needed for later editing.

read the information into an open mic so that both a video and audio slate are recorded. (See Figure 12.8.)

Of course, this formalized slating procedure is not always possible, especially with fast-breaking news. If a production crew has an opportunity to record a criminal being apprehended, you certainly would not want to take a chance on missing the crucial action while you prepare a proper slate.

Recording

Once the slate is recorded, with the camera still rolling, the director should say "Action," and after waiting several beats, the talent should begin. After the segment is recorded, all talent on camera should hold their positions for at least five seconds while the camera continues to roll. These beginning and ending procedures are crucial for the editing function in that they provide adequate *pads* for maintaining proper pace. If you, as the director, are satisfied with the take, you should proceed to whatever is being taped next. If the take is not acceptable, shoot it again.

Logging

Someone, usually the script supervisor, should keep a careful production log of every shot; this should include the scene number (which should be the same as the scene number on the script and the slate), take number, description, length of shot, and any special comments. (See Figure 12.9.) The script supervisor

Slate	Count In	Count Out	Comments
University Security Office Seg 3 Shot 4 Take 3	Lt. Jones. 253 "My Job...	270... this problem."	Best one
Security Office Intro. Meyer Seg 3 Shot 1 Take 1	275 "Lt. Jones...	287... no parking."	
——————— Cassette #2 ———————			
Parking lot student #1 Seg 4 Shot 1 Take 1	025 "Well everyday...	037... no spaces."	Stumbled over words
Parking lot student #1 Seg 4 Shot 1 Take 2	045 "Everyday...	051... really mad."	
Parking lot student #2 Seg 4 Shot 2 Take 1	059 "I don't see	071... parking ticket."	

PRODUCTION Campus Parking   PAGE 2

SHOOTING DATE 8 Nov   PRODUCER Evans

Figure 12.9

Excerpt from sample production log.

should indicate if a take is bad so that the editor does not have to bother looking at it. Often, particularly if the taping procedure is hectic, this **logging** is done after shooting is complete.

Continuity

In a complicated shoot, such as a drama, the script supervisor's main job is keeping track of *continuity*. He or she makes notes concerning what the actors were wearing, where certain props were set, and which hand actors used to make certain gestures. If the actor was wearing a tie when he knocked on the door in the scene shot on Monday, he should be wearing that same tie when he enters the living room in the scene shot on Thursday. If the interviewee's hand was clutching the book he was holding during the long shot, his hand should be clutching the book for the close-up that will be edited into the shot.

Shot Variety

One of the most important production techniques associated with field shooting is that of making sure enough varied shots are taken, so that they can be used during editing to present a meaningful story or to create cut-

aways that will avoid jump cuts. For example, when a director shoots a dramatic scene, it is customary to record a cover shot of all the action in the scene (for example, a man and woman arguing). The director also records close-ups of the man delivering his lines and the woman delivering hers. These shots may be followed by **reaction shots** of both characters listening to what the other is saying and perhaps close-ups of some items pertinent to the argument—the clock, a baby's toy. Similarly, for a news story, you should include shots of interviewers, interviewees, and items relevant to the story, such as the smashed car or flames of a fire.

Handling Talent

A common problem in many news or documentary shootings is people who do not want to be on television. Usually these are people who are in the news in a negative or controversial way and, as a result, try to avoid being interviewed. The degree to which these people should be pursued depends on the nature of the assignment, the context and reputation of the program, and the personalities of all involved. Some people do not want to be on TV because they know they come across poorly. If these people are not crucial to obtaining the message, they should not be used—they may be self-fulfilling prophecies. And certainly, there is little justification for pursuing an interview with the grieving relative of a person who has just been killed.

At the other end of the spectrum is the common problem of unwanted talent. Random people do not wander into a studio very often, but when a shoot is being conducted on a city street, the curious are bound to appear. If a drama is being taped, crew members (or off-duty law officers) are often hired for crowd-control purposes—placed at the edges of the scene to keep onlookers out of the shot. But there is no guaranteed way to keep people out of shots that involve fast-breaking news stories. Egomaniacs and self-proclaimed clowns who strut around in the background and make faces (or obscene gestures) at the camera can be a real nuisance. If the director deals with these people in a firm but pleasant manner, such behavior can sometimes be modified.

Handling Crew

As with a studio shoot, the director must work to build *camaraderie* among the crew members. Poor interpersonal relationships can damage a field shoot because usually people cannot get away from each other. In some instances, they are stuck together for days or weeks.

Because the director is on the set at a location shoot, he or she cannot give commands (zoom in, pan left) during recording—they would be picked up on the mic. The director and the crew must work out shot composition and other details ahead of time.

Editing Aesthetics

The directorial role during postproduction is obviously greater for field shoots than for studio productions because material shot single-camera film style must be edited. In fact, the actual show is made in the editing room. Because of the generally uncontrolled conditions during shooting, postproduction can be a tedious prospect. It can also be quite rewarding, however, if preproduction and production have been carried out effectively and the potential for a successful program is apparent.

Most of the aesthetic principles regarding studio camera shots (see Chapter 4) certainly apply in field shoots. However, some of them take on even increased importance. For example, the concepts of **axis of action** must be watched even more closely in the field because so many shots are taped out of order. The director must be able to envision shots that will be edited together even though they may not be recorded immediately after each other. For example, if a long shot of someone running is recorded before lunch and a close-up of the person running is shot after lunch, the camera must not **cross the line** of the long shot when it is used for the close-up. Otherwise, when the two shots are cut together, the person will appear to change direction. Similarly, it is easy to shoot material that will violate the **three-to-one cutting ratio** when you do not shoot **wide shots, medium shots,** and **close-ups** one after the other.

But the compensating factor is that when you shoot single camera, you can take the time to carefully construct each shot so that it enhances your message and appeals to the eye.

12.5 | Cameras

Most of the aesthetic principles of picture composition apply in the field as well as in the studio. So do the general principles dealing with **f-stops, depth of field, focusing,** and **filters** (see Chapter 5). However, in a studio, once cameras are set, the characteristics under which they shoot remain fairly constant. White balance set at the beginning of a studio program, for instance, can be depended on to give accurate color throughout a taping. Such is not the case with field production.

White Balancing

White balance must be reset frequently as lighting conditions change, because the white balance control adjusts the basic video level to suit the composition of the light that is available for an individual shot. It "reads" a designated item as *white* and then readjusts the electronics associated with the other colors so that they will render true color.

As the sun peeks in and out of clouds, the light source changes, and white balance needs to be readjusted. The changes in the sun's **color temperature** over the course of a day also require changing white balance as does going from outdoors to indoors or vice versa. Fortunately, white balancing is easy—many cameras automatically white-balance as changes in color temperature occur. If your camera does not adjust automatically, you can do the white balancing manually with the push of a button. Your main white-balancing problem may simply be remembering to do it. Also, if you are going to adjust the white balancing manually, you must remember to bring something white to the shoot to be used for **reference white**—a piece of paper, a white sweater.

Filters

A related item very easy to forget in the process of field shooting is the changing of the *filter* on the camera filter wheel. As mentioned in Chapter 5, many cameras have three filters—one for indoor 3,200 K **(Kelvin)** light (which also works for outdoor sunrise and sunset), one for sunny daylight, and one for cloudy outdoor shooting. When you move from outdoors to indoors, or vice versa, you must change the filter, or your footage will have a decided orange or blue cast.

Gain

Many portable cameras have **gain** switches to use in instances of low light. This boosts the electronics so that the camera "sees" better in the dark. However, because using this switch makes the picture grainier, it should be used only when it is absolutely impossible to add light—generally in the covering of a news story.

Power

Another problem in the field is the power source for the camera. Most cameras can be operated either on regular *AC* (household alternating current) or on *batteries*. AC is more reliable, but cameras do add wattage to electrical circuits that may already be taxed from your portable lights.

Batteries have a disadvantage in that they run out of charge—usually when you are in the middle of shooting your most important scene. If you use batteries, make sure the battery is fully charged before you are scheduled to take the camera on location. While in the field, make sure you are not unintentionally discharging the battery when you are not shooting. By all means, disconnect the battery while you transport equipment from one location to another. Some cameras have a *standby* position that keeps the electronics operational but cuts down on battery use. This should be used while shots are being set up and rehearsed. Cameras differ as to how they conserve on battery power, so be sure to find out when the battery is and is not engaged on your particular camera.

Camera Mounts and Movement

Keeping a picture steady on a portable camera can be a problem. You usually do not have the luxury of the sturdy **pedestals** and **cranes** available in a studio. What you are more likely to have is a three-legged **tripod** and/or a shoulder.

Some cameras (especially digital ones) have built in **image stabilization** that operates either digitally or optically. The former digitally magnifies part of the image and tracks it during camera movement. It then compensates for the movement and keeps the picture steady even if the operator's arms are moving. Optical systems have a gyro sensor that detects camera movement and then adjusts the path of incoming light. Image stabilization does not, however, handle large movement variations.

Body braces also can assist you in holding the camera still. (See Figure 12.10.) You can also hold the camera in your hands or place it on your shoulder and brace your elbows or back against a wall or table. But even the strongest and steadiest of people cannot create images that are as still as those that come from a camera mounted on a tripod.

Pans, tilts, and **zooms** can all be executed very effectively on a tripod. However, assuming you do not have the benefit of a field crane, movements such as **trucks** and **dollies** do require the human body to simulate wheeled movement. Improvised dollies and trucks can sometimes be achieved with wheeled conveyances such as a child's wagon or a grocery cart.

Camera operators and directors must be willing to reposition the camera frequently for both aesthetic and informational purposes. This requires effort and muscle on the part of the person operating the camera, but it is needed for everything from reaction shots of the

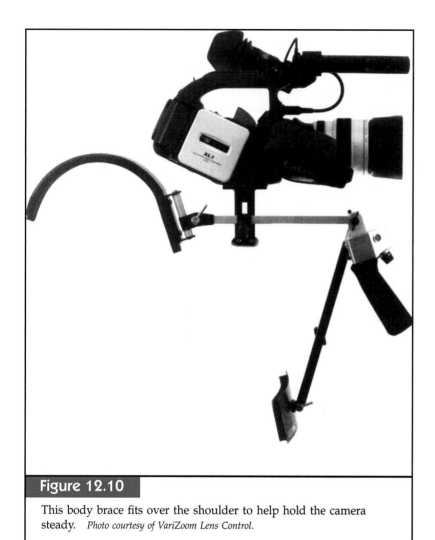

Figure 12.10

This body brace fits over the shoulder to help hold the camera steady. *Photo courtesy of VariZoom Lens Control.*

reporter reasking questions to low-angle shots to convey a sense of power.

Camera Care

Care of the camera must also be a high-priority item for the camera operator. The high level of activity and unanticipated problems on any location production occasionally mean that some of the usual equipment precautions may be temporarily forgotten. Cameras are very vulnerable to the careless treatment they may be given on a field shoot. The lens should be capped between scenes and whenever the camera is moved, because stray objects such as pebbles can accidentally strike a camera. If you are operating the camera, you should realize that you are in charge of a rather delicate piece of equipment that must remain operational for many future projects.

12.6 Lighting

Although lighting in the field is difficult, there is one very distinct advantage that location lighting has over live-on-tape lighting—location lighting allows each shot to be lit individually. When a studio program is shot with three cameras simultaneously, lighting must be general enough that it provides acceptable illumination for any camera shot. Often in multiple-camera shooting, compromises have to be made in setting the lights, and few shots are really properly lit. With location shooting, however, the camera is stopped after each shot, and the lights can be reset to light the next shot optimally.

The basic **three-point lighting** approach is appropriate for field shoots as well as in the studio. Likewise, contrast ratio, color temperature, and other principles of lighting (see Chapter 6) apply, at least in theory, to location work. Once again, problems occur when dealing with uncontrolled situations. In this case, the problems associated with lighting indoors are quite different from those found outside.

Indoor Location Lighting

Since lighting **grids** are far from common in university classrooms, corporate offices, hospitals, and other locations, the crew must bring portable lighting apparatus to the field shoot. *Portable lights* (see Figure 12.11) are usually mounted on stands that can then be placed in positions roughly approximating those of the basic **key, fill,** and **backlights.**

Figure 12.11

This Lowel portable lighting kit contains the lights and supporting equipment needed for effective field production. *Photo courtesy of Lowel-Light.*

Often this is difficult or impossible to accomplish because of lack of space or because the light stands will show in the camera's picture. The backlight is particularly tricky, because it is essentially impossible to position it correctly without having the stand visible in a long shot. Occasionally, clip-on lights can be clamped onto a door or tall piece of furniture to serve as a backlight. However, many field productions are shot with only key and fill lights.

In fact, many news shoots use only one light; it is mounted on the camera and is used only for basic illumination. The result is a very flat, washed-out effect that is, nevertheless, better than shooting a silhouette. The lighting instruments taken on a field shoot are usually limited, too. **Scoops, ellipsoidal** spots, and even **Fresnels** are too bulky to lug along. The main portable lights used are **broads** (see Chapter 6), but their beams are somewhat difficult to control.

Lighting Control

Lack of a **dimmer board** adds to the control problems. To increase or decrease the intensity of a light, the stand must be moved in accordance with the principles of the **inverse square law** (see Chapter 6). However, space limitations may hinder this. Often you can use **scrims, barn doors, flags,** and other devices to help diffuse or shape the light.

Power

Another big problem is securing adequate electrical power. A studio is specially wired in anticipation of the power that will be needed to meet extensive lighting demands. People's homes and offices are not. Lighting properly with key, fill, and backlights all plugged into one circuit is almost guaranteed to blow the circuit breaker.

For this reason, it is particularly important to learn ahead of time where the circuit breakers are, how many amps each circuit is rated for, and which outlets are on which circuit. You should also become familiar with the basic formula *watts = volts × amps.* (This is often referred to as the "West Virginia" formula, $W = VA$.) The watts will be written somewhere on the lamp of your lighting instrument—such as 500 or 1,000 watts. Amperes should be indicated on the circuit breaker—usually 10, 15, or 20 amps. Voltage is regulated by the power company and in most ordinary circumstances is 110 volts. (In industrial settings, it may be 220 volts.) Therefore, if the circuit breaker is rated for 10 amps and the voltage is 110, you can plug in lights totaling 1,100 watts on that circuit. To be on the safe side, use a figure of 100 for the voltage (this also makes the arithmetic easier). So a 20-amp circuit could handle 2,000 watts.[4]

However, you cannot assume your lights can use the whole circuit. You must consider the total wattage of all appliances and devices on the circuit. The office copier or the home refrigerator may be using the same circuit that you want to plug into. One group of students was taping at a factory; they had been recording without problems for an hour or so when suddenly the lights went out. Lunchtime had arrived and the employees began using the company microwave oven that was on the same circuit as the lights.

Usually you must plug lights into at least two separate circuits, and generally this means using plugs in two different areas. In many homes and offices, outlets in one room are all on the same circuit, and you may have to go several rooms down the hall to use a different circuit. This means you must take along extension cords.

Safety

The use of extension cords raises another issue—the problem of safety. First, make sure that the extension cords you plan on using are rated for the electrical load you expect to plug into them. Using cords that are not heavy-duty will result in tripping the circuit breaker—or worse yet, starting a fire.

Also, electrical cable strung all over the floor is likely to cause people to trip, often unplugging the light and/or bringing down the light stand (as well as causing bodily injury). Where cords must be laid along the floor, cover them with a wide tape to help ensure that they will not be tripped over. Ideally, you should run the cords along the walls and up over doorjambs. (See Figure 12.12.) For this purpose, you must bring along heavy-duty tape—preferably something like *duct tape* that has a very strong adhesive. Where cords must be taped to painted surfaces, it is best to use *masking tape* that will not peel off paint when it is removed.

Lights also create a safety problem because of their heat. They should not be placed where someone is

Figure 12.12

Crew member taping a power cord above a doorway to ensure that no one will trip over it during the recording.

likely to bump into them accidentally. Also, they should not be placed where they are touching curtains or paper and could thereby start a fire. At the end of a shoot, they should be turned off *first* and packed away *last*. This gives them time to cool before crew members must handle them.

Available Light

One other problem associated with shooting indoors comes from available light. If at all possible, you should turn off all regular lights and just use the **quartz** or **high-frequency fluorescent** lights from your portable lighting kit. However, sometimes available lights can be used for general illumination if they are of a color temperature close to 3,200 K (see Chapter 6). Regular incandescent lightbulbs can usually be used, but office or home fluorescents should definitely be turned off. Not only may they result in a recording with a blue tint, they may also create a hum or buzz on the sound track.

Outdoor light coming through windows should also be avoided, if at all possible, because it is about 5,500 K—far bluer than the 3,200 K quartz lights. The problem is not with the outdoor light itself but with the fact that you are *mixing* types of light—daylight and quartz. If you set the camera's filter for quartz light and some of your light source is from daylight, your footage will look blue. If you set the filter for daylight, the footage will be orange. **Gels** are made to place on windows to change the color temperature of the outdoor light, but they are expensive and difficult to install. A simpler solution is to avoid mixing the types of light. If you cannot shoot in a windowless room, close the window drapes or shades.

Outdoor Location Lighting

If you are shooting outside, your main source of light is the *sun*. This has both advantages and disadvantages. You do not need to worry about light stands or power requirements. However, you have no control over the sun. It changes position; it can be overly intense; it darts behind passing clouds. Its color temperature changes as the day progresses so that scenes shot at noon will not match scenes shot at 5:00 P.M. Not only will these scenes have a color switch, but they are also likely to show different lengths of shadows, different molding of facial features, and different amounts of glare. This is a particular problem if long shots are taped at noon while close-ups, which are to be intercut, are not shot until 5:00 P.M.

Additional Lights

Sometimes the sun is so bright that you need *extra* lights. This seeming contradiction is caused by the fact that a bright sun can wash out facial features. It acts, in essence, like a very bright key light. To counteract this, you can add artificial lights to create the effect of a fill. Of course, these lights have to be the same color temperature as daylight.

One way to do this is to cover the quartz lights used indoors with special filter gels that convert the

Figure 12.13

As an example of a technique used in portable lighting, these four 12,000-watt HMI instruments were focused through a scrim to produce a soft, flat illumination for an interior scene.

3,200 K light to more than 5,500 K. However, the filters cut down on the efficiency of the light, so more lights than normal are needed. Another way is to use **HMI** or **HID** lights that are made to produce 5,500 K light. To minimize problems from the sun passing behind clouds and changing color temperature as the day wears on, you can actually use large HMI floods to create an artificial source of sunlight, even for interior scenes. (See Figure 12.13.)

If auxiliary lights are needed, getting power to them can be a problem. Powerful battery-operated lights do exist, but they are not commonly or inexpensively available.

Reflectors

Another alternative for obtaining light from a different direction is to use a **reflector.** A commercially available *foil reflector* (see Figure 12.14) can be used to bounce sunlight onto a subject's face from almost any direction. And if the sun is behind the subject (functioning as a backlight), you can place the reflector in front of the subject to provide a satisfactory key light. Even if a professional reflector is not available, you can use any

Foil reflector. The two-sided reflector is a valuable part of outdoor location shooting. The partitioned foil-leaf side (shown) produces a soft diffused light. A smooth silver paper surface on the other side produces a brighter, more intense light. *Photo courtesy of Mole Richardson.*

large piece of white material (a white poster board, for example) to provide some light from a complementary direction. (See Figure 12.15.) Obviously, the more highly polished or reflective the surface of the reflector is, the more efficient it will be.

12.7 Audio

As with other technical components, many of the elements of field production audio are the same as those for studio audio; any differences are caused primarily by the uncontrollable elements of the outside world. As a starting point, ask the same questions concerning frequency, amplitude, pickup pattern, construction, and positioning for both studio and field productions (see Chapter 7).

Microphones

Sometimes the answers are different, however. Generally, microphones need to be more directional for field locations because of all the extraneous noise. By the same token, mics that are less sensitive (and therefore need to be located closer to the talent) are desired, because they will pick up less of the background noise. Also, because of the transportation jolts and rough handling that field equipment is subjected to, mics for location shoots usually are of a more rugged design—**dynamic** rather than **condenser.** *Quality* and *frequency response* often have to be sacrificed for *dependability* and *ruggedness.*

Fishpoles and **hand mics** tend to be used most frequently in the field. Fishpoles (see Figure 12.16) are common for dramas, where the mic should not be seen in the picture. Hand mics are common in interview situations, where the presence of the mic is accepted. Another type of mic, the **shotgun,** is used in situations where the subject being taped is far from the camera and cannot be miked easily (a lion in the jungle or a man on a horse). Shotgun mics are highly directional and can pick up sound from long distances. However, because of the high directionality, they must be pointed at the subject accurately so that they pick up the desired sound. Wireless mics come in very handy when subjects need to move around a great deal.

At times you may want to attach the microphone to the camera to eliminate the need for someone holding it. This is usually *not* a good idea if you are recording speech, since the camera is located at some distance from the person talking and is likely to pick up noises close to the camera much more efficiently than it picks up the talent. A camera mic is acceptable if you are picking up crowd noises or other nonspecific sounds.

Control Equipment

The sophisticated control-room equipment that produces clean, well-balanced sound is not available at a remote site. There usually are no **patch bays, equalizers,**

Figure 12.15

In this setup, reflectors are being used to bounce the sunlight onto the two actors sitting on the sand, providing both fill and backlight.

Figure 12.16

The audio operator is positioning the fishpole so that it will pick up sound as well as possible without getting in the shot. *Photo courtesy of Amy Phillips.*

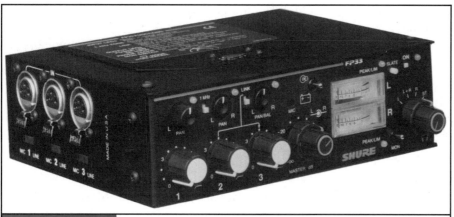

Figure 12.17

A portable audio board can help enhance the audio of a field production.
Photo courtesy of Shure.

or **filters.** The camcorder often has only a "ballpark" meter and some headphones. Audio on a location shoot is only *transduced* and *recorded*—and usually *monitored*. Channeling, selecting, and altering (Chapter 1) are all accomplished in postproduction, and yet great care must be taken to keep recording levels within a consistent range so that they can be matched when edited. Any differences in the levels of sounds will become very obvious when different shots are assembled in the editing process.

One way to ensure consistent levels is to use the **automatic gain control (AGC)** available on most tape recorders. This automatically raises the volume of sounds that are soft and lowers the volume of loud sounds. AGC is *not* always the solution to keeping audio levels within a consistent range, however. This is because AGC cannot distinguish between desired and undesired sound; it boosts anything that is low. Therefore, when no one is speaking, the level of the background noise is automatically amplified, producing a hissing or roaring effect. Because there is a built-in delay factor of one second or so, the effect is most noticeable at the beginning of segments or during long pauses.

Audio **balance** is particularly difficult if two people are talking and one has a very soft voice while the other has a booming voice. AGC cannot completely compensate. Sometimes the better solution is to record each person through his or her individual mic onto a

separate track; then try to match the volumes in postproduction.

To control a large number of different audio sources that need to be recorded at the same time, you will need to take a portable audio mixer on location with you. (See Figure 12.17.) You can then feed several mics through the board, set their levels individually, and record this mix-down on the video. However, setting up such an audio board takes additional space and time, both of which are often unavailable on a field shoot. Also, if the shoot is taking place in a small area, you must be careful to listen for **phase** problems caused by placing the mics too close together.

Another way of creating more control is to record the audio on a separate recorder, such as a **DAT.** An audio operator can then give undivided attention to the audio being recorded on that DAT, something that a person operating a camcorder cannot do. During editing, the sound from the DAT can be synched with the picture and incorporated into the edit along with music and sound effects.

Wildtrack

Audio operators on location should generally record some separate **wildtrack** sound—background sound from the location recorded with no specific voices. Sometimes this is for a specific purpose. For example, a narrator may be standing next to a machine that is important to the story line, but the machine has a distinctive sound. In the final edited program, shots that include the machine are to have a voice-over narration, which is to be recorded later in the studio. If the director wants to have the sound of the machine as a part of the background under the narration, then a wildtrack of that sound must be recorded for a later audio mix.

At other times the wildtrack sound is just general background noise that can be used to cover abrupt transitions during postproduction editing. Good sound operators make a practice of recording numerous pieces of wildtrack as protection against unforeseen editing problems.

Extraneous Noise

The audio operator must also listen carefully to the sound that is occurring and being recorded while a take is being shot. The human brain *subconsciously* filters out unwanted sound. The noise of an airplane flying overhead often goes unnoticed by two people engaged in conversation; they effectively hear only each other. But this **selective attention principle** does not work with a recorded presentation. An unnoticed airplane recorded on an audio track will come through loud and clear on playback. For that reason, the audio person must listen intently and stop production if an unwanted noise is too evident.

In many ways, a person operating audio on a field shoot must have a disciplined "feel" for audio. He or she must have enough experience to know how something will sound in the final edited program.

12.8 Graphics and Sets

Graphics and sets receive less attention in field shooting than in studio shooting. Graphics are usually added after the fact, and sets are determined by the nature of the location.

Graphics

Some consumer cameras have built-in **character generators** so that titles can be included during taping, but these are generally used only for slating/identification purposes. Graphics in a camera can actually be a

problem. More than one student has forgotten to turn off the day/date function of a consumer camcorder and had it appear, very inappropriately, on all the footage shot for a drama. Occasionally, you may need to shoot a chart that appears on a wall or some similar graphics to use as a cutaway, but these are not likely to be designed for television, so the camera operator must frame them as well as possible under the circumstances.

If actual physical charts or illustrations are to be included in a program, they are better shot in a studio where lighting can be *controlled*. Most graphics, of course, are computer generated (see Chapter 8). All of these will be incorporated into the program during the postproduction editing.

Sets

Sets, as such, do not usually exist either. The main reason you go on a location shoot is to obtain realistic scenery and settings that are not possible with constructed sets in a studio. However, unless you find some very cooperative people or you are willing to pay a great deal of money, you cannot usually change much in a location setting. You *can* clean up someone's desk so that the clutter will not be visually distracting, but you *cannot* readily change the color of the walls, the location of trees, or the placement of windows.

When shooting interior scenes, windows do present particular problems in that they cause glare and interfere with proper lighting. The best advice is to *avoid* shooting into windows. However, it may not always be possible to avoid a passing shot of a window; perhaps it is absolutely necessary to pan with the talent while he or she walks across a room, passing in front of a window. In such a situation, you should consider disabling the automatic **iris** control; set the **f-stop** manually for the best interior (nonwindow) lighting, and keep it consistent as the talent passes in front of the window. This will result in an overexposed background through the window, but the alternative (if the automatic iris is left on) is to allow the talent to turn into a silhouette when passing in front of the window.

In one sense, the setting is much easier (and less expensive) to deal with in a remote location than in a studio, because very little, if anything, needs to be constructed. However, an improper setting can totally

Figure 12.18

Hallway to be considered for a location shoot. How many problems can you spot if you plan on using this hallway for a location production? How will the mixture of indoor and outdoor light affect color temperature and white balance settings? What can be done about the potential glare? How will the automatic iris function as the talent walks along the corridor, moving in and out of extremely bright spots? What will be the safest angles to use?

destroy the concept and atmosphere of your program. (See Figure 12.18.) You can wind up with the wrong colors, architecture, traffic flow, and so forth. Therefore, you may have to spend many hours scouting and searching for just the right setting.

Real locations are invariably much "busier" than studio sets; they have a lot of elements that are extraneous to what you will be taping—furniture, wall coverings, appliances, and so forth. As a result, you must pay particular attention to make sure you do not wind up with shots that have light switches or flowerpots that look like they are growing out of someone's head.

12.9 Video Recording

Most modern-day field production is undertaken with digital camcorders. Therefore, the camera and VCR are the same piece of equipment, and the camera operator also becomes the videotape recorder operator. A button that is easily accessible when someone is holding the camcorder turns the recorder on and off.

However, there is a definite trend toward tapeless recorders—ones that use a video disc or hard drive instead of videotape. This is a trend for studio recorders, too, but it has even more advantages for field recorders because it enables the camcorders to be lighter, less power hungry, and more rugged. In addition, field footage is usually edited with nonlinear editing equipment, so the files from a hard drive recorder can be dumped into the editing computer quickly and easily.[5]

Setup and Connections

Although the camera and recorder are one unit, there are still connections that need to be made to it, regardless of whether the signal is being recorded onto a tape or hard drive. For example, the audio should be routed separately from an external mic whenever possible because, as discussed previously, the microphone should be as close as possible to the talent. The video recorder input for a microphone may be an **XLR, BNC, phone, RCA,** or **miniphone connector** (see Chapter 7). Make sure you check before you leave to confirm that the connector on the end of the microphone cable is the same as that required by the recorder. If it is not, get an **adapter** that will convert from one type of connector to the other. You will also want to connect headsets into the earphone output on the camcorder, usually with a miniphone connector.

Monitors are sometimes attached to recorders so that the director can see what the camera operator is framing. Possible connectors for this are the BNC, S-Video, or F-type (see Chapter 10), so again you should make sure the proper cables and connectors are brought to the location to connect the recorder and monitor. Monitors can be unwieldy because, when they are connected to the camcorder, they must be moved if the camera is moved. This can inhibit the camera operator's flexibility. The viewfinder of most camcorders can serve as a viewing device. After something is shot, it can be played back through the viewfinder so that the director can check it. This takes time, however, so many field shoots take place without monitoring. This requires trust and complete communication between the director and the camera operator.

One good approach to the discipline of field production is to lay out all of the cables and connectors you will need for your particular assignment and then plug everything together and operate it before you leave the checkout area, just to make sure you have everything.

Recording Procedures

The camcorder operator should set the audio level and check all controls before taping begins. It is good practice to make sure the machine has been up to speed at least 10 seconds before anything crucial is taped and, likewise, to keep the machine running for about 10 seconds after the shot is completed. A videotape recorder should not be left in *pause* for long periods of time, because this will wear the oxide off the tape and clog the video heads.

During taping, the person in charge of recording should be watching all the "vital signs," most of which appear on indicators in the viewfinder monitor—end-of-tape warning, battery condition, low light, and so forth. In most instances, this person will also be framing shots and listening to the headphone to make sure the audio is recording properly—unless, of course, the audio is being recorded on a separate recorder.

Because the person is doing so many tasks, he or she must be extra careful to make sure the recorder part of the camcorder is operating properly. The best of shots will be useless if they are not recorded properly.

12.10 Editing

Many of the options and operations of editing are the same for multicamera and field production (see Chapter 11). What is different, however, is the emphasis placed on the editing process and the expanded role of audio editing.

The Editing Process

Because much of the editing done in conjunction with studio-based production is intended to correct mistakes made during production or to put together short roll-ins to be played during production, the editing can usually be accomplished rather quickly. Such is not the case with material shot single camera. The program is *literally* put together during postproduction—a process that is often long and drawn out. Much of the strength—and discipline—of a good director is an ability to generate the sense of momentum and enthusiasm needed to complete a production. In live television, the relentless clock focuses everyone's attention; in single-camera postproduction, the constant pressure of a knowledgeable guiding hand is needed.

Although many professional editing sessions involve only the producer or the director working in conjunction with the editor (or even the editor working alone with only a detailed set of notes), student postproduction sessions should, as much as possible, become a *learning process* for the entire team. Without proper organization, however, this process can drift into noisy chaos. The important thing is that someone must be acknowledged as being in charge. This may be the producer, the director, or the editor, but it should be someone who understands the basic structure of the project.

Most of the editing connected with field production is accomplished in nonlinear editing systems (see Chapter 11). However, it is not always completed in an editing suite. ENG footage is often edited in the van that the reporter and camera operator

Figure 12.19

A van used for electronic news gathering. The editing equipment is in the back of the van, the microwave relay is on the top, and the panel on the side can be used for connecting the van to a power source.

travel in. (See Figure 12.19.) Once the footage is shot, the two enter the van and work in tandem; the camera operator transfers the footage through **Firewire** from the camcorder to the nonlinear editing system (usually located in the back of the van) while the reporter compiles the script. Together they piece together the appropriate visuals, and the reporter often adds voice-over narration. Sometimes this edited package is sent from the truck **microwave** transmitter back to the TV station to be incorporated into the news program.

For other types of productions (dramas, documentaries, etc.) an on-set editor may use a laptop computer to edit a series of shots that have just been recorded. The director can look at the edit to see if additional material needs to be shot in order for the scene to work effectively. It is much less expensive to discover that something needs to be redone while all the setups are in place than to try to bring cast and crew back several weeks later for pickups.

Audio Editing

For a studio production, audio is usually mixed while the program is being taped. Music is brought in at the beginning and end of the show, and sound effects are incorporated as the production is under way. Single-camera productions shot without benefit of a sophisticated audio board do not lend themselves to audio mixing during the production phase. Obtaining good dialogue, interview audio levels, or on-camera narration is all that can really be expected in the field.

As a result, for professional single-camera productions, audio editing is sometimes undertaken separately from video editing. While one person is editing the picture and the principal dialogue shot in the field, other people are attending to music and sound effects. Dramatic productions are the most complicated from an audio point of view. Someone, often the director, must first determine where audio elements are needed. Where will the music be brought in and taken out? What sound effects are needed? Which sounds taped in the field need to be rerecorded because they are not good enough? Once all this has been decided, a musician may be asked to compose the music, someone obtains effects from sound-effects CDs, and sometimes members of the cast are brought back into a studio where they record their lines over again—a process known as **automatic dialogue replacement.**

After all the sounds have been gathered, they are placed on a **multitrack** tape or in a computer, either one that is being used to edit the picture or one with a program to edit audio. Here the sounds are positioned so that they are heard where they are needed during the production. They are also mixed together so that they are in a proper volume relationship with each other—the music is lowered when an actor is talking, the gunshot's volume is raised so it stands out from the rain in the background. The average TV drama, commercial, documentary, or top-flight industrial production has a final sound track that is the result of the skilled mixing of anywhere from 16 to 32 or more separate sound tracks.[6]

Most student productions do not incorporate this many tracks, but it is important that the preparation for the sound track start with the very first planning of the shape of the project. The director and producer should question each other continually as to the exact details of how each sound or combination of sounds (on-camera narrator, voice-over narrator, background noise, music, sound effects, etc.) is to be achieved. Some of the sound work can be accomplished while production is still under way. For example, if you know you are going to need the sound effect of a dog barking, you can find it well ahead of the day you need to mix it with other sounds. You may have heard the phrase "We'll fix it in post." This is an invitation to audio disaster. If you have not thoroughly thought out the procedure during preproduction planning, it is often too late to fix it in postproduction.

12.11 Remote Truck Productions

Productions undertaken from large remote trucks bear resemblance to both single-camera field production and studio production. They also have unique characteristics of their own.

The crew is usually larger (and brawnier) than for either studio or field productions. There are cables, mounting devices, lights, and many other things to carry and position. Cleanup is an extensive operation because all cables need to be coiled and everything needs to be packed neatly. (See Figure 12.20.) Space is at a premium in the truck so there is no room for sloppiness. If the event is being broadcast live, there may be crew members to make sure the signal is getting to the station or the satellite. Trucks often have both microwave and satellite dishes on their roofs so that they can send and receive signals. In addition, someone may be needed to oversee the generator if that is what is providing the power for the truck.

The content of many events that are covered with trucks is often not network or station generated. It is a football game, parade, concert, or other event that would go on even if there were no TV coverage. In fact, the TV entity must usually pay for the right to televise the event and abide by certain requirements of the responsible agency—something that adds to the work of the TV producer. Preproduction is very important so that all the elements needed will be at the right place at the right time. Sketches of the location are valuable for determining camera and microphone placement. Producing a truck shoot can involve not only making lists but making *lists of lists.*

The director's job is similar to his or her job in the studio in that there are multiple cameras. But the work can be more intense because many truck broadcasts are live and there is no chance to edit, even if the mistake is blatant. The director may be stationed a long way from the camera operators—in the truck that is outside the stadium with no overall view of the playing field, at the beginning of the parade with no direct view of the parade route. A simple **intercom** system often isn't adequate. Walkie-talkies and cell phone are added tools that the director and crew members need to operate.

A truck shoot is likely to have a number of associate directors preparing different types of shots for the director. One AD may be assessing all the cameras that have crowd shots, looking for those with particular human interest. Another AD might be setting up the instant replays while another is overseeing cameras that have been assigned to get close-ups of the coaches. The chatter

Figure 12.20

Once the remote coverage of a beach volleyball tournament was complete, crew members had to coil all this cable used for cameras and other equipment.

that goes on among the ADs and the director may sound like bedlam, but it is usually a well-organized pattern that people who have worked together often have established. Even with help from ADs the director must pay *very* careful attention to a vast array of monitors and quickly select the most appropriate shot of the moment.

There are likely to be many more cameras for a truck shoot than for a studio shoot. The area of action is usually vast, and since the event is unscripted, cameras need to be situated many places to cover whatever happens. Most of the cameras are connected to the truck through cables. Some facilities that host events frequently (such as sports stadiums or concert halls) have permanent wiring within the walls so that the truck can be hooked up outside the facility and cameras can be connected within the facility. In other instances, all the cable must be strung from truck to camera positions. **HDTV** signals need greater cable capacity, so a number of venues are rewiring with **fiber optics** to accommodate this technology. Often, however, it is the broad-

casters that must run the fiber optics. Sometimes not all cameras are connected to cables. Camera operators who wander around the facility getting close-ups of the action may have cameras that send their signals back to the truck in a wireless fashion that uses an antenna. This gives the camera operators greater mobility.

Lighting is more likely to resemble field production than studio production because the lighting used is available light or special lighting brought by the TV crew. Often it is impossible to control the lighting to the extent you can in field production, however. Trying to diffuse the sharp sunlight over an entire baseball field would be an exercise in futility. *Weather* is a definite factor that affects lights and other aspects of production. Finding a method for getting up-to-date weather reports is often part of the preproduction process for truck shoots.

A truck shoot is likely to involve many microphones, some of which need to be positioned in unusual places. There is often the need to pick up crowd noises, the referee, and the band as well as the people who are announcing the event. Sometimes you need to tie into the public address system that the event organizers are using so that your TV coverage can include such things as the official race results or the concert. You may need to send out live audio in many different forms—5.1 **surround sound** for the HDTV broadcast, **stereo** for **SDTV**, **mono** for an international feed. Added to the audio operator's job is the trend to have audio effects for graphics, slow motion, and other effects—something that wasn't done in the past.

The graphics operator on a truck remote is usually very busy, especially during a sports event. Many statistics can be prepared before the telecast and then brought up as needed, but it is impossible to predict all the graphics needs, so the operator usually needs to build graphics during the telecast. Then there are the "normal" things—balls and strikes, first downs, time remaining—that need constant updating.

The technical director also keeps very busy at the switcher. It is rare that a remote covered by a truck can undergo any rehearsal, so the TD can plan for some events but doesn't really know what to expect—and neither does the director. Remote broadcasts are usually laden with special effects so the director and the TD must develop an effective shorthand that enables the shots the director wants to get on the air.

Even if an event is broadcast live, it is also usually recorded so that there is a record of it for future use. With sports, for example, many of the highlights that appear in the sports part of a newscast are from the recording of the game. In addition, short bits are recorded for instant replay and often material recorded prior to broadcast (interviews with celebrities, background information on the performers) is played back during the broadcast.

It is not uncommon for parts of the telecast to be edited so they can be shown later in the broadcast. Halftime highlights, reviews of basketball shots by one

particular player, or crowd reactions to a particular song are often edited as the taping is in progress. This, of course, means that an editor must be a member of the crew. *Adrenalin* flows freely during most truck shoots, but that is part of what makes them a desirable, bonding experience for members of the crew.

Discussion Questions

1. What are the main differences between lighting in a studio and lighting on location, both for a field shoot and a remote truck shoot?
2. Give the advantages and disadvantages of a large crew versus a small crew on a location shoot.
3. How is a director's job different in the field, on a truck, and in the studio?
4. What are the challenges audio operators face in the field compared with those in the studio?

Notes

1. There is no information that parallels Chapter 9 on the switcher because switchers are generally not used for field production. Some switchers run on DC power, but generally material is "switched" when it is edited.
2. Historically, most of the people given these jobs were female, so the term *script girl* was used in early times. For many years the script supervisor was the only woman on most film crews. Although the functions of script supervisor are very important, this is still a low-paying job.
3. These prices were compiled from a number of rental catalogues, including those of the following: Birns and Sawyer (323-466-8211), Ametron (323-466-4321), Bexel (818-841-5051), and Raleigh (323-466-3111).
4. "Watt Exactly Is a VA?" *TV Technology,* 5 April 2000, 48.
5. "Tape Gone in a Year?" *TV Technology,* 23 July 2003, 10.
6. Some professional music recording sessions use in excess of 100 different tracks.

CHAPTER 13

Video on the Internet and Optical Discs

Throughout this book's first 12 chapters, you have seen how the conversion to **digital** is changing the process of video production. In most cases, however, these changes have been evolutionary. Digital cameras, **video servers,** and **nonlinear editors,** for example, are certainly great innovations, but they do not fundamentally change how video professionals work or how the viewer ultimately sees the finished program. More often than not, the new digital technologies merely provide video professionals with faster or higher-quality ways of doing the things video professionals have always done.

But the rise of digital is also offering entirely new ways of distributing video and audio information, regardless of whether the production is undertaken in a studio, in the field, or with a remote truck. For its first half-century, video was viewed exclusively on television sets—the signals distributed through the air, over a wire, or on a videotape to the viewer's home. Now, as video technology continues to merge with computer technology, we can watch television on our computer screens and use media such as optical discs to record and play back video on both our computers and our televisions. Perhaps even more significant, the **Internet** can be used to make video available any time a viewer wants it. Would you like to watch a story from yesterday's evening newscast? No problem if the video is available on the station's website.

These new delivery systems hold the potential to fundamentally change how viewers watch television, and even change what "television" means. Their inherent **interactivity,** or ability to be actively controlled by viewers, adds another dimension to video production. Where productions for traditional television normally have a set beginning, middle, and end, for example, interactive productions might play differently for different people. Perhaps your story could end *either* with the boy getting the girl or with the boy losing the girl—depending on what the viewer wants.

The *disciplines* of using these new delivery systems include the fundamental concepts already discussed throughout this book. Aesthetically good shot framing, quality sound pickup, coherent graphic design, and logical editing, for example, are as important in interactive delivery methods as they are on traditional television. The availability of impressive "bells and whistles" does not lessen the need for discipline in using them. The *techniques* of using these new delivery systems include a basic understanding of how they work, as well as how video and other information must be prepared for them.

It is beyond the scope of this chapter to discuss *all* types of interactive systems, especially advanced ones like video games and virtual reality simulators. It is also beyond the scope of this chapter to address in detail all aspects of interactive systems such as Web-page authoring and the use of text, graphics, and multimedia elements. Instead, this chapter concentrates on making video and audio available on nonlinear media, namely the Internet and computer optical discs, as it presents the following topics:

- Basic principles of interactivity and dynamic content, and how they affect video and other information delivered via the Internet and computer disk (13.1)

- How links, screens, and menus are used to deliver interactive content (13.1)

- Basic principles of using video on the Internet, including streaming technology (13.2)

- How Web pages are created to provide access to Internet-based video and audio information (13.2)

- Basic techniques for recording video onto computer-based optical discs (13.3)

13.1 Interactivity and Dynamic Content

As mentioned at the beginning of the chapter, most traditional media are **linear,** meaning that their content has a specific beginning, middle, and end. Such media are also static; their content cannot be changed by the consumer of the media. For instance, when you watch an episode of your favorite sitcom, you normally begin watching at the start of the program and watch until the end, and you cannot affect the content of the program. Certainly, you *could* record the program on videotape and then skip around to various parts, but this would be a tedious process, and the result probably wouldn't make much sense. And even then, you would not be able to actually change the show's content.

Interactive media, on the other hand, are characterized by their **nonlinear** design and **dynamic content.** You have already seen the term "nonlinear" used in the reference to editing and storage systems, and its meaning in this context is similar: A nonlinear presentation does not have to proceed in a predetermined order. This is where the concept of interactivity comes in. Interactive media presentations are normally designed to allow the consumer to "navigate" through them. The consumer does not merely passively take in the media content but rather actively controls how it is presented. Thus, the media have dynamic content—the same presentation may be experienced by different people in different ways, changing according to each consumer's wishes. For that reason, consumers of interactive media are usually referred to as *users*, because that term implies actively employing something—putting it to use—rather than the passivity connoted by terms such as "viewer" or "listener."

You have already used interactive media when you have surfed the Internet or played a **DVD (digital versatile disc)** at home on your television. The Internet is perhaps the ultimate interactive medium, allowing users to "move" through cyberspace to find what they're looking for—be it stock quotes, the day's news, or entertainment. On a smaller scale, most movies on DVD allow the user to choose which scenes he or she wants to watch or even view alternate endings. An increasing number of DVDs also feature so-called bonus material—interviews with the actors, the original trailers for the movie shown in theaters, or running commentary by the director as the movie plays.

Links, Screens, and Menus

Later in the chapter, we will discuss various ways to facilitate this type of user control, but for now it is helpful to understand the concepts of **links, screens,** and **menus.** A link is a control element that "connects" one part of a presentation to another. When the link is activated—usually by clicking on it with a mouse or selecting it with a remote control—it triggers a designated action. For instance, a **Web page** may include a line of text, "Click here to see the video clip," which is designated as a link to a video clip. Thus, when the user clicks the mouse on that line of text, the video clip plays. Links may be used to move the user to a new location in the presentation, allowing him or her to quickly "jump" to a new screen. Text designated as a link is often called **hypertext.**

Pictures also may be defined as links. When the user clicks on the picture with the mouse, something happens. Different parts of a picture may be defined as different links. For instance, an interactive presentation may display a picture of the solar system on the screen. When the user clicks different parts, different things happen; for example, a click on Mars might display additional information about Mars and a more

Buttons that allow users to control video clips can be designed to look like the familiar controls found on a VCR.

detailed picture of the planet. Clicking the sun may cause the picture to animate, showing how the planets revolve around the sun. Graphics used in this manner also are called **image maps.**

The most common type of link is the button, which is a small graphic made to look like a button on an appliance. Buttons may be labeled with text ("Continue" or "Stop," for example), or they may have small pictures that define their function (a red hexagon to represent "Stop," for example). On the Internet, video clips are often accompanied by a series of buttons that mimic the functions on a VCR, as shown in Figure 13.1. Thus, users can "pause," "play," "rewind," or "stop" a clip by pressing the appropriate button.

Different portions of interactive presentations are often referred to as *screens;* in Internet-based systems, these screens are usually called Web pages. Screens may contain different types of information such as text, pictures, or video clips, as shown in Figure 13.2.

Menus are screens that allow the user to make choices. The **main menu,** also called the **home page** on Internet-based presentations, is usually the first screen that the user sees, and from this menu he or she makes a selection. Figure 13.3 shows how a user could select from among three different portions of an interactive presentation using a main menu. Complex presentations may have multiple menus; a DVD might have a main menu from which the user can choose among playing the movie, setting audio options, or viewing

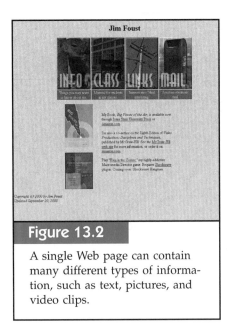

Figure 13.2

A single Web page can contain many different types of information, such as text, pictures, and video clips.

bonus material. If the user selects the bonus material link, he or she may then be taken to a submenu screen, allowing the selection of actor bios or director commentary. The actor bios link might present another submenu allowing the user to choose links to the bios of individual actors in the movie.

Challenges of Interactive Media

The nonlinear nature of interactive media can present challenges for people who create it. Producers of traditional video presentations have more control over how their presentations will be viewed—as discussed, such

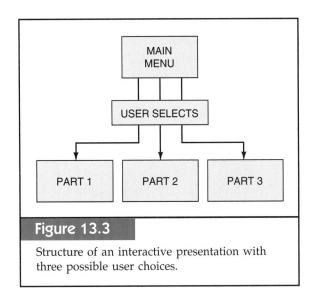

Figure 13.3

Structure of an interactive presentation with three possible user choices.

presentations usually have a defined beginning, middle, and end. Interactive media producers, on the other hand, in essence give over to the user many aspects of program control. Thus, an interactive presentation must be designed so that it makes sense even if the user does not choose to consume it linearly. For example, a television station might choose to make its reporter **packages** available in video form over its website. However, without the news anchor's lead-in to the package, it might not make sense to the user. Thus, the station would need to either include the lead-in as part of the video or provide a text-based introduction to the package on the Web page.

The best interactive presentations also are designed to *encourage* user "exploration," thus taking advantage of the interactive medium's potential. In other words, they make it easy and rewarding for users to navigate their way through the presentation. If the purpose of the presentation is to inform the user, it allows the user to find easily the specific information he or she is looking for; if the purpose of the presentation is to entertain, it makes the experience of using the presentation enjoyable for the user.

13.2 Using Video on the Internet

In a little more than a decade, the Internet went from being a technical curiosity to a major influence on nearly every aspect of everyday life. The Internet's ability to store and make readily available a nearly infinite amount of information has made it a valuable resource for commerce, education, and entertainment. The information offered on the Internet also comes in a variety of forms—text, graphics, sound, video, and multimedia—and these forms are able to intermingle nearly seamlessly. A single Web page, as you've already seen, can contain text, graphics, and video.

Video, however, has remained something of a "Holy Grail" among digital media. Its high resource and **bandwidth** requirements, as discussed in Chapter 10, make distributing it over the Internet more of a challenge than less resource-intensive media like text and pictures. Today, video information can be distributed over the Internet, but its quality is not up to even **standard-definition** broadcast standards. This doesn't mean that video over the Internet cannot be a useful tool, just that the quality expectations—at least for the time being—are different from traditional video production. In the future, as the speed of Internet connections improves and as better **compression** methods develop, we may see higher quality and even **high-definition** video readily available on the Internet. For now, however, it is important to understand that sacrificing the quality of video we've come to expect for traditional broadcast applications is a fact of life for Internet-based video.

How the Internet Works

Before we look at the actual process of putting video and audio information on the Internet, it is useful to discuss briefly the basic concepts that make the Internet work. Many of these concepts have a direct bearing on how video is stored, delivered, and viewed over the Internet.

Although the terms "Internet" and "**World Wide Web**" are often used interchangeably, the two terms actually have different meanings. The Internet is a worldwide **network**, or connection, of computers. The World Wide Web (**WWW**) refers to the set of technologies that places a graphical interface on the Internet, allowing users to explore the network using their mouse, icons, and other visual elements rather than having to type obscure computer commands. In fact, it was only with the advent of the WWW in the early 1990s that the Internet, which traced its roots to 1950s national defense experiments, really began to enter mainstream life.

The Internet's system of interconnections allows one computer on the network to access information on any other computer connected to the network. It also allows many different computers to access one another's information at the same time using the same connection lines. It does this by dividing digital information into "chunks" called **packets.** Each packet is a small amount of digital information that flows over the Internet on the way to its assigned destination. A picture file going from a computer in Germany to a computer in the United States, for example, might be broken up into several hundred packets that then flow individually across the network. At the receiving end, the packets are reassembled into the picture file.

Each computer on the Internet has a unique electronic "address" that identifies it to other computers on the network. This address is typed as a **uniform resource locator (URL),** normally beginning with the "http://"designation. For example, http://www.mhhe.com is the URL for the Internet site of this book's publisher. URLs can be expanded to include subdirectories and files as well. For example, the URL "http://personal.bgsu.edu/~jfoust/classes.html" refers to a particular file on the author's website.

As discussed previously, the Web page is the basic unit of information structure on the WWW. A Web page is actually a computer file that contains "pointers" to other Web pages and media files, as shown in Figure 13.4. Web pages are created using a computer language called **Hypertext Markup Language (HTML),** as discussed later in this section. When an HTML file is loaded into a **browser,** a program used to "read" Web pages, it displays the individual text, links, and media files.

We also know that bandwidth is an important consideration on the Internet, especially when it comes to distributing video information. The actual interconnections between major Internet computers, the so-called backbone of the Internet, consists of very high-bandwidth **fiber optic** and cable connections. However,

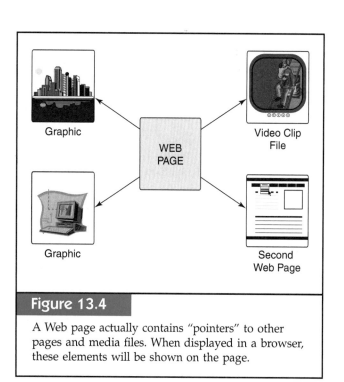

Graphic

Graphic

WEB PAGE

Video Clip File

Second Web Page

Figure 13.4

A Web page actually contains "pointers" to other pages and media files. When displayed in a browser, these elements will be shown on the page.

a significant bandwidth bottleneck often occurs at the end user's computer. Many people use a phone-line-based **modem** to connect to the Internet, and this offers very low bandwidth. Other options for home Internet access include cable modems, which allow Internet access through cable television service, satellite-based Internet services, or Integrated Services Digital Network (ISDN) and Direct Subscriber Line (DSL) services that transmit data over telephone company lines.[1] These services allow much faster speeds, but usually at a significantly higher monthly cost.

Internet Video—Downloading and Streaming

As discussed in Chapters 10 and 11, digital video can be recorded, distributed, and played back as files. These files are just like word-processing files or graphic files, only much larger. We usually refer to video files on the Internet as **clips,** just as we do the individual segments on a nonlinear editing system (see Chapter 11).

Video files (and their accompanying audio) can be sent over the Internet in two basic ways: **downloading** and **streaming.** When downloading, the video file is sent to the user in packets, which are then reassembled by the user's computer and saved to the hard drive. The video cannot be viewed until the entire file has been downloaded and saved. For a very large file, this might mean the user could not see the video for several minutes or even hours. Streaming still sends the data in packets, but the packets are structured so that the individual **frames** of the video are sent sequentially. This means that the user can view the file and hear its audio as it is coming into his or her computer. Most streaming formats, in fact, do not actually save the file to the user's hard drive at all. Streaming has the major advantage of allowing the user to begin watching the clip almost immediately, with no need to wait for the entire file to finish downloading.

Downloading Formats

Digital video can be recorded, distributed, and played back in a wide variety of formats. To view these files in a browser, you need to have an appropriate "plug-in," or helper program, installed. On PC computers, the video format can normally be determined by looking

Extension	File Type
.avi	Audio Video Interleaved
.mpg	MPEG
.mpeg	
.m2p	
.m2v	
.svd	
.vob	
.mov	QuickTime Movie
.rm	RealMedia Video
.wmv	Windows Media

Figure 13.5

Selected video file formats. The "extension" at the end of a computer file's name can be used to identify what format it is.

at the end of the file name for its *extension*, as shown in Figure 13.5. If you have the appropriate viewer installed on your computer, it will usually open automatically to display the video file you've selected.

The Audio Video Interleaved (AVI) and Quick-Time formats originated on Windows and Macintosh computers, respectively. Today, viewers are available for both formats on both types of computers. An AVI player (Windows Media Player) is installed as part of most versions of the Windows operating system, while a QuickTime player comes as part of the Macintosh operating system. Both AVI and QuickTime use proprietary compression methods to make video files smaller.

Files encoded in **MPEG-1, MPEG-2,** or **MPEG-4** formats also can be played back on PCs or Macintoshes with an appropriate player. Newer versions of Windows Media Player and the QuickTime player can play many types of MPEG files.

Choosing among these different formats may come down, for the most part, to personal preference. Since Windows-based PCs are so ubiquitous, AVI is perhaps the safest choice for ensuring that end users will have the software to view the files. However, the various flavors of MPEG may provide greater flexibility in creating files that have the best quality and the lowest bandwidth.

Streaming Formats

The two main streaming formats are Windows Media and RealMedia. In addition, QuickTime, although strictly speaking not actually a streaming format, behaves like one.

To play Windows Media files, you need the Windows Media Player, which, as noted, is installed with newer versions of the Windows operating system. To play RealMedia files, you need the RealMedia Player, which is available from RealNetworks[2] or is installed with some video programs.

Again, the choice between the two competing formats is in large part a personal decision. Since the Windows Media Player is now installed in all versions of Windows (which is the operating system used by more than 90 percent of computers), you can safely assume most potential users will have it. RealNetworks, however, had a head start in the streaming video game, so its software is also found on a high percentage of computers.

Creating Video for the Internet

The actual process of creating video for use on the Internet is largely the same whether you plan to download or stream. The main difference will be the software program that you use to create the digital file. Most nonlinear editing systems, for example, have one or more onboard plug-ins that allow you to create various types of media files from a finished editing project. The "Export Timeline" menu on the Adobe *Premiere* editing program, for example, allows you to create an AVI file (*M*ovie), MPEG-1 or MPEG-2 file (Adobe MPEG Encoder), a RealMedia file (Advanced RealMedia Export), or a Windows Media file (Advanced Windows Media). (See Figure 13.6.)

Other freestanding programs allow you to create various types of downloadable and streaming media files as well. RealNetworks' *Helix Producer Basic* is available for free from the company's website, and it allows you to create streaming RealMedia files from AVI files and other formats. Perhaps the most versatile media creation program is Discreet's *Cleaner XL*, which allows conversion among AVI, QuickTime, MPEG-1, MPEG-2, MPEG-4, Windows Media, and RealMedia formats. (See Figure 13.7.) It also supports

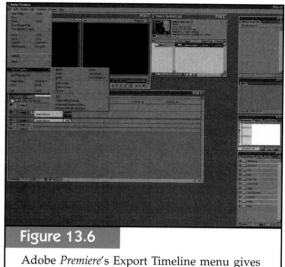

Figure 13.6

Adobe *Premiere*'s Export Timeline menu gives the user several choices for exporting edited information. *Adobe product screen shot reprinted with permission from Adobe Systems Incorporated.*

Kinoma, a video format designed for use on palm computers.

Setting Video Options for Downloading

A variety of options are available for creating downloadable video files for the Internet. How these options are set determines, to a great degree, how much space the finished data file will take up and how the video will look to the end user.

Figure 13.7

Discreet's *Cleaner XL* allows conversion among many different video formats. *Photo courtesy of Discreet, a division of Autodesk, Inc. © 2003.*

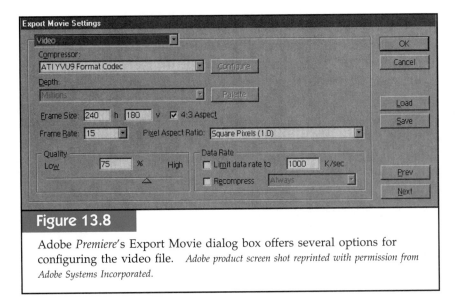

Figure 13.8

Adobe *Premiere*'s Export Movie dialog box offers several options for configuring the video file. *Adobe product screen shot reprinted with permission from Adobe Systems Incorporated.*

These option settings will vary according to the software you're using, but generally with AVI files you can control the following variables:

Type of compression/compressor. There are a number of different compression schemes for AVI files, depending on the program. The best one to use depends on your particular application—you might find it useful to review Section 7.2, which discusses the pros and cons of the most popular compression methods.

Frame size. You can set the size of the video frame, in pixels. In most cases, you will want to preserve the aspect ratio of the original video. For 4:3 ratios, 176 × 132, 240 × 180, 320 × 240, and 640 × 480 are commonly used. The larger the frame size, the larger the file.

Frame rate. This determines the number of frames displayed in each second of video. Frame rates of 24–30 fps are ideal, but most Internet users have gotten used to frame rates around 15 fps. Anything less than 15 fps begins to look jerky and stilted. The higher the frame rate, the larger the file.

Quality. Many programs allow you to set an overall quality level for the video clip. Higher quality will use less compression, often producing a clearer picture. Not surprisingly, higher quality also creates larger files.

Figure 13.8 shows these and other settings available in Adobe *Premiere*'s Export Movie dialog box. Once the options have been set, you simply give the file a name and tell the program where on your hard drive you want to save it. The program will then create the file.

Setting Video Options for Streaming

The settings available for streaming formats are similar to those for downloading. However, in streaming formats we are less concerned about the size of the file and more concerned about data rate. Higher data rates require higher bandwidth, and if we are to achieve successful and uninterrupted streaming, we will have to be careful not to exceed the available bandwidth. For this reason, in some cases (such as the frame rate) the software will determine the best setting based on bandwidth conditions at the time of streaming.

Figure 13.9 shows the Advanced RealMedia Export window in *Premiere*. Starting at the top left of the window, we have the "Audio Format" selector, which sets audio quality based on whether the clip contains voice only (lower quality) or music (higher quality). The "Video Quality" selector allows us to choose whether we want to emphasize smooth motion of the clip (a higher frame rate) or the sharpest video image (more detail in each frame). The setting shown, "Normal Motion Video," provides a compromise between the two.

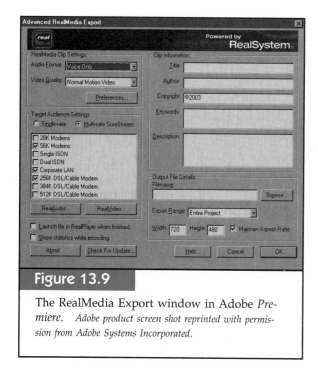

Figure 13.9

The RealMedia Export window in Adobe *Premiere*. *Adobe product screen shot reprinted with permission from Adobe Systems Incorporated.*

Below these choices are the "Target Audience Settings," which determine video parameters based on how the end user will connect to the Internet. For regular phone modem users, lower-quality files will be created, while users of cable modems will get the highest-quality files. Clicking the "RealAudio" or "RealVideo" buttons allows us to override these default settings. Generally, it is not a good idea to do this.

To the right, we can add **metadata** about the clip, such as the author of the clip, date, title, and keywords. This information, as discussed in Chapter 10, can help us organize large quantities of clips through **asset management.** Just below the metadata fields, we can type a filename for the clip to be created—we want to end the name with the extension ".rm" so that we (and the software) know it's a RealMedia file. Clicking the "OK" button creates the clip.

Putting Files on the Internet

For video clips to be available on the Internet, we must copy them to an appropriate server computer. This process will vary based on who is providing the server space. For example, your university may provide students with space on a special server where they can store HTML and other files. Since space is limited

and lots of students want to post information on the Internet, most universities will only allow each student to put so much data on the server. If you are getting space from a commercial Internet Service Provider (ISP), you may have more space available.[3] Remember, video files, no matter what the format, take up a lot of space. You will need to check with your instructor, computer administrator, or ISP to see how much space is available to you.

Creating a Web Page

To allow others to actually view the video, you will need to create a Web page that contains a link to the streaming media file. HTML is a text-based programming language, which means you can use a simple word processor to create your pages. For advanced programming, you can use a Web-authoring program like Macromedia *Dreamweaver* or Microsoft *FrontPage*. Web-authoring programs automatically write the HTML coding based on pages you lay out on the screen.

There is actually a midpoint step between the HTML file and the media file called the "RAM file." The RAM file will, in our case, be a very simple text file that actually contains the location of the media file. Using the RAM file is rather redundant in our example, but in advanced applications it can be used to provide other content along with the media clip as it plays (for example, a bar chart illustrating what a speaker in the media clip is talking about).

The RAM file, too, can be created using a simple word processor or text editing program. Just type the complete URL of the video clip on the first line:

http://www.example.com/~jfoust/housetour.rm

This particular line is a hypothetical example. You, of course, would have to replace this address with the actual address of your clip. Then, save the file, making sure it is in "plain text" or "ASCII" format. This option, which is usually accessible in the "Save" dialog box of word processors, removes unnecessary formatting commands that word processors insert into documents. If the file isn't saved as "plain text" or "ASCII," it won't work as an HTML file. We also want to be sure to name the RAM file with a ".ram" extension, such as "housetour.ram," and save it onto the server in the same location as our media clip.

```
1  <html>
2  <title> Sample Streaming Video Page </title>
3  <h1 ALIGN="center"> Welcome to the Video Page </h1>
4  <p align="center">
5  <h3 ALIGN="center"> Click <a href="housetour.ram"> here </a> to see the video clip. </h3>
6  </html>
```

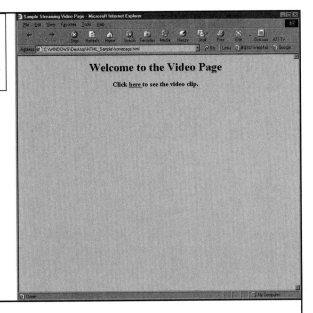

Figure 13.10

Simple HTML code and resulting page. On the left is the HTML coding, and on the right is the resulting page viewed in a browser. The numbers to the left of the code lines are not actually part of the code; they are shown to explain what each line in the program does. Line (1) identifies the file as an HTML script. Line (2) is the page's title, which appears at the very top of the browser window (not on the page itself). Line (3) inserts the first text line, centered on the page. Line (4) inserts a paragraph return. Line (5) inserts another line of text in a smaller font size, centered on the page. Note also the linking code that designates the link to the file "housetour.ram." Line (6) designates the end of the HTML file.

Now, the HTML file will link to the RAM file (housetour.ram), which in turn opens the video clip (housetour.rm). Figure 13.10 shows a simple HTML file that creates the page shown when viewed in a browser. This HTML file would be created and saved (with an ".htm" or ".html" extension) as a plain text file on the server in the same location as our RAM file and media clip. It is well beyond the scope of this chapter to provide a comprehensive primer on writing HTML, but the figure's caption provides a brief explanation of what each line in the file does.[4] For our purposes, the most important part is line 5, which contains the link to the RAM file. The link commands actually enclose the word *here* so that when the user clicks the word, the RealMedia player will open and play the clip, as shown in Figure 13.11.

The page itself is actually somewhat boring visually, but it illustrates the basic process of making available a streaming media clip. We could enhance it a bit by showing a frame of the video on the Web page itself, giving the user an idea of what will be seen when the clip is played. If you refer back to Figure 13.6, you'll see

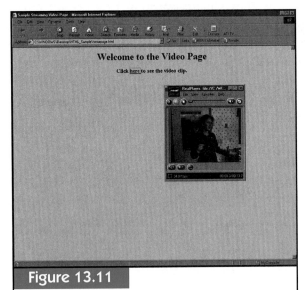

Figure 13.11

When the user clicks on a video clip's link, the player program automatically launches to play the clip.

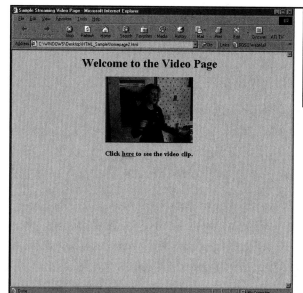

1	\<html\>
2	\<title\> Sample Streaming Video Page \</title\>
3	\<h1 align="center"\> Welcome to the Video Page \</h1\>
4	\<p align="center"\>
5	\<img src="still.jpg" align="center"\>
6	\<p align="center"\>
7	\<h3 align="center"\> Click \<a href="housetour.ram"\> here \</a\> to see the video clip. \</h3\>
8	\</html\>

Figure 13.12

Here, the page in 13.10 has been modified to add a visual interest to the page by inserting a still frame from the video clip. The page still functions as before—the user clicks the word *here* to play the video clip. The still frame is inserted by the code in line (5).

that one of the options in *Premiere*'s Export Timeline feature is exporting a frame of the presentation as a still picture. Thus, we could create this picture and save it to the server in the same place as our video clip, RAM file, and HTML file. Then, we could modify our coding as shown in Figure 13.12 to create the page shown.

Working with other media formats is similar. If we are just providing an AVI or MPEG file to be downloaded by the user, we can cut out the middle step of creating the RAM file. For example, we could replace line 5 of Figure 13.10 with this line: \<h3\>Click \<a href="housetour.avi"\>here\</a\> to download the clip. This would download the AVI file to the user's computer if he or she clicked the word *here*. Of course, we would have first had to create the AVI file "housetour.avi" and save it to the server.

13.3 Using Computer-Based Optical Discs

Video and audio in digital form can be stored on any type of computer media. Of course, the files are usually much too large to fit on media like floppy disks, but

CD-ROMs and DVD discs are well suited to digital video and audio data. In fact, you may not have thought about it, but the DVD disc containing your favorite movie is really nothing more than a storage medium for digital data. Your DVD player merely interprets and decodes this data into video and audio.

The process of creating video for use on optical discs is quite similar to the process of creating video for use on the Internet. For that reason, this section in some ways builds on Section 13.2. Some of the same formats, in fact, that are used to make available video and audio over the Internet also can be used to put video and audio onto computer optical discs.

Types of Optical Discs

Although all optical discs do the same basic thing—store digital data—there are important differences among different types. In some cases the same physical disc—such as a CD-ROM—can be used in a number of different ways.

Video CDs

A **video CD (VCD)** is created using a CD-ROM disc. It uses MPEG-1 encoded video and can hold about an hour of video and audio. The quality of VCD video is somewhat marginal; depending on the source material, it may be a little worse or about the same as a standard VHS tape. The maximum screen resolution of VCD video is 352 × 240. Video CDs can be created using a CD-ROM recorder (usually called a **burner**) and appropriate software and can be played in many newer DVD players or on a computer with a CD-ROM drive and appropriate software.

Super Video CDs

A **super video CD (SVCD)** is an enhanced version of the VCD, created on a CD-ROM disc. It uses MPEG-2 compression, and its quality (maximum screen resolution 480 × 480) is closer to that of a DVD than that of a VCD. However, it can hold only about a half-hour of video and audio. SVCDs can be created using a CD-ROM burner and appropriate software. SVCDs can be played in many newer DVD players (although not as many as can play standard VCDs) and on computers with CD-ROM drives and appropriate software.

DVDs

DVDs provide the best quality of the three disc types, using fairly high data rate MPEG-2 compression. The maximum screen resolution for DVD is 720 × 480. DVD discs look very similar to CD-ROM discs, but they are in reality completely different, holding about eight times the data. The quality can be varied, but even at the highest available data rate a DVD can hold an hour of video and audio. Many commercial DVDs use a dual-layer format that allows them to double the amount of data stored on a single disc.

Another complication involved in creating DVDs comes from the fact that there are two competing blank-disc formats. DVD-R and DVD-RW discs came out first, but DVD+R and DVD+RW discs have the support of many of the largest manufacturers.[5] The two formats are not compatible with one another, although many players can play both types of discs. In some cases, a DVD burner can burn either the − or + format, but not both. As far as how much data can fit on the disc and the quality of the video and audio, there is no difference. It is merely a matter of how the data is electronically recorded onto the disc.

DVDs can be created using a computer with a DVD burner and appropriate software, or with one of the increasing number of home DVD recorders. They can be played back on most newer DVD players and on computers with DVD drives and appropriate software. Of course, you need to make sure the player supports the DVD format (+ or −) you're using.

Video Data Discs

VCDs, SVCDs, and DVDs are all designed to be played back on *either* computers or DVD players. For that reason, the discs have to be created in a very specific way—it is important, for example, that folders and files on the discs have certain names and that the video and audio be in certain formats. However, if you do not need to play a disc on a DVD player, you can simply create a **video data disc** using either a CD-ROM or DVD.

Video data discs are just that—discs with video and audio files in any desired format. As long as you have the appropriate software on your computer, you can access and play the files. Because they are not constrained by the required parameters of VCDs, SVCDs, and DVDs, they can sometimes hold more data. The downside, of course, is that they are useless in DVD players.

Creating Optical Discs

Many nonlinear editing programs have built-in tools for creating VCD, SVCD, and DVD discs. Some high-end editing systems, however, do not include these tools. In these cases, you can simply purchase a relatively low-cost program such as Roxio's *Easy CD & DVD Creator* or Pinnacle's *Studio Deluxe* to create the disc files from AVI or MPEG data output by the editor.

Most of these types of programs will offer one or more default settings for each type of disc, and it is best to not stray from these defaults. As noted, VCDs, SVCDs, and DVDs need to be created in very specific ways to allow them to work properly. For that reason, it is best to go with the default settings. If you are creating a video data disc, of course, you will have more leeway to tweak the parameters to exactly what you want.

In most cases, creating the video disc will be a two-step process. The software will first **render** the video in

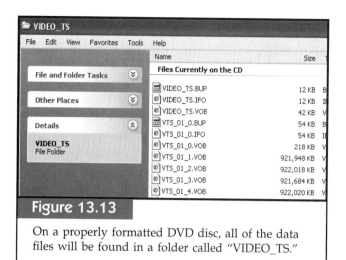

Figure 13.13

On a properly formatted DVD disc, all of the data files will be found in a folder called "VIDEO_TS."

Figure 13.14

A sample program in Pinnacle's *Studio Deluxe*. The menu contains links to the three clips in the program's timeline. *Screen shot courtesy of Pinnacle Systems, Inc.*

the appropriate format, then write it to disc. These programs are configured to automatically create the right types of files and file names and to put them in the right directories on the disc. On a DVD disc, for example, all of the data files go into a folder called "VIDEO_TS," as shown in Figure 13.13.

Using Menus

VCDs, SVCDs, and DVDs allow the use of menus to facilitate user control. In most cases, the menu will be the first thing a user sees when he or she puts the disc in a player. If there are no menus on the disc, the video will simply start to play.

VCD and DVD authoring programs usually have built-in tools for creating menu screens. Menu links can point to other menus (as discussed in Section 13.1), or to different video clips. You can configure the video clips so that they play and then return to the menu or so that they play and then go on automatically to the next clip. VCD and SVCD menus are a bit less advanced than DVD menus, allowing link selection only by typing in numbers on a remote control, not by using arrow buttons to move from link to link.

Figure 13.14 shows a sample program in Pinnacle *Studio Deluxe*. As you can see, the program has three separate sections, and a menu containing links to each of the three sections. Most programs like this one offer many tools for configuring the look and operation of menu screens.

A Wrap-Up

When producing a video program (regardless or how or where it is going to be distributed), a traditional *wrap-up* is given to a performer about 15 seconds before he or she has to finish talking. It means that there is very little time left to wrap things up, quickly summarize, and say good-bye. Perhaps it is appropriate that we wrap up quickly at this point.

This text has been concerned with the *techniques* of video production. If it has been successful, it has also gotten into the *disciplines* of handling these various elements. Discipline has been defined in several ways throughout this text. As much as anything, it can be considered a matter of attitude.

Attitude toward learning and improving is one major ingredient of discipline. If you truly want to learn as much as you can about the business of video, you will gain quite a bit from this course. You will observe intently. You will try conscientiously. One of the most important secrets of learning in a course such as this is the ability to admit areas of temporary ignorance and then ask questions or seek experiences to fill in those areas. If you are unsure about audio patching, ask to have it explained to you. If you are insecure with the switcher, get all the experience you can as technical director. If you have never placed a video on the Internet, start with something simple and work up from there. Do not try to bluff your way through; no one gets very far in that manner.

Attitude toward communication is important. Unless you have a strong feeling for the pursuit of communication—unless you really have a deep desire to succeed in communicating a message—you are in the wrong field. Television is not just a business of glamour or money or excitement. It is the business of communication. For example, every program starts with a specific purpose—a clear-cut idea of what is to be attained in the production. Until you begin program planning with this attitude, your productions may be slick and polished, but they most certainly will turn out to be meaningless and devoid of any substance.

Finally, *attitude toward a professional obligation must be considered.* The terms "professional attitude" and "professionalism" are bandied about with little thought as to their implications. We use the terms here to imply more than just a means of earning a livelihood. We challenge the student to think of professionalism in the original sense of the three learned professions (law, medicine, and theology), which carry a strong societal obligation. The true professional is one who is dedicated to high principles and a sense of community benefit. If you are committed to this kind of self-giving professionalism, you certainly will be more likely to leave your mark on the field of video production.

Discussion Questions

1. What are some advantages of interactive media? What are some ways video and audio can be effectively integrated into interactive presentations?
2. Find some websites that offer streaming video and look at (and listen to) some of it. What format is it in? What is the size of the frame? What is the overall quality like? Does it play smoothly or are there pauses? How does the speed of your particular Internet connection affect these things?
3. Look at the nonlinear editing system(s) used at your school. Do they offer output for the Internet and optical disc? If not, are there other programs available to create video and audio for these media?
4. To get an internship or job, you may want to put together a "demo reel" that shows your best video production work. Although demo reels have traditionally been recorded on videotape, how might you create a demo reel on the Internet or using an optical disc? What kinds of menus would you use? What would be the advantages and disadvantages compared with tape?

Notes

1. DSL transmits data at high speed over regular telephone lines. ISDN requires a digital data line, which most telephone companies offer for an additional cost.
2. http://www.realnetworks.com.
3. America Online (AOL) and the Microsoft Network (MSN) are two examples of national ISPs. There are also a number of local and regional ISPs, providing various levels and speeds of Internet access.
4. There are literally thousands of books and Web-based resources that can help you learn HTML more comprehensively. For a start, try Chuck Musciano and Bill Kennedy, *HTML and XHTML: The Definitive Guide,* 5th ed. (Sebastopol, CA: O'Reilly and Associates, 2002); and Elizabeth Castro, *HTML for the World Wide Web,* 5th ed. (Berkeley, CA: Peachpit Press, 2002).
5. The designation "R" refers to a disc that can be recorded once—it cannot be erased or rerecorded. The designation "RW" refers to a disc that can be recorded, erased, and rerecorded over and over. These designations are used for both CD-ROM discs and DVD discs.

Glossary

above-the-line Costs for creative and performing personnel (such as the producer, writer, director, musicians, and actors).

A/B roll A linear editing system that is capable of performing dissolves, wipes, and other transitions.

actors TV talent who perform as someone other than themselves.

AD See *associate director* and *assistant director*.

adapter A connector that converts from one type of connector to another (e.g., from phone to RCA).

AFM See *audio frequency modulation*.

AGC See *automatic gain control*.

agents People who find work for actors, writers, and others engaged in creative aspects of the media business.

air monitor (1) In video, the TV set in the control room that shows the video signal currently on the air. The air monitor receives its signal not directly from the switcher but over the air (in broadcast situations) or through an RF cable (in nonbroadcast situations). (2) In audio, the speaker that allows an operator to hear the transmitted broadcast signal.

altering Changing a video or audio signal so that it is different from the original signal that was transduced.

amplify To magnify an audio or video electrical signal for mixing, distribution, and transducing purposes.

amplitude The height of a sound wave. Amplitude determines the volume of the sound. The higher the amplitude, the louder the sound.

analog A method of representing video or audio signals using a "wave" of continuously varying value.

animal handler A person who makes sure dogs, cats, horses, and other animals do what they are supposed to for a TV production.

animation A sequence of graphics that rapidly cycles to create the illusion of motion.

aperture The opening in the camera lens that determines how much light will pass through.

arc shot A combination trucking, panning, and dollying movement in which the camera is moved in a semicircle around a subject while the camera head remains pointed toward the subject.

arm move To move the boom arm of a crane left or right.

art director A person who deals with the look of sets and other artistic aspects of a television program.

aspect ratio The ratio of the height of a television screen to its width.

assemble editing A process in which video, audio, and control track information are simultaneously recorded onto a videotape.

asset management The process of cataloguing and using video on servers in the most efficient manner possible.

assistant director A person who helps a director; the term is most likely to be used in relation to a film director, whereas associate director is used in studio-based television.

assistant producer See *associate producer*.

associate director The person who keeps track of timing for a program and assists the director in other ways.

associate producer A person who helps the producer with any of a number of production chores.

asymmetrical balance An informal arrangement of elements in a camera shot or graphic in which an important object placed close to the center of the picture is balanced by one or more objects of lighter visual weight some distance from the center.

ATSC A series of digital television formats developed by the Advanced Television Systems Committee. ATSC formats are intended to eventually replace NTSC in the United States.

audio board See *audio console*.

audiocassette recorder A piece of equipment that uses tape encased in a small housing, which threads itself, as a recording medium.

audio console The piece of equipment that is used to gather, mix, select, and amplify sounds and send them on to their next destination.

audio frequency modulation A method of recording audio on a videotape by combining it with video information in helical-scan tracks. Using this method, the sound cannot be separated from video for editing.

audio operator A person who sets mics in a studio or location setting and/or operates the audio console.

audition A separate audio speaker that is not tied to what is being mixed by the audio console or sent over the air.

auto key A key effect in which one source is used to establish the shape of the key hole, and another source or sources are then inserted into the hole.

automatic dialogue replacement Rerecording dialogue for a production after the principal shooting is over because, for some reason, it was not recorded properly when it was shot.

automatic gain control An internal control device, for either audio or video signals, that automatically increases or decreases the strength of the incoming sound or picture to maintain optimum signal strength.

automatic iris A camera setting that continuously alters the aperture in response to changing light levels.

automatic white balance A camera setting that automatically adjusts the camera's white-balance setting for differing lighting conditions.

auxiliary send A routing bus on the audio console used to feed external processing gear, multitrack recording equipment, or other audio equipment.

axis of action An imaginary line that extends the path in which a character or object is moving, with the result that if one camera is on one side of the line and another is on the other side, cutting from one camera to another will make the person or object appear to change direction.

axis of conversation An imaginary line that connects two persons talking to each other with the result that, if one camera is on one side of the line and another is on the other side, cutting from one camera to another will make the person appear to change position.

B

background light General lighting on the set behind the talent.

backlight A highly directional light coming from above and behind a subject, adding highlights, shape, and separation from the background.

backplate The part of a condenser mic that is electrically charged.

backtime The process of timing a piece of audio and/or video so that it can be started at a precise time and end at the properly appointed time.

balance In audio, the achievement of the correct ratio among several sound sources; in video, a picture composition where the various portions of the screen appear to have equal weight.

balanced cables Audio cables that have three wires, one for positive, one for negative, and one for ground.

bandwidth The amount of information that can be carried by a given method of signal transmission. The higher the bandwidth, the more information that can be carried.

bank See *bus*.

barn doors Movable metal shutters, attached to the front of a lighting instrument, that are used to limit the area of the projected light.

base light An overall lighting that produces enough light for the cameras to yield an acceptable picture. It does not provide any modeling or effects; it is simply illumination.

batch capture The automated recording of a series of video and/or audio clips to a nonlinear editing system.

batten A counterweighted lighting grid that can be raised and lowered so that lights can be worked on near the studio floor.

beam splitter The optical device in a color camera, consisting of a prism and mirrors, that separates the incoming visual image into the primary colors of blue, red, and green.

below-the-line Costs for technical and production personnel and for equipment, facilities, and services.

bidirectional A microphone that picks up sound from two directions.

bin A storage area for clips on a nonlinear editing system.

bit An individual unit of a digital signal that can have a value of either "off" (0) or "on" (1).

bitstream A stream of digital information, such as video, audio, or other data.

black (1) A synchronized video signal that contains no picture information—a blank screen. (2) To record control track and a synchronizing signal onto a videotape.

blocking The process of planning and coordinating all movement and positioning of talent and production equipment before a production begins.

blocking diagrams Drawings directors make to help them visualize where actors and cameras should be placed.

BNC connector A bayonet-type connector used for video and sometimes for digital audio.

body time The length of a program not including closing credits and titles.

boom (1) Any device consisting of a movable base, an adjustable stand, and a long arm for suspending a microphone above and in front of a performer. (2) An arm of a crane that can be used to move a camera up and down or sideways. (3) To move a camera with a boom arm.

boundary mic See *pressure zone mic*.

breakdown sheets Different pieces of paper or computer screens that list what will be needed for each shot, such as actors, props, and special effects.

brightness An indication of where a color would fall on a scale from light (white) to dark (black).

broad A rectangular floodlight.

browser A program that is used to view interactive media presentations on the World Wide Web.

burner A device used to write digital data to a CD-ROM or DVD.

bus A group of buttons on a video switcher representing the available video inputs.

business Actions that actors perform while they are delivering their lines in order to add realism or strengthen particular ideas.

byte A group of digital zeros and ones that have a particular meaning.

C

cables Coverings that contain wires that transport the signals needed for audio and video production.

call sheet A posted list that lets cast and crew know when and where they should report.

camcorder An integrated unit that combines a camera and a videotape or other recorder.

cameo lighting A type of lighting where the performer is lit but the background is not.

camera control unit The part of a studio camera used to adjust the video quality of the camera.

camera mount The support mechanism, such as a tripod, pedestal, or crane, that holds the camera mounting head and the camera itself.

camera operator The person who frames the shots for a production.

capacitor The part of a condenser mic that stores electrical energy and permits the flow of alternating current.

capture Recording video and/or audio information to a nonlinear editing system.

cardioid A microphone that picks up sound in a heart-shaped pattern.

carpenter A person who builds sets.

carrier wave A specific range of frequencies used to carry an electronic signal from a transmitter to a receiver.

cartridge recorder Audio or video equipment that records or plays back material on tape that is on a continuous loop in a self-contained unit.

cassette A plastic case containing reels that hold audio- or videotape.

cassette recorder Audio or video equipment that records or plays back material on tape that has both the supply reel and take-up reel in a self-contained case.

casting Deciding who will act various roles in a television program.

casting agencies Companies that can be hired to select people for various roles in a production.

catwalk A structure above or around a lighting grid on which technicians can crawl to position lights.

CCD See *charge-coupled device.*

C-clamp A metal clamp with a pivot adjustment for attaching lighting instruments to a lighting grid.

CCU See *camera control unit.*

CD player Equipment that plays back discs on which sound has been recorded digitally.

CD-R A compact disc player that can also record once.

CD-ROM An optical disc that can be used to store digital information. CD-ROMs can normally hold about 700 megabytes of data.

CD-RW A compact disc recorder that can record over the disc many times.

CG See *character generator.*

channeling Moving signals from one place to another.

character generator An electronic device used to display lettering on the television screen.

character generator operator A person who builds computer-generated graphics and operates the equipment that enables them to appear on-air; often called a graphics operator.

charge-coupled device A microchip inside a camera that transduces visual energy in the form of light into electrical energy.

choreographer A person who designs dance movements.

chroma key A special effect in which a designated color (usually green or blue) is used as a key to determine what picture information is to be cut out of the picture with the foreground image.

chrominance The color information (hue and saturation) of a video signal.

clip (1) A segment of video and/or audio stored as a discrete unit in a nonlinear editing system. (2) A digital audio phenomenon where sound that is overmodulated disappears or is intermittent.

clip window A window on a nonlinear editing system used to manipulate video and/or audio clips.

close-up A view of a subject from a relatively short distance. A close-up of a person, for instance, might include only the person's face.

coaxial cable Camera and video cable with a central insulated conducting wire and a concentrically arranged outer wire.

codec (coder-decoder) A device that performs the functions of both a decoder and an encoder.

coil The part of a dynamic microphone that vibrates within the magnet, setting up an electrical charge.

cold edit An edit made without setting in or out points but by simply pressing the "record" button. It is normally used at the beginning of a videotape.

color bar generator The part of the camera or switcher or other piece of equipment that produces the basic colors—red, blue, green, yellow, cyan, and magenta.

color bars An electronically generated pattern of vertical color strips that can be used to standardize and calibrate the color values of all cameras and monitors.

color temperature The relative reddish or bluish quality of a light source, as measured in degrees Kelvin.

compact disc player See *CD player.*

component A method of video signal distribution in which the signal is separated into two or more separate signals representing chrominance and luminance elements of the signal.

composer The person who creates the music for a production.

composite A method of video signal distribution in which the three basic video elements (hue, saturation, and brightness) are combined into one signal.

compression A process used to make digital audio or video data more compact.

compression ratio The size of the original digital signal compared with the size of the compressed digital signal. The higher the compression ratio, the more effective the compression method.

compressor An electronic device used to lessen the distance between the highest and lowest audio volume levels.

condenser A high-quality mic whose transducer consists of a diaphragm, backplate, and capacitor.

connectors Metal housings that allow audio or video or other signals to travel from one cable to another.

continuity Maintaining a consistent and unobtrusive progression from shot to shot in terms of screen direction, lighting, audio, props, graphics, and other production details.

continuous image compression A digital video effect in which a video image is shrunk to a smaller size in real time.

contrast ratio The relationship of the brightest area to the darkest area in a given camera shot, as determined by reflected light readings.

control room The area where all video signals are mixed. The director and technical director (and other crew members) control all program elements from this location.

control room rehearsals A rehearsal with the director seated where he/she will be calling the shots, rather than in the studio.

control track The portion of a videotape that contains the sync information that keeps all elements in a proper timing relationship.

convergence A term used to define the coming together of technologies with previously differing applications to create a digitally based video system. This process involves such things as broadcasting, cable TV, telephones, satellite transmission, and the Internet.

cookie See *cucalorus.*

copyright The exclusive right to a production or publication.

corner insert A video effect in which one video input is placed in the corner of another video input.

costume designer The person who decides what the clothing that actors wear should look like.

countdown Numbers from 10 to 2 that are placed on a videotape before the program material so that the program can be cued to come in at the right time.

crab dolly A small studio crane that can move on tracks.

crane (1) A large camera mount with an extended boom arm for a camera and a seat for a camera operator, all placed on a large, four-wheeled base. (2) To move the boom arm of a crane up and down. (3) A shot produced by craning a camera.

crawl A graphic effect in which lettering moves horizontally across the screen.

crossfade To bring in one sound slowly while taking another out slowly.

crossing the line Having one camera shot come from one side of the axis of action/conversation and another camera shot come from the other side. If the two shots are cut together, the material in the shot will appear to change direction.

cross-keying A lighting technique that uses one light for several purposes, such as a key light and a backlight.

cross-pair miking A stereo mic setup that uses two cardioid mics placed like crossed swords.

CU See *close-up.*

cucalorus A metal or wooden cutout pattern that is placed in front of a spotlight to produce a shadow effect on a scenic background.

cue button A control on an audio board that allows an operator to hear a sound without transmitting or taping it. It is used to prepare sound before it is to be aired or taped.

cue cards Sheets of cardboard with the script written on them that are held next to the camera lens so that the talent can look at the camera and read the script.

cue track A track on a videotape that can be used to record time code or additional audio information.

cut An instantaneous change from one video source to another; also called a take.

cutaway A shot edited into a program to prevent a jump cut. A cutaway shot does not show the focus of action, but rather something related to the main action. For example, a cutaway shot of the audience could be placed between two shots of a politician speaking at a podium.

cuts-only An editing system, normally with only one playback tape machine and one record machine, that is capable of performing only cut transitions between edits.

cutting for information Making a video edit in order to reveal new information to the viewer. For example, cutting from a medium shot of a magician on stage to a close-up when he holds up a particular card from a deck.

cutting on action Making a video edit at a point when some action takes place; for example, when an actor turns toward another actor.

cyc See *cyclorama.*

cycle per second A basic unit of frequency measurement for electromagnetic and acoustic waves; now usually referred to as *hertz.*

cyclorama A large, continuous, smooth backing, usually made of cloth, that may cover two or three walls of a studio.

D

DA See *distribution amplifier.*

daily hire Someone who is hired to work only one day or a few days at a time as opposed to someone who is a regular staff member at a particular company.

DAT See *digital audiotape.*

data rate The amount of information being sent simultaneously in a digital video or audio signal, usually measured in megabytes per second (Mb/s).

DAW See *digital audio workstation.*

dB See *decibel.*

decibel (1) A unit of measurement of sound that compares the relative intensity of different sound sources. (2) A unit of measurement for video that relates to the output gain.

decoder A device used to uncompress a digital video signal.

defocus A camera transition in which the picture on the on-air camera becomes fuzzy.

demographics Information that pertains to vital statistics of a population group, such as age, marital status, income, and geographic location.

depth of field The distance between the nearest point at which objects are in focus and the farthest point at which objects are in focus in a camera shot.

diaphragm (1) The vibrating element in a microphone that responds to the compressed air molecules of sound waves. (2) The adjustable mechanism that controls the size of the lens aperture.

digital A method of representing video or audio signals that uses discrete "on" and "off" pulses. The value of a digital signal at any point can be either "off" (0) or "on" (1).

Digital material can be reproduced with little to no degradation of signal.

digital audiotape Tape that gives high-quality sound because it records information in numerical data bits and bytes. It is a small tape because it records horizontally.

digital audio workstation A stand-alone computer that can be used to record, store, edit, sweeten, and mix sounds.

digital cart A piece of equipment meant to replace the analog cartridge player. It stores audio selections in files on a hard drive and can be programmed to bring up any files in any order.

digital delay A unit that holds a signal temporarily and then allows the signal to leave. It is often used for talk shows so that something a participant says can be halted before it goes on the air.

digital versatile disc An optical disc that can be used to store digital information. Digital versatile discs can normally hold between 4.7 and 10 gigabytes of data. Depending on how data is written on the disc, it can be played back using either a computer or a set-top DVD player.

digital video effects Special effects accomplished through digital technology in which elements of video can be manipulated, resulting in pictures that change size, move across the screen, or are altered in other ways.

digitization The process of converting analog data, such as an audio or video signal, into digital form.

digitizing pen An electronic pen used to create computer graphics by "drawing" on a graphics tablet.

dimmer board A lighting control unit, operated on the same principle as a rheostat, that determines the intensity of a light by controlling the amount of electric current flowing to the instrument.

dimmer circuit One fader of a dimmer board that brings up one or several lights.

director The person in charge of the creative aspects of a TV program and all the procedures that occur in the studio or field.

dissolve A simultaneous fading out of one picture while fading in to another.

distortion A muddy sound caused by playing a sound at a higher volume than the equipment can handle.

distribution amplifier A power amplifier that increases signal strength as an electronic signal is traveling from one place to another.

dolly To move the camera and its mount closer to or farther from the subject.

dolly shot A shot produced by dollying the camera.

downloading Transferring digital data from a computer network such as the Internet to a personal computer.

downstream keyer Part of a switcher used to create a key on a signal after it has gone through all other switcher manipulations.

dress rehearsal The final, full rehearsal before the actual production take—using all sets, props, and costumes—designed to be conducted straight through without interruption.

drop frame A mode of time code that periodically "skips" a frame number to compensate for the fact that NTSC color video actually runs at 29.97 frames per second, and not exactly 30 frames per second.

dry run A session where the director and talent work together on the basic staging of a program without actually doing a full rehearsal.

dub (1) To make a copy of a tape or disk. (2) A copy of a tape or disk.

DV A compression system that uses only intraframe compression and is thus particularly well suited to editing.

DVD See *digital versatile disc.*

DVD-R A digital versatile disc player that records.

DVE See *digital video effects.*

dynamic A rugged microphone whose transducer consists of a diaphragm connected to a movable coil.

dynamic content A characteristic of interactive media that allows a presentation to change according to a user's wishes.

dynamic range The difference between the softest and loudest

sounds a piece of equipment can handle.

E

earphones Tiny speakers that cover or are inserted in the ear so that one person can hear sound coming from equipment.

ECU See *extreme close-up.*

edit controller An electronic unit used to synchronize and operate the videotape recorders in a linear editing system.

edit decision list A computerized file containing information about edits. The file can be used within the computer, printed out, or used to re-create an edited program using another editing system.

editor The person who assembles raw footage into a final program.

EDL See *edit decision list.*

electron gun A device in the rear of a television picture tube that shoots electrons to the front, making phosphors on the front of the screen glow.

electronic news gathering The use of single-camera portable equipment to record news events and other actualities.

electronic still store A system of storing video frames in digital form, indexed for each retrieval.

ellipsoidal A spotlight with a reflecting mirror at the back of the housing that enables it to create a very directional, well-defined beam.

ELS See *extreme long shot.*

encoder A device used to compress a digital video signal, or to digitize and compress an analog video signal.

ENG See *electronic news gathering.*

equalization Emphasizing, lessening, or eliminating certain audio frequencies.

equalizer A unit that adjusts the amount of amplification given to certain audio frequencies, such as high, middle, and low frequencies.

ESS See *electronic still store.*

essential area The area left after cropping 25 to 30 percent from the outer edges of the screen. Graphics and other crucial screen elements should always be placed within the essential area, as the edges of the screen may be lost by the time the image is seen by the home viewer.

establishing shot A long shot used at the beginning of a scene or program to relate the subjects and/or circumstances to one another.

event video The production of tapes dealing with special occasions, such as birthdays and weddings.

executive producer A person who oversees several TV productions.

extender An optical device placed between the lens and the camera to extend the focal length of the lens. A 2X extender, for example, doubles the focal length of a lens.

external key See *auto key*.

extreme close-up A very close shot of a person or object used to intensify drama or to show close detail.

extreme long shot A shot in which the characters are so far away that they are not distinguishable as specific individuals.

F

---

facilities request form A sheet that someone fills out to reserve studio and/or equipment time.

FACS See *facilities request form*.

fade The gradual bringing in or taking out of an audio or video source.

fade-in (1) For video, a dissolve transition—normally used at the beginning of a program or program segment—in which a picture gradually fades in from a black screen. (2) For audio, the gradual bringing in of a sound.

fade-out (1) For video, a dissolve transition—normally used at the end of a program or program segment—in which a picture gradually fades away to a black screen. (2) For audio, taking a sound from full up to silence.

fader The audio console control that raises and lowers volume by controlling the amount of resistance going through the system.

fader bar A handle unit on a video switcher that allows the operator to manually change from one bus to another.

fc See *foot-candle*.

feedback A high-pitched squeal that results from accidentally feeding a program monitor into a live microphone, causing an instantaneous overamplification of the system.

fiber optic A transmission cable that uses transparent strands of glass or plastic instead of copper or other metallic wire.

fibre channel A network system that is popular for use with digital video and audio data.

field In interlace scanning, one-half of a complete frame of video. NTSC interlace scans the odd-numbered scanning lines, then the even-numbered scanning lines, creating a complete frame every ⅟30th of a second.

field of view The size or scope of a shot, indicating how much is encompassed.

field production Television production, usually consisting of single-camera recording and postproduction editing, that takes place outside of the studio.

fill light An unfocused and diffused light used to complement the key light, coming from the side opposite the key to fill in dark areas and soften the shadows.

film-style script A script that is organized by scene with description written on the width of the paper and dialogue centered in the middle.

film-style shooting Taping the way movie makers have traditionally filmed by using one camera and resetting the camera and lights for each shot.

filter (1) A glass or gelatin element mounted in front of a light or in front of a camera imaging device that compensates for changes in color temperature, or in other ways changes the color of the light. (2) Equipment or code within a computer program that cuts out a particular frequency or frequency range of an audio signal.

Firewire (IEE-1394) A digital interface that allows the simultaneous transfer of audio and video information.

fishpole A small lightweight arm to which a microphone is attached, to be handheld by an audio assistant outside of the picture frame.

fixed-focal-length lens A lens that is one specific focal length, as opposed to a zoom lens.

flag A rectangular cloth-covered or metal frame placed in front of a lighting instrument to produce a precise shadow on one side of the light beam.

flat (1) A standard staging unit, constructed of a frame covered with cloth or hardboard, often used to represent walls of a room or the exterior of a building. (2) When all audio frequencies are recorded equally well.

floodlight A lamp fixture that creates diffused light that covers a wide area.

floor director See *stage manager*.

floor manager See *stage manager*.

floor plan A drawing done to scale that shows where various set flats and furniture are to be placed in the studio for a particular production.

floor rehearsals Rehearsals where the director is in the studio rather than in the control room.

floor stand A microphone holder that rests on the floor and has a pole that can be adjusted to various heights so that someone standing can talk into the mic; a stand that holds a light that projects from ground level.

focal length The viewing range of a given lens. The higher the focal length numerically, the narrower the field of view.

focus To make an image look sharp and distinct.

follow shot A camera shot in which the camera follows a moving subject, usually keeping the same distance from it.

follow spot A light of high intensity that is most commonly used to follow a performer as he or she moves around a stage area.

font A set of consistently designed lettering and characters.

foot-candle A unit of light measurement equivalent to the amount of light falling upon a surface one foot away from a standard candle.

fps See *frames per second.*

frame A complete television picture.

frame rate The number of frames in each second of video. The NTSC frame rate is 30 frames per second, while ATSC formats have frame rates ranging from 24 to 60 frames per second.

frames per second The unit of measurement for frame rate.

frame synchronizer An electronic component that is used to synchronize external video sources such as satellite feeds with the synchronization created by in-house components.

freelance Working by the hour or day on one project at a time and without being an employee of any particular organization.

free run A time code mode in which the time code numbers continue to increment even when video is not being recorded.

frequency The number of oscillations per second (hertz) of an electromagnetic wave that, in the audio range, determines the pitch of the tone and, in the light range, determines color.

frequency response The range of pitches (frequencies) that any particular piece of audio equipment can pick up or reproduce.

Fresnel A light with a well-defined lens; the beam width is varied as the bulb is moved toward and away from the lens.

front focus The lens focus that is obtained by zooming in tightly on a subject and then focusing.

f-stop A notation that indicates the size of the lens opening; the higher the f-stop number, the smaller the opening and vice versa. The smaller the lens opening, the less light that enters the lens.

full screen A graphic that covers the entire area of the screen.

fundamental The main frequency of a particular sound.

G

gain Volume of an audio signal or amount of amplification of a video signal.

gel A thin translucent, colored material such as gelatin or plastic that can be mounted in front of lighting instruments to produce specific color effects.

generation The term used to denote a taped copy of another recording. A copy of a first-generation (original) tape recording, for example, is called a second generation.

giraffe A small boom that consists of a counterweighted arm supported by a tripod on casters.

graphics generator An electronic device used to create and display titles, charts, and other graphics on the television screen.

graphics operator A person who creates words, drawings, and some visual effects that are incorporated within a production.

graphics tablet A pad used with an electronic pen to create drawings on a computer.

green room The place in a studio complex where people who are about to appear on a TV show can wait.

greensperson Someone who keeps plants looking alive and fresh on a set.

grid Pipes near the studio ceiling from which lamps are hung.

grip A person who carries things such as cables and set pieces.

group assign switch A control on each input channel of an audio board that allows the operator to group some audio inputs together so they can be controlled separately from other audio inputs.

guide pin The part of an XLR connector that is used to line up the male and female conductors accurately.

guilds Organizations that set wages and working conditions that production companies must adhere to for people (usually above-the-line people) whom they hire.

H

hand mic A microphone that a person holds to speak or sing into.

hard drive The part of the computer on which information is stored.

harmonics See *overtones.*

HD See *high-definition television.*

HDTV See *high-definition television.*

head clog A problem caused by small particles from a videotape becoming lodged in the video heads. Leaving a videotape recorder in "pause" mode for long periods of time can lead to head clogs.

headroom The space between the top of a subject's head and the upper edge of the camera frame.

headsets Ear coverings and small mouthpieces connected together; crew members wear them so they can communicate with each other, and equipment operators wear them to hear the sound from their equipment without disturbing others.

helical scan A method of videotape recording that records video and/or other information in a slanted pattern on the tape.

hertz A basic unit of frequency measurement for electromagnetic and acoustical waves, named after Heinrich Hertz.

HID See *high-intensity discharge lamp.*

high-definition television A television format with more lines of resolution and a wider aspect ratio than standard-definition NTSC television.

high-frequency fluorescent lamp A low-energy, long-lasting light that puts out reds, greens, and blues in a consistent manner to produce 3,200 K light that oscillates between 25,000 and 40,000 cycles per second.

high-intensity discharge lamp A 5,600 K light that does not use much power.

high-key lighting Lighting that is generally bright and even, with a low key-to-fill ratio.

high-speed fluorescent lamp See *high-frequency fluorescent lamp.*

HMI A hydrargyrum medium-arc-length iodide lamp that is balanced for daylight and is often used outdoors as a supplement to the light from the sun.

home page The main menu of a World Wide Web–based interactive presentation.

horizon line The horizontal line in a camera shot that indicates that the camera is level.

horizontal sync pulse A video signal that controls the movement of a scanning beam from the right side to the left side of the screen at the completion of a line of scanning.

HSF See *high-speed fluorescent lamp.*

HTML See *Hypertext Markup Language.*

hue The color tint.

hydrargyrum medium-arc-length iodide lamp See *HMI.*

hypercardioid A narrow pickup pattern in an elongated heart shape.

hypertext In interactive media, text that is designated as a link.

Hypertext Markup Language A text-based computer language used to author interactive media presentations for the World Wide Web.

hyphenate A person who undertakes two jobs, such as producer-director or writer-director.

Hz See *hertz.*

I

IFB See *interruptible feedback.*

image expansion A digital video effect in which a portion of a video input is "magnified" to a larger size.

image map In interactive media, a picture that is designated as a link or series of links; different parts of a picture may trigger different links.

image stabilization An internal camera feature that keeps the image relatively still through digital or optical means.

image stretching A digital video effect in which a portion of a video input or the entire video input is stretched to a larger size or shrunk to a smaller size vertically and/or horizontally.

import To bring digital video, audio, or other information into a nonlinear editing system or computer program.

incident light Light coming directly from the source of illumination.

indecency Something that is offensive (usually in a sexual way) to members of the community in which it is shown.

ingest To bring digital video data into a video server.

in-house Producing a program using equipment and facilities that belong to the company desiring the production.

in point The designated start point for an edit.

input selector switch A switch on a videotape recorder used to select from among inputs to be recorded.

insert editing An editing process that allows video and individual audio tracks to be recorded independently of one another.

insert track information An area of the videotape used in some formats to record data for automated functions, editing, and audio dubbing.

interactive Methodology whereby the person operating a media program has control, to some extent, over the content of the presentation.

intercom A closed-circuit audio network connecting all production personnel with headsets.

interformat A videotape editing system that uses tape machines of two or more different tape formats.

interframe compression A video compression method that analyzes each individual frame of video as a separate entity.

interlace scanning A scanning method in which half of a frame is scanned at a time, creating a field. Two fields combine to create a complete frame every $\frac{1}{30}$th of a second. Interlace scanning is used in NTSC television, and in some ATSC formats.

internal key See *self key.*

Internet A worldwide network of computers.

interruptible feedback An audio setup that allows the talent, wearing a small earpiece, to hear program audio or receive instruction from the director or someone else.

intraframe compression A video compression method that analyzes frames of video in groups, discarding information that does not change from frame to frame.

invasion of privacy Not leaving someone alone who wants to be left alone or presenting information about a person that he or she does not want divulged.

inverse square law A principle of physics that states that when the distance between a light (or an audio source) and its point of perception is cut in half, its intensity will be increased fourfold.

iris The part of the lens that allows light to pass through.

ITI See *insert track information.*

J

jack (1) A hinged stage brace attached to the rear of a flat. (2) A female connector.

jog/shuttle knob A control on a videotape recorder used to visually search through a videotape at rapid or slow speed.

jump cut An effect—usually undesirable—in which a person or object changes position from one shot to the next.

K

K See *Kelvin.*

Kelvin The scale of measurement used to measure frequencies so that color temperature can be determined.

key A generic term for any number of special visual effects whereby video signals from two or more sources are electronically combined in such a way that one image looks like it has been cut out and placed on top of the other image.

key bus A bus on a video switcher used to select from among various key sources and create various types of key effects.

key light The primary source of illumination falling on a subject that is highly directional and produces a definite modeling or shaping effect with well-defined shadows.

keystoning An undesirable distortion created when a camera is not precisely perpendicular to the flat object being shot. Keystoning is normally undesirable but can be used intentionally for artistic effect.

kicker Additional light, usually a spotlight, coming from the side and slightly to the rear of the subject.

kinescope An old-fashioned film recording of a TV program made by adapting a film camera to record from the face of the TV tube.

kook See *cucalorus.*

L

lav See *lavaliere.*

lavaliere A small mic that can be worn near the neck.

layering The process of placing video elements "on top" of existing elements during the editing process.

LCD See *liquid crystal display.*

LD See *lighting director.*

lead room Additional framing space in a camera picture on the side toward which a subject is looking or moving.

LED See *light emitting diode.*

libel To say something destructively negative about a person that is false.

light emitting diode An electron tube that puts out light; it can be used in audio to show the amount of volume a sound has.

lighting director The person who oversees the lighting of the set and makes lighting changes, if they are needed, during production.

lighting grid See *grid.*

light meter A photoelectric device that measures the amount of light falling on a specific area.

light plot A floor plan that indicates the lighting requirements—location, type, and function of each instrument—for every staging area in the studio.

limbo lighting A type of lighting where the performer is seen clearly, but the background appears to be vague or nondescript.

limiter An electronic device used to cut off audio levels when the volume is too strong.

linear Progressing in a specified order over time; used to describe a program such as a TV show that has a specified beginning, middle, and end.

linear editing A method of video editing that progresses from the beginning to the end and usually

uses videotape for playback and recording.

line feed An audio amplification input for equipment, such as a videotape recorder or an audiotape recorder, that has already been amplified.

line level An audio amplification level for equipment, such as a videotape recorder or audio recorder, that has already been amplified.

line producer A person who is on the production set representing the producer by making sure the program finishes on time and on budget.

lines The number of horizontal rows of pixels in a video picture. The more lines, the higher the resolution of the picture.

link In interactive media, an object that—when activated by the user—triggers an event.

liquid crystal display A television display composed of crystal cells that can be electrically charged to display a picture.

location scout Someone who looks for appropriate places to shoot a remote TV production.

logging Writing down what is on a videotape, including the content of each shot, the in points and out points, and comments about the quality of the shot.

longitudinal time code A method of recording time code into one of the horizontal tracks on a videotape.

longitudinal tracks Information tracks on a video- or audiotape that are recorded parallel to the edge of the tape.

long lens A lens with a high focal length, creating a narrow field of view.

long shot A camera view of the subject from a relatively great distance, usually showing the subject in its entirety.

lossless A method of compression that does not degrade the quality of the signal.

lossy A method of compression that causes degradation in the quality of the signal.

low-key lighting Lighting that is dark and shadowy with a high key-to-fill ratio.

LS See *long shot.*

LTC See *longitudinal time code.*

luminance The brightness information in a video picture.

luminance key See *self key.*

M

macro flange The part of a zoom lens used to set macro focus.

macro focus A feature found on some zoom lenses that allows the operator to focus on objects very close to the lens.

magnet The part of a microphone that creates a field that produces an electric current.

main menu The opening screen of an interactive media presentation.

makeup artist The person who applies makeup to performers and actors.

manual white balance Setting white balance on a camera by aiming the lens at a pure white object, then pressing the appropriate button on the camera.

master An original videotape recording.

master control The primary engineering control center where all video and audio signals are ultimately channeled; program input, camera controls, and transmitter distribution often are handled from this location.

master fader The volume control on an audio board that is located after all the input channel controls and after any submaster controls.

M/E See *mix bus.*

medium shot A view of the subject from a comfortable distance between a wide shot and a close-up.

menu In interactive media, a screen that allows a user to choose from a series of options.

metadata Additional information that can be saved with digital video and audio clips to help in identifying and indexing them.

mic feed The relatively low strength for an electronic signal produced by a microphone prior to several stages of later amplification.

microwave High-frequency radio waves that are often used to send signals from a remote location back to the TV studio.

mid-side miking A method of stereo miking with the mic forming an upside-down T. The stem of the T is a supercardioid mic, and the top can be either one bidirectional mic or two supercardioid ones.

MiniDisc A 2.5-inch optical-magneto disk that can be used to record, store, and edit digital audio material.

miniphone connector A small audio connector with a sleeve and tip.

mix To combine and balance two or more audio signals through an audio console or two or more video sources through a switcher.

mix bus A bus on a video switcher used to set up special effects and transitions.

mix/effects bus See *mix bus.*

mix-minus An output from an audio board that is missing at least one of its elements so that the element can be recorded.

modem A device that allows computer-generated information to be sent over phone lines.

moiré effect Distracting visual vibration caused by the interaction of a narrow striped pattern and the television scanning lines.

monaural Sound coming from only one direction.

monitor A TV set for viewing material produced during TV production as opposed to broadcast signals; also used to refer to audio speakers.

monitoring Listening to or viewing sound or picture as it is being manipulated.

mono See *monaural.*

Motion-JPEG (M-JPEG) The first compression method designed for video information. It has since been largely replaced by newer compression methods.

mounting head A device used to attach the camera to the camera mount. A mounting head facilitates camera movements such as pans and tilts.

MPEG-1 A compression method designed to store VHS-quality video on CD-ROM discs. It is also used often for video on the Internet.

MPEG-2 A series of compression schemes for digital video. It is the most widely used method of compression for digital television.

MPEG-4 A compression method designed for video, audio, and multimedia transmitted over computer networks.

MP3 player A piece of equipment that can play compressed audio that can be sent over a computer.

MS See *medium shot.*

multiple source See *A/B roll.*

multitrack Tape or a tape recorder capable of holding a large number of audio signals, such as 8, 16, or 24, in parallel with each other.

music licensing company An organization that collects money from stations or production groups that use music and then distributes that money to composers and record companies.

mute A control that turns off an assigned channel of an audio console.

N

ND See *neutral density.*

network A group of computers linked together electronically so that they can share data.

neutral density A camera filter that reduces the amount of light hitting the charge-coupled device without affecting the color temperature.

neutral shot A "head-on" shot of a moving object that can be placed between two shots in which the object's screen direction has changed.

noise Unwanted sound or static in an audio signal or unwanted electronic disturbance or snow in a video signal.

nondimmer circuit A switch that turns a light off and on but cannot adjust its brightness.

non-drop frame A method of time code that does not "skip" any frame numbers. Using this method, one hour of video according to time code will actually be one hour + 3.6 seconds long due to the fact that NTSC color video actually runs at 29.97 frames per second and not exactly 30 frames per second.

nonlinear Having the ability to progress independent of time constraints and in a number of different ways; used to describe an interactive media presentation in which the user can control what parts of the program to view and when.

nonlinear editing A method of video editing that uses computers and random-access media for recording and playback.

normaled Having inputs and outputs of an audio patch bay permanently wired so that sound goes from one to the other if it is not sent somewhere else by a patch cord.

NTSC The original television standard approved in the United States in the 1940s that is still in use today. The letters stand for National Television System Committee.

O

obscenity Material that depicts sexual acts in an offensive manner, appeals to prurient interests of the average person, and lacks serious artistic, literary, political, or scientific value.

off-line An editing mode used to create a preliminary rough cut of a product before the final product is edited using on-line editing.

off-mic Distorted sound that occurs when noise from outside a mic's pickup area is transduced and amplified.

omnidirectional A microphone that picks up sound from all directions.

on-line An editing mode used to create a finished product.

open-ended edit An edit in which no out points are set. At the conclusion of the edit, the operator must manually stop the tape machines.

outboard equipment Pieces of equipment that are used in conjunction with the audio board, such as CD players, DAT recorders, and digital carts.

outline A general listing of what will be included within a program, usually in sentence fragment or paragraph form.

out point The designated ending point for an edit.

overtones Acoustical or electrical frequencies that are higher than the fundamental tone.

P
---

pacing The overall speed at which edits are made in a program. Fast pacing means there are a lot of edits.

package A self-contained news story that includes a reporter's voice, sound bites, and video footage.

packets Small "chunks" of digital data that travel over the Internet or other computer networks.

paintbox A device used to create graphics for television.

painter A person who applies paint to a set either before or after it is assembled.

pan (1) To turn a camera horizontally by rotating the camera mounting head. (2) The shot produced by panning a camera. (3) A rectangular floodlight.

pan handle The handle extending toward the rear of the camera with which the camera operator controls movement of the camera.

pan knob A control that shifts an audio signal from the left speaker to the right speaker for stereo mixing. For a mono mix it is usually placed at the 12:00 position.

patch bay A board with numerous terminals (inputs and outputs) through which various audio, video, or lighting signals can be connected by patch cords to other channels or circuits.

patch board See *patch bay*.

patch cord A cable with connectors on both ends that is used to go from one connector on a patch bay to another.

PCM See *pulse code modulation*.

peak In audio, to reach the high point of volume level for a particular sound sequence; the ideal place to peak is at the 0 position on the VU meter.

pedestal mount A camera mount, usually used in studio productions, that facilitates smooth movement of the camera across the studio floor and a limited range of camera height adjustment.

perambulator A large three-wheeled movable platform that holds a mic operator and a mic in such a way that the mic can follow action throughout a studio.

performance release A form signed by people appearing on video giving the production company the right to distribute their performances.

performers TV talent who are on as themselves, not acting the part of someone else.

persistence of vision A human phenomenon whereby the brain retains images for a short period of time so that still images that are projected very quickly look like moving images.

perspective In audio, the matching of visual and sound distance.

phantom power Current sent to a condenser mic from the audio console.

phase The relationship of the positive and negative portions of the sine waves of two different electrical signals to determine to what extent their oscillations are synchronized. Sounds that are out of phase tend to cancel each other out, resulting in silence or on and off sound.

phone connector A connector with a sleeve and tip that is used for patch bays, among other things.

pickup shots Material recorded after an entire program or sequence is recorded that can be edited in to correct some element of what was shot.

pilot A taped production of one representative program from a proposed series of programs.

pinned Rays of a spotlight focused into a narrow beam of intense light.

pitch (1) A meeting during which people with a program idea try to convince other people to buy their idea. (2) The highness or lowness of a sound, determined by the frequency of the sound wave.

pixel One of the small, illuminating "dots" that make up a picture on a television or computer screen. Short for "picture element."

PL See *intercom*.

plasma A technology for TV screens that consists of two glass panels with gas between them; voltage activates the gas, which then activates colored dots.

playback The process of retrieving electronic signals from a tape or disk and turning them into sound and/or images.

playout The server in a television station designed to play the information appearing on air.

plug A male connector.

pop filter A metal or foam ball placed over the top of a mic to minimize plosive sounds.

position jump A cut between two cameras in which a person or object appears to change position from one side of the screen to the other.

posterization A digital video effect that reduces the number of color shades in a picture, raising the contrast level.

postproduction The period of time, after individual program segments have been produced and recorded, when elements of a program are assembled.

pots Round knobs on an audio board that control the volume.

preproduction The period during which preparation and planning are undertaken for a television program.

preread The capability of some digital videotape recorders to simultaneously read existing information on a tape while recording new information onto it. Preread allows dissolves, wipes, and other transitions to be achieved using only a single playback and a single record machine, as well as the layering of video elements.

preroll The process by which an edit controller rewinds source and recording decks before performing an edit. This allows all machines to achieve proper speed and synchronization before the edit is performed. Normally, an edit controller prerolls 3 to 10 seconds before the in point of an edit.

presence The authenticity of a sound in terms of perceived fidelity and distance.

preset bus A bus on a video switcher used to select the next video input to be placed on the air.

preset white balance A camera setting that allows the user to select one or more predetermined white balance settings for various lighting conditions.

pressure zone mic A flat microphone that consists of a thin pickup plate that, when mounted on a table or ceiling, uses the surface it is mounted on to collect sound waves.

prestudio rehearsals Rehearsals with the talent in a rehearsal hall or other location before coming into the studio.

preview To look at an edit before it is actually recorded to make sure it is correct.

preview bus A bus on a video switcher used to set up video effects and transitions before they are put on the air.

preview line An output of a video switcher that allows the operator to set up and view effects before they are put on the air.

preview monitor A video monitor that shows the preview line output of a video switcher.

primary colors Red, blue, and green.

private line See *intercom*.

process amplifier An electronic component that stabilizes the levels and removes unwanted elements from a video signal.

producer The creator and originator of a television program, usually in charge of elements such as writing, music clearance, financial considerations, and hiring the director.

production The stage during which all the shooting for a TV program is undertaken.

production assistant A person who undertakes small miscellaneous duties during a production such as getting people coffee and distributing scripts.

production designer A person in charge of the overall look of a film or video.

production house An organization that produces various types of video material—commercials, corporate videos, broadcast programs, educational programs.

program bus The bus on a video switcher used to select the video input(s) that are put on the air.

program line (1) The output of a video switcher that is the signal being put on the air or recorded. (2) A window on a nonlinear video editor used to assemble audio and video elements.

program monitor (1) A video monitor that shows the program line output of a video switcher. (2) An audio speaker on which you can hear the output of the audio board.

program time The total length of a show.

progressive scanning A scanning method that scans a complete frame with each complete pass of the scanning beam. Many ATSC formats and most computer monitors use progressive scanning.

promotion Calling attention to something in an appealing and formal way so that people will watch.

prompter The generic term for TelePrompTer, a mechanical device that projects the moving script, via mirrors, directly in front of a camera lens. It allows talent to read the script as they look into the camera lens.

prompter operator The person who makes sure the script is appearing on the right part of the prompter screen so the talent can read it properly.

prop Something on a set that is actually used or manipulated by an actor during a production.

propmaster The person who sees that all props are purchased and in their places on the set.

proposal Several written pages that describe the purpose, goals, objectives, target audience, and planned segments of a proposed TV series or program.

proximity effect The boosting of bass frequencies as a sound (particularly a male voice) gets closer to a cardioid mic.

psychographics Information pertaining to lifestyle characteristics of a group of people, such as their desire to preserve nature.

public domain The legal condition covering copyright that says that when material is old enough it can be used without copyright clearance being obtained.

pulse code modulation A method of sampling analog audio information and converting it to digital form. It is used in some digital videotape formats to record audio information along with video information in helical-scan tracks. However, unlike audio frequency modulation, pulse code modulation allows separation of the audio information for editing.

push-off A digital video transition in which the first picture is "pushed" off the screen by a second picture.

PZM See *pressure zone mic*.

Q

quantization The number of bits that each sampled unit of an analog signal is placed into. All else being equal, higher bit levels result in a digital signal that is a truer representation of the original analog wave.

quartz-halogen lamp See *quartz lamp*.

quartz lamp A lamp with a tungsten filament and halogen gas in a quartz or silica housing.

R

rack focus A camera shot that starts with one object in focus, then changes to focus on another object.

radio frequency A carrier wave on which radio and television signals can be superimposed for transmission.

RAID A series of computer hard disks wired together to act as one large hard disk. Often used in video servers.

random access A storage medium that allows nearly instantaneous access to any portion of the stored data.

rate card A listing of costs for renting equipment or a facility.

ratings Data based on statistical sampling that tells the percentage of people who watch a particular program.

RCA connector A connector with an outer sleeve and a center shaft.

reaction shot A shot that shows someone responding to what someone else is saying or doing.

recording Using audio and/or video electronic signals to arrange iron-oxide particles on the magnetic recording tape or computer disk or laser inputs on a disk so that they can be retrieved later.

recording head The part of an audio- or videotape recorder that records information onto the surface of the tape.

recording tab A small plastic tab on a videotape that is used to prevent accidental erasure (recording over) of a tape. When removed or in a designated position, the tab prevents a videotape recorder from recording on the tape.

record run A time code mode in which the time code numbers increment only when the video is being recorded.

Redundant Array of Independent Disks See *RAID*.

reel-to-reel A type of audiotape recorder for which the tape must be threaded from the source reel to the take-up reel.

reference white A white object, such as a piece of paper or a T-shirt, that can be used on location to white balance a camera.

reflected light Light bounced back from the surface of an object.

reflector A shiny device or light-colored surface used to bounce light back into a scene.

remote/local switch A switch on a videotape recorder used to select how the machine is controlled. When in "local" mode, the machine responds to controls on the front panel; when in "remote" mode, the machine responds to signals coming from a remote source connected electronically to the recorder. Remote mode is used to allow an external edit controller or computer to control the videotape machine.

remote production Taping video material or airing it live away from the studio usually with numerous cameras and a truck that serves as a control room.

rendering The process by which a computer creates a complex video transition or other effect.

residuals Payments that actors, producers, and others receive when a program is rerun.

resolution The fineness of detail that can be produced by a given television system. The higher the resolution, the more detail that can be reproduced. Higher resolution systems use a greater number of pixels to reproduce pictures.

reverberation Sound that has bounced off a surface or various surfaces more than once or sound that has been processed so it sounds like it has bounced off surfaces.

review To look at an edit after it has been recorded to make sure it was executed correctly.

RF See *radio frequency.*

robotic camera control A computerized unit that allows one or more cameras to be controlled from one location.

robotic cameras Cameras that are controlled remotely and do not have a camera operator behind them.

roll A graphic effect in which lettering moves vertically on the screen. A roll is often used at the conclusion of a program to show closing credits.

roll-in A short bit of material, such as a news story, that is played, usually from a VCR, into a longer program, such as a newscast.

rough cut An assemblage of video and audio, created with off-line editing, that will eventually be used as the model for creating the edited master of a program with online editing.

router A device that allows a digital signal to be sent to a number of different locations.

routing switcher A simple audio or video switcher used to select from among two or more different signals.

rule of thirds A principle of composition that divides the TV screen into thirds, horizontally and vertically, and places objects of interest at the points where the lines intersect.

rundown A list of various segments that will be included in a program.

S

SA See *studio address.*

safety chain A steel chain on a lamp housing that should always be attached to the lighting grid so that the housing will not fall if it comes loose.

sampling The process used to convert an analog signal into digital form by measuring the value of the analog signal at various temporal points and converting that value into digital information. All else being equal, a higher rate of sampling results in a digital signal that is a truer representation of the original analog wave.

sampling rate The frequency at which an analog video signal is sampled to convert it to digital form.

sandbag A heavy weight placed on the brace of a flat to hold the flat in place.

saturation The strength or intensity of a color—how far removed it is from a neutral or gray shade.

scanning The process of reproducing a video picture by illuminating individual pixels that make up the screen; also, the process that a charge-coupled device uses to transduce visual energy into electrical energy.

scoop A floodlight that contains a single bulb in a bowl-shaped metal reflector.

screen In interactive media, the building block of an interactive presentation; the amount of information that can be displayed on a computer monitor at one time, including various media elements such as video, text, or graphics.

screen direction The direction a subject is facing or in which a subject or object is moving.

screenplay A script that is for a movie.

scrim A translucent filter, often made of fiberglass or fine screening, used in front of either a spotlight or floodlight to soften and diffuse the light quality.

script The written guideline from which a TV program is produced.

script supervisor A person who keeps notes during production so that continuity is maintained and the material shot can be edited properly.

SD See *standard-definition television.*

SDI See *serial digital interface.*

SDTV See *standard-definition television.*

search A method of moving quickly from one point on a videotape to another while viewing the images contained on the tape.

secondary colors Colors created by combining two primary colors in equal amounts. Secondary colors are cyan, magenta, and yellow.

SEG See *special effects generator.*

segue To cut from one sound at full volume to another sound at full volume.

selecting Choosing which audio or video signal is to be recorded or aired, usually through an audio board or a switcher.

selective attention principle The ability of the human ear to filter out unwanted noise so that a person can concentrate on the particular sound he or she wants to hear.

self key A key effect in which the video source cutting the key is also inserted into the key hole.

serial digital interface A method of transporting digital video and audio information over a cable.

serif A small extension found on the tips of letters in some font styles.

server A computer-based unit used to store and retrieve video signals in digital form.

servo capstan The part of a recorder that pulls the tape through the machine at the proper speed.

set designer The person who determines the environment where the production takes place.

set dressing Something on a set that is similar to a prop but is not essential to the action. It is there to add atmosphere or interest.

set light General lighting on the scenery or other background behind the talent.

setup The electronic adjustment of a video signal.

shader See *video operator.*

shaping Altering an audio signal by controlling volume, filtering out certain frequencies, emphasizing upper or lower pitches, creating an echo effect, and so forth.

shooting schedule A sheet that lists what is to be accomplished each day of production and the major elements needed to accomplish it.

short lens A lens with a low focal length, creating a wide field of view.

shotgun A highly directional microphone used for picking up sounds from a distance.

shot log A list of shots contained on a videotape.

shot sheets Lists of shots in a program that can be attached to the back of a camera so that the camera operator knows what he or she will be shooting.

signal processing Changing elements of sound or picture, such as frequency response and gain, so that the resulting signal is different from the original one.

signal-to-noise ratio The relationship of desired sound to undesired electronic sound. The higher the ratio, the purer the sound.

silhouette A type of lighting where the background is lit but the performers are not.

skew A control on a videotape recorder that adjusts the tension on a tape to correct for when the top part of a video picture appears to "bend" to the right or left.

slant-track recording See *helical scan.*

slate An identification procedure whereby date, scene, segment, and other information necessary for editing or for identifying a tape are recorded at the beginning of the taped material.

sleeve An outer part of a number of connectors, such as phone, miniphone, and RCA.

slug A title for a news story, usually written at the top of the page.

SMPTE Society of Motion Picture and Television Engineers. Usually used in conjunction with time code.

S/N See *signal-to-noise ratio.*

snake A connector box that contains a large number of microphone input receptacles.

snap zoom A camera shot that very quickly (almost instantly, in some cases) zooms in or out. Snap zooms are normally performed manually, after disengaging the zoom control's motor drive.

snoot A circular metal object placed in front of a light to pinpoint the light onto a particular area of the set.

soft contrast filter A camera filter used to create a fuzzy effect.

softlight A lamp that has the bulb positioned in such a way that the light is reflected on the back of the lamp housing before leaving the fixture.

solo The control on the audio console that silences all channels except the one that has been selected.

sound designer A person who decides the overall effect of all the aural elements of a show, such as sound effects and music.

special effects Complicated actions, such as flames or flying people, executed on a set by people qualified to do them.

special effects generator The part of the video switcher that can be used to create special electronic effects, normally through the use of digital video effects.

speech bump A frequency response characteristic of a mic that enables it to pick up speech frequencies better than other frequencies.

split edit An edit in which the video and audio portions have different in or out points.

split screen A special effect with the screen split into two or more sections, with a picture from a different input filling each portion of the screen.

spotlight (1) A concentrated light that covers a narrow area; it usually provides some means for varying the angle of the illumination by moving the bulb within the housing. (2) A special effect in which one part of the picture is lighter (brighter) than the rest of the picture; it is often used to highlight a particular portion of the screen.

spot server A server used to store commercials.

spread To focus the rays of a spotlight to a relatively wide area so that the light is less intense than when the light is in the pinned position.

staff People who are employed by a particular production organization and receive regular weekly wages regardless of what project they are working on.

stage manager The director's key assistant in charge of all production concerns on the studio floor.

staging See *blocking*.

standard-definition television With the advent of high-definition television, this term is used to refer to NTSC television and ATSC formats that have a 4:3 aspect ratio.

star filter A camera filter used to create a "star" effect that radiates from bright spots on the screen.

start-and-stop rehearsal A full facilities rehearsal with cameras operating, designed to be interrupted to work out problems as the production progresses.

stereo Audio that is recorded, transmitted, and played back through two separate (left and right) channels to simulate binaural hearing.

stock footage Scenes of various types that can be purchased to insert into a production.

storyboard A series of simple drawings or computer-generated frames that lay out visually the content of a commercial or program.

streaming A method of sending video, audio, or other digital data over a computer network in sequential form so that the end user can begin playing the information before it finishes downloading.

streaming video A method that allows moving video to be viewed over the World Wide Web or an intranet.

strike Cleaning up a set after a production.

stripboards Large boards or computer-generated sheets that summarize the scenes, locations, and actors needed for each day of production.

striping The process of recording time code onto a videotape.

strip lights A series of pan lights or low-wattage bulbs mounted in a row of 3 to 12 lights in one housing, used as a specialized floodlight for lighting a cyclorama or other large background area.

studio The primary room devoted to video production containing all the paraphernalia for sets, lighting, cameras, microphones, and so forth—the space where all acting or performing takes place.

studio address A public-address loudspeaker system, allowing those in the control room to talk directly to the studio floor.

studio production TV program creation that takes place in a controlled environment meant for it as opposed to production that takes place in the field.

subcode An area on a videotape used by some formats such as DVCPRO to record time code information.

submastering Controlling groups of sound inputs, such as separate inputs from each percussion instrument in an orchestra, separately from other groups of sound inputs, such as all the strings.

super See *superimposition*.

supercardioid A very narrow microphone pickup pattern, often used to record sounds that are at a distance.

superimposition A picture resulting from the simultaneous display of two pictures that are partway through a dissolve.

super video CD A CD-ROM-based disc that can hold about 20 minutes of video at a quality higher than VHS but lower than DVD.

supervising producer See *line producer*.

surround sound Audio that comes from five or six speakers or more placed around a room.

SVCD See *super video CD*.

sweetening The process of adding pickup shots and enhanced audio information after a production has been shot.

switcher A device consisting of selection buttons and control levers that permits the selection and combining of incoming video signals to form the final program picture.

symmetrical balance A formal arrangement of elements in a camera shot or a graphic, usually with the most important element centered in the picture and other objects placed equidistant from the center.

sync generator A device that produces a synchronizing signal (sync pulse) that serves as a timing pulse to coordinate the video elements of all components in a video system.

syndication A process by which programs are distributed to individual stations that air them when they wish as opposed to network programs that are generally aired by all network affiliated stations at the same time.

T

table stand A mic holder that sits on a table or tablelike setting so that one or more people can talk into it.

take An instantaneous switch from one picture to another; also called a cut.

talkback mic A microphone located in the control room that allows the director, audio operator, or others to communicate with people in the studio who can hear the studio monitor.

tally lights Small red indicators on a camera to let the talent and camera operators know that the camera is on the air or recording.

TBC See *time-base corrector*.

TD See *technical director*.

technical director The production person who operates the switcher.

technical rehearsal A rehearsal intended mainly for the equipment operators so they know how to position their equipment during the recording of a program.

telas An interruptible feedback system that can be used in a studio but not out in the field because its sound cannot travel that far.

telephoto lens See *long lens*.

TelePrompTer See *prompter*.

three-point lighting The traditional lighting setup that incorporates a key, a fill, and a backlight.

three-to-one cutting ratio A principle that states you should not take to a shot that is three times larger or three times smaller than the preceding shot.

three-to-one rule A microphone placement principle that states that, if two mics must be side by side, there should be three times the distance between them that there is between the mics and the people using them.

tilt (1) To pivot the camera vertically by pointing the camera mounting head up or down. (2) The shot produced by tilting a camera.

timbre A distinctive quality each voice or musical instrument has caused, to a large degree, by overtones.

time-base corrector An electronic component that takes the video feed from a video recorder, encodes that signal into a digital form, and then reconstructs an enhanced synchronizing pulse and video signal for distribution and playback.

time code An address system used to assign each frame of video a unique numerical designation in the format hours:minutes:seconds:frames, such as 23:03:58:23.

time code burn-in A dub of video footage that has time code information displayed on the screen.

time code generator A device used to create running time code to record with video information. Time code generators are built in to many videotape recorders, and they are also available as separate units.

time code reader A device used to read time code information.

timeline An area of a nonlinear editing system used to assemble video clips, audio clips, and other information into a completed program.

timing sheet A form that helps the AD keep track of the running times of various portions of a program and other time elements so that the program ends at the appropriate time.

tip The end of some connectors, such as phone and miniphone.

tone A one kilohertz sound used to calibrate equipment volume levels so that the sound will have a consistent volume each time it is played or recorded.

tone generator An element in an audio board or other piece of equipment that produces a constant one kilohertz sound that can be used to set consistent volume levels on different pieces of equipment.

tracking control The control on a videotape recorder that adjusts the video head to put it in the optimum position when a tape is played back.

transducing Receiving energy in one form (sound waves or light energy) and converting it into another form of energy (electromagnetic signals).

transfer editing Any form of editing in which a signal is transferred (dubbed) from one tape to another.

transition A method, such as a cut, dissolve, or wipe, of getting from one shot to another.

transparent The term used to describe the ability of digital signals to be distributed and manipulated without loss of quality.

treatment Several written pages that describe the main premise and elements of a series or movie.

triax A cable used to connect a camera to a camera control unit.

trim (1) To adjust an in or out point of an edit frame by frame. (2) To make final adjustments on lights. (3) To make slight sound adjustments in audio.

tripod A three-legged camera mount, sometimes equipped with casters to facilitate camera movement.

truck (1) To move the camera and its mount laterally to the right or left. (2) A shot produced by trucking the camera.

tungsten-halogen lamp See *quartz lamp.*

turntable A piece of equipment for spinning records and converting the groove vibrations into electrical energy.

two-column scripts Scripts with video in the left-hand column and audio in the right-hand column.

U
---

ultracardioid A very narrow microphone pickup pattern, often used to pick up sound from a distance.

unbalanced cables Audio cables that have two wires, one for positive, and one for both negative and ground.

uniform resource locator A standardized system of typing Internet addresses.

uninterrupted run-through The rehearsal of an entire show without stopping for anything except major problems; minor problems are fixed later.

unions Organizations that set wages and working conditions that production companies must adhere to for people (usually below-the-line people) whom they hire.

unit production manager A person who schedules and determines the cost of equipment and facilities.

UPM See *unit production manger.*

URL See *uniform resource locator.*

V

VCD See *video CD.*

VCR See *videocassette recorder.*

vectorscope A piece of diagnostic equipment used to adjust the color qualities of a video signal using color bars.

vertical interval A brief time during the scanning process when the scanning beam turns off and is repositioned at the top of the screen to begin scanning a new frame.

vertical interval time code A method of recording time code information into the "blank" area during the vertical interval.

vertical sync pulse The portion of the sync signal that controls the movement of a scanning beam from the bottom to the top of the screen.

video capture Hardware and software that allow a personal computer to convert video into digital form.

videocassette recorder A magnetic-electronic recording machine that records audio, video, and control track signals on a videotape enclosed within a container.

video CD A CD-ROM-based disc that can hold about an hour of video at a quality comparable to VHS tape.

video control A knob used to adjust the level of video coming into a videotape recorder.

video data disc A CD-ROM or DVD disc used to store video information in digital form.

video disk A round storage device that can hold video and audio signals in such a way that they can be randomly accessed.

video effects Complicated actions for a movie or video that are created in a computer.

video gain A control used to boost the overall brightness of the picture being produced by a camera.

video operator A person who makes technical adjustments on a camera using a camera control unit located at some distance from the camera.

video output control A control that increases the gain of a video signal so that a camera can obtain a picture in low lighting conditions.

video recordist See *videotape operator.*

video server See *server.*

videotape operator The person who records and/or plays back video material during production.

videotape recorder A device used to record video and audio information onto a magnetic tape.

video track The portion of a videotape on which video information is recorded.

virtual sets Studio sets that are computer generated and filled in electronically behind performers who stand in front of a blank background.

VITC See *vertical interval time code.*

volume unit meter A display meter that shows the relative volume of an audio signal.

VTR See *videotape recorder.*
VU meter See *volume unit meter.*

W

walk-through rehearsal An abbreviated rehearsal, conducted from the studio floor, to acquaint the talent and/or crew with the major outline of the production.

waveform An electronic representation of a signal.

waveform monitor A piece of diagnostic equipment used to evaluate the brightness qualities of a video signal.

Web See *World Wide Web.*

web page An interactive media screen designed for use with a web browser.

white balance An electronic adjustment of a camera to compensate for differences in color temperatures so that a pure white object appears as pure white.

wide-angle lens See *short lens.*

wide shot See *long shot.*

wildtrack Background noise recorded at a site so that it can be mixed in with other sounds during postproduction.

windscreen See *pop filter.*

wipe A transition in which a geometric pattern gradually replaces one picture with another.

wireless Any system that sends audio or video frequencies through the airwaves as opposed to through cables.

World Wide Web The set of technologies that places a graphical user interface on the Internet.

WS See *wide shot.*

WWW See *World Wide Web.*

X

XLR connector A professional-quality balanced connector with three prongs.

XLS See *extreme long shot.*

Z

zip drive A computer drive that has more storage capacity than a floppy but less than a CD-ROM.

zoom A camera shot during which the focal length of the shot is adjusted as the shot is in progress.

zoom lens A variable-focal-length lens that, through a complex optical system, can be smoothly changed from one focal length to another.

zoom mic A microphone that can change its direction pattern gradually from cardioid to super-, hyper-, or ultracardioid.

Suggestions for Further Reading

Alten, Stanley R. *Audio in Media*. Belmont, CA: Wadsworth, 2001.

Anderson, Gary H. *Video Editing and Post Production: A Professional Guide*. Woburn, MA: Focal Press, 1998.

Austerberry, David. *Technology of Video and Audio Streaming*. Boston: Focal Press, 2001.

Barr, Tony, Stephen Kline, and Edward Asner. *Acting for the Camera*. New York: HarperCollins, 1997.

Benedetti, Robert. *From Concept to Screen: An Overview of Film and Television Production*. Boston: Allyn and Bacon, 2002.

Boston, Jim. *DTV Survival Guide*. New York: McGraw-Hill, 2000.

Brown, Blain. *Motion Picture and Video Lighting*. Stoneham, MA: Focal Press, 1996.

Browne, Stefen E. *Nonlinear Editing Basics*. Woburn, MA: Focal Press, 1998.

Cartwright, Steve R. *Pre-Production Planning for Video, Film, and Multimedia*. Boston: Focal Press, 1996.

Compesi, Ronald J. *Video Field Production and Editing*. Boston: Allyn and Bacon, 2003.

Cury, Ivan. *Directing and Producing for Television*. Boston: Focal Press, 2002.

Dancyger, Ken. *Techniques of Film and Video Editing*. Boston: Focal Press, 2000.

De Bruin, Ronald, and Jan Smits. *Digital Video Broadcasting: Technology, Standards, and Regulations*. Boston: Artech House, 1999.

Eargle, John. *The Microphone Book*. Boston: Focal Press, 2001.

Farris, Linda Guess. *Television Careers: A Guide to Breaking and Entering*. Fairfax, CA: Buy the Book Enterprises, 1995.

Fauer, Jon. *Shooting Digital Video*. Boston: Focal Press, 2001.

Filoreto, Carl, and Lynn Selzer. *How to Get a Job in TV News*. New Haven, CT: Mustang Publishing, 1998.

Fitt, Brian, and Joe Thornley. *Lighting Technology*. Boston: Focal Press, 2002.

Flynn, Deras. *Guide to Creating Digital Video Like a Pro*. San Francisco: TechTV Press, 2002.

Gates, Richard. *Production Management for Film and Video*. Newton, MA: Focal Press, 1995.

Gawlinski, Mark. *Interactive Television Production*. Boston: Focal Press, 2003.

Grant, August E. *Communication Technology Update*. Boston: Focal Press, 2002.

Gross, Lynne S., and Larry W. Ward. *Digital Moviemaking*. Belmont, CA: Wadsworth, 2004.

Hilliard, Robert L. *Writing for Television, Radio, and New Media*. Belmont, CA: Wadsworth, 2000.

Hyde, Stuart W. *Television and Radio Announcing*. Boston: Houghton Mifflin, 2001.

Kehoe, Vincent J. R. *The Technique of the Professional Make-Up Artist*. Stoneham, MA: Focal Press, 1995.

Kindem, Gorham, and Robert B. Musburger. *Introduction to Media Production: From Analog to Digital*. Woburn, MA: Focal Press, 2001.

LeTourneau, Tom. *Placing Shadows: The Art of Video Lighting*. Woburn, MA: Focal Press, 1998.

Luther, Arch C. *Video Camera Technology*. Boston: Artech House, 1998.

Maier, Robert G. *Location Scouting and Management Handbook*. Newton, MA: Focal Press, 1994.

Medoff, Norman J., and Tom Tanquary. *Portable Video*. Boston: Focal Press, 2002.

Miller, William. *Screenwriting for Film and Television*. Boston: Allyn and Bacon, 1998.

Millerson, Gerald. *Video Production Handbook*. Boston: Focal Press, 2001.

Pohlman, Ken C. *Principles of Digital Audio*. New York: McGraw-Hill, 1995.

Rabiger, Michael. *Directing Film Techniques and Aesthetics*. Boston: Focal Press, 2003.

Reese, David E., and Lynne S. Gross. *Radio Production Worktext*. Boston: Focal Press, 2002.

Tarrant, Jon. *Digital Camera Technique.* Boston: Focal Press, 2003.

Thompson, Roy. *Grammar of the Shot.* Oxford: Focal Press, 1998.

Tucker, Patrick. *How to Act for the Camera.* New York: Routledge Press, 1993.

Ward, Peter. *Picture Composition for Film and Television.* Oxford: Focal Press, 1996.

Watkinson, John. *Introduction to Digital Audio.* Boston: Focal Press, 2002.

Zettl, Herbert. *Sight-Sound-Motion: Applied Media Aesthetics.* Belmont, CA: Wadsworth, 1999.

Zettl, Herbert. *Television Production Handbook.* Belmont, CA: Wadsworth, 2003.

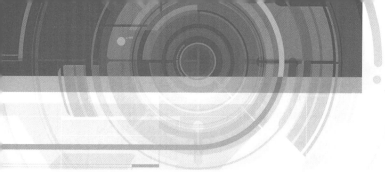

Index

Reaction shot, 94, 284
Reality, 130
RealMedia, 307
Recording, 11, 227–248
    analog audio, 163, 165
    digital audio, 163–165
    digital video signals,
        227–229, 233–236
    for field production, 283,
        293, 295–296
    procedures, 296
    on servers, 236–239
    sound, 162, 177–180
    video signals, 228–233
    videotape principles for,
        239–243
Recording head, 239
Recording tab, 246
Record run, 231
Redundant Array of Inde-
    pendent Disks
    (RAID), 238
Reel-to-reel recorder, 165
Reference white, 286
Reflected light, 126, 128
Reflector, 290–291
Rehearsal, 80–81, 250, 283
Remote/local switch, 246
Remote production, 4, 15,
    7–9, 298–300
Render, 258, 312
Residuals, 50
Resolution, 12–13, 50, 99,
    101–102, 200, 235
Reverberation, 174
Review, 265
RF, 229–230, 244
Ripple, 261
Riser, 120
Robotic camera, 32, 116, 149
Roll, 187
Roll-in, 40, 238, 251
Rough cut, 251, 257
Router, 238
Routing switcher, 208
Roxio *Easy CD & DVD*
    Creator, 312
Rule of thirds, 120, 190
Rundown, 56–58, 277

S

SA. *See* Studio address
Safety chain, 144, 149–150
SAG, 61
Sampling, 163, 233, 235, 241
Sandbag, 199

Sarnoff, David, 14
Satellite, 5–6, 13, 162,
    166, 298
Saturation, 102–103, 191,
    228–229
Scanning, 99–100, 230
Scene shop, 199
Schedule, 66–68
Scoop, 135, 137, 140,
    146–147, 288
Screen Actors Guild, 61
Screen direction, 90–91, 270
Screenplay, 53
Scrim, 134, 146, 288
Script, 51–60
    for field production,
        276–277
    forms of, 52–60
    marking of, 78, 87
    news, 52, 57
    performers' handling of, 44
Script supervisor, 275, 283
SD. *See* Standard definition
SDI, 101–102, 257
SDTV. *See* Standard
    definition
Search mode, 245
Secondary colors, 102
SEG. *See* Special effects
    generator
Segue, 175
Selecting, 10, 205, 293
Selective attention
    principle, 294
Self key, 212
Serial digital interface (SDI),
    101–102, 257
Serif, 191
Server, 6, 162, 188, 228,
    236–239, 250, 255
Servo capstan, 243
SESAC, 69
Set designer, 42
Set dressing, 200–202, 204
Set light, 139
Sets, 183–185, 195–204
    for field production,
        294–295
    and other production
        elements, 202–204
    permanent, 196–197
    physical, 196–200
    pictorial functions of,
        184–185
    removable, 198–200
    storage of, 6
    for studios, 4, 7
    virtual, 195–196

Set up, 224
Shader, 32
Shadow, 141–142, 161, 178
Shape, 130, 146–147
Shaping, 174–175
Shooting schedule, 68, 280
Shortcut, 165
Short lens, 103–104
Shot, 88–91, 115,
    117–119, 285
Shotgun microphone,
    161–162, 291
Shot log, 253
Shot sheet, 78, 124
Shure, 155
Signal flow, 244
Signal processing, 174
Signal to noise ratio, 162–163
Silhouette lighting, 131,
    142–143
16:9 aspect ratio, 120–121
60 Minutes, 251
Skew, 246
Slant-track recording, 239
Slate, 84, 283
Slaved camera, 250
Sleeve, 166
Slow motion, 258
SMPTE, 230
S/N, 162–163
Snake, 166
Snap zoom, 109
Snoot, 147
Society of Motion Picture and
    Television Engineers
    (SMPTE), 230
Soft contrast filter, 110
Softlight, 135, 143
Solo, 175
Sound. *See* Audio
Sound designer, 42
Sound effects, 297–298
Sound wave, 154
Speakers, 5, 9, 11, 177. *See
    also* Monitors
Special effects generator, 42,
    205, 219–220, 271, 300
Speech bump, 155
Spin, 220
Split edit, 260–261
Split screen, 211, 215
Spotlight, 132–134, 137–140,
    142, 211
Spot server, 238
Spread, 133, 137
Squeeze, 220
Staff position, 28–39, 61, 84,
    149, 275

Stage manager, 28–30, 84, 275
Staging, 76
Standard definition, 13
    and aspect ratio, 121, 193
    and cables, 166
    contrast ratio, 128
    and editing, 252, 256, 267
    formats, 98
    for graphics, 185–186
    and the Internet, 304
    lenses, 102
    lighting, 143
    with servers, 237
    sets for, 199
    shots, 88, 116
    and switchers, 207
    for truck production, 300
Standby, 224, 286
Star filter, 110
Start-and-stop rehearsal,
    81–82
Stereo, 156–157, 167, 170,
    177, 300
Stock footage, 70, 278
Stop down, 106
Storyboard, 58–60, 78, 277
Streaming, 262, 306–310
Strike, 40
Stripboard, 68, 282
Striping, 231
Strip light, 134, 140, 147
Studio, 4–7, 82
Studio address, 5, 26, 81
Studio floor rehearsal, 81
Studio production, 4–6
Studio sync, 231
Subcode area, 243
Submaster, 176
Super, 211
Supercardioid microphone,
    156–157, 162
Superimposition, 211
Super video CD, 313
Supervising producer, 50
Surround sound, 156–157,
    174, 300
SVCD, 313
S-Video, 244, 296
Sweetening, 251
Switcher, 205–225, 230
    advanced functions,
        220–223
    analog, 205–206
    basic design of, 208–216
    basic types of, 206–208
    computer-based, 208
    in the control room, 5
    for editing, 249, 262